Mockingbird

Mockingbird

A PORTRAIT OF HARPER LEE

Charles J. Shields

HENRY HOLT AND COMPANY
NEW YORK

HENRY HOLT AND COMPANY, LLC
PUBLISHERS SINCE 1866
175 FIFTH AVENUE
NEW YORK, NEW YORK 10010
WWW.HENRYHOLT.COM

HENRY HOLT® AND 🅷® ARE REGISTERED TRADEMARKS OF HENRY HOLT AND
COMPANY, LLC.

DISTRIBUTED IN CANADA BY H. B. FENN AND COMPANY LTD.

LIBRARY OF CONGRESS CATALOGING-IN-PUBLICATION DATA

SHIELDS, CHARLES J., 1951–
  MOCKINGBIRD : A PORTRAIT OF HARPER LEE / CHARLES J. SHIELDS — 1ST ED.
    P. CM.
  INCLUDES BIBLIOGRAPHICAL REFERENCES (P.   ) AND INDEX.
  ISBN-13: 978-0-8050-7919-7
  ISBN-10: 0-8050-7919-X
    1. LEE, HARPER.   2. AUTHORS, AMERICAN—20TH CENTURY—BIOGRAPHY.   I. TITLE.

PS3562.E353Z94   2006
813'.54—DC22
[B]   2005046799

HENRY HOLT BOOKS ARE AVAILABLE FOR SPECIAL PROMOTIONS AND PREMIUMS.
FOR DETAILS CONTACT: DIRECTOR, SPECIAL MARKETS.

FIRST EDITION 2006

DESIGNED BY MERYL SUSSMAN LEVAVI

PRINTED IN THE UNITED STATES OF AMERICA

2 4 6 8 10 9 7 5 3 1

To my mother, Jeanne, and father, Charley,
with deepest gratitude

Though justice be thy plea, consider this,
That, in the course of justice, none of us
Should see salvation . . .

—Portia in *The Merchant of Venice,* Act 4, Scene 1

Contents

Introduction 1

1. *The Making of Me* 11

2. *"Ellen" Spelled Backward* 31

3. *Without "Finishing Touches"* 60

4. Rammer Jammer 83

5. Atticus *Becomes* To Kill a Mockingbird 112

6. *"See NL's Notes"* 136

7. Mockingbird *Takes Off* 180

8. *"Oh, Mr. Peck!"* 203

9. *The Second Novel* 232

10. *Quiet Time* 264

Notes 287

Bibliography 311

Acknowledgments 323

Index 325

Mockingbird

Introduction

"As a reader I loathe Introductions," Nelle Harper Lee once wrote. But, with apologies to the subject, I must say that one is necessary for this book, the first ever about the woman who gave the world *To Kill a Mockingbird,* one of the most influential pieces of fiction produced in the United States. In a "Survey of Lifetime Reading Habits" conducted by the Book-of-the-Month Club in 1991, researchers found that *To Kill a Mockingbird* ranked second only to the Bible "as making a difference in people's lives." Forty-six years after its publication, the novel still draws almost a million readers annually. Maybe that is because its lessons of human dignity and respect for others remain fundamental and universal.

This book aims to capture a life but is not a conventional biography, because—despite her novel's huge impact—Lee's writing life has been brief, and her personal life has been intensely private. She wrote only one book, her Pulitzer Prize–winning perennial bestseller, and then, after a brief moment in the spotlight, disappeared from the public eye. She has not sought fame, then or since, although around the time of *To Kill a Mockingbird*'s publication she did grant interviews.

Unlike her lifelong friend Truman Capote (perhaps even because of his example and experience), Harper Lee has never appeared comfortable in the limelight. In fact, not only does she not solicit attention, she also actively discourages it, refusing to speak in public and turning down all requests for interviews and all forms of cooperation with writers and reporters. In our era of relentless and often prurient self-exposure by some approval-hungry personalities, Lee prefers silence and self-respect. That is not to say she is furtively reclusive; though she enjoys her solitude, she is not some modern-day Emily Dickinson. She lives a normal life, replete with community activities, many related to her church. Lee is "like someone you'd meet in any small town," as Professor William Smart of Sweet Briar College, in Virginia, expressed it. And Smart has known Lee for forty years.

Consequently, this book has been produced without Lee's help, although I have repeatedly solicited it. She has declined with vigor, even to the extent of refusing to respond to my attempts to check facts by mail. Despite her desire for privacy, I believe it is important to record Lee's story while there are still a few people alive who were part of it and can remember. I have tried to balance her desire for privacy with the desire of her millions of readers who have long hoped for a respectful, informative view of this rarely seen writer.

This book is based on six hundred interviews and other sorts of communication with Harper Lee's friends, associates, and former classmates. It's also the product of four years of research into the papers of her friend Truman Capote, which include Lee's notes for his book *In Cold Blood* (for which she served as research assistant); the papers of Lee's literary agent; the archives of national and local libraries; and hundreds of newspaper and magazine articles. Until the mid-1960s, Lee was generous about granting interviews. I had to "put on my reporter's hat," as my late father, a journalist, liked to say, in order to trace this life, and I have tried to be as careful and as scrupulous as possible. I have sometimes made the decision to overlook topics that may have interested some, rather than to rely on psychologizing that I am not qualified to do or to risk producing errors that might find their way into future accounts of Lee.

I want readers to be introduced to the author and get a sense of what makes her tick: the things that influenced her when she was growing up during the Depression in Monroeville, Alabama, for example; the reasons why classmates regarded her with awe; the traits of nonconformity and almost ferocious independence that distinguished her in college; the steps that led to her dropping out of law school and moving to New York to write; the sense of loyalty that drew her to Truman Capote's side when he was researching his "nonfiction novel," *In Cold Blood;* the sense of humor that sustained her while she was scrutinized by the media because of the success of *To Kill a Mockingbird* and the film based on it; and, finally, the reasons why she never wrote another novel.

As I was researching this book, I tended to be asked the same questions by interested friends. The first was "Is Harper Lee still alive?" Yes. *"Nail Har-puh,"* as her name is pronounced in her hometown, spends most of the year in Monroeville, and a few months in New York in the apartment she has maintained for the past forty-five years. Her eldest sister, Alice, ninety-four, who is one of the most highly regarded attorneys in Alabama, shares a house with Nelle in Monroeville. Residents are accustomed to seeing the two ladies puttering around the First United Methodist Church, where they have been members all their lives; at the country club where they enjoy the lunch buffet and the opportunity to see friends; and at various favorite diners around town. Nelle refuses to talk about *To Kill a Mockingbird* in social situations, and friends warn strangers not to bring it up. She has been known to leave the room if pestered about the novel.

The second question I was asked was "Is she married?" The answer is no. That question was almost always followed by "Is she gay?" I do not necessarily make a connection between being unmarried and being gay. I cannot say if she is homosexual (she was friends with Capote and other openly gay people), heterosexual (she and her literary agent, Maurice Crain, were devoted to each other), or just not open to long-term romantic relationships. I do know, on the other hand, of her ability to charm others and cultivate friends—though she also has a temper, and as a child, had a reputation for bullying. I am not sure what labels Lee would apply to herself, except "woman," "Southerner," and perhaps "writer."

The final question I was continually asked was "Why didn't she write another novel?" This was the big question I had asked myself in the first place, and which led to the adventure of writing this book.

After reading it, I hope you will come away with at least some idea of why she never published another novel after *To Kill a Mockingbird.*

YEARS AGO, WHEN I was an English teacher in a large high school near Chicago, I taught *To Kill a Mockingbird* to freshmen. That's a good time to be introduced to it, because students at that age are crossing the bridge from childhood to young adulthood, as the young characters in Lee's novel are. In-class discussions of the novel tend to be lively, and assigned essays are weighty with insights and opinions. It's a very rich text to teach.

If you don't remember much about the novel, here's a summary:

To Kill a Mockingbird is really two stories. One is a coming-of-age tale told from the point of view of Scout Finch, a girl of about nine, and her slightly older brother, Jem. The second story concerns their father, attorney Atticus Finch, who has been appointed to defend a black man, Tom Robinson, falsely accused of raping a white woman.

There are also two broad themes: tolerance and justice. The first is treated through the children's interactions with Arthur "Boo" Radley, their mysterious and maligned neighbor; the second is illustrated by Atticus's courageous moral stance in defending Tom Robinson to the best of his ability, despite the racial prejudices of the town. Tying the themes together is a homespun piece of advice that Atticus gives Scout: "If you just learn a single trick, Scout, you'll get along a lot better with all kinds of folks. You never really understand a person until you consider things from his point of view. . . . Until you climb inside of his skin and walk around in it." This appeal to recognize the humanity in everyone is practicable in normal day-to-day relations with people, even those we dislike, and, as Atticus powerfully demonstrates, in courtrooms where juries must sit in judgment of their fellow men and women.

The plot of the coming-of-age story revolves around Boo Radley, who is rumored to be a kind of monster living in a shuttered house down the street from the Finches. Scout, Jem, and their next-door neighbor Dill Harris engage in pranks to make Boo show himself. Unexpectedly, however, Boo responds to their interest by reciprocating with small acts of kindness and consideration. They come to feel affectionate about their unseen friend.

The Tom Robinson plot is fairly straightforward. As a black man,

Tom doesn't have a ghost of chance of being acquitted of raping a white woman, and Atticus knows he will lose the case. Still, the attorney faces up to the challenge, even stepping between a lynch mob and his client, though racist taunts are directed at Atticus's children.

The two plots intersect on a Halloween night not long after the trial is concluded. The drunken father of the girl Tom was accused of having raped ambushes the Finch children because Atticus exposed his ignorance and vices during the trial. He intends to kill the children, but they are saved by the angelic intervention of Boo Radley. Atticus is persuaded by the sheriff not to involve Radley in a homicide case (the children's attacker was killed during the struggle), because it would be cruel, he argues, to subject a pathologically shy man to a sensational trial that would, in any case, end in his acquittal. Atticus is unsure of the moral implications until Scout likens the choice to something her father once said: it's a sin to kill a mockingbird "because mockingbirds don't do anything but make music for us to enjoy." Scout escorts Radley back to his home and safety.

IN THE LATE 1990S, I left the teaching field to write biographies and histories for young adults. Historical and cultural figures such as Gandhi, Captain Cook, novelist Amy Tan, and filmmaker George Lucas were relatively easy to write about because of the wealth of information available about them. So, as a challenge, I started casting around for someone worthy of an adult book, but about whom not much was known. My thoughts returned to Harper Lee.

It was astonishing how little appeared about her in ordinary reference books. Encyclopedias carried two or three paragraphs, and often the facts were contradictory. She either had a law degree or she didn't (she doesn't); she either attended Oxford University for a year or for a semester (she attended only for a summer); she attended on a Fulbright scholarship (wrong and often repeated); her family is descended from General Robert E. Lee (fanciful, but not true).

For almost a year I myself wondered if I had enough information to flesh out a full-length book. Lee's growing up in Monroeville was colorfully eccentric but unremarkable except for what she heard, read, saw, and thought about. Although her family was upper-middle-class, the impact of the Depression turned Monroeville into a narrow world. "We had to use our own devices in our play, for our entertainment,"

Lee said later. "We didn't have much money. Nobody had any money. We didn't have toys, nothing was done for us, so the result was that we lived in our imagination most of the time."

Harper Lee and Truman Capote became friends as next-door neighbors in the late 1920s, when they were about kindergarten age. From the start they recognized in each other "an apartness," as Capote later expressed it; and both loved reading. When Lee's father gave them an old Underwood typewriter, they began writing original stories together. Capote moved to New York City in the third grade to join his mother and stepfather, but he returned to Monroeville most summers, rekindling his friendship with Lee.

In high school she was fortunate to have a gifted English teacher, Gladys Watson-Burkett, who introduced her to challenging literature and to the rigors of writing well. Lee's preferred authors became nineteenth-century British writers, with Jane Austen as her favorite. Nelle once remarked that her ambition as a writer was to "become the Jane Austen of south Alabama."

She spent her freshman year of college at Huntingdon College, a Methodist school for women in Montgomery, but transferred to the University of Alabama in 1945. Unable to fit in with the sisters of the sorority she joined, she found a better community of friends on the campus newspaper. Eventually, she became editor in chief of the *Rammer Jammer,* a quarterly on-campus humor magazine. Her junior year, she entered the university's law school but was unhappy about this career choice. Despite her father's hopes that she would become an attorney like her sister Alice and practice in Monroeville, Lee went to New York in 1949 to become a writer.

She spent eight years at odd jobs until friends loaned her enough money to live on for a year so that she could write full-time. Even so, the manuscript she showed Tay Hohoff, an editor at J. B. Lippincott, resembled a string of stories instead of a novel. Two and a half years of rewriting followed, under Hohoff's guidance. At last, *To Kill a Mockingbird* was completed and slated for publication in July 1960. Lee opted for the name "Harper Lee" on the book's cover because she didn't want to be referred to erroneously in the press as "Nellie." In the meantime, Truman Capote asked her to accompany him to Kansas as his "assistant researchist" on a project for the *New Yorker* magazine.

Their intense partnership as they researched the murder of a farm family in Holcomb, Kansas, resulted in *In Cold Blood* (1965), one of the outstanding nonfiction works of post–World War II literature. Capote slighted Lee, however, by hardly acknowledging her help.

To Kill a Mockingbird appeared to highly favorable reviews and quickly climbed to the top of bestseller lists, where it remained for more than eighty weeks. In 1961, the novel was awarded the Pulitzer Prize. A film adaptation was released in 1962, starring Gregory Peck, and received three Academy Awards.

Although fans of *To Kill a Mockingbird* waited for the second novel about a southern town that Lee said she was writing, it never came. She also researched a book similar to *In Cold Blood,* about a part-time reverend in Alexander City, Alabama, who was accused of killing five people for their insurance money and was later murdered himself by one of his victims' relatives. But she dropped the project in the 1990s.

Initially, that was about all I could uncover.

To FIND PEOPLE WHO may have known Lee at one time, I occasionally relied on unorthodox methods that were surprisingly effective. To begin with, I joined an online reunion service and contacted everyone listed who had attended Lee's schools during the years she was enrolled. This yielded some correspondents. The Huntingdon College alumni directory carried not only names and addresses but, in many cases, e-mails. Thus, I added more names to my list of people to talk with and write to. The alumni directory of the University of Alabama was available on CD, again with mailing addresses and e-mails. One day, I recall e-mailing three hundred Alabama alums and receiving dozens of helpful and informative replies in return. There was also a university yearbook from 1945 available for sale on eBay, making it possible for me to pair names in the alumni directory with Lee's former sorority sisters.

Next, as a result of Google searches turning up key words, I visited the archives of Columbia University; the New York Public Library; the Fales Library at New York University; the University of Virginia's network of libraries; the Library of Congress; the National Archives, in College Park, Maryland; the Harry Ransom Humanities Research

Center, at the University of Texas at Austin; the Museum of Mobile; the Hoole Library, at the University of Alabama; and the Duke University libraries. Through an online database at the University of Virginia, I located perhaps one hundred articles from national newspapers about *To Kill a Mockingbird* and e-mailed them to myself.

Now I was ready to get down to some real research, because there's still no substitute for interviewing people, examining materials firsthand in archives, and visiting locations associated with the person being written about. These steps alone took an additional two years.

As my research mounted, it seemed clearer to me that the question of what became of Lee's career had to do the nature of creativity—and the power of community. As a young woman in her early thirties, Lee was fortunate to come in contact with a handful of people in the arts who believed in her. After years of trying to write a novel, she was suddenly, through the generosity of friends, given money to live on for a year so she could write full-time. Then she was introduced to an agent who nurtured her talent. Next, her manuscript landed in the hands of an editor who recognized an unpretentious, hardworking writer and was willing to take her on as a kind of apprentice.

None of this is to take away from the value of *To Kill a Mockingbird,* but only to make the point that Lee had to put herself in league with people who could help her, who formed a circle around her and helped her create a book that would outlive all of them by decades, perhaps centuries. Over the years, unfortunately, Lee's "family" of helpers grew old and died. After the success of *To Kill a Mockingbird,* she felt under pressure and came to dislike many of the demands of fame. Although she worked on a second novel for some time, her muse then became more tentative, and she finally gave up. If there's a lesson to be learned, it's that artists are not Byronic types who emote on windy cliffs. (As G. K. Chesterton said, I seem to recall, an artistic pose is a sure sign of an amateur.) Producing a novel, like any creative effort, is demanding, usually solitary work. Certain people and circumstances are conducive to aiding the work. In Lee's case, these people were especially necessary, and replacements for them could not be found.

I have come to believe that Harper Lee was inspired by love to create her great novel—love for the world of the South, for her little town, for her father and her family, and for the values she found among the people she most admired. She was lucky enough to have captured many of the things she most wanted to replicate her first time out. Many writers have done much less after many books. Maybe she was, in some sense, satisfied. Maybe her deed was done.

The Making of Me

IT STARTED TO SNOW IN THE NORTHEAST AT ABOUT DAWN ON March 3, 1960.[1] All day, brisk winds whipped snow into mounds. Temperatures plunged to the twenties. In the seaside town of Wildwood, New Jersey, gusts of forty miles an hour tore a world-famous racing schooner, the *Atlantic,* from its moorings and set it asail and heaving like a bronco in the green waves.

In New York City, telephones went dead in all five boroughs as weather-related calls overwhelmed switchboard operators. The Lincoln Tunnel choked with the swell of outbound traffic until, by midafternoon, forward movement had halted. Cashiers at the Port Authority Bus Terminal refused to sell any more tickets to the twenty-five thousand stranded New Jersey commuters. Some office workers chose to wait out the storm by having dinner in town. Taverns were packed with patrons six deep at the bars. Restaurateurs, exhausted, warned of waits of two hours or more. By 10:00 P.M., yellow Checker cabs were crunching through the fourteen-inch snow with weary or inebriated passengers heading for nearby hotels. All night, two thousand snowplows from the garages of the Department of Sanitation headed into the streets, mounted by 7,500 workers. The next morning, New Yorkers rose from their beds and peeked at the sky. It was still snowing.

On York Avenue in Manhattan, between East Eighty-first and Eighty-second streets, the freezing air rang with the cries of snowball fights between children. From the window of her apartment at 1539 York, Nelle Harper Lee could see ambushes about to be sprung from behind doorway stoops and retreats taken to the safety of parked cars. A young woman who had grown up in the dry wire grass and piney woods region of southwestern Alabama, she had never, in her ten years in New York, witnessed such deep snow accumulating over a single night.

Somehow, though, a surprising March snowstorm seemed in keeping with the dramatic, absolutely unexpected events that were turning the thirty-three-year-old woman's life around. After two and a half long years of writing and rewriting, her first novel, *To Kill a Mockingbird*, had recently been chosen as a selection by both Reader's Digest Condensed Books (a coveted honor in those days) and the Literary Guild (another tough nut to crack). When her agent, Maurice Crain, called with the news, he had chuckled happily. He thought she would enjoy hearing the introduction written by the editor of the Literary Guild, John Beechcroft.

This month we offer our members another discovery—*To Kill a Mockingbird* by Harper Lee. It is a first novel and shows the sincerity and intensity that so often marks an author's first book. The author calls it "a love story pure and simple," and it is the story of a small town and of a way of life that were close to the author's heart. Harper Lee was born in a small town in Alabama, and as she writes, the reader feels she is writing about people and places at once dear to her and unforgettable.

To Kill a Mockingbird is the story of the Finch family: Jean Louise, known as Scout, her brother Jem, and the boy she has decided to marry, Dill Harris. Her father Atticus Finch was a lawyer and a member of the State Legislature. . . . The great mystery of the neighborhood was the Radley home. Gloomy, always shuttered, packed with mystery, the home fascinated Scout and Jem and Dill.

No one ever went inside its gate, and what lives were led there were the subjects of wild rumor.

Although Atticus Finch was a small-town lawyer, born and bred in Maycomb County, and had never been farther north than St. Louis in his life, he was a deeply sophisticated man in his knowledge of humanity. At the same time he was a man of unfaltering good will and humor. Because he was what he was, and because he lived where he lived, he and his children were plunged into a nightmare of events that marked their lives for the rest of their days.[2]

Crain's news had arrived a few days earlier, before the snowstorm. After putting down the phone, Nelle hadn't been able to sit still. Torpor would have been a sign of ingratitude—the only thing that would do was for her to take the Lexington Avenue express subway down to Crain's offices, on Forty-first Street, in Midtown, and share her happiness, bring a bottle of wine—something! She wrapped herself in the only presentable calf-length wool coat she owned and went out hatless. She abhorred anything on her head.

The temperature was in the upper twenties, and she had a five-block walk to Lexington Avenue. But she was tall, with a long stride, and could cover the distance in minutes. The wind blew back her short chestnut hair, showing a wistful face with features that her intimates might have recognized as inherited from her father, A. C. Lee, a lawyer back home in Monroeville, Alabama. Of her two older sisters, the one most often referred to as "pretty" was Louise. Alice, on the other hand—petite, disarmingly birdlike, and endowed with a remarkable wit—shared Nelle's dislike of cosmetics and perfume. The Lee sisters' only brother, Edwin, had died in 1951, the same year as their mother, Frances.

On this snowy day, though, Nelle was almost certainly not preoccupied with painful losses. Reaching Lexington Avenue, she turned north to get the Eighty-sixth Street express stop. She was startled by a police officer blowing his whistle and pointing at her. She glanced around uncertainly, incredulous that anything she might be doing would draw the attention of a traffic cop. But this one meant business.

"Yes, sir?" she said reflexively, her southern manners coming to the fore.

"You walked against the light. Couldn't you hear the cars?"

"Cars?"

He made her recite her name and address, then ripped off a ticket from his pad and handed it to her with a peremptory "Be careful."[3]

The incident rankled for a few minutes, but by the time she was standing on the subway platform with the train swooshing in front of her like a grimy silver dragon, the effect had worn off. As the train lurched forward, she sidled past people until she found an available seat. A tendency toward motion sickness always prevented her from reading on the train, so she spent the trip thinking and studying people.

Four months before, when she had turned in the final version of her manuscript to J. B. Lippincott publishers, there had been no indication that she should expect to be so happy, although the publisher seemed optimistic. The advance copy of her novel sent to reviewers by the company's publicist included this note: "Please set aside an evening or two real soon to read *To Kill a Mockingbird*. I'd be very happy to know your reaction. . . . We are rushing this paperbound copy to you so that you may share with us the rare fun and lift in the discovery of a new, fresh talent."[4] Her childhood friend, Truman Capote, had contributed a blurb for the review copy. "Someone rare has written this very fine first novel, a writer with the liveliest sense of life, and the warmest, most authentic humor. A touching book, and so funny, so likeable." But everyone at Lippincott had conscientiously done their best to rein in Nelle's expectations, too. During her thirty years on Printers Row, Nelle's editor, Tay Hohoff—a lifelong Manhattanite in her sixties—had seen too many young hopefuls crushed by rejection. Trying to prepare her new writer for anything, she had warned, "Don't be surprised, Nelle, if you sell only two thousand copies—or less. Most books by first-time novelists do."[5]

But now, suddenly, *To Kill a Mockingbird* was finding itself in impressive company: some of *Reader's Digest*'s recent picks had included Fred Gipson's *Old Yeller,* John Hersey's *A Single Pebble,* and *A Rockefeller Family Portrait,* by William Manchester. Being selected by the Literary Guild, Crain said, practically guaranteed that Nelle's novel would be a commercial success.

* * *

THE YEAR HARPER LEE moved to New York City, 1949, E. B. White wrote, "No one should come to New York to live unless he is willing to be lucky."[6] As every newcomer knew, the giant city had riches worth having, but at the time of Nelle's arrival there was practically no decent place to live. The wartime housing shortage hadn't abated yet, and thousands of residents were living in Quonset huts on former military bases in Manhattan Beach, Brooklyn, Fox Hills, and Staten Island. Hundreds of thousands more were doubled up with relatives. Apartment dwellers weren't budging because rent control ensured that they already had the best deals they could get. NO VACANCY signs were as ubiquitous as drawn-down window shades.

Overcrowding was a fact of life—there was standing room only on Midtown buses and lines of businessmen outside restaurants at noon. Cases of polio had risen 300 percent from the previous year, to 2,446 cases, making 1949 the worst year for the disease since 1931.[7] A Marine Corps veteran living with his wife in Queens described the kind of living situation that gave rise to disease: "Seventy dollars a month, hardly furnished, stall shower, ice box. The door down to the basement got water rats. They were banging on the door."[8]

If these reports were not enough to make expectant travelers to New York reconsider, there was the sheer size of Gotham to reckon with as well. Eight million people lived in the six hundred square miles of the five boroughs. The savvy among them knew how to navigate the city's twenty bridges, eighteen tunnels, seventeen scheduled ferries, fifteen subways, and the city bus lines. Or, if they didn't, they weren't bashful about hailing one of eleven thousand taxis. Getting lost could be hazardous. In 1949, twenty thousand children and adults were reported stolen or missing—last seen somewhere on New York's 6,000 miles of streets or 650 miles of shoreline.

From the air, New York City resembled a colossal outcropping of rock crystal scraping the clouds. But beneath the city's 630,000 manholes was the detritus of millions of human beings living in one place. Sewer inspectors working low tide between midnight and 8:00 A.M. cleared the catch basins of broken watches, Christmas trees, jewelry, murder weapons, false teeth, and the occasional glass eyeball. Living in this trash were rats as big as cats, long assumed to be the lords of the underworld until one night a worker saw an alligator swimming sinuously toward him. The city hunted down dozens of the reptiles in the ensuing weeks, all of them dumped into the sewers by pet owners.[9]

Nelle Harper Lee arrived in the city at age twenty-three. Her send-off from Alabama had not been festive, mainly because of her parents' reservations about her departure. Her mother, easily thrown off-kilter by emotional and health problems, imagined the direst scenarios befalling her daughter. Her father was crestfallen that his youngest child had burned her bridges by dropping out of law school in midyear at the University of Alabama a semester short of graduation. He had counted on her joining her sister Alice at his firm, Bugg, Barnett & Lee. At the time, A. C. Lee had been almost seventy, semiretired, and had entertained fond hopes that Nelle would replace him at the firm as part of his legacy. But she wanted to go to New York to write, an ambition that struck him as obstinately romantic, especially when the Lees already owned the *Monroe Journal,* the only newspaper in town.

He probably didn't have the heart to tell her that he feared she would be perceived as the proverbial southern hick coming to the big city. As soon as she said, "Sho' enough?"—Alabamians never understood what was so risible about that—northerners who thought they knew all about the South would have her pegged. Southern stereotypes ran rampant up North, that was clear: On the popular Fred Allen radio show, a Connecticut-born actor named Kenny Delmar was doubling-up audiences with his rendition of a blustering, pontificating southern politician named Senator Beauregard Claghorn. "When in New York ah only dance at the Cotton Club," intoned Claghorn solemnly. "The only dance ah do is the Virginia reee-ahl. The only train ah ride is the Chattanooga Choo-Choo." On the Jack Benny program, bandleader Phil Harris, a native of Indiana, pretended to be a crass, thick-headed, illiterate Southerner who drank too much. His signature song was "That's What I Like About the South."

Mr. Lee certainly had reason to fear that Nelle would return home with her spirit broken. As a worldly wise gentleman who had lived more than threescore years, he knew that lightning didn't often strike in the same place twice—and Monroeville had recently already produced one literary star.

Growing up in Monroeville, Nelle had been as close as a sister to the boy next door, Truman Capote, whose first novel, *Other Voices,*

Other Rooms, had been published in 1948. As children, they had played, wrestled, fought, and even written childish stories together. As the years passed, their friendship had not lost its power. Mr. Lee suspected that Nelle's desire to emulate Capote was what was drawing her to New York. Mr. Lee liked Truman—he had given him a pocket dictionary that the boy carried around with him until the covers fell off. In earlier years, he had felt sorry for Truman when his divorced parents dumped him on relatives in Monroeville. He wished him well in his literary success. But he wasn't so certain that he wanted Truman's dreams rubbing off on his daughter. If Nelle thought she could get a book written, accepted, and published in a finger snap—well, she had another thing coming. He believed that one day his prodigal daughter would return, and he would find it hard to resist saying, "I told you so."

None of this had made any difference to Nelle. She had passed up registering for the law school exams in spring, and since they wouldn't be coming around again for another year, why not try her luck in New York now? Mr. Lee could think of a hundred reasons "why not," but they would all fall on deaf ears. So he loaded his daughter's things into his black Chevy and, after she bid the family adieu, drove her down South Alabama Avenue—where Nelle had played tag, caught fireflies in jars, shot marbles, and stolen fruit from the neighbors' trees—to the railroad depot in Evergreen. They passed rickety picket fences, one-hundred-year-old trees, and homes where people had been born, lived, and died without ever feeling the need to venture far.

To a pair of young eyes, Monroeville was just a dusty old hamlet. Even after electric power had arrived in 1923, the town still had hung back languidly in the nineteenth century. When Nelle was a child during the Great Depression, the sawmill whistle at noon announced when it was time for the midday meal, and when it blew again at five o'clock, wives checked their progress on making supper. The metallic clink of blacksmiths' hammers rang from several shady alleys. Down by the warehouse docks, near the Manistee and Repton railroad depot, horse- and mule-drawn drays were as common as internal combustion trucks. During spring and fall, gardeners shared "pass-around perennials"—cuttings, seeds, and root dividings—throughout the neighborhood, knitting properties together with undulating blankets of calla lilies, coreopsis, dianthus, gladiolas, phlox, and fragrant chocolate vines. No one locked their doors; food was brought over in times of sickness or trouble. In hot weather, a friendly wave from a porch beckoned passersby to come on up for a glass of sweet tea. Ladies would get their work done in the morning, then get dressed in midafternoon and go to a neighbor's porch for visiting. News gleaned from church, a local fraternal dinner, and family events, and the weather, of course, provided dependable topics for conversation. (With as many as ten households on the same telephone party lines, everyone knew everybody else's business anyway.) Some talk was unwelcome in polite company, however, such as the goings-on at the Wild Boar, a honky-tonk outside of town; or how a pint of bootleg liquor was for sale anytime from a certain shed in the alley on North Mount Pleasant Street.

At dusk, especially in the late summer, the dry air sparkled with sawdust from the mills. In winter, when the red clay streets turned sloppy, cars splashed along in axle-deep tire ruts like chariots on Roman roads. The week before Christmas, most farmers didn't mind strangers trespassing on their land, so long as they cut just one tree, respected the fences, and closed the gates when they left. Come nightfall, Monroeville's sole watchman began his quiet rounds in the square.

Nelle would have all this to remember whenever she looked back. But that was not where her gaze was directed on that day in 1949. With his daughter in the passenger seat, Mr. Lee had turned south out of the square, and left Monroeville behind, the white dome of the courthouse receding in the rearview mirror. At Repton, he caught Route 44 going twenty-four miles west to Evergreen. The Louisville and Nashville Railroad steamed almost daily into Evergreen, pulling a line of Pullman cars. From there, his headstrong daughter could begin the 1,110-mile journey to New York City.

SHE FOUND AN AVAILABLE cold-water flat on the East Side in the Yorkville neighborhood, seven blocks east of Central Park, and a block and a half west of the East River, not far north from where Truman had rented his first New York apartment a few years earlier. The way he began *Breakfast at Tiffany's* would describe any hopeful writer like himself or Nelle starting out in that section of the city in those days: "one room crowded with attic furniture, a sofa, fat chairs upholstered in that itchy particular red velvet that one associates with hot days on a train. . . . The single window looked out on a fire escape. Even so, my spirits heightened whenever I felt in my pocket the key to this apartment, with all its gloom, it still was a place of my own, the first, and my books were there, and jars of pencils to sharpen, everything I needed, so I felt, to become the writer I wanted to be."[10]

Nelle's neighborhood was an old German-Czech-Romanian low-rise community of rathskellers, grocery stores, newsstands with papers in East European languages, Brauhauses, delicatessens, coffeehouses, flower shops, drugstores, and German-language movie theaters. Geraniums and catnip grew in window boxes; ivy and myrtle on brick walls; boxwood, yew, and laurel in tubs around sidewalk cafés. A block from her door was a branch of the New York Public Library built in 1902 and considered one of the most elegant architectural designs in the city. A few of the better restaurants, such as the Café Geiger, attracted tourists with loud polka music on weekends and fräuleins serving pigs' knuckles and sauerkraut, plockwurst, or Bavarian sauerbraten. In the cellar taverns where Deutsch-speaking men preferred to drink their lager in peace, a regular topic of conversation was the fallen Nazi Party or, on a happier note, the legend of local boy Lou Gehrig.

On Nelle's street, children dashed in and among cars after balls and called to friends to come out and play. There weren't enough garbage cans supplied by the city, so some protesting residents dumped their trash in the gutters.[11] On windy days, cyclones of newspapers, bread wrappers, and cigarette cellophane whirled through the air. In the heat, squashed fruit stank and the flies were as big as raisins.

Nelle needed a job, of course—Capote thought he could find her one as a writer, but that didn't pan out—and got one in a bookstore.[12] A bookstore was barely within the orbit of the literary world, but at least she would meet writers there. Or so she imagined. On the other hand, the tedium of unpacking boxes of books, shelving them, and ringing up sales was odious. Quickly, she learned one of the first lessons of living in New York: a job that barely pays the rent isn't worth it. After a long week's work and her rent payment, she was left with only about twenty-five dollars with which to purchase soup and stew for her hot plate. Her father, somewhat mollified that she had a job at least, would not have been pleased to see her walloping parking meters to dislodge a coin for a slice of pie at a Horn and Hardart's

Automat.[13] Her finances improved in 1950 when she took a position as a ticket agent at Eastern Airlines because she was required to join the Brotherhood of Railway Clerks union. Overnight, her salary doubled. After she learned the ropes at Eastern, she moved over to British Overseas Air Corporation (BOAC) because employees could fly to Britain at a discount, an adventure she liked to think about.

In the evenings, she sat down at the detached door she was using for a huge desk and wrote. At first, the din of the city was hard to shut out: taxis blowing their horns, trucks and fire engines roaring by, and radio shows squawking unintelligibly through open windows. On sultry nights, people sat outside, smoking and talking until all hours. With time, however, she was able to ignore the noise and settle into reveries. For subject matter to write about, she abided by the advice given to most novices: "write about what you know."

She might have written her version of the tale of the toy airplane, for instance. One Christmas, Truman had received an expensive "model airplane large enough to sit in and pedal like a bicycle," he recalled in his short story "One Christmas." "It was green and had a red propeller. I was convinced that if you pedaled fast enough it would take off and fly! Now wouldn't that be something! I could just see my cousins standing on the ground while I flew about among the clouds."

Nelle and Truman's cousin Jennings Faulk Carter had the same idea, according to Jennings in Marianne M. Moates's *A Bridge of Childhood: Truman Capote's Southern Years.* Only they decided to enhance the take-off phase by pushing the Trimotor Ford model off the roof of a tin-roofed barn. Knowing that Truman would never approve, they waited until he was away visiting. Then they got out a ladder and, with much grunting and perspiring, hauled the toy up on the roof. Jennings got in and Nelle volunteered to add additional thrust from behind. Jennings braced himself for takeoff.

Pedal, Big Boy! Pedal! Nelle screamed as she gave the plane a tremendous shove.

Everything was under control. The Trimotor Ford sailed off the edge of the barn. *I was flying!* then all of a sudden, instead of gliding over the pigpen and fence and landing on the grassy spot, the plane started to drop. *Bloop!* Holding on for dear life, I still hadn't lost control. There were two big hogs lying in the pond. One had heard the racket of the plane rattled down the topside of the tin roof, and she raised her head out of the water just in time to see the plane ram her side with a big *Whomp!* She'd never walk straight again.

The other old hog was excited, too, and as she stood up in shock, the plane careened off the first hog and hit her head-on. I sailed out of the plane into the water, and the plane went under the hog. Mud, trash, and manure slopped everywhere.

Nelle grabbed Jennings and pulled him from the wreckage. Then came the sorrowful task of explaining to Truman what they'd done. "We looked over the plane, all muddied, scrunched up, and hog-stomped. 'It'll never fly again,' [Jennings] said, realizing that what the crash hadn't done the hog had finished." Since he was Truman's cousin, he decided it was up to him to offer an apology.

I'm real sorry, Truman. Nelle and I are sorry we took it out and let something happen to it.

I'm glad you weren't here to see me cry, Big Boy, Truman said. I cried hard over my plane, probably more than anything in the world. I wish I was a magic person, then I'd fix it back. I'd make a lot of things right again. But then I guess there's no such thing as magic anymore.[14]

As a story, it would not, perhaps, be on par with something from the pen of Sherwood Anderson or Edgar Lee Masters. But Nelle Lee had a mission. She wanted to show the world where she was from; she hoped to write about the ripples of incident and character in her small town. Then again, perhaps writing about the red dust and sweet tea of her Deep South also comforted her. Because as weeks on her own grew into months, and then into years, she was learning another lesson of big-city life, that it is more than possible to be lonely among millions of people.

THE ARTS SCENE IN 1950s New York was tailor-made for socializing—there were all-night apartment parties with jazz recordings by Chet Baker, Charlie Parker, or Miles Davis playing in the background, poetry readings in basement clubs, and coffeehouses where no one looked askance at a joint being passed around. Some hipsters were still taking the A train to Harlem's Jungle Row, as it was called, for yardbirds and strings (fried chicken and spaghetti) and dancing at the Savoy Ballroom or Small's Paradise, but that had become pretty passé. Half a million Negroes lived in Harlem, but most of the big clubs were owned by whites now and would admit whites only. Nelle wasn't a swinger, though, even if she could have afforded it. The only way she could loosen up in groups was to have a few drinks of her favorite bourbon—a practice that would have upset her father, had he known about it. Mr. Lee was a strict Methodist and, as everyone in Monroeville knew, "as dry as an old bleached bone."[15]

A party-loving bunch of ex-Alabamians were living in New York, but they took Nelle's measure and found her lacking in essential cool. One of the chief revelers was Eugene Walter, a modern-day Puck from Mobile who kept a stuffed monkey under a glass bell jar and who was finishing a novel, *The Untidy Pilgrim*, soon to win the 1954 Lippincott Prize. "All the Southerners in New York would get together about every ten days or two weeks and cry over Smithfield ham," Walter said. "There was a community, like a religious group except it wasn't a church. Southerners always, by secret gravity, find themselves together. . . . You always knew, if there was any kind of trouble, that was like [having] cousins in town."[16] Nelle put in an appearance at these gatherings from time to time, often accompanied by Truman toting a bottle of scotch, but to most everyone else in the room she seemed to be an ordinary, self-effacing young woman in worn-out jeans and a tomboy haircut, ill at ease among sophisticates. "Here was this dumpy girl from Monroeville," remarked Louise Simms, an Alabamian and wife of jazz saxophonist Zoot Simms. "We didn't think she was up to much. She said she was writing a book, and that was that."[17]

It was through Truman, however, that she finally made two close friends. It happened in autumn 1954, when the chrysanthemums were in glorious full bloom in Central Park, during rehearsals of the Broadway musical *House of Flowers* at the Alvin Theater on West Fifty-second Street. Nelle wouldn't normally have found herself in the wings of a theater examining the mysteries of light boards, scrim, cables, and pulleys. But Truman had brought her along. He had co-written the the show's book and lyrics with Harold Arlen, composer of "Over the Rainbow" for *The Wizard of Oz*. As Truman's tagalong friend for the day, Nelle got to listen to run-throughs of songs and dance numbers for the show. The storyline was centered on a comic competition between the madams of two bordellos in the West Indies and a young romance that blossoms, defying the show's atmosphere of cynicism about love.

Helping to freshen up some of the lyrics was another young migrant to the New York arts scene, Michael Martin Brown, originally from Mexia, Texas. Michael was almost exactly the same age as Nelle's late brother, Edwin. After a stint of teaching, he had turned to composing and writing lyrics for a living. And in 1954 he was enjoying life at the top of his form. A novelty song of his, "Lizzie Borden (Fall River Hoedown)," had become a showstopper for the Broadway revue *New Faces of 1952*. The Chad Mitchell Trio had radio listeners all over the country chanting the chorus:

> 'Cause you can't chop your poppa up in Massachusetts
> Not even if it's planned as a surprise
> No you can't chop your poppa up in Massachusetts
> You know how neighbors love to criticize.[18]

"He was brilliant and lively; his one defect of character was an inordinate love of puns," Nelle wrote later for *McCall's* magazine. "His audacity sometimes left his friends breathless—who in his circumstances would venture to buy a townhouse in Manhattan?"[19] With his wife, Joy, and two small sons, Michael lived in a late-1800s two-story, seven-room townhouse at 417 East Fiftieth Street, refurbished in the contemporary 1950s style and dominated by his ebony grand piano. He enjoyed nothing better than dropping down on the piano bench and performing numbers from his cabaret act for the entertainment of his guests.

Drollery was Michael Brown's favorite type of humor, and Nelle had it in abundance, a trait that tended to go unnoticed at the gabfests she attended in other people's apartments. Since she lived only a ten-minute subway ride north of the Browns, Michael invited her over to meet his wife.

Joy Brown turned out to be not a young mother in tired dishabille chasing her two toddlers around the townhouse but an "ethereal, utterly feminine creature," in Nelle's eyes.[20] She had trained with the

School of American Ballet and danced with several companies, including the Ballet Russe de Monte Carlo and Les Ballets de Paris. But motherhood suited her, too, and she had hung up her slippers, so to speak. She also was a guilt-free chocolate lover who insisted on whipping up a big batch of fudge during at least one of Nelle's increasingly frequent visits. The three friends sang show tunes at Michael's piano or gorged on one of Joy's latest concoctions in front of the fireplace. "Common interests as well as love drew me to them," Nelle wrote. "An endless flow of reading material circulated amongst us; we took pleasure in the same theater, films, music; we laughed at the same things, and we laughed at so much in those days."[21] Michael and Joy listened as Nelle vouchsafed to them her hopes for becoming a writer, and they applauded the stories she read to them in a tremulously embarrassed voice.

DECEMBER 1956 ARRIVED AND Nelle was still working for BOAC. Not much had changed in her life, in fact. She was still struggling to make ends meet and squeeze in time to work on her fiction. In previous years, she had tried to schedule Christmas vacations so she could spend time with her family. She would arrive at the railroad station in Evergreen, bearing gifts like a female magus from the East, and be reunited with Alice and her father. Then she would take a few days to drive the 187 miles to Eufaula, Alabama, on the Georgia state line, to visit her sister Louise and her family. For Nelle, a trip to the balmy South acted as a vaccination against the long, dark, slushy months of winter about to descend on the Northeast.

But this year, word came down from BOAC's head office that though she could take Christmas Eve and Day as vacation days, she would be needed to handle the holiday rush. Her disappointment brought on a sudden bout of homesickness.

> New York streets shine wet with the same gentle farmer's rain that soaks Alabama's winter fields. . . . I missed Christmas away from home, I thought. . . . I missed the sound of hunting boots, the sudden open-door gusts of chilly air that cut through the aroma of pine needles and oyster dressing. I missed my brother's night-before-Christmas mask of rectitude and my father's bumblebee bass humming "Joy to the World."[22]

When the Browns heard that Nelle would be alone on Christmas Eve, they invited her over to stay the night and the following day, too, until it was time for her to leave for work.

Early Christmas morning, Nelle, habitually a late sleeper, opened one eye to see a small early-riser in footie pajamas commanding her to rise and shine. Downstairs everyone had already gathered at the foot of the Christmas tree and was preparing to distribute presents. Michael had built a crackling fire in the fireplace. The Browns were in an especially happy mood because Michael had received a financial windfall from his musical comedy special *He's for Me,* starring Roddy McDowell, slated to air on NBC in July. Things couldn't be better.

The adults never exchanged expensive gifts because Michael and Joy, knowing that Nelle couldn't afford them, had suggested that bargain treasures should be the order of the day for special occasions. That way, finding and giving offbeat presents would be part of the fun. This Christmas, Nelle was pleased with herself because, ever the Anglophile, she had purchased for Michael, for thirty-five cents, a portrait of Sydney Smith, the eighteenth-century founder of the *Edinburgh Review*; and for Joy, she'd rooted through used-book stores for a year until she found a complete set of the works of Lady Margot Asquith, an English wit who had once quipped, "Lord Birkenhead is very clever but sometimes his brains go to his head." With pride, Nelle handed out her gifts. And then there was a pregnant pause . . . nothing came her way in return. The Browns, smiling to themselves, let her twist in the wind a little a bit.

Finally, Joy said, "We haven't forgotten you. Look on the tree."

Poking out from the branches was a white envelope labeled "Nelle." She opened it. The note inside read, "You have one year off from your job to write whatever you please. Merry Christmas."

"What does this mean?" she asked.

"What it says."

Several seconds passed before she found her voice. "It's a fantastic gamble. It's such a great risk."

Michael smiled. "No, honey. It's not a risk. It's a sure thing."

She went to the window, "stunned by the day's miracle," she remembered later. Her friends had given her, she realized, "A full, fair chance for a new life." Not through "an act of generosity, but by an act of love. *Our faith in you* was really all I had heard them say."[23]

A few weeks later, Nelle wrote rapturously to a friend about the Browns' offer:

> The one stern string attached is that I will be subjected to a sort of 19th Century regimen of discipline: they don't care whether anything I write makes a nickel. They want to lick me into some kind of seriousness toward my talents, which of course will destroy anything amiable in my character, but will set me on the road to a career of sorts. . . . Aside from the et ceteras of gratefulness and astonishment I feel about this proposition, I have a horrible feeling that this *will* be the making of me, that it will be goodbye to the joys of messing about. So for the coming year I have laid in 3 pairs of Bermuda shorts, since I shall rarely emerge from 1539 York Avenue."[24]

She would have to carefully budget the Browns' gift of money, but it was enough to pay for rent, utilities, and canned groceries destined for the hot plate. She quit her job at BOAC, and soon her writing regime fell into place: out of bed in the late morning, a dose of coffee, and then to work—all day long until midnight sometimes. All she needed was "paper, pen, and privacy."[25] In these monastic conditions, her output soared.

THIS WAS HOW HARPER Lee, after all her nights of burning the midnight oil, found herself taking the Lexington Avenue express to Maurice Crain's office. This was how she found herself—full of expectation on that snowy morning in 1960—hearing the disembodied voice over the loudspeaker announcing "Forty-second Street, Grand Central!" She rose and exited to the platform, following shoppers, businesspeople, and slightly bewildered out-of-towners through the spokes of the turnstile, then up the stairs, gusted by fresh air, and onto the sidewalk. In department store windows, female mannequins sported bloused bodices, colorful billowing skirts, and cotton suits with kimono-cut sleeves—the fashions for the coming season—in contrast to the passersby bundled up in winter clothes against the nippy wind. Every time a customer opened a department store's big doors, a perfumed zephyr blew over the shoots of crocuses, narcissus, hyacinths, and tulips in garden boxes near the entrance, which seemed to be the only breath of spring sustaining them.

Maurice Crain shared offices at 18 East 41st Street with his wife,

Annie Laurie Williams, an agent who specialized in handling film and dramatic rights for literary properties. She worked closely with Mavis MacIntosh and Elizabeth Otis of MacIntosh and Otis, located on the floor below, an agency that had grown rich on one client alone: John Steinbeck. The two women had taken on Steinbeck when he was still an unknown, and he reciprocated by never changing agencies, despite eventually becoming one of the bestselling writers of the mid-twentieth century.

Williams had started in the business in the late 1920s, a young woman from Denison, Texas, a bleak cattle railhead near the Texas-Oklahoma border. After attending a dramatics school in Chicago, she came to New York expecting to become an actress.[26] When that didn't work out, she went into the publishing rights side of theater and film instead. At four foot ten and with a taste for Texas high plains clothes—lace-collared Edwardian blouses, cameos, and long skirts— she had impressed novelist Howard Fast as a "woman with a face and figure like Mae West and a mind like a steel trap."[27] Publishing was a gentleman's occupation in the twenties and thirties, as it would continue to be until the fifties at least.

But Annie Laurie Williams was no gentleman, and she made no bones about wanting to make money in the business. Her first successful sale was Lloyd C. Douglas's *Magnificent Obsession,* which became a hit movie in 1935. "That took nerve," Williams said later, "because no movie executive at the time wanted to buy a book by an unknown Lutheran minister."[28] In 1936, Williams had convinced Margaret Mitchell that *Gone With the Wind* would also make a fine movie, despite Mitchell's skepticism. She left the Atlanta-born journalist aghast when she turned down an offer of $35,000 for the film rights to Mitchell's book from 20th Century Fox, and another from Warner Brothers of $40,000. She held out for $65,000—the equivalent of $850,000 in 2005—and got it. (Mitchell never forgave Williams for her audacity, perhaps one of the only times an American author has held a grudge against the agent who made her wealthy.) Williams's track record improved for John Steinbeck, for whom she secured $300,000 in 1942 from 20th Century Fox (the equivalent of $3.5 million in 2005) for his novel *The Moon Is Down,* at that time the highest sale price on record for screen rights. To a reporter's query about whether it was true that her Hollywood deals for Clarence Day's

Life with Father, John Hersey's *A Bell for Adano,* and Kathleen Winsor's *Forever Amber* amounted to $800,000 worth of literature sold in a single day, Williams dead-panned, "Frankly, I don't do that much business in a whole week."[29]

She and Crain had no children, but to anyone with eyes, they were enough for each other. They had met in the 1930s when Crain, another Texan from the ranching town of Goodnight, was a city editor with the *New York Daily News.* He liked Williams's looks and spunk; she liked his bluff charm and confidence. When the United States entered World War II in 1941, Crain, despite being almost forty, enlisted. "Pops," as the other Army Air Corps cadets called him, made staff sergeant on B-17s as a ball turret gunner. On May 17, 1943, while flying with the 401st Squadron of the Ninety-first Group out of East Anglia, Crain's plane, the *Mary Ruth,* was shot down over the Ruhr Valley. After eluding capture for five days, he was eventually shipped via boxcar with hundreds of other prisoners to Stalag XVII-B near Krems, Austria, the camp later made famous by the film *Stalag 17.* He remained there until liberated by American troops eighteen months later.

The war left Crain with two peculiarities: He was extremely fastidious, always keeping his office immaculate and highly organized as if, for some reason, he might not be back. Second, he hated wasting time. He seemed to feel deprived of an adequate share of it. After a long day at the office, he chided Williams if they were late for Sardi's, their favorite restaurant, in the heart of the theater district on West Forty-fourth Street. He liked to arrive at the stroke of eight o'clock. For relaxation, they had a weekend getaway place in West Hartland, Connecticut: the Old Stone House, built in 1745. At first, neighbors mistook Crain for a hired laborer, with his short, powerful frame. He was always performing some manual task—pushing a wheelbarrow full of rocks or ramming a post-hole digger into the ground for a new stretch of fence.[30] His idea of taking a break was lighting a fresh Camel cigarette, of which he went through a couple of packs a day.

NELLE TOOK THE ELEVATOR up to Crain and Williams's offices, eager to begin celebrating their fantastic luck of having *To Kill a Mockingbird* selected by Reader's Digest Condensed Books and the Literary Guild, four months before the novel's scheduled publication, in mid-July. "I could just imagine what went on in that office," wrote Crain's sister-in-law Pamela Barnes to Nelle, several weeks later. "I am sure if that had happened to me I would just have swooned."[31]

Nelle was still feeling high from her visit to Midtown when she stepped off the subway train at Eighty-sixth Street a few hours later. She didn't keep a journal, but she was an avid letter writer and needed to get back to her apartment to send descriptions of the day's events to friends and relatives as soon as possible.

Then, as she was crossing an intersection, the same cop who had ticketed her earlier blew his whistle at her sharply. "C'mere, lady!" he shouted.

She came over to him, thinking he had hadn't forgotten about their encounter and wanted to give her one more rap on the knuckles for good measure.

"Are you deaf?"

"No, sir," she said meekly.

"Can't you *hear* the horns?"

"Yes, sir, I'm sorry—"

He wrote her up again.[32]

She tucked the second ticket into her pocketbook beside the first and continued on her way, pulled to earth again from Olympian heights by one of New York City's finest.

Several days later, the big snow of Friday, March 3, fell. A brief warming trend lasted over the weekend, causing icicles to fall hundreds of feet from dripping building cornices and stick like glass daggers in snowbanks. Some residents in Nelle's neighborhood strained at pushing their cars out of parking spaces along the street, and cursed the snowplows that roared past abruptly, blocking them in again with dirty slush up to their cars' rocker panels. It was a good weekend to stay inside.

Nelle, a baseball fan, settled in with the Monday morning *New York Times* and noted with interest that the weather in St. Petersburg had been frosty, too. Yankees manager Casey Stengel wasn't getting in the workouts he'd planned. Adding to his problems, Mickey Mantle and Tony Kubrek were still holding out on their contracts. A bright light was a new player, Roger Maris, who had just signed from the Athletics and would be taking over left field.

As she was considering venturing outside again to restock her pantry, the phone rang. It was Crain.

"Are you sitting down?" he began. "Because I've just hung up the phone, and guess what? Annie Laurie's instincts were right about Hollywood. On top of everything else, I've just received a call—"

"No!" Nelle blurted out. "Don't tell me until I get across that intersection!"[33]

"Ellen" Spelled Backward

"GET *OFFA* HIM!" NELLE ROARED. "GET OFF NOW!" SHE peeled the older boys from on top of their prey, uncovering beneath flailing elbows and knees her friend Truman Capote, lying on his back, red-faced and tearful, in the sandpit of the Monroeville Elementary School playground. The bigger boys had been playing a game called Hot Grease in the Kitchen, in which they demonstrated their territorial prerogative by standing with arms crossed in front of the sandpit as they announced, "Hot grease in the kitchen, go round, go round!"

Every other child had been wise enough to obey the injunction except Truman, who saw in the challenge a dazzling opportunity to get attention. With fists clenched and chin held high, he had marched toward the line, then broken through it, feeling the boys drag him down on all sides like Furies. Pain, darkness, and muttered curses between clenched teeth enveloped him for a few seconds. Then Nelle hauled him to his feet and escorted him away from his antagonists, glancing backward as if daring any of the others to pursue.[1]

But the boys knew better than to try that. Though she was only seven years old, Nelle Harper Lee was a fearsome stomach-puncher, foot-stomper, and hair-puller, who "could talk mean like a boy."[2] Once, three boys tried to challenge her, charging her individually like knights galloping toward her. Each ended up facedown, spitting gravel and crying "Uncle!" within moments. "In my mind's eye I can still see the fire in those big brown eyes as they stared dead ahead," recalled George Thomas Jones, who, as a sixth-grader, witnessed the brawl. "Her teeth clenched in jaws set as only could be akin to a full-blood bulldog. Her tiny hands balled into tight fists as she strode defiantly from the playground back toward her fourth-grade classroom."[3] Truman later based the character "Ann 'Jumbo' Finchburg . . . a sawed-off but solid tomboy with an all-hell-let-loose wrestling technique" on his friend Nelle in his short story "The Thanksgiving Visitor."[4]

Young men were not automatically her enemies, however. Those who appreciated her talents paid her the highest compliment they could think of: "She was just like a boy!" enthused Taylor Faircloth, a resident of Atmore, Alabama, where Nelle spent summers visiting her mother's sister, Aunt Alice McKinley. "She would come down and stay sometimes three or four weeks in the summer. In a small town, everybody knew everybody, and we just kind of roamed around like wild animals—we had no boundaries. She got rid of all her surplus hair in the summertime, and she could climb tall trees. When we played 'capture the flag' at night, she held on longer than anybody!"[5]

Although boys might venerate this behavior, girls generally did not. A youngster whom she bowled over at first base, ripping her dress in the process, called her a bully who acted like she knew more than anybody else. Maybe she did, but that was no excuse for the way she acted.

No one could dispute that Nelle was quick on the draw out on the playground, but she outstripped nearly all others in the classroom, too. Her vocabulary was prodigious, her skepticism a constant bother to teachers accustomed to quiet children who swallowed the material like guppies. Freda Roberson would turn around in her desk to watch in awe whenever Nelle would start in asking her usual slew of impertinent questions.[6] Mrs. Leighton McNeil, one of Lee's elementary school teachers, journeyed ten miles to Monroeville every morning on dirt roads from Frisco City. Early on, she was astonished to hear little

Nelle greet her at first as "Leighton." When the child was upbraided about it, she expressed confusion. At home, she explained, she called her father by *his* first name.[7]

Actually, anything about school, protocol, and organized activities went against Nelle's grain. "One year, there was an agricultural parade, in which schoolchildren were dressed up to represent products of the county," said Jane Hybart Rosborough, another of Nelle's classmates. "I wore a fertilizer sack and wasn't happy about it. My friend Sara Anne McCall was a ham."[8] Later, in *To Kill a Mockingbird,* Nelle appropriated the agricultural pageant for her novel, poking fun at the notion of dressing a child as a ham whose cue to appear in the pageant is "Po-oork!"[9] Alice Lee, thinking about her sister's antiauthoritarian streak, said simply, "Anyone who knows her well will tell you that she is a very highly individualistic person. She isn't much of a conformist. . . . Nelle was extremely bored by part of the school curriculum."[10]

So, in the eyes of her classmates, Nelle's taking on the job of guardian angel to Truman Streckfus Persons—as Capote was known then—was further proof of her particularity: Truman, as surely as every kid at Monroeville Elementary knew that night followed day, was a sissy, a crybaby, a mamma's boy, and so on. Moreover, if he had worn a sandwich board to school with the words HATE ME painted on it two feet tall, the advertisement would have been redundant. His clothes extended that invitation from a block away. It was the 1930s, the Great Depression, when children went to school in hand-me-downs that had been patched, taken down, taken up, or taken in several times. A girl in a flower-print dress of cotton made from a fifty-pound flour sack had nothing to be ashamed of then. Many children came to school with no shoes, their dirty heels thumping on the smooth pine floors. Consequently, when Truman's Aunt Jennie, the owner of a millinery in town, outfitted Truman in Hawaiian shirts, white duck shorts, blue socks, sandals, and Eton caps from the best department stores in Mobile and Montgomery, he looked, as one teacher expressed it, "like a bird of paradise among a flock of crows."[11] The implied insult to the other children could not be ignored. Boys gave him his comeuppance by rubbing cockleburs into his fine blond hair and bruising his milky skin.

Yet Truman was Nelle Lee's pilot fish—at school and in their neighborhood. And she looked after him not only because she was a head taller but because they complemented each other. "Nelle was too rough for the girls, and Truman was scared of the boys, so he just tagged on to her and she was his protector," said Charles Ray Skinner, a boyhood friend of Nelle's brother, Edwin. It was more than symbiosis, though. They were bound together, as Nelle would express it much later, looking back, "by a common anguish."[12]

NELLE WAS GOING ON five years old the summer she became acquainted with Truman, who was almost six and living with his aunts, the Faulks. Barefoot, Nelle enjoyed teetering along the top of the low rock wall that separated the Lee and Faulk properties. Next to the wall grew a twin-trunk chinaberry tree supporting a tree house. From this outpost, Nelle could spy on Truman ambling among the lilacs and azaleas. "Beautiful things floated around in his dreamy head," she would later write of him, when Truman became Dill, the lonely boy next door in *To Kill a Mockingbird*. "[H]e preferred his own twilight world, a world where babies slept, waiting to be gathered like morning lilies."[13]

Whatever his imaginative gifts, however, at first glance Truman hardly seemed the ideal candidate for friendship for a girl like Nelle. She was a female Huck Finn with large, dark brown eyes and close-cropped hair. Besides, she already had a playmate among her three siblings: her ten-year-old brother, Edwin. As a big brother, Edwin was a little sister's dream. Friends saw him horsing around in the backyard with Nelle, and he was good to her.[14] But when he left for an afternoon game of ball on the courthouse lawn, she was out of luck. Next oldest in line was Nelle's sister Louise, a freshman in high school. An attractive girl and a smart dresser, Louise enjoyed a burgeoning social life through 4-H and youth activities at the Monroeville Methodist Episcopal Church. But she was too old to play with Nelle, as was Alice, the Lees' eldest daughter, who was in her early twenties and working full-time at the *Monroe Journal*.

In fact, on the whole block of South Alabama Avenue there were no real peers for Nelle. A little girl lived across the street from the Lees briefly, but she moved away. To the south of the Faulks lived ex-Confederate Captain and Mrs. Powell Jones, whose house was best avoided. The Joneses were very old, and Mrs. Jones, an invalid in a wheelchair, could often be heard raising her voice at her beleaguered husband. Children passing by were not exempt from her imprecations, either. (Many Monroeville residents would later recognize in Mrs. Jones the model for Mrs. Dubose in *To Kill a Mockingbird*, who tormented Scout and Jem with her vicious taunts.) To the north of the Lees lived Mr. Hendrix, a druggist, and his wife. Their children were grown.

Under these circumstances, Nelle turned to Truman, who, it seems, was overjoyed. Before long, Truman's aunt Marie Faulk Rudisill, his mother Lillie Mae's sister, noted that the two children could often be seen climbing up into the tree house that was off-limits to meddlesome people known as "grown-ups."[15] Nelle was best at shooting marbles, while Truman excelled at swiping jacks off the sidewalk so fast that his hand was a blur. He was not coordinated, actually—the label "sissy" was undeserved, he just wasn't interested in the kinds of things most boys were—but was quick, agile, and determined, and could leap up on a rock wall and turn cartwheels. Kids at school called him "Bulldog" because he had an underbite, a moniker he lived up to by head-butting adversaries and knocking them down. Eugene Walter saw him do it in the lobby of the Lyric movie theater in Mobile, only Bulldog sailed in a bit low that time and collided with the other boy's genitals.[16]

The "common anguish" that bound Truman and Nelle may have become clear to each other in an unspoken way not long after they met. It isn't too much of a stretch to say that neither Nelle nor Truman fit the mold of what a parent had in mind for a child—and, in both cases, it was their mother.

Nelle, who was so unconventional at every turn that she left her teachers and classmates feeling nonplussed, came from a traditional Deep South family. She was the daughter of Amasa Coleman Lee and Frances Cunningham Finch. Amasa Lee, born July 19, 1880, in Georgiana, a village in Butler County, Alabama, was near the middle in a brood of nine: six boys and three girls, two of whom died in childhood. His family called him "Coley." It's highly doubtful that these Lees are related to the famous Virginia tidewater Lees that include Robert E. Lee, as sketches of Harper Lee usually claim. A. C. Lee's line starts with John Lee, Esq., born in 1695 in Nanesmonds, Virginia. A.C.'s father, Cader Alexander Lee, was a Confederate veteran who fought in twenty-two battles, including Gettysburg, as a private with the Fifteenth Alabama Regiment. General Lee may have tipped his hat to one of his most valiant soldiers, as well he should have, but that's as far as current genealogical research will take us about the relationship.[17] Coley's mother, the former Theodocia Eufrassa Windham, was sister to a kinsman of Cader Lee's killed at the battle of Malvern Hill, in Virginia.

Coley's upbringing was Methodist, with a stringent dose of Calvinism—meaning his parents frowned on drinking, card playing, and other time-wasting behavior. On Sundays, his father hitched up the horses for a three-and-a-half-mile trip from their farm in Chipley, Florida, to services at the local Methodist church. The message delivered there—the idea that salvation was only the first step in fulfilling a moral obligation to help reform humanity—became Coley's central philosophy. But chores on the farm took precedence over philosophizing or books. Some winter evenings he ran out of daylight before finishing his lessons. Luckily, though, he was an independent reader. At sixteen, he passed the examination to teach, and for three years did so, at a school near Marianna, Florida.

After his stint of teaching, Coley—who was now introducing himself as "A. C. Lee"—shook the dust of Florida from his heels. Eager for advancement, he relocated to Alabama's Monroe County, where sawmills were chewing into the piney woods, filling the air with their ear-splitting whine and the vinegary smell of fresh-cut lumber. A series of better-paying jobs brought him to Finchburg, Alabama, as a bookkeeper at the Flat Creek Mill. The postmaster there, James Cunningham Finch, had named the settlement for himself. While attending church one day, young A.C. was introduced to the daughter of Mr. Finch and his wife, Ellen Rivers Williams: nineteen-year-old Frances, a tall, well-educated young woman. They married in the bride's home on June 22, 1910.

Nelle's mother's side of the family began in Virginia, resurfacing in Monroe County, Alabama, in the early 1800s, probably as part of the migration of farmers who could no longer afford good land along the mid-Atlantic seaboard. Nelle's grandfather, James Cunningham Finch, the postmaster, grew up on his parents' farm near Belle's Landing, but the family of his wife, Ellen Williams, owned a plantation nearby, about halfway between Montgomery to the north and Mobile to the south. The land was excellent, bordered as it was by the Alabama River. Steamboats arrived to offload goods and take on the Williams's cotton. Slaves stood at the top of the hill and slid the four-hundred-pound cotton bales down a steep chute to stevedores, who halted them before they fell overboard or were lost in the drink.

Although Postmaster Finch's family was not as gentrified as the Williamses, he and Ellen tried to rear their children in circumstances as elevating as they could afford. When their daughters—Nelle's mother, Frances, and her sister, Alice—reached fifteen, their parents enrolled them in the new Alabama Girls' Industrial School in Montevallo, a progressive institution for whites campaigned for by Julia Tutwiler, a feminist leader in Alabama educational and penal reform.

The school was unusual, as it served as both a vocational and a finishing school. All the girls enrolled in English, Latin, and other basic high school courses. Then they could add elective classes, including stenography; photography; typewriting; printing; bookkeeping; indoor carpentry; electrical construction; clay modeling; architectural and mechanical drawing; sewing; dressmaking; cooking; laundering; house, sign, and fresco painting; home nursing; and "other practical industries."[18]

Frances Finch, Nelle's mother, excelled in the school's music program and appeared as a pianist and vocalist in concerts and recitals. On her way to class, she could be seen, like all her classmates, wearing the school uniform of a navy blue dress and a cap trimmed with white cord and a tassel. Trips off campus into Montevallo were forbidden without a chaperone. The school catalog warned, "It is understood that pupils are not here to enter society, but to be educated, therefore they are not allowed to correspond with gentlemen, and visits from them is positively prohibited under penalty of expulsion."[19]

With such an education, when Frances Finch married thirty-year-old A. C. Lee, she was an artistic, some might say bourgeois, young woman who looked forward to the genteel life her ambitious husband could provide. Throughout her life, family members often used the word *gentle* to describe her.[20]

A.C. did not disappoint her. In 1912, two years after their marriage, the Lees moved to Monroeville, then a town of seven hundred and fifty residents. There, A.C. quickly demonstrated that a small fish in a small pool could find itself generously enlarged.

The town hadn't changed much from the days of the Civil War, when a Confederate soldier passing through had identified it as the "most boring place in the world."[21] But Monroeville, already three generations old, finally seemed about to live up to its destiny. The year the Lees arrived, the first locomotive of the Manistee and Repton Railroad reached the downtown on freshly laid tracks, the brainchild of Monroeville businessmen J. B. Barnett, L. J. Bugg, and J. A. Kaufmann. The *Monroe Journal* proclaimed, "They will endeavor to establish through freight and passenger rates with the Louisville and Nashville Railroad, which will be a great convenience to all concerned."[22] The M&R did indeed begin hauling freight and passengers east from Monroeville to Manistee Junction, where it joined like a tributary the mighty Louisville and Nashville Railroad, which had missed the little town by only four miles.

A. C. Lee's reason for moving his wife and newborn child, Alice, less than two years old, from Bonifay, Florida, to Monroeville was that he was now financial manager for the law firm Bugg & Barnett, handling their majority interests in the M&R.

The benefits of the railroad's arrival had been staggering to the small town. After 1912, brick structures began replacing old weatherbeaten wooden buildings, providing the appearance of real permanence. Although the underpinning of the town's economy was still only a smattering of humble but necessary industries—a sawmill, a cotton ginnery, a gristmill, a fertilizer plant, a machine shop, lumber mills, and a waterworks plant—an enormous new county high school opened the same year the railroad arrived. It seemed to attest to the local bondholders' conviction that prosperity and a better future lay ahead for the town's young people.

A.C.'s career flourished in Monroeville, and specifically in the offices of Bugg & Barnett. First, he acquitted himself well as a financial manager. Then by "reading for the law" under the tutelage of his employers, he passed the bar examination in 1915. Steadily, he was ascending the rungs of respectability: from teacher in a country school, to bookkeeper, to financial manager, to attorney. The firm changed its name to Bugg, Barnett & Lee. His family was growing, too. Alice Finch Lee had been born in 1911; then Frances Louise Lee in 1916;

Edwin Coleman Lee in 1920. Despite his responsibilities as a family man, A.C. registered for the draft at age thirty-eight on September 12, 1918, when American forces were suffering their worst losses in France during World War I. "Although I was quite young at the time," recalled Alice, "I remember the anxiety among adults when it looked as though married men with dependents were facing the draft. Also do I remember vividly the rejoicing when the events of November 11, 1918, were celebrated in our small town," because an armistice had been declared.[23]

But Nelle Harper Lee, born April 28, 1926, the youngest of four children—the roughhousing boss of the playground who scampered up trees—put a crimp in the upper-middle-class home life that her parents had been expecting. By naming her "Nelle," a fanciful backward spelling of her grandmother Ellen's name, it was as if the Lees had introduced a changeling into the staid Finch-Lee line. Deliberately or not, she rebelled at everything her mother valued. With both heels dug figuratively into the ground, Nelle would not go willingly into the "pink cotton penitentiary" of girlhood, as the nine-year-old narrator of *To Kill a Mockingbird,* Scout Finch, characterizes it.[24] The charms of Miss Tutwiler's Alabama Girls' Industrial School—dressmaking, cooking, laundering, home nursing, and house, sign, and fresco painting—would not have held her attention long. She couldn't even accept, without squabbling with her teachers, the three *R*s offered at the public school down the block. Hence, Frances Lee and her stubborn daughter lived in two different worlds. The situation was further strained emotionally when Mrs. Lee began to show signs of mental illness.

"We went to Mrs. Lee's practically every day," said Marie Faulk Rudisill, who was Alice Lee's age and lived next door with Truman and the rest of the Faulks. "She was very kind and very sweet to us. Always had a watermelon for us out on the back porch, but she didn't talk to us at all. I never saw her even speak to one of her children. She got up in the morning and started playing that darned piano all day long, or going outside on her front porch and tending to her nasturtiums in flower boxes on the end of the porch. Those were the only things I ever saw Mrs. Lee do, but as far as providing companionship for the children that wasn't so because Mrs. Lee never left the house."[25]

From the time she was small, Nelle mainly knew her mother as an overweight woman with a host of demons, some of which resembled symptoms of what is now known as bipolar disorder. The "gentle soul" of the household could become inexplicably upset or unaccountably happy at the drop of a hat. On certain days, Miss Fanny "seemed withdrawn" to visitors: she might remain blank-faced in response to a greeting, as if she didn't know the person, or only nod in reply.[26] On other occasions, she would veer to the opposite pole, her mind racing, words tumbling and gabbling out. During these periods of mania, she even shouted instructions to people on the street. One day, Mrs. Lee spotted someone walking past the house at a good clip despite the beastly hot weather. She charged out on the porch and, pointing out another passerby sauntering along, shouted, "Walk like her!"[27]

Capote disliked Nelle's mother; she was an "eccentric character" and an "endless gossip," he thought. He pilloried her when he was ten years old in a story titled "Old Mrs. Busybody" and submitted it to the *Mobile Register* for a children's writing contest. Frances was the character Old Mrs. Busybody, "A fat old widow whose only amusement was crocheting and sewing. She was also fond of knitting. She didn't like the movies and took an immediate dislike to anyone who did enjoy them. She also took great delight in reporting children to their mothers over the slightest thing that annoyed her. In other words no one liked her and she was considered a public nuisance and a regular old Busybody." Over the next twenty-seven pages, Mrs. Busybody endures a visit from her atrocious in-laws (showing comical forbearance at their fights, drinking, and boorishness like the grande dame in Marx brothers movies) until they leave on the train for their home in "Slumtown."[28]

It was so true to life, Capote claimed, that when the story appeared in the newspaper, he instantly became a notorious character on South Alabama Avenue. "I'd walk down the street and people on their front porches would pause, fanning for a moment. I found they were very upset about it. I was a little hesitant about showing anything after that. I remember I said, 'Oh, I don't know why I did that, I've given up writing.' But I was writing more fiercely than ever."[29]

The Lees coped with Frances's "nervous disorder," as they preferred to call it, as best they could. For several years, in June, Mr. Lee sent his wife on a lengthy vacation to Orange Beach on the Gulf of Mexico, under the watchful eye of his secretary, Maggie Dees, a single woman who lived on their street. During these times, he sent Nelle to the home of his sister-in-law, Mrs. Alice McKinley, in Atmore, hoping for a little peace and quiet for a few weeks. Alice, whose nickname in the family was "Bear," shifted some of her father's burdens onto herself by acting as his substitute helpmate in practical affairs. Louise, nicknamed "Weezie," concentrated on an active social life and swept problems at home into the background. Edwin, simply called "Brother," was a loner who stuck close to a few good friends and kept his head down. (Nelle, the baby sister, was called "Dody," for reasons known only to her family.) A.C. responded to his wife's maladies, and their impact on his family, with a stiff upper lip. A cerebral, contemplative man, he went about his business without complaint, probably reasoning that everybody had some kind of cross to bear and that in the scale of things he had much to be grateful for.

As a help to Mrs. Lee, the household was run along simple lines. "She had a Negro woman who came in every day and cleaned up for her," said Rudisill.[30] Hattie Belle Clausell walked over to South Alabama Avenue from the Negro part of town.[31] She kept the house organized with a sort of Spartan plainness: there were no rugs to vacuum or shake out, the chairs were cane-backed, the iron bedsteads had been painted white, and the pine floors gleamed from regular rubbings with oil.[32]

When Nelle barged through the screen door after a day of play, sunburned and grass-stained, it was usually Hattie, instead of Nelle's mother, who ordered "Miss Frippy Britches" out of her hand-me-down overalls, to be scrubbed in the tub, combed, and given supper in the kitchen.

Even so, over the years, despite the precautions taken to help maintain Mrs. Lee on an even keel, her condition deteriorated. Sympathetic neighbors began using terms such as "hardening of the arteries" and "second childhood" to describe her behaviors. "She used to go out but they didn't permit her to go out," said Rudisill. "She tried to go out and walk around town but they put a stop to that. They had to watch Mrs. Lee. They kept her in the house or on the premises."[33]

Frances Lee's "nervous disorder" deprived Nelle of affection while she was growing up and approval from one of the most important figures in a child's life. In fairness, Monroeville, especially during the years of the Great Depression in the 1930s, was not a healthy environment for someone like Frances. The image of a troubled woman marking time by playing the piano or reading all day is a lonely one.

But her severe mood swings almost certainly undermined the constancy children need to feel secure. It's likely that Nelle regarded her unhappy mother with sympathetic but confused feelings. When it came time to write *To Kill a Mockingbird,* Nelle wiped the slate clean of the conflict between herself and her mother. Since she could not be her mother's daughter, so to speak, in the novel, the fictional Finch family has no mother. Or, rather, it did have, but "Our mother died when I was two," says Scout, "so I never felt her absence."[34]

"I THINK MRS. LEE loved people," Rudisill said, "but she had a very hard time expressing it."[35]

In Truman's case, the evidence that he and his mother were mismatched is even more apparent. He couldn't have misinterpreted the meaning of her behavior toward him: she abandoned him; she simply didn't want him. Truman's unhappiness began in fact even before he was born.

His mother, Lillie Mae Faulk, while still in her teens, had enjoyed the reputation of being a "rare beauty" while she was growing up in Monroeville.[36] Through the glass booth at the Strand movie theater on the town square where she sold tickets, boys gawked at her as if she were something wonderful on display. Then, in the spring of 1923, her prince, Archulus Julius Persons (pronounced "PEER-sons"), arrived in a chauffeur-driven Packard Phaeton. He was in town visiting fraternity brothers from college. As a suitor, Arch had a few peccadilloes: he was a feckless huckster, a disbarred lawyer, and a world-class liar. But Lillie Mae was smitten, even if her paragon did wear spectacles as thick as magnifying glasses. More and more often that summer, Persons knocked on the door of the Faulks' home, next door to A. C. Lee's house, where the object of his affection resided with four cousins—three unmarried sisters and a bachelor brother—who shared her surname.

On August 14, 1923, silver-haired probate judge Murdoch McCorvey Fountain granted a marriage license to Arch, not quite twenty-six, and Lillie Mae, his bride-to-be, just sixteen. Less than a week later, on a sweltering day, a Baptist minister married the pair in the Faulk home as guests consumed gallons of lemonade. At the piano, Nelle's mother played a sonorous repertoire of classical music.

It only took a few weeks for the love knot to unravel. In New

Orleans, where the couple was kicking up their heels in the French Quarter, Arch confessed to his child-wife that he was in "straitened means"—that is, he was practically broke. Yes, he was formerly a lawyer, but he had been accused of unethical conduct. (His main line of work, as would become clear over time, was hustling to make a buck.) Tearful and humiliated, Lillie Mae returned alone to the big Faulk house. Arch stayed behind in New Orleans, probably suspecting, with good reason, that Jennie Faulk, Lillie Mae's cousin, would brain him with a skillet if he dared show his face in Monroeville. Once before, years earlier, she had horsewhipped a man she didn't think fit to court her younger sister, Callie.

Thirteen months after the marriage, on September 30, 1924, Truman Streckfus Persons was born. Arch—apparently back on the scene temporarily—chose the name Truman after one of his college friends. "Streckfus" was an obsequious gesture toward Arch's latest employer, the Streckfus Steamship Line, a fleet of old-fashioned paddle wheelers that offered hot jazz by Louis Armstrong and other musicians during trips on the Mississippi and Ohio rivers.

But the marriage was doomed. During the next several years, threats of divorce smoldered as Lillie Mae and Arch both pursued extramarital affairs. By the time the union ended in 1931, Truman had become a tiny piece of collateral damage. His mother, determined to immerse herself in cosmopolitan excitement and sophistication, booked hotel rooms in New Orleans and Mobile, where she locked Truman in by himself when she went out, instructing the hotel staff to ignore his hysterical screams.[37] Arch was a rare presence.

Between 1928 and 1930, Truman was shunted more and more often to Monroeville to stay with his mother's cousins, the Faulks. By the summer of 1930, Lillie Mae and Arch had sent him to live in Monroeville indefinitely. Freed from the burdens of parenthood, Arch whisked away in a rented limousine in pursuit of get-rich-quick schemes while Lillie Mae flew like a butterfly to New York, having won an Elizabeth Arden beauty contest. Truman started throwing red-faced tantrums, legs flailing in the air. Once, he found a bottle of perfume Lillie Mae had left behind in a bureau drawer, and he quaffed it like an elixir that would magically draw his mother back to him.[38] (Truman later averred that he never cared much about seeing his shiftless father.)

Besides perceiving Truman as a millstone, Lillie Mae had a grudge against him, which he refused to feel contrite about: he acted effeminate. As he grew older, his mother openly resented that her boy was not conforming to her image of what a son should be: a rough-and-tumble hearty. "Lillie Mae continually attacked him for behavior she thought effeminate and improper," wrote Truman's aunt Marie Faulk Rudisill in *Truman Capote*. "She rode him constantly."[39]

"Truman, I swear, we give you every advantage," his mother raged, "and you can't behave. If it were just failing out of school, I could take it. But, my God, why can't you be more like a normal boy your age? I mean—well, the whole thing about you is so obvious. I mean—you know what I mean. Don't take me for a fool."

So he was trapped both ways. Craving his mother's love, he missed it keenly; on other hand, there was an aspect about him that he couldn't change, and it repelled her. Like Nelle, he was who he was.

If Nelle and Truman's "common anguish" had been limited to their mothers, they might have channeled their energies into relationships outside the home instead. But they were in a double bind. In Truman's phrase, they were also "apart people," different from most other children their age.[40] A classmate of theirs at Monroeville Elementary School recalled seeing them play a word game before the start of the Saturday matinee at the Strand Theater. "They were a little above the rest of the kids in town," she said simply.[41]

This can be interpreted as Nelle and Truman thinking they were better than everybody else. In their defense, Monroeville during the Depression in the 1930s was not much to be above. The cultural index, or standard of living, in the South at the end of the 1920s was already the lowest in the nation. The region was at the bottom of the list in almost everything: ownership of automobiles, radios, residence telephones; income per capita; bank deposits; homes with electricity, running water, and indoor plumbing. Its residents subscribed to the fewest magazines and newspapers, read the fewest books; they also provided the least support for education, public libraries, and art museums.[42] When the stock market crashed in 1929, Monroeville drifted back into the economic twilight preceding its two golden decades between 1910 and 1930.

Even so, if Nelle's father, A. C. Lee, and Atticus were alike in "disposition," as she later claimed, A.C. would likely not have encouraged his children to rank themselves above others because of their ancestry or social position. While many Southerners were preoccupied with tracing their roots back centuries, Mr. Lee apparently didn't care. For a questionnaire he completed for the state archives during his political career, he was asked for "Remarks on Ancestry. Give here any and all facts possible in reference to your parents, grandparents, great-grandparents, etc., not included in the foregoing, as where they lived, offices held, Revolutionary or other war service; what country the family came from to America, where first settled, county and State; *always* give *full* names." He typed a succinct answer. "Haven't complete data on great-grandparents, but they moved from South Carolina about a hundred years ago to Dale county, Alabama."[43]

Likewise, when Atticus, an atypical Southerner who evinces a tolerant skepticism toward the past and its traditions, is pressured by his sister, Aunt Alexandra, to tell Scout (Jean Louise) and Jem about their "gentle breeding," he does so without enthusiasm:

> Your aunt has asked me to try and impress upon you and Jean Louise that you are not from run-of-the-mill people, that you are the product of several generations' gentle breeding . . . and that you should try to live up to your name. . . . She asked me to tell you you must try to behave the little lady and gentleman that you are. She wants to talk to you about family and what it's meant to Maycomb County through the years, so you'll have some idea of who you are, so you might be moved to behave accordingly.[44]

Scout, never having heard her father speak so strangely, bursts into tears. Atticus tells her to forget what he has just said and bids the children a humorous goodnight. Perhaps in Nelle's family, her father also discouraged notions of superiority based on background. This would partly explain her lifelong dislike of pretense.

In any case, as Nelle remarked later, during the Depression, there were no "strivers," anyway—"life was grim for many people who were not only poor but hungry, and their wants were absolutely basic." In such an atmosphere, there was little to nourish youngsters' imaginations, whether a child was precocious like Nelle and Truman or not. There was no library in Monroeville or ongoing activities outside of church. There were no books to take home from school because it had none to loan. Movies at the Strand Theater tended to be escapist Westerns, adventures, or romances because people wanted to forget their problems for a few hours. In most households, the outside world was funneled into the living room via radio or newspaper only. "This was my childhood," Nelle said. "If I went to a film once a month it was pretty good for me, and for all children like me. We had to use our own devices in our play, for our entertainment. We didn't have much money. Nobody had any money. We didn't have toys, nothing was done for us, so the result was that we lived in our imaginations most of the time."[46]

One way "apart people" with time on their hands could feed their imaginations was by reading. The books were provided by their respective families. Truman's cousin Jennings Faulk Carter recalled how Nelle and Truman's shared love of reading created a bond that put them in splendid isolation.

> The year I began school, Truman and Nelle were knee-deep reading Sherlock Holmes detective books. Even though I hadn't learned to read with their speed and comprehension, we three would climb up in Nelle's big tree house and curl up with books. Truman or Nelle would stop from time to time to read some interesting event aloud. We'd discuss what might happen next in the story and try to guess which character would be the culprit. Sometimes Truman called me "Inspector." Nelle was "Dr. Watson."[47]

Hearing stories read aloud was another passion. *The Rover Boys,* written by Edward Stratemeyer, was a favorite series, despite the stories' ridiculously stilted dialogue—"'Hello, you fellows!' shouted a voice from behind the Rover boys. 'Plotting mischief?'" At least they featured a girlfriend-sidekick named Nellie. A better choice, in Nelle's opinion, was the *Seckatary Hawkins* books by Robert F. Schulkers. The series is centered on a boys' club on the Kentucky River; the plots usually revolve around a suspicious new boy, slandered by rumor or blamed without evidence, who later comes out on top by dint of his character. He seems to embody the club's motto, "Fair and Square." "When we were a bit too young to read, Brother, who was a voracious reader," Nelle said, "would read many, many stories to us. Then we'd dramatize the stories in our own ways, and Truman would always provide the necessary comic relief to break up the melodrama." Later, when Nelle was old enough to read the *Seckatary Hawkins* series on her own, she wrote to the publisher requesting a club membership form. In her childish handwriting she signed the pledge: "I shall always be fair and square, possessed with strength of character, honest with God and my friends, and in later life, a good citizen."[48]

Sometimes her ideals were tested: As a friend, Truman could be a handful. Throughout his life he would exhibit the habit of testing the devotion of those who tried to care for him. Even early on, Nelle was no exception. She wouldn't let him get under her skin, though, even when he marred a nice afternoon spent cutting out magazine pictures of kites by raging at her.

" 'Stop that, Nelle. Keep your hands off my pictures. I hate you, Nelle. I really do.'

'You shut up, you silly little shrimp, or I'll knock your silly block off.' "[49]

He couldn't push her far.

When this sort of pleading failed, he tried shaming her into letting him have his way by playing the victim. But she had older siblings and didn't have an only-child's expectation of special treatment. His bawling accusations that she was being mean to him drew angry physical retaliations. In *To Kill a Mockingbird,* the narrator, nine-year-old Scout Finch, flails at her brother, Jem, yelling, "You ain't so high and mighty now!" a reenactment of some of the contests between Nelle and Truman. "She was bigger than Truman. Lots bigger," said Jennings's mother, Mary Ida Carter. Nelle would hurl him to the ground, as if to demonstrate that weakness made one the legitimate prey. "She was tough on me," Truman later said.[50]

Unable to overcome her in physical contests, he tried other methods to manipulate her. Once, he concocted a fabulous scheme to make her jealous. Still smarting from one of their fights, Truman decided to run away with another girl he knew, an older girl named Martha Beck. They hitched to Evergreen, probably with the idea of getting on the train and lighting out for parts unknown. But they were spotted and brought home by suppertime.[51]

Yet despite their spats, separations, and grudging reconciliations, the two friends remained inseparable. They swam in the pond at

Hatter's Mill Creek, where speckled trout tickled their legs. Sometimes they hiked the dirt road that led to Jennings's farm. They liked it when Truman's aunt Mary Ida spread the kitchen table with homemade biscuits, jam, butter, and fresh milk to welcome them. And if nothing else, they could always walk to the town square.

Two blocks north, South Alabama Avenue became the east edge of the town square, an even larger landscape for Nelle and Truman to explore. (In those days, three sisters worked the local switchboard—Thelma and Lillian Lamb, and Wilka Croker—and, like guardian angels, they could locate any child for a worried parent. More than one teenager talking on the phone was surprised to hear the operator break in and say, "Betty Jean! Your mother's looking all over for you. Get home!")

On the perimeter of the square were shops providing simple goods and services—hardware parts, jewelry repair, dry goods, and so on. The Barnett and Jackson Hardware Store was always worth a brief visit. The owner, Gus Barnett, had a wooden leg and never minded hiking up the cuff of his pants to satisfy children's natural curiosity. A good long hour, though, could be spent gazing at the panoply of household, children's, and gift items in M. Katz's Department Store. Meyer Katz was a Russian Jew born in Kiev who had worked his way up from peddler on foot in southern Alabama to his position as an established and patriotic merchant. "The only free cheese is in a rat trap!" he was fond of saying. He also had the ironic distinction of selling the local Klan their sheets in the 1920s. When an abashed Klansman said that maybe he shouldn't buy his robes from a Jewish storeowner, the unflappable Katz replied, "That's all right because you know who I am and I know who you are. And you know that if you buy them somewhere else you will have to pay more for them."[52] In *To Kill a Mockingbird,* Atticus recalls that the Klan paraded by "Mr. Sam Levy's house one night but Sam just stood on his porch and told 'em things had come to a pretty pass, he'd sold 'em the very sheets on their backs. Sam made 'em so ashamed of themselves they went away."

Also on the square was the Home Café, changed by Nelle to the O.K. Café in her novel, "a dim organization on the north side of the square." Mrs. Dubose, trying to intimidate Scout, points an "arthritic finger at [her]—'What are you doing in those overalls? You should be in a dress and camisole young lady! You'll grow up waiting on tables if somebody doesn't change your ways—a Finch waiting on tables at the O.K. Café—hah!'"[53]

On Sundays, families who could afford it ate boardinghouse style for fifty-five cents at the Simmons Hotel on a side street off the square. Fifteen minutes before the midday meal of chicken, mashed potatoes, okra, corn, gravy, cornbread, and pie, a Negro boy in a white suit rang a bell vigorously at the curb.

And there were three pharmacies on the square, all featuring soda fountains where cold drinks cost five cents. The name of the newest drugstore had been chosen through a contest. Alice Lee had won the first prize of five dollars by combining "Monroeville" and "Alabama" into Monala. Sometimes, the prospect of soda fountain ice cream dangled in sight when a tin can on a string descended like bait from a second-floor window of the jail across from the courthouse. It meant that a prisoner up there needed someone to run an errand. In the bottom of the can would be money for cigarettes, or a soda, and enough left over for a tip.

In the center of the square and dominating everything by its size was the Monroe County Courthouse, which was always open to the public. A genial, moonfaced man named Judge Nicholas Stallworth had conceived it. He was convinced that Monroeville, the "hub of Southwest Alabama," needed a courthouse worthy of the distinction. And he persuaded the town council to agree, so that in 1903, work got under way. But the first shovelful of dirt turned up bad luck: the architect or one of his assistants had lost the blueprints and a new set had to be drawn. Then, during construction, a realization hit like a thunderbolt: no one had instructed the workers to dig a basement. As the costs continued to mount, predictions flew that the jumbo courthouse—a citadel of brick, four-stories high and capped by a white clock tower shaped like a bishop's miter—was destined to be a white elephant. At the next election, the voters turned Judge Stallworth out of office, nicknaming his legacy "Stallworth's Folly."[54]

There was nothing foolish about the courthouse's interior, however. On the contrary, it was, as the *Monroe Journal* boasted, "one of the handsomest and most conveniently appointed in the state and one that would do credit to a county far exceeding Monroe in wealth and population." With its double set of tall slender windows, curving side aisles, second-floor gallery suitable for a choir, and rows of wooden benches like pews, the courtroom gave the impression of a small church with New England ties. Its tin ceiling was stamped with patterns of dogwood blossoms. The pine floor, tight as a ship's deck, had been treated with coats of black gum to withstand the boots of country folk. At the front was a dais, eight-sided like a small stage and enclosed by white balusters, where lawyers presented their forensic performances before the judge's bench. To the judge's right sat the jury box. Visitors to the courtroom tended to whisper in reverence. From the gallery, Truman and Nelle could watch Mr. Lee below performing the functions of a title lawyer. Truman later complained that sometimes Nelle only seemed interested in hanging around the courthouse and playing golf.

Nevertheless, in his emotionally unstable world, Nelle presented him with a steadfast friendship. Her faithfulness was something she never hesitated to prove. Truman touched in her a desire to see underdogs treated "fair and square"—a sentiment that would be important to her throughout her life. Because of her loyalty, some of Truman's loneliness gradually abated: he had a good friend and didn't feel so alone.

WHILE NELLE AND TRUMAN were still youngsters of elementary school age, the flint of their imaginations was sparked by a simple act of thoughtfulness. Instead of a bond of "common anguish," this would be another creative bond, such as reading books or acting out stories. Nelle's father gave them a typewriter.

Recognizing that his daughter read better than any of her classmates—Truman, he may or may not have heard, was whacked on the palm with a ruler his first day of school for reciting the alphabet—Mr. Lee gave them the 1930s equivalent of a word processor: a rugged, steel-chassied, black Underwood No. 5 typewriter. It looked like an accordion lying on its back, and every mechanical thing it did was visible. Depressing a key lever raised the corresponding letter from the semicircular comb, shifted the carriage, and resulted in a satisfying "Clack!" as the letter struck an ink ribbon and imprinted its shape on a sheet of paper. Just operating it was fascinating.

But that was not Nelle and Truman's ambition. They wanted to use it to write stories.

At first, Truman had to assuage Nelle's skepticism about laboriously tapping out stories with one finger versus writing them by hand. He explained to her that typing was what real writers did, instead of printing in block letters. She countered that making up stories and repeating them was the quickest way of all. Again, he baited her with the status of being a real writer, like the authors of their favorite books. Apparently, his logic won her over.[55]

Most children probably would have begun by creating original fairy tales. But an invasion of fairies in down-and-out Monroeville seemed farfetched. Anyway, the two friends' favorite books, the *Seckatary Hawkins* series, were about the adventures of a boys' club on the banks of the Kentucky River. That wasn't so much different from their hometown. Why couldn't Monroeville—their neighborhood, in fact—do just as well for a setting? This would also dovetail with another of their favorite activities—people watching. They knew more about "Doc" Watson, the dentist, and his family across the street, for instance, than they would ever know about trolls and so on. As a result of this line of thinking, the residents of South Alabama Avenue unknowingly became dramatis personae in the first stories of Truman Streckfus Persons and Nelle Harper Lee, authors—one of whose earliest efforts (since lost) bore the provocative title "The Fire and the Flame."[56] One child would dictate the story slowly while the other typed, and then they would switch places. Looking back, Nelle was of the opinion that small-town life "naturally produces more writers than, say, an environment like 82nd Street in New York. In small town life and in rural life you know your neighbors. Not only do you know everything about your neighbors, but you know everything about them from the time they came to the country."[57]

There was certainly no lack of interesting people to cast as characters on South Alabama Avenue. At the top of the list were Truman's people, the Faulks. Jennie Faulk had built the rambling, two-story house next door to the Lees as a communal dwelling for her three siblings: sister Callie, two years younger than she; brother Bud, who managed a little farm and had acquired the nickname "Squire" Faulk among the wags in town; and sister Sook, who, despite being white-haired, had the mind and disposition of a fourteen-year-old girl. All four were middle-aged or older, but they quarreled like teenagers. In contrast to the restraint of the Lee household, the Faulk residence was a stew of door-slamming, tearful arguments, accusations, shouting, delicious schemes to subvert authority, and mock remorse when one was caught red-handed. Jennie had appointed herself head of the household, and refused to budge on matters unless she deigned to let Callie have her way; Sook, rarely comfortable with anyone except children, traded her status as the eldest for scraps of kindness and respect. Drawing nearest to her were Nelle, Truman, and Jennings Faulk Carter, whose affection she welcomed. The three children spent many happy hours sitting at Sook's feet, being fed, like open-mouthed birds, cookies dipped in coffee; or sitting in her lap and making up long, fantastic tales. When the *Mobile Register* landed on the porch, they opened to the "funnies" and read their favorite strip together, *Hambone's Meditations,* in which cartoonist J. P. Alley lampooned, among other subjects, the Ku Klux Klan, the Republican Party, and all political elections.

The Faulks had secret pleasures, too, that Nelle and Truman could ferret out if they stalked their adult prey carefully enough. Sook, the prolific baker of fruitcakes later immortalized in Truman's story "A Christmas Memory," was discovered to enjoy a discreet pinch of Brown's Mule tobacco tucked in her cheek. Politely, she'd dab away the dark juice from her lips with a cotton handkerchief.[58] Also, despite the fact that the consumption of liquor would seem anathema in the Faulks' Baptist home, Nelle and Truman ambushed Jennie and Sook sneaking good long pulls from their separate stashes of Kentucky bourbon or sometimes pouring splashes into their iced teas.

Worth spying on, too, was the sagging residence on the cinder-strewn path that ran behind the Faulk and Lee homes. Spreading the bushes apart revealed one of the queerest-looking persons in town: a woman bedecked with a tipsy wig, red makeup, and wads of cotton stuffed in her toothless mouth. Anna Stabler could not be readily categorized as Negro or white. Rumored to be the daughter of a Negro maid and former probate judge I. B. Slaughter, she did a little cleaning now and then for the Faulks. For these reasons, probably, she was permitted to live in town instead of in Clausell, the Negro section of Monroeville. The whine of her animated fiddle music induced the children to draw nearer. Truman took a particular liking to her. He begged Jennie to buy him a guitar. Then, when he had mastered a few chords, he would steal outside to strum and sing with Anna. In concert, they sounded like two cats. Truman later took Anna as the model for Catherine in *The Grass Harp*: "She lived in the back yard in a tin-roofed silvery little house set among sunflowers and trellises of butter-bean vine. She claimed to be an Indian, which made most people wink, for she was dark as the angels of Africa. . . . Most of her teeth were gone; she kept her jaws jacked up with cotton wadding."[59]

But for sheer mystery and speculation, no source was richer than the tumbledown Boleware place just two doors south of the Lees', past Captain and Mrs. Powell Jones's place, its backyard flush against the playground of the elementary school. It was a dark, ramshackle structure with all the paint fallen off. What went on inside was a matter of conjecture, because the shutters were always closed as if the house were asleep. Children held their noses while walking by, or crossed to the other side of the street, to avoid inhaling evil vapors that might be emanating from chinks between the house's boards.

The owner was Alfred R. Boleware, sixty, a merchant, an influential man in town, but a prig and a cheapskate. To him, Shakespeare's Uncle Toby might have said, "Dost thou think, because thou art virtuous, there shall be no more cakes and ale?" And he would have answered, "Yes." He was married to Annie, two years his junior. They had three children—Mary and Sally, both in their late twenties, and Alfred, Jr., a few years younger than his sisters and nicknamed "Son."[60]

Boleware wouldn't spend a dime on his house, or its raggedy yard of tangled pecan trees, broken scuppernong arbor, truck garden, and other externals usually associated with hill people. But his sagging realm belonged to him, and no one was permitted to put a foot on it without his permission. A well-hit ball from the schoolyard that arced over the heads of the outfielders and landed in the Bolewares' weeds might as well have rolled into a minefield. Everyone knew better than to retrieve it. When the pecans ripened and fell, old man Boleware stood in the backyard, arms crossed, as if daring any pipsqueak on the playground to risk life and limb to steal one.

Adding to the mystery of the Boleware house was that every day Mary and Sally emerged from their father's lair looking fresh as daisies. They waved to Nelle and Truman like beauty queens on parade floats, and then continued on their way downtown to their respective jobs as a dental assistant and secretary. This unaccountable behavior left

Nelle and Truman astonished. How could the ogre have beautiful daughters? And what about Son, who was said to be languishing inside, a prisoner in his own home, tied to a bedstead by his father?

Son's fate sounded like a campfire tale, but it was essentially true. He and two schoolmates—Robert Baggett and Elliott Sawyer, the sheriff's son—had been taken before Judge Murdock McCorvey Fountain in 1928 for breaking school windows with a slingshot and burglarizing a drugstore. Fountain decided that such enterprising young men could benefit from a year at the state industrial school. Baggett's and Sawyer's parents concurred, but Boleware proposed something else for his boy. He asked the judge to turn Son over to him, because Boleware could guarantee that his lad would never trouble the community again. Something about the look in Boleware's eye convinced Judge Fountain, and Son went home with his father.[61]

After that, Son Boleware was rarely seen by anyone ever again. At first, friends from the high school would crawl on elbows and knees to his bedroom window to talk to him. Word got around that he would gladly do football players' math for them. In return for his help, team members took him for rides in the darkness after midnight. But eventually, all the young people Son had known moved on, and he was forgotten. Occasionally, as the years went by, his shadowy figure would appear on the porch after dusk. Some neighbors reported hearing a parched voice from the Boleware place cry, "Caw, caw!" and incidents of Peeping Toms were blamed on him. Once, Nelle had seen him resting in the shade and didn't find him so strange. But, essentially, Son Boleware was erased from Monroeville forever. "Mr. Boleware ruined his son's life, I guess because it was shaming him," said Charles Ray Skinner, a friend of the Lee family.[62] "The man was *mean.*" Or as Calpurnia, the Finches' housekeeper, says bitterly in *To Kill a Mockingbird,* when the body of "Boo" Radley's father is taken away in a hearse, "There goes the meanest man God ever blew breath into."[63] In 1952, Son died of tuberculosis. The marker placed at his grave in the First Baptist Church cemetery reads, TO LIVE IN HEARTS WE LEAVE BEHIND IS NOT TO DIE.

NELLE AND TRUMAN HAD more than enough to write about on South Alabama Avenue, whether they chose to exaggerate their material or not. Soon, the Lees and the Faulks saw them lugging the

Underwood No. 5 back and forth as they alternated offices between houses. The tree house would have been the ideal spot to write, but the twenty-pound typewriter would have been as hard to shove up there as an anvil.

So it was that the two children began the journey that would change their lives in so many ways, but also intensify their separateness from others their age. They kept their ears and eyes open for the nuances of life in their small world. They were writers. Sometime later, Nancie B. Robinson came over to Nelle's house to play games. "There was an old typewriter on the desk in the room, and Nelle grabbed some paper and put it in the typewriter. Truman started telling a story, and while he talked Nelle typed it. Well, they would not let me help with the story, so I just grabbed my paper dolls and went home!"[64]

But the splendid friendship between Nelle and Truman was interrupted suddenly in the mid-1930s, when Lillie Mae belatedly exercised her partial-custody rights and took Truman to New York City, where she was living with her second husband, Cuban American businessman Joseph Capote. From then on, until he was about eighteen, Truman returned to Monroeville summers only. Arch Persons fought a Parthian battle to have full custody of his son, but his attempts to portray himself as a proper father were complicated by his run-ins with the law. In 1935, Joe adopted Truman, and the ten-year-old took "Capote" as his surname. Lillie Mae, who had changed her name to Nina, enrolled Truman in a tony prep school.

The Lees, too, with such a bright and assertive child on their hands, could have sent Nelle to a private school. Some Monroeville parents had the means to send their children out of town to private schools in Birmingham and Montgomery. Nelle's parents, however, knew that she was a nonconformist and bored with school already. There was a chance that if she were to attend a private school, she might be pigeonholed as a hopeless troublemaker. The Lees were too tenderhearted to resign her to a lonely fate like that. Instead, it seems that her father took her in hand.

To people outside the family, Mr. Lee did not seem the type to minister to a rowdy child young enough to be his granddaughter. "Mr. Lee seemed to me to be much more of an intellectual than a physical man," said Joseph Blass, one of Mr. Lee's caddies on the golf course.

"The image of shooting the mad dog or of facing down the crowd of rough necks has never quite rung true to me. The strong intellectual stand, though, seems very natural."[65]

"Mr. Lee was detached," Truman Capote's aunt Marie Faulk Rudisill said, "not particularly friendly, especially with children. . . . He was not the sort of father who came up to his children, ruffled their hair, and made jokes for their amusement."[66] In Mr. Lee's presence, said former resident Harriet Swift, "you didn't feel comfortable with him. But he was nice."[67]

Blass thinks the era had a good deal to do with Mr. Lee's standoffishness. Professionals such as doctors and lawyers were expected to display a degree of gravitas around others. "People seeing him in the normal course of affairs might interpret his formal habits of speech and behavior as signs of coldness and distance," Blass said. "For example, he and my father were good friends and golfing buddies, but I don't believe either ever called the other by his first name. Those were different times."[68]

Mr. Lee was of slightly taller than average height with flat, pugnacious features like a boxer's. But his large-eyed, impassive expression, accentuated by a pair of large, round glasses, seemed permanently impressed on his face from his days as a bookkeeper. Every weekday morning, like clockwork, he could be seen coming down the steps of the Lees' bungalow dressed in a rumpled three-piece suit. Passing beneath the tangle of fig trees, crape myrtle, and pecans in the front yard, he turned left to walk the two blocks north to his law office above the bank in the town square. Had someone on the street pointed him out as a minister, a scholar, or a professor, instead of one of the most prominent businessmen in town, it would have seemed appropriate. His mannerisms were those of someone always preoccupied with his thoughts.

Stopping to converse with him required patience. His manner of speaking was almost comically precise and deliberate. He did not make conversation as much as offer pronouncements that began with "ah-hem!" progressed to "uh," and sometimes, for emphasis, ended with "ah-RUM!"[69] It was as though every matter he was invited to discuss had a potentially grave aspect, and he wanted to limit his personal liability by choosing his words with absolute care. He much preferred listening to talking, often while sucking thoughtfully on a piece of hard candy. He also had a distracting habit of absentmindedly fumbling with things, including his watch, a fountain pen, or his special favorite: a tiny pocketknife that he flipped with his thumb and caught like a coin. Once, a hardware store clerk waited while Mr. Lee flipped different penknives until he found one with exactly the right weight and balance.[70] It soothed him to do it.

He did not grope for words, however, when writing editorials for the *Monroe Journal.* In addition to being an attorney, in 1929 he had purchased a partnership in the newspaper. Founded in 1866, the *Monroe Journal* was not one of the more influential organs in a state that boasted the *Mobile Register,* the *Montgomery Advertiser,* the *Birmingham News,* and the most widely read Negro newspaper in Alabama, the *Birmingham World.* But it was a dependable guide to local goings-on in the county: a weekly farrago of mishaps, odd bits of local and national news, letters from readers, arrests, marriages, visits by out-of-town kin, births, and deaths. Residents of Monroe County looked to it as their source of local information and opinion. As the *Journal*'s editorialist, Mr. Lee used the paper as a bully pulpit from which to address his favorite topics: taxes, overreaching government, drinking, hooliganism, and political corruption.

Nor did he mince words in person when moved to indignation. One night in August 1934, just weeks before a state election, one hundred members of the Ku Klux Klan gathered in the parking lot of Monroeville Elementary School to make a show of force. Marching up South Alabama Avenue in serried rows toward the courthouse square, the hooded figures passed the Lee property. A.C. came down off the porch, his suspenders hanging in loops to his knees, and confronted the local grand dragon. He warned him that he would give them a drubbing in one of his editorials. After an exchange in the street that lasted a few minutes, Lee and the grand dragon struck a compromise. The marchers dropped the militant pose and walked the rest of the way like pedestrians.[71]

Jennings Faulk Carter tells a different story. According to him, Truman was having a Halloween party and some members of the Klan tried to break it up because they heard Negroes disguised in costume had been invited to attend. When they grabbed a young white man completely hidden by silver-painted boxes as part of his robot costume, Mr. Lee "waded into the middle of the sheet-covered Klansmen, who had gathered in the middle of the road holding their torches high."

> The Klansmen didn't offer any resistance to Mr. Lee, a big, strong man who had the respect of everybody in town. He was a member of the state legislature, editor of the *Monroe Journal,* and an upstanding citizen. No one wanted to be the one to cross him. When Mr. Lee got to the center of the activity, he came face-to-face with a Klansman wearing a hood with green fringe. This was the Grand Dragon. . . . Mr. Lee turned to address the crowd of Klansmen. "See what your foolishness has done? You've scared this boy half to death because he wanted to believe something that wasn't true. You ought to be ashamed of yourselves."[72]

Either way the story is told, it's clear that Nelle witnessed at least one demonstration of her father's relatively liberal values about racial issues during her formative years.

On Sundays, Lee the public man took a few moments to be alone with his thoughts during services at the Monroeville Episcopal Methodist Church. Congregants noted that he preferred to sit in front by himself. Later during the service, in his capacity as deacon, he would rise to lead his fellow worshippers in long improvised prayers, tapping the pew with his penknife to create a cadence for his deep, somnolent voice.

His beliefs were rather hidebound, at least in midlife, built as they were on the conviction "that the destiny of this world in the years before us is very largely in the hands of the rather small percentage of mankind that have come to accept the Christian religion, and have recognized that in reality this is our Father's world, and that the way of life He has provided is the only way that holds any promise of endurance. And that way of life includes the acceptance of his rules and regulations for all creation, including mankind."[73]

Few people studying one of the most influential men in the community while he was speaking about God and obedience in such terms could have guessed correctly what kind of parent he was. The truth was, despite his reserve in public, A.C. was a fond and indulgent father. At home, he encouraged Nelle to clamber up on his lap to "help" him read the newspaper or complete the crossword puzzle.

They invented a word game, which they played together while Nelle toyed with A.C.'s pocket watch (and she did call him "A.C."). One of them would think of a word and provide two clues: one letter in the word and the total number of letters. Then the other would have to guess the word. Nelle's vocabulary shot up as a result. And when it came to disciplining his youngest, Mr. Lee used a light hand, overlooking her misdemeanors. He spared the rod, preferring to reassure her—even if it meant being too lenient at times—that she was growing up in a home where she was loved. Perhaps he leaned in this direction because he knew, as only a parent in Mr. Lee's situation could know, that he was the buffer between Nelle and her unstable mother. "Nelle just trotted at her father's heels, up and down the street," said Marie Faulk Rudisill.[74]

By the age of twelve, Nelle Lee had grown into the fascinating and bumptious young person whom Truman used as the model for Idabel Tompkins—a forceful personality, quick with a dirty joke, haughty, and angry about the constraints of her gender—in his first novel, *Other Voices, Other Rooms* (1948). When Joel, the main character, expresses embarrassment about undressing in front of Idabel, she retorts,

> "Son," she said, and spit between her fingers, "what you got in your britches is no news to me, and no concern of mine: hell, I've fooled around with nobody but boys since first grade. I never think like I'm a girl; you've got to remember that, or we can't never be friends." For all its bravado, she made this declaration with a special and compelling innocence; and when she knocked one fist against the other, as, frowning, she did now, and said: "I want so much to be a boy: I would be a sailor, I would . . ." the quality of her futility was touching.[75]

t   h   r   e   e

Without "Finishing Touches"

NELLE ENTERED MONROE COUNTY HIGH SCHOOL IN SEPTEM-
ber 1940, with the United States' entry into World War II only a year
away. All around her, the engines of the nation's economy were finally
revving up after years spent idling during the Great Depression.
When war finally erupted, in December 1941, Monroeville awoke
from its sleepy, magnolia-shaded lassitude, roused by a sense of national purpose. The Lees found a number of ways to pitch in, doing
more than many families. A.C. assisted his former law partner, J. B.
Barnett, now president of the Monroe County Bank, in chairing local
war bond drives; Alice volunteered for the Red Cross; Louise had settled down for the duration of the war in Eufaula with her infant son
to await her husband's return from duty; and Edwin suspended his
studies at Auburn University in 1943 to join the Army Air Corps. In
addition, the governor appointed A.C. to the state Alcohol Beverage
Control Board. Knowing Lee's views about alcohol consumption,
newspaper editors all over the state had a field day commenting about
giving a teetotaler oversight for liquor.

Nelle, only sixteen during the first full year of the war, navigated adolescence according to her own lights. Generally, she ignored conventions that applied to most girls, going her own way. Although she had a beau or two, everyone in her high school class of 120 students saw that she didn't make an effort to employ tried-and-true feminine wiles to entice boys. In a photograph taken her sophomore year, in spring 1942, she stands with her English class on the steps of the high school. Unlike nearly all of the other girls, she isn't wearing lipstick, her hair doesn't look as if it's seen a curling iron recently, and her chin, held high, gives her unsmiling face a truculent expression.

She was not about to give in to Lotharios, either, teenage or adult, who discovered that Nelle Lee had outgrown her overalls and turned into what men used to call a "spitfire." One day, Truman's footloose father, Arch Persons, drove up the dirt lane to Jennings Faulk Carter's house out in the country, eager to show off his new red Buick convertible. Everyone greeted him, including Nelle and Truman. Arch only nodded at his son, but he "immediately noticed Nelle, who by this time had grown into a tall teenager about as big as he was," said Jennings. "Truman and I saw Arch's clawlike hand slip way down Nelle's back as he hugged her. Nelle stiffened, acted surprised, then backed away."

Ever the con man, Arch let the kids practice driving down to the mailbox at the end of lane, until finally he took off with Nelle alone in the car. "A few minutes later Arch returned, driving by himself and holding a handkerchief over his nose," Jennings said. It was bleeding.

Later, at Truman's house, Jennings wanted to know what had happened. Nelle shrugged. "I drove up to the mailbox and he got fresh. So I hit him in the schnozzle. Then I got out of the car and walked home."[1]

Classmates pegged Nelle as someone unlike anyone else they knew: someone who it wasn't all that easy to warm up to but who was definitely a person to be reckoned with. As the years went by, she quieted down in class, but she could still flick her wit with a snap that smarted. "You took her as she was. She wasn't trying to impress anyone," said Claude Nunnelly.[2]

Being conventional just struck her as illogical at times. In high school, Nelle and her friends Anne Hines and Sara Anne McCall stopped to watch some boys their age choose teams for a pickup game of football on the courthouse lawn, for instance. Over the boys' protests, Nelle insisted that they put her on a team, too. A. B. Blass, Jr., one of the captains, gave in and added her to his side, figuring she'd last for a play or two. Hines and McCall appointed themselves cheerleaders, one for each team. On the first play, the center snapped the ball to Blass, and he instantly handed it off to Nelle. As she took off, one of the opposing players ran around the end to intercept her. Instead of dodging, Nelle straight-armed him out of the way and continued sprinting downfield toward the goal line.

Blass put his hands on his hips disgustedly. "Nelle, we're playing touch!"

"Y'all can play that sissy game if you want to," she shouted over her shoulder, "but I'm playing tackle!"[3]

On the other hand, she was not immune to expectations just for the sake of being contrary. Higher education was in the picture for all the Lee children, and Nelle looked forward to it as the next step after high school. It was the same for most of her upper-middle-class friends, most of whom were the sons and daughters of professionals. One of the boys playing touch football that day on the courthouse lawn was Rayford Smith. Since childhood, he had wanted nothing except to follow in the footsteps of his father, Dr. Rayford Smith, Sr., who, by the end of his fifty-year career, would deliver more than three thousand babies—one by the smoky light of a burning pine torch in a backwoods cabin. (Dr. Smith's tally of births amounted to more than the entire population of Monroeville in the early forties.) Nelle's friend Sara Anne McCall had already chosen to attend Huntingdon College, a Methodist women's college in Montgomery. A. B. Blass, the touch football quarterback, could talk of nothing except applying to the school of his favorite college team, the University of Alabama.

So Nelle's decision to attend college would not have surprised her classmates. But those who looked at her and saw only her iconoclastic nature and desire for independence would probably never have suspected her admiration for two adults, both of whom had begun to exert a powerful influence over her choice of careers and vision of her future. They were two women with a go-it-alone attitude. And Nelle had a strong desire to follow their lead in some yet-undefined way. This dilemma over which direction to take would eventually lead to a decision that would number among the most critical of her adult life.

The first of her two role models was her high school English teacher, Miss Gladys Watson. Like an apprentice learning the craft of language, Nelle willingly submitted to Miss Watson's instruction. Tall, blond, and angular, with hipbones that protruded under her warm-weather dresses, Miss Watson lived with her parents across the street from Nelle in a two-story yellow house with a deep, wide veranda that ran around three sides. Her father, "Doc" Watson, was a dentist, a three-hundred-pound giant of a man. Outside of being one of the best teachers of two generations of students at Monroe County High School, Miss Watson was also a quilter and a gardener. Neighbors were accustomed to seeing her in her parents' yard pruning the lilacs, tending the potted succulents on the porch, and yanking out pernicious weeds in the grass, her fair face hidden beneath a big straw hat. She remained single until late in life, preferring to devote her time to reading and teaching.

Because Monroe County High was a rural school, the faculty numbered about a dozen teachers. Students had Miss Watson for three years, for sophomore through senior English, which also included a semester on British literature. And most of her students counted themselves lucky in later years to have had a triple dose of "Gladys," as a few called her behind her back.[4] "I adored her," said Sue Philipp, a friend of Nelle's. "She was very strict. She gave you two grades. One was for your grammar in a paper—and you got a whole letter taken off for any mistake, and that included commas. So I would usually get a C for grammar and an A for writing." English professors at state universities in Alabama were known to remark to some of their most proficient undergraduates, "You must have taken Miss Watson."[5]

Her classes always began with students receiving a blue grammar rules booklet—a sort of early Strunk and White *Elements of Style*—which Miss Watson had personally selected. It was going to be their Bible, she told them—they should never lose it.[6] She skewered mistakes on their papers by indicating in the margin the page number in the blue booklet where that particular problem was treated. Then the paper had to be rewritten and handed in with the mistakes corrected. Comma splices—joining two complete sentences with a comma—she let it be known, were the most egregious mistakes anyone could make, tantamount to a confession that the writer did not understand the least thing about grammar. She confessed to her students that after seeing a comma splice, she was always tempted to give the writer an F and not read any further. Grammar, she explained over and over, was not a pointless academic exercise, but a tool. Knowing the rules was the quickest route to better writing. Grammatical writing also was the key to developing a clear and euphonious *style* of writing. She had students read their compositions aloud so that everyone could hear how good writing had three Cs: clarity, coherence, and cadence. As she listened, she leaned forward, sucking on an earpiece of her pink tortoiseshell glasses and interjecting now and then, "That was good, very good."[7] Little did her students know that in her heart she would have given anything to be a writer herself.[8]

Sometimes, when her charges had grown weary of gerunds and the active versus the passive voice, and their writing hands had grown stiff from overuse, she would read them a story, a poem, or a scene from a play. Probably as a result of practice, she was a particularly gifted reader of Chaucer in the original fourteenth-century English. As she read *The Canterbury Tales* aloud, the voices of the Middle Ages emerged for her students, who were able to visualize people, taverns, shrines, and waysides of a land that had disappeared long ago.[9]

Nelle worshipped her. From the time that Miss Watson came into her life, Nelle became devoted to British literature. After school, she spent time in the library looking up information in an encyclopedia about topics Miss Watson had mentioned. And there was also one well-thumbed copy of *Pride and Prejudice* in the school library's collection that opened for Nelle the intimate world of Jane Austen.[10]

Whether Miss Watson perceived Nelle as a budding writer is hard to tell, especially since Monroe County High School had no school newspaper or yearbook to showcase the talents of stellar English students. But if being in print really mattered to Nelle, she easily could have been—in her father's newspaper, the *Monroe Journal.* As fond as he was of his children, Mr. Lee wouldn't have turned down a submission from his hopeful daughter. However, except for a poem titled "Springtime," which Nelle wrote when she was eleven, no byline of hers appeared in the *Journal.*[11] After Truman moved away, she wrote only in secret, though not in a journal. Her desk at home contained personal essays, short stories, and limericks. But she never dared share them with her parents or siblings, because in a family as literate as hers, she dreaded the possibility that her efforts would fall short.

Her second role model was her sister Alice. Alice Finch Lee, the eldest of the Lee children, reminded many Monroeville residents of her father made over. In most families, the son was the heir apparent to a business, store, or farm. If there were no sons in the family, then a son-in-law could uphold the tradition of nepotism. But Alice broke the mold. She seemed destined and determined to follow in her father's footsteps.

Alice and Nelle were as alike, Capote once cracked, "as a giraffe and a hippopotamus."[12] Alice was a petite, birdlike young woman who wore black glasses like her father's and seemed as uninterested in cosmetics as Nelle later came to be. But she was a grade-getter in school, conservative, and the essence of tact. All through school she remained at the head of her class, and in 1928 she graduated from Monroe County High School at age sixteen. That fall, she enrolled at the Women's College of Alabama, a Methodist institution in Montgomery, enjoying the privilege of becoming the first member of her family to attend college. Her freshman year, 1928–1929, was one of the happiest times of her life, she has said.[13]

Unfortunately, her freshman year was her only year in college in Montgomery. The stock market crash in October upended her plans—at least that's what she told friends. The truth was, A.C. had plans of his own. For years, because of his wife's poor health, he had been compelled to push ahead without the support of a helpmate. Now that Alice was entering adulthood—and she was clearly a very capable young woman—he began to shift more and more of his professional duties to her. And she quickly rose to meet his requirements.

The year she left college was also the year A.C. purchased a partnership in the *Monroe Journal.* As a smart business move, he cut Alice in as the fourth of four partners, giving the Lees half interest. Alice was only eighteen, but her father had every faith in her. He put up the cash, completed the legal paperwork, and appointed her associate editor.

He needed her to hold down the fort while he went off adventuring in state politics. Three years earlier, in 1926, he had announced, midway through his ten-year tenure on the town council, that he would run as Democratic representative to the state legislature. In a lengthy advertisement appearing in the *Monroe Journal,* Lee assured the electorate that his candidacy was "not prompted by any political or selfish motive, but with the sincere purpose to contribute to the general welfare." Politically, he was a centrist, an advocate of states' rights, and a fiscal conservative. In the August primary, he thumped his opponent, another Democrat, 281 to 116 (the Republicans had not bothered running a candidate for seventy-five years), and in the November election, he won his legislative seat handily.[14] As he was required to be in the state capital regularly, Alice was the obvious choice to be his ear to the ground in Monroeville.

In addition, A.C.'s business interests were prospering. Since 1923, he had been pivotal in helping the town council electrify all of Monroeville. As a result, in 1929—the year he and Alice became newspaper owners—Riviera Utilities Corporation moved its headquarters to Monroeville and appointed A. C. Lee as its corporation counsel for the entire state. If that weren't enough, he also had accepted a post as director on the Monroe County Bank. His time was at a premium, and Alice was needed as his right hand.

Alice also had her work cut out for her on South Alabama Avenue. The job was "keeping the home fires burning," as she later put it.[15] Her siblings, Louise, Edwin, and Nelle, were then thirteen, nine, and three, respectively, and the stress of raising them seemed to exacerbate Frances Lee's mood swings. Negro housekeepers could straighten up, do laundry, and make meals, but Mrs. Lee required attention, too. Alice had to take over.

All of these roles she stepped into for the sake of helping her father, to whom she was devoted. If she entertained any thoughts of marriage, she would almost certainly have required a larger pool of eligible men than Monroeville could offer. But for the next seven years, from 1929 to 1936, she put her young life on hold while she worked side by side with her father at the *Journal* and helped him manage at home.

Meanwhile, A.C. toiled away in the Alabama legislature on a career that was not exceptional: he was too inflexible to make a good politician. His only guideposts on the statehouse floor were his principles and his two special interests: finance and morality. During the twelve years he represented Monroeville and its environs, he was proudest of making good on a campaign promise to push through a budget bill that put county fiscal systems on a pay-as-you-go basis, thus reducing deficit spending.[16] He also sponsored a bill that substantially raised the pension amount awarded to several thousand Confederate soldiers and their widows still living in Alabama in the 1930s. These were not bills put in the hopper by a firebrand; they reflected his principled approach to fidelity and responsible government.

On another matter, this one concerning sexuality and the law, he drew on the teachings of the Bible, as he interpreted them, to give him guidance. In 1935, he voted in favor of a "therapeutic sterilization law," or compulsory sterilization, affording due-process safeguards for "those suffering from perversions, constitutional psychopathic personalities or marked departures from normal mentality." This category included any inmate of a penal institution or insane asylum whose "physical, mental or moral condition" would be improved, such as a "sexual pervert, Sadist, homosexualist, Masochist, Sodomist, or any other grave form of sexual perversion."[17] He also voted in favor of an amendment to ban voluntary sterilization for the purposes of contraception.[18] Another issue that was something of a personal hobbyhorse with him was alcohol consumption. In editorials for the *Monroe Journal*, he inveighed against federal enforcement of Prohibition, calling on the state of Alabama and its citizens to do a better job of educating young people about the dangers of drinking.

When the 1938 election approached, however, he decided he would not run again. After ten years in the statehouse, he was treading water politically. His personal life offered greater rewards. After more than twenty years on the public scene, he was one of the most prominent figures in southern Alabama. "My father is one of the few men I've known who has genuine humility, and it lends him a natural dignity," Harper Lee was quoted as saying in a 1961 *Life* magazine article. "He has absolutely no ego drive, and so he is one of the most beloved men in this part of the state."[19] In his hometown, he was unquestionably a guiding spirit as a highly regarded attorney, newspaper publisher, bank director, civic leader, and church deacon. Louise and Edwin had become responsible young people; Nelle was in middle school. Also, there was the other side of the ledger to consider: he was coming up on sixty years of age, and feeling he should concentrate his energy. For a man with many responsibilities, some of them no longer necessary, it was time to take stock.

Alice moved away from Monroeville in April 1937 to begin belatedly a life of complete independence at age twenty-six. For a year and a half, she found work as a clerk in the newly created Social Security division of the Internal Revenue Service in Birmingham. With time, given her talent for shouldering administrative tasks, it's likely she would have moved up quickly, especially since Social Security, as a governmental agency, was destined to grow into a huge bureaucracy.

But then, suddenly, Mr. L. J. Bugg, of Bugg, Barnett & Lee, died. With Bugg departed, a once-in-a-generation opening was available in the law firm. A.C. discussed with Alice the idea of her returning to Monroeville—conditional upon her completing law school, of course—as a new partner. She hesitated.

She asked him whether he thought folks in town would view her as A. C. Lee's "little girl" or a person with an identity in her own right. He answered that by the time she completed law school, she would be older than thirty and would have been absent from town for a long time. Who would think of her as someone's "little girl"? This mollified her. But she was also concerned that folks might not take a female lawyer seriously—there were fewer than two dozen or so in the entire state, and most practiced in Montgomery, Birmingham, or Mobile, where professional women were not unusual. To this, A.C. had no direct answer. Instead, knowing Alice as he did, he appealed to her love of a challenge. "You won't know unless you try," he said.[20]

In 1939, she enrolled in night classes at the Birmingham School of Law. It was a demanding regime she set for herself: doing a full-time job during the day, and in the evenings, sitting through lectures on torts, contracts, real estate, and criminal statutes. Working on her degree part-time, she nevertheless completed her last semester of classes at the end of four years. Finally, in July 1943, during World War II, she was ready for the Alabama bar exam. On a muggy Monday morning, Alice and three 4-Fs—men who had failed the physical for active duty in the armed forces—presented themselves as candidates for the legal profession at the Whitley Hotel in Montgomery.[21]

Over the next four days, there were four examiners and thirteen exams. On the last day, the examiner advised them that they would be notified of the results by telephone the following morning.

In Alice's apartment the next day, the phone rang early. She had passed. A.C. was elated when he got the news. Not many weeks later, Alice Lee had taken her place in the law offices of Bugg, Barnett & Lee (the name stayed the same), eager to begin. As a country lawyer just starting out, she was prepared to take practically any case that came through her door. But through a remarkable stroke of luck, a stampede of clients beat a path to her. On December 31, 1942, the federal government had passed the first income tax law in United States history, named the Victory Tax. With no certified public accountant in Monroeville, word spread that Miss Lee had worked for the IRS. In fact, she knew very little about tax preparation, but characteristically she stepped into the breach and studied at night. The "tax lady," as she became known around town, saved the day.

So, as her father had predicted she would, Alice established her own identity in Monroeville as a professional to be counted on. But there was still the question of whether people would take her seriously as an attorney—someone fit to give advice on weighty issues of law. On this score, she faced much more of a challenge. In the beginning, few clients brought her cases of any consequence, and her fellow barristers in southern Alabama treated her as a curiosity. She looked too delicate for the fray of forensic battle; but more to the point, she was a woman in a small town. None of the leading civic organizations in Monroeville—the influential Kiwanis Club, for example—accepted women. Church and school committees were all that were open to her. Hence, she was shut out of the higher circles of power in Monroeville, and in the county, for that matter.

Then one day, she received a call from a Mobile attorney whose rhetorical powers had helped him build an important reputation in the profession. He told Alice that he had a wrongful death suit in the docket for the next session of the circuit court in Monroeville—would she assist him? She was most pleased to accept. As it turned out, however, what the attorney really had in mind was someone to serve as his legal assistant. During the trial, Alice sat quietly at the table watching the old pros in action. Presiding was circuit judge and Monroeville native Francis W. Hare, a veteran of the Spanish-American War and a friend of the Lee family. With testimony taken, and both sides having made their arguments to the jury, the trial was clearly winding down. Alice had not said a word. Then Judge Hare made a statement to the jury. "It is customary in cases like this for there to be two speeches on each side. However, we have with us the youngest member of the Bar. And if this young lady would like to address the jury, I will grant her that privilege." Alice rose, walked to the jury box of twelve men, and gave a memorable speech for her side. "Judge Hare had paved the way for my acceptance," she said later, "and I was treated as a member of the Bar and not as an aberration."[22]

Thus, as Nelle approached graduation from high school in 1944 and was faced with making a decision about college and a career, her sister Alice presented an example of a woman who had overcome challenges that would have discouraged anyone less determined. To someone of Nelle's spirit, who always enjoyed a good tussle, physical or verbal, her sister's quietly combative style and choice of law were an inspiration. As far as Nelle's love of literature and writing was concerned, she rationalized that she would be doing a good deal of reading for a profession that was based on words, history, and, of course, writing.

Emulating her sister, in 1928 Nelle enrolled at the Women's College of Alabama, where Alice had spent the happiest year of her life. By now it had been renamed Huntingdon College, for the Countess of Huntingdon, a sponsor of the Wesleyan Movement in England. Nelle wasted no time, signing up for summer classes beginning in June.

A. C. Lee viewed this latest development with undisguised pleasure. Around town, he started telling a little joke. With Mr. Bugg taking his eternal rest, and Mr. Barnett running the Monroe County Bank, the firm of Bugg, Barnett & Lee might have to be changed sometime soon to "A. C. Lee and Daughters, Lawyers."[23]

It's hard to imagine a setting that would have been less appropriate than Huntingdon College for a young woman like Nelle Lee. Perhaps in addition to imitating her sister, she was trying to win her mother's attention by enrolling in a college that was, in some ways, like the Alabama Girls' Industrial School, which prided itself on turning out young ladies.

Huntingdon's fifty-eight-acre campus was located off East Fairview Avenue, in one of Montgomery's most beautiful neighborhoods, Old Cloverdale. The area still felt like the country in those days, despite the proximity of the city, which was only a bus ride away. Each house was unique in design but all were large and substantial and quite southern-looking, with wide aprons of lush green lawns. Sprays of mums, coneflowers, columbines, irises, or day lilies looked glorious in the sunlight. Beneath the heavy trees lay camellias, hostas, jasmine, and impatiens, all tucked into flowerbeds like rows of children.

Husbands parked their automobiles off the street, in garages at the end of private drives.

As freshman girls arrived through the front gate with their families, they saw directly ahead the charming peaks, oriels, and tracery of Flowers Hall, the administration building. To the left and right, extending along a low, semicircular ridge, were all the other important buildings that new girls needed to become acquainted with: the library, the student center and its tea room, two dormitories, and the infirmary. These overlooked a natural amphitheater called the Green, which served as a park, playing field, and the site of an annual May festival, complete with a maypole and May Queen.

Huntingdon was traditional. Although the war had brought rationing of butter, milk, sugar, and other staples, the college, like a safe harbor, guaranteed that solid instruction in the liberal arts and sciences would continue unchanged. The year Nelle arrived, the college's president, Dr. Hubert Searcy, declared, "It may be that our greatest contribution at Huntingdon is to keep alive and strengthen those ideals for which we are fighting. When we see the tragedy of the world at war, we see the need for greater understanding among men, for keener appreciation of the aspects of life that endure, for love of beauty, and acquaintance with music, literature, and art, and a deeper knowledge of the relations of people."[24] Experienced educators taught such subjects as composition, the history of Western civilization, philosophy, and theology. By and large, the Huntingdon faculty was made up of graduates from selective northern institutions: Columbia, Northwestern, Cornell, and Syracuse. Mr. Davidson, professor of sociology, for example, who had done graduate work at Yale, liked to sport his Phi Beta Kappa key on his suit vest. Many of the female instructors were unmarried, and some gallantly said that the students were their family.

The students' Christian education was given symbolic pride of place at the start of every day. Chapel was at 8:00 A.M. Missing services was inexcusable, unless the offender made up the absence by attending church elsewhere. Sometimes the entire student body of five hundred girls listened while Methodist missionaries just returned from China described what they had witnessed—depredations by Japanese forces, starvation, and orphanages overbrimming with children. The lesson cannot have been lost on the students, many of whom were contemplating careers in education, social service, or medicine. Huntingdon's motto was "Enter to grow in wisdom, go forth to apply wisdom in service."

Not surprisingly, given the place and time, another important component of a Huntingdon girl's education was to become adept at the social graces. Dinner was never a haphazard affair. The girls ate at tables of eight. At the head was a female instructor. The food was passed around, and everyone was expected to take at least a small portion out of politeness. The right piece of silverware had to be used for each course of the meal. Now and then the instructor would peek under the table to make sure none of the girls had her legs crossed—feet *flat* on the floor. Once a month, on a particular date, the girls were expected to come down to dinner in evening dress.

Off campus, Huntingdon girls were expected to abide by a dress code that included hats, gloves, dresses, and high-heeled shoes. An appropriate outfit for a day in Montgomery consisted of a skirt, a cardigan worn backward, a string of pearls, a black Chesterfield coat, white gloves, and a white scarf worn in blustery weather. ("We must have looked like a bunch of penguins," one of the fashion-conscious later said.)[25] Inside the dormitories, the girls could wear whatever they chose. But the minute they stepped outside, even to go to class, penny loafers, a dress or skirt, and a blouse at the minimum were de rigueur.

If these descriptions create an image of prim young women who would "get the vapors" like debutantes in whalebone corsets if they saw a glimpse of male leg, that sort of stereotype would be incorrect. As with most young women their age, there was one subject that was never far from these Huntington girls' minds—romance. And few campuses had a better location for fostering hopes of love. Nearby was Maxwell Airfield, "a source of men—a source of dates!" as one former Huntingdon girl happily recalled.[26] Above the campus, four-engine B-24 Liberators or Vutlee BT-13 trainers flying in formation often filled the air. At Maxwell and adjoining Gunter airfields, nearly eight thousand airmen officers—British, French, and American—were in training. And they were the best of the best. Many of these flyers had already proven themselves in twin-engine planes, and now, having been promoted to lieutenants, captains, majors, or even colonels, they were the best of the American "Mighty Eighth" Air Corps.

One of them was Edwin Lee.

UNLIKE HIS SISTER, EDWIN had no trouble abiding by expectations of proper behavior. For Maxwell cadets, the day began at 5:30 A.M., when loudspeakers blared reveille. Exactly twenty-five minutes later—after shaving, dressing, and straightening their personal belongings—trainees hit the "ratline," an imaginary demarcation on the sidewalk, their eyes fixed straight ahead. To enforce discipline, upperclassmen patrolling the ranks judged the silent "zombies," as they were nicknamed, using the West Point system. They hunted for "gigable" offenses—dusty shoes, sloppy salutes, mumbled replies, or ignorance of a regulation, for instance. Cadets who had acquired too many demerits were ordered to take a one-hour hike around the base at a cadence of 128 steps a minute, with a rifle at shoulder arms.

At the end of breakfast, on the order, the trainees marched back to their quarters and were allowed five minutes to give their shoes a quick buff before hurrying to class. Classroom instruction covered math, Morse code, maps, and charts—essentials for pilots, bombardiers, and navigators. At 11:00 A.M., they fell in for military drill until noon. Lunch lasted a little more than an hour, after which smoking was permitted until 1:30 P.M. Then it was chemical warfare class until 2:50 P.M. The next hour and a half was taken up with physical training and calisthenics, and polished off with a two-mile run. After showering at 4:30 P.M., they attended a first aid class until dinner, followed by a fifteen-minute smoke break. By 7:00 P.M. the men were assigned to quarters and hitting the books. During study time, upperclassmen sometimes exercised the right to hassle loafers by ordering them to snap to attention and sing Army Air Corps songs, recite regulations, or say prayers. The only measure of peace and quiet in the day lasted from 9:00 to 9:30 P.M., when many of the men wrote or answered letters.

On weekends, however, swains in uniform made a beeline for the Huntingdon campus. The ones who could get their hands on a car whisked away girls to Hilda's, on Atlanta Highway, a lively restaurant with dinner and dancing. Local young men envied the damn "fly boys," who could always spring for a swell time. But despite the airmen's claims to worldliness, they "came just about as young and inexperienced as the college girls." Or so recalled a woman who was a Huntingdon junior in 1944.

Some cadets, on the other hand, always seemed to strike out where games of the sexes were concerned. In those cases, the older heads in the Army Air Corps brass put plan B into action. They knew there was nothing like a Saturday night dance for getting a bashful young man into the distracting arms of a girl.

During 1944, Maxwell Field hosted eighteen dances featuring popular big bands, including Glenn Miller's. Most of the Huntingdon girls welcomed the open invitations as exciting additions to their social calendars. The base would send trucks, and the girls would clamber on board. At the dance, there were usually three guys for every gal, but with those odds, the young ladies could have a different date every weekend night, if they wished.

Into this welter of social activity, Nelle arrived on the Huntingdon campus as a full-time student in the autumn of 1944. Credits from two summer courses, added to the twelve semester hours she was awarded for scoring at least a B on four entrance exams in mathematics, social science, natural science, and English, resulted in her starting college as a second-semester freshman.[27]

She was assigned to a triple room in Massey Hall, where the housemother was white-haired Mrs. Hammond, or "Mother Hammond," a much-loved figure who enjoyed playing the role of nosey maiden aunt. She wore pince-nez—glasses without temple bars—which pressed the sides of her nose à la Teddy Roosevelt. When a young man arrived to pick up his date, Mother Hammond made a show of examining him up and down as though she had never seen such a specimen. It was rumored she could smell beer at twenty feet. Her authority compelled young men to conform to the spirit of the rules, at least, if not always to the letter. A gentleman caller remembered, "A freshman girl could not leave the dorm in a car with a boy, and had to be in by ten thirty. It didn't take too much thought to figure out that you could park your car a short distance off campus and walk to it with your date."[28]

As she settled into her triple room, Nelle was no different from other adolescents in relishing her newly found freedom. She no longer had to cope with problems at home stemming from her mother's behavior; hardly anyone on campus had a preconceived notion about Nelle Harper Lee from Monroeville, except for a few high school classmates who had also enrolled. (These included Nelle's friend Sara Anne McCall.) A life of independence, fun, books, and ideas—all the things afforded by higher education—awaited Nelle Lee at last. The first quarter she made the honor roll.

There were many fine instructors at Huntingdon, but Nelle's favorite was Irene Munro, whose course on international affairs had extra relevance because of the war. In a number of ways, Professor Munro was like Gladys Watson. She was tall and patrician, a graduate of Wesleyan and Columbia. She and her husband spent every summer at their place in Massachusetts because, she said, they liked the "intellectual energy" of New England. She peppered her lectures with thumbnail sketches of people who had spent their lives in the arts and letters. She impressed upon her students the need always to think critically and emphasized that an education was not a commodity that could be purchased. "If you lost your lecture notes, would you forget everything you're learning here?" she asked several times. "I certainly hope not."[29]

In class was a junior, Jeanne Foote, who struck up a friendship with Nelle when they agreed that Munro's class was the best on their schedule of classes. Foote brought her readings for the class to Nelle's floor in Massey Hall, and the two young women stayed up late discussing them, camped out in the reception area so they wouldn't disturb the others. "Those conversations were very important to me," Foote said. "I don't think that there were others at Huntingdon—whom I knew and had ready access to—who had these same interests."[30]

It was true that Nelle was more sophisticated than most of her classmates about politics and economics; after all, her father was a newspaper publisher and a state representative. Also, aside from six years spent in Birmingham, Alice had lived at home, too. The level of dinner table conversation at the Lees' was probably more elevated than what was normal in most small-town households in Alabama. On the other hand, Nelle was not sufficiently sophisticated—at least in the eyes of most Huntingdon women, and in ways that mattered to them. Acceptability was measured by how closely one hewed to conventions

of taste, manners, and politeness. And by those standards, Nelle's behavior really rankled some of the girls in Massey Hall.

To begin with, her roommates objected to her use of salty language, a trait of hers since childhood and not untypical of precocious
children. Catherine Helms, who lived a few doors down in Massey, remembered getting steamed every time Nelle cursed.

> We were taught that if you had to resort to ugly words, you had a
> very weak vocabulary and needed further English study. Actually
> we were not sure what a lot of bad words meant. We were ladies in
> every sense . . . at least, most of us were. So, a girl who used foul lan-
> guage was a misfit in every sense of the word. Nobody wanted to be
> around her. I never heard any of my friends use four-letter words.
> No one in my family did. Once when my mother was ninety, my sis-
> ter and I were trying to help her with a problem hearing aid and she
> said, "damn." My sister and I were horrified. We didn't know she
> knew the word, however she had read *Gone With the Wind*.[31]

Another aberration was Nelle's smoking—or, rather, the way she
smoked. Smoking was equated with sophistication, and students were
permitted to have cigarettes in their rooms. But a girl passing Nelle's
boudoir did a double take when she saw Miss Lee puffing away med-
itatively on a pipe, like William Faulkner. The image couldn't have
been more at odds with an environment devoted to enhancing girls'
femininity.

And to many of the girls in Massey Hall, Nelle's appearance was
the last straw. It was true that inside the dormitory the girls could wear
comfortable clothes and relax in slacks, for instance, rather than dresses
and skirts. But the girls wondered at Nelle's preference, day in and day
out, for jeans or white Bermuda shorts. Moreover, she did not wear an
ounce of makeup, only brushed her hair instead of curling it, and
evinced no interest in indulging in any kind of beauty regime. By contrast, judging from the pages of Huntingdon's yearbook, her classmates
were attuned to the latest hairstyles and fashions of the Swing Era.

Not even the approach of a social event could force Nelle to conform. She skipped monthly formal dinners rather than be forced to
wear an evening gown. When Saturday night came and the girls left

for a night of dancing, she found other ways to spend the evening. Or she just went home for the weekend. The campus newspaper, the *Huntress,* fails to mention her name except two or three times, despite pages and pages about student skits, engagement announcements, visits by students to friends' homes, class and club elections, or meetings of campus organizations. She even seems to have deliberately avoided showing up for yearbook pictures. Despite belonging to Chi Delta Phi, a literary honor society; the Scribblers Club; and the Glee Club, Nelle doesn't appear in any of those photos.

By midyear, the verdict was all but in: Nelle Lee was different, and not in a fun or delightful way, but in a manner that ignored convention, which could be interpreted as a kind of backhanded insult to everything these young ladies stood for.

"I didn't have anything in common with her because she was not like most of us," said Catherine Helms. "She wasn't worried about how her hair looked or whether she had a date on Friday night like the rest of us were. I don't remember her sitting around and giggling and being silly and talking about what our weddings were going to be like—that's what teenage girls talked about. She was not a part of the 'girl group.' She never had what we would call in the South 'finishing touches.' "[32]

At the end of first semester, Nelle's roommates kicked her out.

Against the larger canvas of the campus, however, she made a different impression. Seen from a distance, traits that set her apart from the normal Huntingdon "penguins" were found intriguing. Walking across campus with her long stride, dressed in a simple navy cotton skirt, white blouse, and the brown leather bombardier's jacket Edwin had given her, she cut a figure that blurred gender distinctions. "I noticed her physically," said Mary Tomlinson, another freshman. "She had a presence. I remember her better than I do anyone else at Huntingdon, except my roommate and maybe one or two other people. Everything about her hinted at masculinity. I think the word *handsome* would have suited her."

"I was struck by her height, athletic ability, and congeniality, and the simplicity of her spring clothes—navy skirt with short-sleeved shirts, and a brogan-type shoe."[33] "Having come from a family of privilege and money, she was unpretentious," added Tomlinson.[34]

Her athleticism caught the attention of team captains, too. For volleyball games, she was first pick when sides were chosen. The solid *thunk!* of her spikes over the net resounded across the Green. Her soccer kicks sent the other team running pell-mell after the ball.

She was not incapable of making friends, either, if given the chance. A chat with her after class revealed a bubbling, subversive wit. From her seat by the edge of Huntingdon's lively social mainstream, she confided that there was nothing she disliked about the place; she just found the experience a little humorous at times. Her conversation was rife with observations of campus life, spun into stories. Exhaling smoke slowly from her cigarette, she would watch the face of her entertained listener with an amused expression. "Every time I think about her, I always think about laughing, I always think about humor," said algebra classmate Martha Brown. Tina Rood agreed: "She really sort of became a recluse—even in school she did her thing—I just remember her as fun, and funny! I can still see her telling wonderful stories with a cigarette dangling from her lips."[35]

It took a while to get to know Nelle Lee, but those who did realized something about her. She just wanted to be comfortable in her own skin. Her cussing was unconscious; the clothes she wore appealed to her because they were practical; she laughed when one of her teasing remarks drew a comeback delivered with equal zest. But she would not stop to seek others' approval. The notion that she should never seemed to enter her head. Her right to live as she pleased was not up for negotiation, even if it ran against the grain of the milieu at Huntingdon. It was nobody's business. "That was an era when you did the proper thing," said Catherine Helms. "And your mother was horrified if you didn't. That was never part of Nelle's persona—she didn't care! It must have taken a colossal amount of courage to be different."[36]

Nelle was not oblivious to other people's feelings, however. According to Mary Nell Atherton, "They turned the lights out in the dorm at eleven o'clock. Many nights, when I had to go to the restroom, which was right across from Nelle's room, Nelle would be sitting outside the door because she said she couldn't sleep and didn't want to disturb her roommates."[37]

A better indication of her sensitivity toward others occurred on February 12, 1945. Half an hour before the girls were to come down in formal attire for a Valentine's Day dinner, a tornado tore through Montgomery, dragging a funnel for thirteen miles that killed twenty-six people and destroyed one hundred homes. The lights stayed off in Massey Hall until almost bedtime. By then, one of Mary Nell Atherton's roommates was too agitated to sleep and kept looking out the window. For the next several days, fear of another tornado kept her awake.

"One afternoon," said Atherton, "Nelle came down to the room because she'd heard my roommate was so afraid she couldn't sleep. She told her, 'I'd be glad to stay up with you and keep you company, because I can't sleep, either.' Nelle was very concerned about people, but she was not one to mix and mingle that much."[38]

And when she committed herself to an activity in advance, Nelle could meet social expectations. The key was whether she chose to do so. That spring, the Glee Club, in which she sang alto, made a performance tour of Methodist churches. One night, she and Emily H. Anthony were welcomed into the ancient home of an elderly couple in which indoor plumbing was a recent improvement. "They had a very, very old car," said Anthony. "And we, of course, put on our evening dresses to sing. They brought out sheets and spread them on the seats so we wouldn't get our evening dresses dirty. I think of it now and smile to think how sweet they were. They were so proud of having us spend the night with them."[39] Like two princesses, Nelle and Emily rode to the church.

And although Nelle was sometimes sidelined socially at Huntingdon, she more than compensated for it by contributing occasional articles to the *Huntress,* the campus newspaper. In April, she was inducted with seven other girls into the campus chapter of the national literary society, Chi Delta Phi. Also that spring, the second-semester edition of the Huntingdon literary magazine, the *Prelude,* featured two vignettes written by Nelle Lee.

These short pieces of fiction, perhaps the first of Lee's ever in print, stand out in the magazine, not only because the voice of a writer comes through, especially in the handling of southern speech, but also because of the rather daring choice of subject matter: racial prejudice and justice, themes that would resonate in her novel. All of the other poems and prose in the magazine treat topics one would expect from young people raised in that era: romance, nature, a portrait of an admired grandfather, and a short story about a historical figure. But Lee's submissions are first glimpses of the landscape that she would make her own in *To Kill a Mockingbird.*

In her story "Nightmare," a Huntingdon girl is daydreaming in class. The droning voice of the teacher sends the girl into a reverie in which she sees herself as a child. She's watching something happening on the other side of a fence through a crack in a board. Suddenly, she hears a "sound which she will hear in her dreams the rest of her life . . . Karrumph . . . Karangarang!" The child runs home and hides in her bed, but hears someone say as he passes under her window, "[D]idn't take him long . . . neck was pretty short . . . best hangin' I've seen in twenty years . . . now maybe they'll learn to behave themselves."[40]

To her southern classmates raised in genteel circumstances, Nelle's decision to write about the hanging of a Negro may have seemed in poor taste and outside the bounds of a college literary magazine. And it's possible she submitted it as a bid for attention, or she may have recognized that a subject with elements of conflict and social significance was worth writing about.

In her second story, "A Wink at Justice," also a clear forerunner to *To Kill a Mockingbird,* she takes a different tack. This time, in contrast to how bigotry permits injustice, she shows justice administered by a wise judge.

"The tiny courtroom reeked of tobacco smoke, cheap hair oil, and perspiration," the tale begins, anticipating a description from *To Kill a Mockingbird*: "The warm bittersweet smell of clean Negro welcomed us as we entered the churchyard—Hearts of Love hair-dressing mingled with asafetida, snuff, Hoyt's Cologne, Brown's Mule, peppermint, and lilac talcum."[41] A swift overview of the courtroom borrows elements from the Monroeville courtroom she knew so well. Then the judge enters, Judge Hanks—a dead ringer for A. C. Lee, right down to his mannerisms: "He carried a pocketknife which he twirled constantly, sometimes thumping it up and catching it. Fine lines ran down from his nostrils to the corners of his mouth. I noticed that they deepened when he smiled. A pair of rimless glasses perched precariously on his short nose."

The case to be decided involves eight Negroes arrested for gambling. Judge Hanks comes down from the bench and orders the men to turn their hands palms up. "He went down the line inspecting each outstretched hand. To three of the men he said, 'You c'n go. Git out of here!' To the other five he barked, 'Sixty days. Dismissed.'" After court is adjourned, the unnamed narrator approaches the judge and asks how he had reached his decision.

"Well, I looked at their hands. The ones who had corns on 'em I let go, because they work in the fields and probably have a pack of children to support. It was the ones with soft, smooth hands I was after. They're the ones who gamble professionally, and we don't need that sort of thing around here."[42]

AS THE END OF her freshman year drew near, Nelle's reputation had jelled. She was not fitting in, and she had evidently resigned herself to that, too. The girls in Massey Hall had noticed that ever since she was kicked out of her first room there, she was often holed up, either in her new room or at the library studying.

When word got around that she would be transferring to the University of Alabama, at Tuscaloosa, northwest of Montgomery and only another couple of hours by car or train from Monroeville, one of her instructors, Dr. Gordon T. Chappell, professor of history and economics, expressed regret to his teaching assistant, Ann Richards. "He had mentioned several students that were doing outstanding work and she was one of them," she said. "He was disappointed that she wasn't coming back to Huntingdon because he thought she had a lot of promise. He was interested in the girls he thought would go far."[43] Because Huntingdon didn't offer a law degree, she would have had to transfer after sophomore year, anyway. But her decision to leave Huntingdon after one year indicates her eagerness to start afresh.

With the coming of warm weather, Nelle became more and more impatient to put Huntingdon behind her. One spring day, A. B. Blass, Jr., arrived on campus to drive his fiancée back to Monroeville. When Nelle saw him, she ran up to the car.

"A.B.! A.B.! You goin' back? Hold on, I'll get my things."

"Yeah, but Nelle—" Blass began. He sighed as she sprinted off.

In a few minutes she was back and climbed into the backseat behind the two lovebirds.

A.B. turned around. "Nelle, I haven't seen my girl for awhile."

"So? Let's go. We can talk about it later."

"You don't understand—"

"You're going home, aren't you?"

A.B. chose his words carefully, overenunciating each one: "Nelle, you've never gone with anybody. We-might-not-go-straight-home, get it?"

Nelle's face clouded over. "Fine!" She got out and slammed the door.

As the car drove away, she shouted, "You'll see A. B. Blass! I'll fix it so you never get into a fraternity at Alabama—just wait!" She stalked off.[44]

During the final week of classes in May, the girls in Massey Hall hugged one another and handed their yearbooks around, seeking farewell messages. In Catherine Helms's book, Sara Ann McCall wrote, "Dear Cobb, It's been fun knowing you. You're one swell girl and I'll never forget you." Another student penned, "Dear Cobb, This year was really swell, and you helped make it so."

Florence Moore handed her yearbook to Nelle. When she returned it, Moore read the following:

> Dearest Flo,
> Thanks for the memories
> of stinking sophomore lit
> of Mrs. Figh's shoes
> that you were so swell
> and now I'll leave you
> with love & all that hell!

"Typical Nelle," Moore said.[45]

f   o   u   r

Rammer Jammer

"TA-*DUM*! TA-*DUM*! TA-DUMPITY-*DUM*!" SANG A HANDFUL OF girls out of the window of Phi Mu house at the University of Alabama in Tuscaloosa. Their voices were loud enough so that the target of their derision could hear every syllable. "She had long flat shoes, long straight hair, a slight slump, probably because she carried a black, portable typewriter in one hand and a stack of books and papers in the other," said one of the choristers, Barbara Moore. "I never saw her with anyone and wonder if she were lonely."[1] The girl they were ridiculing was Nelle.

It seemed inconceivable that with World War II officially ended (on September 2, 1945) and the campus of 7,500 students awash with veterans, any woman would not want to look her best. The university had been "almost a girls' school," remembered Mildred Jacobs, "we gave boys' names to some of the girls so that we could hear the sound of the name."[2] But now the freshman class was filled with men just out of the armed services. "The veterans were not like any of the teenagers that I knew," said Moore. "Most weren't interested in fraternities, but most were interested in dating and getting an education, in that order, and were serious about both subjects."[3]

With this sea of men inundating the university, many coeds hoped to get their "MRS degree" before graduation. The student newspaper, the *Crimson White,* added luster to their fantasies by featuring an undergraduate "Bama Belle" on the front page almost every week—lovely as a Hollywood starlet, sometimes with the enviable distinction of being a gentleman's fiancée. A few were married already and pictured in romantic settings with their husbands, suggesting that a princess had at last found her prince.

But Nelle was apparently uninterested in any of this, which affronted the young women in the fifteen houses along Sorority Row. Her lack of makeup, her flyaway hair and dun-colored outfits would have passed unnoticed had she been an "independent"—someone outside the elite panhellenic organization of sororities and fraternities. But she wasn't. Through an error of judgment on the part of the girls in the Chi Omega house, she had become one of them—a sorority sister.

They were outstandingly pretty, the girls who were taking her in. Chi Omega was a house that "specialize[d] in blondes," proclaimed the university yearbook, "long, short, thin and broad," including Miss Alabama of 1946.[4] "Your sisters were watching you," said Chi O member Polly Terry. "They did not want your behavior to reflect on them."[5] But Nelle's certainly did. In the purely feminine aquifer of sorority life, she floated like a drop of motor oil. "I kind of wondered at the time what she saw in a sorority to join it," marveled Mary Anne Berryman, looking back.[6]

Regardless, with an optimistic heart, Nelle put her name on the Panhellenic Association's list of young women scheduled to visit all the houses on Sorority Row during Rush Week in the autumn of 1945. As she and other rushees came through the door at Chi Omega, the members—all sporting fraternity pins—serenaded them lustily with fraternity and drinking songs. Nelle liked the humor. They invited her back. And a few days later, much to Nelle's surprise (and later theirs), the Chi Os—Nu Beta chapter, founded 1922—accepted her.

The Chi Omegas lived in a two-story brick house painted white and designed in Federal style. On the right-hand side of the main stairway was a flat-roofed sunroom, sometimes used as extra sleeping quarters. Upstairs, the young women slept in bunk beds and got ready for the day by sharing showers and dressing rooms. None of them would have thought of appearing downstairs in the living room other than nicely dressed. Young men visited regularly, and not only to see a girlfriend, either. A masculine voice calling, "Three for bridge!" was an invitation for anyone to come downstairs to play a few hands.

Once the girls had left their bedrooms in the mornings, Negro maids scurried upstairs to dust, sweep, and change the sheets. During mealtimes, the Negro butler, Benny Snoddy, served at table. Nelle usually skipped breakfast; she hated it because she hated eggs. And she let it be known that she hated swing music, too, which was then the most popular kind in America: she thought that numbers by Benny Goodman, Count Basie, and Duke Ellington were frantic and obnoxious. She liked to sing in the shower, but instead of catchy Hit Parade songs such as "Let It Snow," her pretty alto voice carried tunes by Gilbert and Sullivan, composers of nineteenth-century British musicals such as *The Mikado* and *H.M.S. Pinafore*:

> *A British tar is a soaring soul,*
> *As free as a mountain bird,*
> *His energetic fist should be ready to resist*
> *A dictatorial word.*
> *His nose should pant and his lip should curl,*
> *His cheeks should flame and his brow should furl,*
> *His bosom should heave and his heart should glow,*
> *And his fist be ever ready for a knock-down blow.*

The sentiment of these lyrics was not anything like "If I Loved You," from Richard Rodgers and Oscar Hammerstein II's 1945 Broadway hit, *Carousel,* which gave the Chi Omega girls goose bumps when it played on the radio. In fact, as Nelle's sorority sisters tried to get to know her better, they were at a loss to categorize her; she seemed so unlike young women her age. Not a lot about her had changed since Huntingdon. She was still chain-smoking, and she preferred men's pajamas over frilly gowns. "She was a little mannish-looking," recalled Jane Benton Davis. "When girls had long hair and did things with it, her hair was short."[7] Mary Anne Berryman chose the word *matronly* to describe her: "A little bit thick in the middle. Nothing very stylish." However, "She had beautiful large, dark brown eyes that were quite piercing."[8]

In the evenings, the girls chatted about their days and their beaus, but Nelle didn't. "She was just sort of a loner. She just sat there and looked. I don't remember any contact between her and anybody," said Berryman. At mealtimes, "she never entered into any conversations with the girls at the table, but was more of an observer. I always had the feeling that she found us very shallow, silly, and young, in which case she was absolutely right."[9] Most of the girls incorrectly assumed Nelle was a graduate student. She could be amiable and funny, too, remembered Polly Terry, "but she was not going to bounce up to somebody and go, 'Hiya, I'm *Nail!*'" Once, said Terry, "I got fearfully blistered from lying too long in the sun on the roof of the sorority house. I was so blistered and sitting cross-legged on a metal card table in the upstairs lounge, and Nelle drew a caricature of me as Mahatma Gandhi. The girls were very impressed!"[10]

On Friday and Saturday nights, when the other Chi O girls were bustling around, trying to be ready in time for dates or dances, Nelle never had any plans. No one recalled seeing her with a beau. Practically every weekend, she tromped through the living room, golf bag slung over her shoulder, heading out for a few rounds. The way she dressed for eighteen holes raised a few eyebrows—just jeans and a sweatshirt. "That wasn't the way we dressed," said Jane Benton Davis.[11] The pronouncement on Nelle's outerwear was "very different."

Nelle's mannish appearance led to some interesting situations, including one involving a suspected burglar and a night watchman. At about two o'clock one morning, there were noises from downstairs that sounded like a burglar on the premises. Nelle wrote:

> People poured into the lounge with angry expressions on their faces, wanting to know who the hell woke them up. Then Lila said the word "burglar." From nowhere appeared the most complete collection of blunt instruments I have ever seen: coke bottles, tennis racquets, pokers, hair dryers, and even a pair of ice tongs.
>
> But nobody would go downstairs.
>
> Finally someone hit upon the bright idea of calling the police.

The police and night watchman came an hour later. After screaming
at them the pertinent data [the police] reached the admired conclusion that they ought to search the house.

"I was chosen to escort them through the premises," Nelle continued, "and when we got up to the attic the watchman gave me his
flashlight and said, 'You go first.' "[12]

Out of all the girls in the house, Nelle had only one good friend: a
girl she'd grown up with in Monroeville, Sylvia Parnell. Tall and remarkably beautiful, Parnell was held by the other girls in slight awe.
So when Nelle bounded up the stairs after classes to Parnell's room to
spend an hour with her before dinner, the sisters wondered: What on
earth was the basis of that friendship? Parnell, they all knew, acted
"sophisticated"—it was a quality she had acquired on her own; her father owned a big lumberyard in Monroeville and her grandmother
was a seamstress. Nelle was much less confined by provincialism than
many of the other girls, but she wasn't really anyone's idea of "sophisticated," by any stretch of the imagination. Few would have guessed
that part of the reason for her attraction to Parnell may have been that
Sylvia was rather risqué. At an annual costume Shipwreck Party at
the Sigma Nu house, she stunned everyone the moment she walked
through the door. Married by then to the student circulation manager
of the *Rammer Jammer*, the university's quarterly humor magazine,
she entered the room clad only in the shirt of a pair of men's pajamas, which fluttered at the top of her long legs; her husband, bare-
chested, sported only the bottoms. "There was a big to-do about that!"
said Polly Terry.[13]

But no such leniency was accorded to Nelle. She did not have the
Teflon coating of prettiness and enviable behavior to deflect criticism.
"I'm ashamed to admit that we made fun of her," said Barbara Moore,
a member of Phi Mu sorority. "Never around her, but behind her
back. Today she would be called a campus nerd."[14]

After a year in the Chi Omega house, Nelle moved out into New
Hall, one of the female dormitories. She continued to take her meals at
the house sometimes and attended chapter meetings, but her sorority
sisters thought she seemed preoccupied. The reason was she had discovered another, more suitable, group of companions—the avowed
pundits of campus life and its traditions and, most important, the

serious writers. She called them "the most casual colony" at the university, and they greeted her as one of their own. They were "the various editors, feature writers, proofreaders and kibitzers who sling together," as she put it, the University of Alabama campus publications.[15]

NELLE HAD FOUND HER way to the enormous Beaux Arts–style Alabama Union building almost as soon as she arrived on campus in the fall of 1945. The entrance was up a majestic flight of stone stairs at the foot of a row of three-story columns. On the third floor was the office of the student publications, a large room divided by a row of file cabinets acting as a line demarcating journalism from creative writing. On one side sat the staff of the *Crimson White,* the campus newspaper; on the other, the writers and editors for the *Rammer Jammer,* the campus humor magazine, named for the thunderous cheer shouted by Crimson Tide football fans: "Rammer jammer, rammer jammer, rammer jammer!" Nelle introduced herself to one of the *Crimson White* editors, Bill Mayes, "a lanky, Klan-hating six-footer from somewhere in Mississippi."[16] She offered her services as a stringer—someone to cover the odd meeting or event. Unfortunately, most of the news beats had already gone to journalism majors; also working against her was that she had no experience. Undeterred, she went around the wall of file cabinets to the *Rammer Jammer* side of the room. That staff consisted of novice satirists and humor writers, under pressure to produce an amusing quarterly publication. Good submissions were sought after and prized. Nelle got her hand in right away by submitting a few pieces for the homecoming parody—a takeoff on *Esquire* magazine. In the December issue, the masthead listed her as a staff member. Mildred Jacobs, a *Crimson White* staffer, recalled hearing Nelle's voice on the *Rammer Jammer* side of the file cabinets, and years later, when she read *To Kill a Mockingbird,* "I could just hear her talking in the book."[17]

During the following summer, Nelle stayed on campus, catching up on a few credits but also because she knew that the *Crimson White* would be strapped for writers. Pages were hard to fill while the university was in a somnambulant state under the hot Alabama sun. Having written for the *Rammer Jammer,* Nelle had now demonstrated that she could produce. She suggested an idea to Mayes, who was taking over as summer newspaper editor: What if she wrote an at-large column, she asked, that commented on the passing scene—something to lighten up the editorial page? He agreed. For a prelaw student, it was a coup.

She dubbed her column "Caustic Comment," an irregular feature that delivered doses of self-parody, exaggerated descriptions, and long-winded gags. John T. Hamner, destined to become a newspaperman in Alabama, was struck by the tone of "bright, brittle, sophomoric but sharp humor. . . . Her specialty was debunking, taking quick sharp jabs at the idols and mores of the time and place."[18] The column was at its strongest when Lee took aim at inane advertisements on the radio, or the amount of red tape students had to endure; at its weakest when she got on her high horse about something. She didn't bother to rein in her fondness for cursing, either:

> There is a striking difference between University students now and those of five years ago in regard to their interests. Formerly, the minds of the Capstone [University of Alabama] undergrads were almost solely occupied with who belonged to what fraternity and the respective merits of Glenn Miller and Tommy Dorsey as bandleaders.
>
> The high moment in an undergrad's life was the interfraternity dances at the end of each year. He planned for months ahead just who he would escort to each dance, and how many invitations to pre-dance cocktail parties it would be socially acceptable to decline. . . .
>
> Contrast the undergrad of 1946. He doesn't give a damn what kind of pants he wears to a formal, his major interests are not who's pinned to whom or how many quarts per capita his fraternity brothers consume each day. There is an awakening of interest in the lives of students in the things that really count.[19]

In response, at least one subscriber submitted several caustic comments himself, asking, "How did that sneak in?"—in reference to the rather mild expletive *damn*.[20] Another complained, "Irony is delightful; sarcasm is fine; 'Caustic Comment' is the best reading there is—but so much more fun if not slapped on like red paint on an old barn."[21]

It was true that Nelle strained hard to get readers' attention. Trying her hand at a book review, for instance, she interjected some tough talk about race relations, a subject usually avoided in polite company. In her opinion, too many southern writers danced around the "Negro problem"—the preferred euphemism then—and depicted racism romantically: "Almost since the time the first slaves were shipped into the South by the Yankees, various authors have taken it upon themselves to probe, explain and hash over the problems that came with them. The South has been repeatedly embarrassed by the Smiths [in reference to Lillian Smith, author of *Strange Fruit*], Faulkners, Stowes, et al, who either wrote delicately of the mint julep era or championed the dark eddies of 'niggertown.'" For avoiding these pitfalls, Nelle praised the book under review, *Night Fire,* written by a popular instructor on campus, Edward Kimbrough. She relished Kimbrough's portrayal of a character named "Turkey Littlepage, who is reminiscent of all the county sheriffs in South Alabama and Mississippi. Mean, utterly stupid, and with violent prejudices, Turkey tramps through the pages of *Night Fire* as a living memorial to all the miserable incompetents the South elects as enforcers of the law."[22]

Such language was not often seen in print on campus. The University of Alabama in the 1940s, the "Country Club of the South" as it was nicknamed, was a "profoundly conservative community," remembered Ernest Maygarden, a history and political science major.

> Both the student body and the faculty were representative of traditional Southern social and political attitudes, and there was little pressure for any type of change. . . . There were a few faculty members who expressed reservations about some of the prevailing political and social orthodoxies, but they received little student support and were generally regarded as harmless eccentrics. The one subject never discussed, in my experience, was race relations. The prevailing view was that there was no reason to upset the status quo, and most were willing to continue existing conditions indefinitely.[23]

The status quo regarding whites and Negroes was indeed cast in iron in the Deep South. A classmate of Nelle's, Vincent Lauria, an Italian-American from Long Island, inadvertently violated it and was quickly set straight. Boarding a Tuscaloosa bus, he sat down in the back, the "colored" section, where seats were available. The white driver pulled the bus over to the curb. "Stand up here with us or get off the bus!" he shouted, red-faced. At Woolworth's department store, Lauria purchased an item and automatically entered the shortest checkout line, which happened to be the one labeled COL-ORED ONLY. He realized his mistake when "Everybody looked like they were going to kill me."[24]

However, among the "most casual colony" of young writers and journalists at the university, Nelle's opinions learned at her father's knee about bigotry were not unusual. At the end of the summer, "Klan-hating" Bill Mayes prepared to turn over the helm of the *Crimson White* to his successor, Jane Freret, who had been in New York City working as a guest editor for *Mademoiselle* magazine. Mayes's parting shot on the editorial page was "We Bequeath: Our Anti-Klanism." His target was Governor Theodore G. Bilbo of Missis-sippi. Governor Bilbo advocated terrorizing black voters: "I call upon every red-blooded white man to use any means to keep the nigger away from the polls. The best way to keep a nigger from voting is to have a little talk with him the night before."[25]

Mayes responded:

> We just couldn't wind out our editorial term without mentioning our old friend the Klan. Last week, the "man" Bilbo admitted he was a member of that organization. This just bears out our previous contention. When a shrewd politician will boast of his Klan mem-bership, the average citizen may rest assured that the power of that organization is pretty great.... Now is the time to stamp out this malignant growth. If we have any legacy to leave our successor, we would make it a thoroughgoing hatred of Alabama's—and the nation's—Ku Klux Klan.[26]

"Caustic Comment" had never quite ventured so far. But at the end of the summer of 1946, Nelle was given a broader forum for skewering prevailing attitudes about race, in addition to satirizing less volatile topics. She was appointed editor in chief of the *Rammer Jammer*.

THE *RAMMER JAMMER* WAS a better place than the more tradi-tional *Crimson White* to exercise her talents. She "dressed differently, ate differently, talked differently than most. She thought differently, too," said John T. Hamner, "and those differences made her stand out."[27] The humor magazine was wide open for creative writers with an offbeat slant on things. Taking over the top spot was going to be a heavy responsibility, though. That same autumn, the beginning of her junior year, Nelle also enrolled in law school.

At that time, prelaw students who had maintained a C average or better in all their courses could apply as juniors to the University of Alabama law school. Nelle's liberal arts credits from prelaw—including the ones in history and literature from Huntingdon, and the additional ones she picked up the previous summer—were transferred in without a hitch.

The actual process of registering for law school, however, was another matter—at least according to Nelle's exaggerated account of the steps involved. In a humor piece she'd written for the *Crimson White* during the spring, "What Price Registration?" she described entering the august law building, Farrah Hall, and running a gauntlet of men:

> I was eager, to put it bluntly, I told myself that I was entering upon a new thing, a thing which would determine the course of my life. After some ten minutes of fast pacing and indulging in ego-raising exercises, I found myself in sight of a building which seemed to be looking gloomily down at me. There, upon the steps (forty-six of them) sat men, men, men! In some confusion I began climbing those damn steps, amid the usual medley of whistles (I haven't figured that deal out yet; I'm as ugly as sin).

She's sent chasing after paperwork, back and forth across campus, until finally she returns exhausted back at Farrah Hall.

> Promptly at five o'clock Monday afternoon I returned to the desk. "Here's the affidavit," I said proudly. "Huh?" said the said one. "Here's the affidavit. THE AFFIDAVIT!" I screamed. "Oh," he said, serenely probing his right bicuspid. "Well, you're too late. Come back at eight in the morning."
>
> Evidently he caught some faint perception of my inner feelings because he extended a long arm and patted me on the shoulder. "That's O.K., kid," he assured me. "I'm a freshman here myself."[28]

It was a clever send-up of bureaucracy and addle-headed rules, to say nothing of Nelle's skill at pacing a story and creating characters in a few words. A perplexing note is why a twenty-one-year-old coed would describe herself "ugly as sin" in print, unless it was to offer an explanation for why she didn't have any suitors or show any interest in dating. "She never dated," said Betty McGiffert, one of her Chi Omega sisters.[29]

In any case, Nelle sallied forth with equal fervor as both the editor of the *Rammer Jammer* and as a law student. Her quirkiness was a particularly good fit with the humor magazine's reputation, and she enjoyed acting eccentric. She is an "impressive figure as she strides down the corridor of New Hall at all hours attired in men's green striped pajamas," said the *Crimson White* in a front-page article.

> Quite frequently she passes out candy to unsuspecting freshmen; when she emerges from their rooms they have subscribed to the *Rammer Jammer.* . . . Her Utopia is a land with the culture of England and the government of Russia; her idea of heaven is a place where diligent law students and writers ascend after death and can stay up forever without Benzedrine. . . . Wild about football, she played center on the fourth grade team in Monroeville, her hometown. Her favorite person is her sister "Bear". . . . Lawyer Lee will spend her future in Monroeville. As for literary aspirations she says, "I shall probably write a book some day. They all do."[30]

When the yearbook photographer came around to get a shot, Nelle hammed it up by posing as a harried editor glaring at a typewriter, a cigarette burning perilously low in one hand.

She began law school with equal zest. In a front-page article for the *Crimson White,* she enjoined her fellow students to consider enrolling, too, particularly women. "The feminine pulchritude numbers five at the moment, but even more women are going to enroll in the Fall quarter. If you are an earnest student, not afraid of hard work (by that we mean hard, brother) and are of a high moral character (you have to get five affidavits to prove it) the Law school wants you!" She by-lined it "Dody."[31]

For homecoming, in November, she joined in the fun with all the other law students who donned striped pants, morning coats, polka-dot ties, and derbies, a University of Alabama tradition since the 1920s. Wearing her brother's "wing collar and boiled shirt," and a red carnation in her lapel, she entered the parade with her classmates singing to the tune of "Sidewalks of New York":

> *Yeast side, vat side*
> *All around the town*
> *All the lawyers are drinking*
> *All the whiskey they can down*
> *Boys and girls together*
> *Far from the faculty's call*
> *We drink like Hell*
> *And pass out Swell*
> *On the steps of Farrah Hall!*[32]

Riding atop the law school float was Farrah Hall's Negro janitor, Remus Rhodes, the "official mascot," playing popular tunes on an organ and surrounded by four law school cheerleaders throwing candy to the crowd. The *Crimson White* interviewed Nelle and the other female law school students about their plans for homecoming. Making the point that Nelle was following in the family footsteps, the article explained, "Nelle's entering law school just came naturally, since her father and sister are both barristers."[33]

It was demanding preparing for a day's classes in torts, real estate, and contract law; yet along with that, Nelle managed the *Rammer Jammer*'s staff of sixteen, too. "She was a lot of fun; she just made it go," said Elise Sanguinetti, who was one of the self-described "lowly persons" on the magazine staff.[34] Nelle contributed at least one piece to every issue, including "Now Is the Time for All Good Men," a one-act play lampooning a proposed racist amendment to the Alabama constitution.

Her so-called Boswell Amendment would have required prospective voters to interpret the U.S. Constitution to the satisfaction of the local registrar. At the start of the play, Nelle introduces a senator, the Honorable F. B. MacGillacuddy, chairman of the Citizen's Committee to Eradicate the Black Plague, who argues strenuously for the passage of the bill, which is nothing more than a warmed-over post-Reconstruction gambit to disenfranchise blacks at will. Once it passes, however, Senator MacGillacuddy fails the test, too, and is denied the right to vote! He appears before the United States Supreme Court, pleading, "I come to you on a matter of gravest importance. My civil liberties are being threatened. You boys all know me, I was in Congress with most of you. A diabolical group down in Alabama slipped one over on the honest, decent citizens of the state three years ago. . . . Whatta you going to do about it, boys?"[35] As a piece of satire, the play was more mature in style and content than most of what usually appeared in the magazine.

Nelle felt sufficiently confident about her powers to also offer tongue-in-cheek literary criticism. An idea for a takeoff on the state of southern fiction apparently came to her as a result of a speech delivered on campus the previous April by Pulitzer Prize–winning author T. S. Stribling. A graduate of the University of Alabama School of Law, Stribling spoke to young writers about choosing appropriate subject matter for fiction. He reminded them that the socially conscious Southern Renascence movement had replaced the "old massa" school of writing set in the Reconstruction-era South. He cited his bestselling novel *Birthright* (1922) as an example. The protagonist is a Harvard-educated Negro who struggles to survive in his small Tennessee town.

But the South, Stribling insisted, was still the most "writeable" part of the United States "because it has three humorous characters that readers would recognize right away." He then ticked them off: the Negro, the southern aristocrat, and the "hill" man. These three characters, he said, would not tax the reader's mind to interpret. "Characters that need description," he warned, "give the reader one strike against the author in reader interest." The reader's mind should not be exerted, just carried along by the story. "It is best to have your reader without a thought in his head."[36]

By exaggerating Stribling's guidelines, Nelle contributed a withering piece to the *Rammer Jammer* titled "Some Writers of Our Times":

The first and foremost qualifications one must have if [a writer] aspires to the higher brackets of intelligentsia are (1) a sadistic father; (2) an alcoholic mother. He must be beaten into insensibility by the former and ostentatiously loved and hated by the latter in her drunken orgies. Any maltreatment by older brothers and sisters also helps. This comes under the category of The Unhappy Childhood.

An author's environment is important to his training in the gentle art of self-expression. The general trend today is small towns, preferably Southern villages. There must be the annual race riot full of blood & gore which causes violent reactions in his sensitive (I use that word because all writers are supposed to be sensitive) soul. . . . Yes, it is to the writer's advantage if he comes from such surroundings. He has the chance to expose to the public the immoral goings-on in an out-of-the-way village, have himself hailed as the H. W. Beecher of the day, and instigate a movement which would do away with small towns forever.[37]

Having said her piece about extremes in southern fiction in her satire, Nelle can't resist turning next to lampooning writers' egos. The author she chooses to caricature is Truman Capote, who wanders into "Some Writers of Our Times." Since December 1944, he had been working on his first novel, *Other Voices, Other Rooms,* sketching a rough draft in Monroeville while staying with relatives. Evidently, Nelle saw parts of the work-in-progress, destined to create a controversy because of its open treatment of homosexuality.

Nelle was surprisingly knowledgeable about the topic of same-sex love, especially for a young woman raised in a small southern town more than sixty years ago. In another of her pieces for the *Rammer Jammer,* this one parodying the famous, "Yes, Virginia, There Is a Santa Claus" column written for the *New York Sun* in 1897, Nelle writes, "Believe in Santa Claus! You may as well believe in fairies! Of course, there are fairies, but not the kind you read about in Anderson's fairy tales. While we are on the subject, I may as well disillusion you further. The authorities tell us that fairies cannot be seen. Don't you believe it! I saw two of them huddled together reading *The Well of Loneliness.*"[38] The novel, written by English writer Radclyffe Hall, tells the story of a girl born to a wealthy English family who is nicknamed Stephen because of her boyish ways. She falls in love with Mary, a younger woman, and the two live together harmoniously in Paris. Many lesbians in the 1930s, '40s, and '50s encountered their first exposure to other lesbians in the book's pages, although some were offended that Hall portrayed homosexuals as tragic, suicide prone, and alcoholic.

Truman enters "Some Writer's of Our Times," complaining envi-
ously about Edward Kimbrough, whose novel *Night Fire* Nelle had
reviewed for the *Crimson White*:

> "May I thit here?" I looked up and beheld a blonde young gentle-
> man, so I answered certainly. As soon as he was seated he embarked
> upon a diatribe. . . . Any attempt to reproduce vowels would be im-
> possible, but here's what he said: "I thimply refwoose to call that
> man MISTHER Kimbrough. Afther all, I'm thix months older than
> he ith, and there's no thense whatthoever, WHATTHOEVER, in
> calling him that. I've been writing thince I wath eight years old, and
> I'm not going to let him bully ME! . . .
>
> Honey, I'm thuck. My novel ith about a thenthitive boy from
> the time he'th twelve until he ith a gwown man. MISTHER Kim-
> brough thez I've justh got to cut it thum, but all of it ith so poignant
> I justh can't bwing mythelf tho change a WORD of it.[39]

On the whole, "Some Writers of Our Times" is a pretty good piece
of droll humor, although it was probably over the heads (or beneath
the interest) of most undergraduate readers. Fewer still probably understood a reference she makes to a young writer in her Shakespeare
class who was working on a novel. Nelle's instructor for Shakespeare
was Hudson Strode, one of the best-known creative writing teachers
in the country, and the struggling young man is supposed to be one of
his protégés. Nelle could have made fun of Professor Strode himself—
he played the arty, pipe-smoking man of letters to the hilt—but then
she might have been accused of sour grapes. Because for reasons that
have never been adequately explained, Nelle wasn't one of the young
writers at the University of Alabama in Strode's famous workshop.

Born on Halloween in Cairo, Illinois, Hudson Strode grew up in
Demopolis, Alabama, and considered himself a Southerner. After grad-
uating from Columbia University, he had tried acting, but Sir Johnston Forbes-Robertson, one of the greatest British Shakespeareans of
the day, told him he was too short. Strode also had a high, squeaky
voice. Lessons from a voice teacher eventually dropped his register
two octaves into a rich, smooth baritone "that he used brilliantly in his
famed class on Shakespeare's tragedies, making Hamlet's voice boom
through Morgan Hall," remembered Wayne Greenhaw, one of Strode's

writing students.[40] To improve his carriage, Strode walked along the banks of the Alabama River balancing a book on his head. He wore ascots instead of ties and draped a Burberry overcoat around his shoulders like a cape.

His workshop received an average of 1,200 manuscripts annually from students eager for one of fifteen to twenty-five spots available. "If you were chosen, he made you feel as though you had already accomplished a writing feat; you were among the chosen few. At his table, you were sitting with the great," said Greenhaw.[41] The workshop met two nights a week at a big table on the fourth floor of the library, during which students received priceless instruction. "He was always right when a story needed more development," said novelist and Alabama poet laureate Helen Norris. "He had a marvelous sense of what he needed more of: 'Well, I need something *more* there.' "[42]

Thomas Hal Phillips, one of Strode's teaching assistants in the early 1940s, and later a novelist and screenwriter, revered his instructor: "To me, he was *the* master. Once, as we were about to cross campus from his Shakespeare class to the library, I was going down the steps with three or four other people right behind him. I referred to him out loud as 'the master.' He stopped and dressed me down and said I shouldn't call him that. But I defended myself by saying I meant it, I *believed* it."[43]

But the name "Nelle Harper Lee" doesn't appear on the attendance rolls of Strode's workshop. After she won the Pulitzer Prize for *To Kill a Mockingbird,* in fact, she resented reporters' assumption that she had been one of Strode's creative writing students. She was grateful for his Shakespeare class and told him so years later. An interviewer, she wrote to Strode, "asked me what kind of teacher you were. My reply was something like this: 'I don't know what kind of teacher he was, but I know one thing; if you met even half of his demands, you received something in return that stays with you for the rest of your life.' "[44]

So if Nelle was in Strode's Shakespeare class and he was aware of the quality of her writing, then why wasn't she among his twenty-five students in his workshop?

The simple answer might be that she didn't make the cut. With sample manuscripts for the workshop pouring in to be evaluated, anything she might have submitted during 1946–47 would have had about a one in forty-eight chance of being accepted, according to

Thomas Hal Phillips, who reviewed many of the applications. Or, it might have been that she didn't have the requisite fifty sample pages of manuscript ready. Elise Sanguinetti, one of the workshop members at the time and a close friend of Nelle's, said that Nelle didn't have time to write fiction; her output was limited to articles for the *Rammer Jammer.*[45]

And, finally, there's one more possibility—she didn't take Professor Strode seriously. Nelle had a reputation as a "deflater of phoniness" and Strode, with his fey airs of the theater floating around him and his histrionics in Shakespeare class (he acted out the lead parts), struck her as slightly ridiculous, despite the compliments she later paid him. "She thought Strode was pompous," said Helen Norris, who sat near Nelle in Shakespeare class. "She would be almost rude to him."[46] One day, as Strode was holding forth in his mellifluous baritone voice, Nelle drew a caricature of him as Hamlet addressing Yorick's skull. It was so good that the class secretly passed it back and forth, sputtering to contain their laughter. Evidently, Nelle didn't share the opinion of some beginning writers that Hudson Strode was "*the* master."

NELLE CLOSED OUT THE 1946–47 school year by severing her ties with the *Rammer Jammer.* One year as editor in chief was enough. Besides, her law school classes were demanding and she was forced to spend most evenings studying at the library until midnight. When she socialized, she often drank to break through her normal reserve. One of her favorite spots to hang out was the University Supply Store, the SUPe—a combination bookstore and soda fountain, where she liked nothing better than to sit in a booth crammed with young men and talk about football. Nelle played on a powderpuff team of junior and senior girls—"pigskin-packin' mamas," the *Crimson White* called them. One night, John T. Hamner recalled, Nelle was carrying on in the booth a little louder than usual. From her direction, Hamner got a whiff of onion that he imagined was meant to conceal a strong smell of hard liquor.[47]

Classes ended in May, and Nelle went home by train. For once, she didn't stay on campus for the summer session, breaking the pattern she had established several years before. She was needed in Monroeville to help with a happy occasion: the marriage of her brother,

Edwin Coleman Lee, to Sara Anne McCall, Nelle's friend and class-mate since childhood.

Edwin was seven years older than McCall and, according to friends, hadn't given her a second look when they were growing up together. When he graduated from high school, she was still in ele-mentary school. Later, she enrolled at Huntingdon College the same year Nelle did, but Edwin was in the Army Air Corps by then, serving with the Eighth Air Force. In June 1944, he participated in the Nor-mandy invasion, flew support for General Patton's Third Army in Europe, and received the Purple Heart. In 1946, Captain Lee re-turned to Alabama and reenrolled in Auburn University to complete his degree in industrial engineering. There he met Sara, who had transferred from Huntingdon. With so much in common, they hit it off immediately and fell in love. The wedding was set for Saturday, June 28, 1947, in Monroeville.

The weather was hot, and the guests were relieved that the cere-mony at the First United Methodist Church had been scheduled to begin at six o'clock in the evening. Inside the church, garlands of southern smilax and tall baskets of Snow Queen gladioli decorated the aisle and altar. Sara wore a dress with a high collar, full skirt, and long train that was a modern adaptation of an 1860 wedding gown on display in a museum in Richmond, Virginia. The maid of honor was Anne Hines, later to be the mayor of Monroeville; Nelle was a brides-maid. The reception was held outside at the bride's home, an innova-tion that not many folks in Monroeville were familiar with, but the lovely coolness of the evening persuaded them that it was a grand idea. Mrs. Lee, by now quite overweight and probably experiencing the early stages of diabetes, found it best to let well-wishers come to her, where she was seated at the table for the family of the groom.

Everything would have been ideal for A. C. Lee, as patriarch, ex-cept that a month earlier Nelle had raised an issue about her direc-tion in life. Unless he could persuade her to change her mind, her notions would ultimately lead to a major alteration in the Lee fam-ily's fortunes.

The crux of the matter was that she wasn't enjoying law school. She had enrolled, she said later, because "it was the line of least resis-tance," meaning that she realized how strongly her father wanted to welcome another lawyer into the family fold.[48] But she was discovering that she hated studying law—and that was the term she used, *hated*. A friend on the campus newspaper, Carney Dobbs, never doubted that "she could have been a good lawyer. Her mind was so quick, but she just wanted to write."[49]

If she framed her dilemma in similar terms to her father—that writing was winning out over law—he might have countered that, if that were the case, she could take over the *Monroe Journal* from him and Alice. After all, he was almost seventy. He was looking forward to having a little more time for playing golf and serving on various committees in ways that weren't too demanding. Just taking it easy. Weekly deadlines wouldn't permit that, and Alice's law practice was booming. So Nelle could do a real service by her family, the town, and the whole county if she took over the reins of the *Journal* after graduation. She didn't have to join Bugg, Barnett & Lee, either, if she didn't want to. But a law degree was always good insurance.

What Nelle said in reply isn't known. But an episode occurred in the newspaper offices of the *Baldwin Times* in Bay Minette, Alabama, that suggests how she reacted to the idea of running a small-town newspaper. One day in early June, publisher Jimmy Faulkner was sitting at his desk reviewing some copy, when A. C. Lee knocked on his door.

"Jimmy," A.C. said, getting right to the point, "I understand you are interested in establishing a newspaper in Monroeville." Faulkner replied that he wasn't, because the town couldn't support two competing papers.

"Well, how would you like to buy one already in existence?" Lee asked. "I'll sell *The Monroe Journal* to you right now for fifteen thousand dollars." A.C. and Alice had obtained the permission of Edward Salter, who had been the minority part owner of the paper ever since Alice purchased R. L. Jones's share following Jones's death in 1938. So the *Journal* was the Lees' to sell.

Faulkner could hardly believe his ears: he had been dreaming about an opportunity like this. He even had a potential partner lined up: *Baldwin Times* editor Bill Stewart. Faulkner immediately went to Stewart and "asked him if he would like to have half interest in *The Monroe Journal,* and he was quite excited and agreed that he did." Stewart borrowed three thousand dollars from his brother, and Faulkner sold a parcel of timberland he owned for another three thousand dollars. With six thousand dollars in hand, they borrowed another nine thousand dollars, partly from Lee's former law partner, J. B. Barnett, now president of the Monroe County Bank, and the rest from the First National Bank in Mobile. Alice Lee completed the legal paperwork transferring ownership of the *Journal* to Faulkner and Stewart. And so, after eighteen years in the newspaper business, the Lees were officially out of it. (And they took a beating financially. Ten years later, Faulkner sold his half-interest for $115,000; and in the mid-1990s, Stewart sold the paper for $2 million.)[50]

On June 26, 1947, two days before his son's wedding, A. C. Lee's final editorial appeared in the *Journal*:

> The task of a newspaper editor, though his audience may be limited to the small area of a country weekly, is not always easy. If he appreciates the responsibilities of the newspaper he must needs give some thought to his discussions, bearing in mind the possibility that the course of some life may be influenced by the character of his comments. . . . However, we feel that we are entitled to make this observation. As we are bowing out of the newspaper field it is but natural that we allow our thoughts to go back over the years of our service for the purpose of a critical review. And with the added experience of the years we are unable to recall any position we have previously taken on any important question that we would wish to change. Again we express our most profound appreciation for the splendid cooperation accorded us through the years by our good friends throughout the county.[51]

The rest of the summer must have been a bittersweet one in the Lee household. Edwin had made a fine marriage and let it be known that the couple would be settling down in Monroeville. Alice had decided to live at home permanently to help her parents, particularly her mother, whose health required regular visits to Vaughn Memorial Hospital in Selma, seventy-five miles away. Nelle, on the other hand, had thrown everybody for a loop. In August, she boarded the train at Evergreen and rode it north to Tuscaloosa, where she was determined to give law school at the University of Alabama one more try.

About one hundred students were enrolled in law school for the 1947–48 school year, taught by thirteen faculty members, all of whom were "on the younger side," remembered Daniel J. Meador. The number of women, however, he said, totaled fewer than a dozen. The whole group was small enough to fit "in the women's rest room at the same time."[52]

And they could usually be found in there, too, freshening up between classes. Nelle milled around in front of the mirror with the others, but classmate Mary Lee Stapp couldn't recall ever having a conversation with her, "and she wouldn't have initiated it. She never made a great effort to get to know anybody; she had her mind on what she had her mind on."[53] Jane Williams recalled Nelle from criminal law class, saying that Nelle "would not have been noticed except for the fact that she was in a large class of males. She was habitually dressed in a baggy pullover, with a skirt and loafers, her hair pulled behind her ears and no makeup. To say that she was reclusive is an understatement. She was very quiet, spoke to no one—except when the instructor called on her to respond. Even then, she did so with as few words as possible."[54]

She may have been on her guard because the competition was unusually keen. The classes were rife with men whose education had been delayed by the war. They were "gunners"—hard-charging types who wanted to excel and get into practice quickly. The war also had the effect of bunching up talent. Among Nelle's classmates were men and women who would later become leading jurists and politicians, including Howell T. Heflin, chief justice of the Alabama Supreme Court, a civil rights reformer, and a United States senator; Daniel J. Meador, dean of the University of Alabama Law School and assistant attorney general in the U.S. Department of Justice; Claude Kirk, the first Republican governor of Florida in ninety years when he was elected in 1967; Mary Lee Stapp, assistant attorney general of Alabama; and John Patterson, the youngest governor in Alabama's history.

The instruction the students received, by all accounts, was first-rate. The professors, sensing that this group wanted to be pushed, gave their all. Jay Murphy, a showman, would stand on a chair, curl up on the windowsill, or fling a book against the wall when the class was inattentive. "Jumping Jack" Payne, so-named for his energy, "could drive that stuff into your head," everyone agreed.[55] Whit McCoy, an expert with labor and contract law, who later became director of the Federal Mediation and Conciliation Service, was known for being blunt, but able to guide his students to the heart of complex issues; Leigh Harrison and Leonard Traywick could make the law come alive from the depths of hoary legal tomes.

The students, for their part, gave as good as they got. They formed study groups and focused in particular on being able to recall rulings that applied to case studies, without having to resort to sources. At that time, the Alabama bar accepted the "diploma privilege," as it was called: if students passed their exams in every subject, they would not have to take the bar exam. But each instructor's pride in the importance of his subject guaranteed that the final exam in his course would be horrendous. Students brought towels to wipe their perspiring faces, and candy bars to revive their energy.

The women, although they were few in number, demonstrated a tenacity equal to that of their male counterparts. None who attended during the years Nelle was enrolled flunked out. Moreover, they would not be intimated. A certain criminal law professor, for example, tried to fluster female students by pressing them on the indelicate facts of sex crimes. One day, while he was questioning student Marion Goode Shirkey about the details of a rape case, attempting to maneuver her into an explicit description, she cut him off in midsentence: "Look, she said, "you know about the male anatomy—why don't you just tell us?"[56] The class laughed and applauded.

Meanwhile, Nelle continued to linger on the margins, disengaged. "Most of the women who were there knew each other, but most of us don't remember her," said Olive Landon.[57] To drop out, though, would disappoint her father, especially because it would come on the heels of his selling the *Monroe Journal.* The prospect of still another letdown for him, compounded by the dread she felt at facing exams that she might not pass for sheer lack of interest, threw a gloomy light on the way ahead. Unknown to her (though she would have been insulted if she knew), some of her classmates thought that Miss Lee and the law would not be a good match, either. Jane Williams couldn't picture Nelle abiding by the formalities of courtroom protocol. "I think lawyers sort of have to conform, and she'd just as soon tell you to go to hell as to say something nice and turn around and walk away. . . . I just couldn't see her being interested in that sort of thing."[58]

Shortly before his death in 1984, Truman Capote suggested that Nelle had a secret reason for being unhappy in law school. But, typically, he omitted the details, thereby deliberately making his gossip more tantalizing. "She had a great love affair with one of her professors at college, and it did something to her. It didn't end up well," he told a reporter. "It was a law professor. I don't know if [the pain] still exists now."[59] Jane Williams said she heard the same rumor, but she suspects it was unrequited love on Nelle's part, which, if true, would have increased her feelings of being isolated.[60]

In any case, by spring 1948, A.C. was aware that his youngest daughter, for whatever reasons, was not showing anywhere near the same enthusiasm about law that Alice had. So he agreed to provide an incentive—one that would acknowledge Nelle's love of literature. Perhaps, he reasoned, if she could have an experience that showed she was not making a Hobson's choice—law or nothing—she would see what a well-paying career such as practicing law could provide, including the means to travel and write as an avocation. On April 29, 1948, the *Monroe Journal* announced, "Miss Nelle Lee, University of Alabama law student and daughter of Mr. and Mrs. A. C. Lee of Monroeville, has been accepted as an exchange student at Oxford University in England during the coming summer. She will sail from New York on June 16."[61]

It would be a pilgrimage to the land of Nelle's favorite authors: Austen, Stevenson, Lamb, Fielding, Butler, and all the others, who until now had lived for her only between the covers of books. And perhaps it would break the spell of her unhappiness.

STUDENT EXCHANGES WITH EUROPEAN countries were a new idea after the end of World War II, and eagerly supported by Congress and a host of religious and social-service organizations. On one level, the purpose of such exchanges was to promote mutual understanding between the American people and other cultures, and, according to the legislation authorizing them in 1948, "to correct misunderstandings about the United States abroad." On another level, exchanges appealed to secular and nonreligious organizations such as the American Friends Service Committee and the Future Farmers of America as opportunities to send young people abroad in the name of promoting peace and goodwill.

In April 1947, the Department of State arranged with the Maritime Commission to assign two C-4 troopships, the *Marine Tiger* and the *Marine Jumper,* to study-abroad programs that summer. The rock-bottom accommodations of troopships ensured that student passengers could travel to their destinations—Southampton, Plymouth, Genoa, Cherbourg, or Danzig, for instance—as inexpensively as possible.

Things got off to a rather slow start. When the *Marine Jumper* sailed out of New York Harbor in June 1947, only 105 students were aboard. (Adding poignancy to the hopefulness of this little delegation was the arrival three weeks later of seven vessels in a single day carrying 2,920 European refugees.)[62] Nevertheless, by the end of the summer, three thousand students had participated. In June 1948, when Nelle was scheduled to leave, organizers were confident that ten thousand American students would sail by August.

On the other side of the Atlantic, European universities responded to student exchanges with fervor, anticipating that a minor renaissance of learning was about to start, to say nothing of the fees that thousands of middle-class American youngsters would pay to enroll. Students could choose from three-week international courses at German universities; classes on German-Austrian culture near Salzburg; classical and archaeological studies in Naples; art and music appreciation courses in France; or courses about Shakespeare, Elizabethan drama, or European civilization at six British universities, including Oxford. Nelle applied to the Oxford summer program through the Institute of International Education and enrolled in the university's Extra-Mural Studies Summer School program, "European Civilization in the Twentieth Century."

On the morning Nelle arrived at the docks preparing to board the *Marine Jumper,* there was a festive Pied Piper feeling in the air. Nearly six hundred young people were hugging their parents, posing for snapshots, and waving as they climbed the steep gangway. The ship, among the largest transports built during the war, was one and a half times the length of a football field, seventy-one feet wide, and still painted drab olive gray from the days when it ferried legions of soldiers to and from Europe. The only indication that times had changed was a band of red, white, and blue painted on the ship's funnel. Nelle found a spot on one of the double bunks in the passengers' quarters; one shower served thirty-five people—"just like you'd expect in the army," commented one of the students.[63]

Then the hawsers were pulled in, and the ship got under way, assisted by a tugboat or two to point the ship's bow toward the Atlantic. When New York had at last dipped below the horizon, coordinators from the institute assembled the students for a series of orientation programs. They congratulated the young people on their initiative and then, aided by films, provided lengthy sessions about the students' destination countries—their religions, social life, and economic problems after the war. A Harvard undergraduate continuing on to Le Havre, France, watched the proceedings with a jaundiced eye:

> I met, in the student category, Quakers, Youth Hostelers, Adventure Trailers, one delegate to the World Council of Churches, and huge numbers of young tourists going abroad ostensibly for study in London, Paris, Copenhagen, Geneva, and elsewhere. Their groups held orientation programs on the ship 25 hours a day, passed out reams of literature, held foreign language courses daily, and generally showed their eagerness to promote International understanding and prevent future war. All these idealists, unhappily, seemed naively unaware of the economic conflicts which will probably cause another war. The pamphlets dealt with racial and religious misunderstandings, not with oil fields in Arabia.[64]

Meals on board were filling but greasy; after a dinner of duck and gravy a few students had difficulty staying on their legs. There was no curfew, so the main deck on starry nights was usually dotted with travelers lying on their backs, feeling the thrum of the ten-thousand-horsepower turbine underneath them as the ship rolled through the swells at fifteen knots.

On Friday, June 25, Nelle was awakened by a loudspeaker announcement that passengers should prepare for landing at Plymouth. After hastily eating breakfast, she waited until 9:00 A.M. for a motor launch to pull alongside.[65] Then, she joined one of the departing groups and was ferried to the customs warehouse. Officials and porters loudly explained how to locate luggage. Their English sounded so strange that many of the young Americans wondered if what they were hearing was indeed their mother tongue. After finding her bags, Nelle listened to a clerk at the money-exchange counter run through the British monetary system: pounds, crowns, shillings, pennies, farthings, and so forth. It was incomprehensible to her. When it was her turn to purchase a ticket for the train to Oxford, she held out her hand and murmured like the others, "Take what you need."

A four-hour train ride brought the spires of Oxford within sight, by which time the students were so hungry that they were bartering rolls and fruit saved from breakfast. As the train crossed the Isis River, on the west side of the university, Nelle could see Christ Church's octagonal Tom Tower, whose seven-ton bell has rung 101 times every night at 9:05 to mark curfew since the late 1600s. No doubt a fleeting thought of Miss Watson crossed Nelle's mind as she entered the epicenter of English intellectual life dating from the reign of Henry II. The welcoming dinner that evening was held in a centuries-old hall amid stained glass, carved beam ceilings fifty feet overhead, and wood-paneled walls.

Although Nelle was enrolled in the seminar on twentieth-century literature, she was permitted, as all the students were, to attend any lecture she wanted to on philosophy, politics, economics, or general topics. It's doubtful that such an array of scholars could be assembled today for a six-week summer session. The panoply of almost seventy lecturers included novelists Elizabeth Bowen and Joyce Cary; A. J. P. Taylor, one of the most controversial historians of the century; pianist and music critic William Glock; historian H. R. Trevor-Roper, just making a name for himself by documenting the last days of the Third Reich; and J. B. S. Haldane, a pioneering geneticist who expanded Darwin's theories of evolution. In addition to lectures that Nelle was required to attend on Virginia Woolf, T. S. Eliot, Russian poetry, Thomas Mann, Gerard Manley Hopkins, and Jean-Paul Sartre, for example, there also were at least three other lectures to choose from every day, on such topics as free will, truth, political theories and moral beliefs, communism, modern painting, and the history of Oxford University.[66] For a young woman like Nelle, raised in a rural and economically depressed part of the United States, it was a feast for the mind. One day in the Bodleian Library, she walked among rows and rows of centuries-old volumes, more than three million in all, including original manuscripts of Old English poetry and prose dating from *Beowulf,* and even earlier.

After that experience, Nelle lasted only one more semester in law school. She knew she couldn't go on. "She fell in love with England," her sister Alice said later.⁶⁷ She had walked streets known to writers she admired and imagined herself in their company. What she needed to do now was to write earnestly. Truman had done it, and his first novel, *Other Voices, Other Rooms,* published exactly a year earlier, had established him. She couldn't hope to duplicate his success the first time out, but she had to make a start. Staying in law school was pointless, particularly when there was a strong possibility she might fail the exams because she just couldn't muster the will to study for them.

Over the winter holidays she told her father what her plans were: to drop out of law school, go to New York, find a job, and write. A.C. made it clear that he was prepared to pay for law school, but he was not going to subsidize a pack of daydreams. At the end of the first semester of her senior year, Nelle withdrew after taking no degree—not even a bachelor's, since she had begun law school her junior year and didn't take the final exams. For a short while she lived at home and saved money. But within a few months, in 1949, having "got an itch to go to New York and write," as Alice said later, trying to put the best spin on how suddenly the Monroeville-centered Lee family had splintered, twenty-three-year-old Nelle Lee moved to New York.⁶⁸ Her place was a cold-water flat in Manhattan, at 1539 York Avenue, two blocks from the East River, with an iron fire escape where she could sit and think on hot nights.

But breaking her ties with Monroeville was not as easy as that. Her mother's health was poor and continued to decline. One winter evening in 1951 in Selma, Alabama, an alumna of Huntingdon College recognized Nelle walking along by herself, lost in thought. The woman pulled over and offered her a ride to wherever she was going. Nelle asked to be taken a few blocks to the hospital—her mother was there. It was clear that she was preoccupied with worry and the two rode in silence the rest of the way.⁶⁹

Mrs. Lee never left the hospital, and on June 2 she died. Nelle was only twenty-five, not an adult long enough to have resolved the biggest emotional mystery of her upbringing, which was why her mother practically ignored her. It was true her mother was beset by a "nervous disorder," as the family euphemistically called it. But how far did that go in explaining the absence of normal attachments between parent and child? What little Nelle knew about her mother, she seemed to later pour into the character of Aunt Alexandra in *To Kill a Mockingbird*: "She was not fat, but solid, and she chose protective garments that drew her bosom up to giddy heights, pinched in her waist, flared out her rear, and managed to suggest that Aunt Alexandra's was once an hour-glass figure. From any angle it was formidable." Borrowing from her mother's upbringing and behavior, Lee writes, Aunt Alexandra "had river-boat, boarding-school manners . . . and she was an incurable gossip," echoing Capote's description of her in "Mrs. Busybody." And then the final, most telling parallel with her mother: "Aunt Alexandra would have been analogous to Mount Everest: throughout my early life, she was cold and there."[70]

No sooner had the Lee family begun to recover from the long-expected passing of Frances, than they suffered a second blow that staggered them. Six weeks after the death of their mother, Edwin Lee died at age thirty. The previous March, he had been recalled to duty in the Army Air Force and assigned to Maxwell Airfield. Then, on the morning of July 12, he was discovered dead in his bed in the officers' quarters. An autopsy conducted by army medical officers concluded that the cause of Major Lee's death was a cerebral hemorrhage. A few of the servicemen attending the funeral mentioned that Edwin had been playing a strenuous game of softball the afternoon before.

At the funeral in Monroeville the following day, presided over by Reverend Ray E. Whatley, several hundred mourners dressed in black surrounded the grave on all sides, including three ministers representing the major Protestant denominations in town. The July heat was suffocating, although the service had been delayed until 5 P.M. Standing beneath the awning shading the grave site was Edwin's widow, Sara, who was holding by the hand the couple's three-year-old daughter, Mary; Sara's sisters-in-law, Nelle, Alice, and Mrs. Louise Connor, her husband, Herschel, and their eleven-year-old son, Hank. Between the sisters, they handed back and forth Edwin's nine-month-old son, Edwin, Jr. Nearby, A.C., seventy-one years old and bent under the weight of a double load of grief in such a short space of time, bore up as best he could.

The service concluded about 6:30 P.M. The three other attending ministers, A. Cowan Lee, L. Reed Polk, and Richard Kell, complimented Reverend Whatley on his handling of the service, one of his first as the newly appointed minister of First United Methodist. Though not a forceful man, Reverend Whatley always made a point of looking people in the eye and giving them a firm handshake. He remained by Edwin's grave for nearly an hour, receiving introductions to many of the people in his 376-member congregation.

Without Edwin, who had been living in Monroeville, the brunt of family affairs fell upon Alice, so aptly nicknamed "Bear." Louise had family responsibilities more than two hours away in Eufaula; and A.C. was getting on in years. From a purely practical standpoint, it must have seemed that Nelle, the youngest child—off in New York and working low-wage jobs while she wrote fiction—was not doing her share.

In fact, the issue would become a test of wills between Nelle and Alice, the eldest of the siblings, in the years to come.

Atticus Becomes
To Kill a Mockingbird

FOR YEARS NELLE JUGGLED A SERIES OF UNREWARDING JOBS in New York—bookstore clerk and then ticket agent for two airlines— all the while writing at night and on weekends. Meanwhile, the city had subtly polished some of the rougher edges of her personality that had alienated her from people when she was younger. Becoming independent had relieved her of the need to kick over her traces at every opportunity. Her sense of humor, so cutting in college, had evolved into a more self-deprecating wit. But most important, step by step, with the help of friends, she had been moving toward the goal of being published.

By November 1956 she had completed a handful of stories that satisfied her: "The Land of Sweet Forever," "A Roomful of Kibble," "Snow-on-the-Mountain," "This Is Show Business," and "The Viewer and the Viewed."[1] The next step, advised her friend Michael Brown, the former teacher from Texas turned Broadway composer and lyricist, was to show her work to an agent. And he had someone in mind for her, too: Annie Laurie Williams. Hoping for the best, Nelle typed a copy of each of her five stories and arrived with them at Williams's suite the week after Thanksgiving.

"I walked around the block three times before I could muster the courage to go in and give the stories to the agent," Nelle remembered. "At the time, I was very shy. Finally, I rushed in, left the manuscripts with the secretary, and left. I prayed for a quick death, and forgot about it."[2]

Actually, Brown had steered her to the wrong person, but he was not too far off. Williams handled film and dramatic rights for books, plays, and musicals—and this was why Brown knew of her. He had shown her the outline of a musical he was working on called *Jack O'Diamonds*.[3] The person Nelle needed to see was Maurice Crain, Williams's husband, who worked in an adjoining office. He represented literary properties.

Nevertheless, Williams followed through with the mysterious submission and invited Nelle to visit her. Trying to recover from her confusion during the appointment, Nelle offered that she was a "very good friend of Truman Capote's."[4] This was yet another gaffe, but she couldn't have known it. Williams had handled some of Truman's work and had found him difficult to manage because he went off on long junkets to Europe without letting anyone know his itinerary. There had also been the matter of his insisting on examining all financial statements himself, probably a reaction to his parents' spendthrift ways when he was a child. But Williams was gracious and assured Nelle that her husband, Maurice, would read her submissions. The conversation drifted into small talk.

Ten days after her rocky start with Williams, Nelle returned, this time because Maurice Crain had invited her to dinner. She was startled, but it was typical of Crain, whose emotional reserve belied a gentlemanly and thoughtful nature. (The secretaries in the office, all of them Williams's sisters, teasingly called him Old Wooden Face behind his back, because he acted grumpier then he was.)[5] In addition, Crain may have taken a shine to this nervous young woman with the soft southern accent because his mother went by "Nellie"—Helen Greene Nellie Berryman. It's likely they met at Sardi's, Crain's favorite restaurant for relaxing. He complimented Nelle on her ability to tell a good story. One of her submissions in particular, "Snow-on-the-Mountain," about a boy who revenges himself on an old scold in the neighborhood by ripping up the story's eponymous flowers, was especially good. But the others needed more work. At this point, "Snow-on-the-Mountain" was the only story he thought he might be able to place.[6] The others he was returning to her with the caveat that short stories were hard to sell. Novels were easier, in fact—"Had she thought about one?" he wanted to know.[7]

She had, of course—most writers do at some point—but the investment of time was daunting. She had already spent seven years on this batch of submissions. In addition, the demands of working full-time put free time to write at a premium. She told Crain she would think about it. After they parted, she buoyed up her spirits by thinking about how she could share this big news during her annual Christmas visit home to Monroeville, only a few weeks away.

That Christmas, however, was the one when the Browns bestowed their generous check on Nelle, the check that allowed her to write full-time. The Browns' generosity was a "miracle," Nelle said, and "an act of love."

Liberated from having to work nine to five, she returned to Crain's office in January 1957 with both a short story, "The Cat's Meow," and the first fifty pages of a novel, *Go Set a Watchman,* a title that suggests the scene in the novel when Atticus Finch sits outside the town jail, guarding his client from a lynch mob. A week later, she was back again, this time with one hundred more pages. From then on, she dropped off about fifty new pages with Crain every week through the end of February.[8] Two months of back-and-forth revisions followed between author and agent until, in early May, Crain judged that the manuscript was in suitable shape to send out. But he had never liked the title *Go Set a Watchman.* It sounded like the novel had to do with clocks or something. What about just titling it after the main character, Atticus? Nelle had chosen the name after Cicero's best friend, Titus Pomponius Atticus, a "wise, learned and humane man," as she explained later.[9] She didn't object to the change—she thought it was better, in fact.

And so an unsolicited manuscript bearing the title *Atticus* arrived at the offices of J. B. Lippincott, a firm that had not had a number-one bestseller since Betty MacDonald's *The Egg and I,* fifteen years earlier. In the meantime, Nelle—not wanting to waste a day of her writing sabbatical—surprised Crain at the end of May with 111 pages of a second novel, *The Long Goodbye*.[10] Days later, he phoned her with good news: Lippincott had requested to meet with her about *Atticus*. Her pen froze.

THE LIPPINCOTT EDITORS WHO assembled to meet Nelle were all men except one: a late-middle-aged woman dressed in a business suit with her steel gray hair pulled tightly behind her head. Her name was Theresa von Hohoff—but she preferred the less Teutonic sounding "Tay Hohoff." She was short and rail thin with an aristocratic profile and a voice raspy from cigarettes. Her eyesight was failing, and her devoted assistant, Margaret Carroll, was taking up as much slack as she could.[11]

As a child, Hohoff had been raised as a Quaker in a multigenerational home where "thee" and "thou" were used.[12] The Quakers' social consciousness had never left her, and outside the office she was completing a book of her own, *A Ministry to Man,* a biography of John Elliot Lovejoy, one of the leaders of the settlement house movement for impoverished immigrants in New York. One of Hohoff's principal delights was working with eager young authors, such as Thomas Pynchon. But she also spent time with her bookish husband, Arthur, and—and this was a near obsession—adopted cats in need of homes. As she studied the "dark-haired, dark-eyed young woman [who] walked shyly into our office on Fifth Avenue," her instincts told her she would like her.[13]

To Nelle, the meeting was excruciating. The editors talked to her for a long time about *Atticus,* explaining that, on the one hand, her "characters stood on their own two feet, they were three-dimensional." On the other, the manuscript had structural problems: it was "more a series of anecdotes than a fully conceived novel." They made a number of suggestions about how Nelle could address their concerns. Turning her head back and forth to acknowledge the remarks from this roundtable dissection, Nelle obediently nodded and replied in her gentle Alabama voice, "Yes, sir. Yes, ma'am."[14] She assured them that she would try. Finally, they wished her luck on a revision and hoped to see her again.

Hohoff hoped they hadn't discouraged her. Even though Nelle had never published anything, not even an essay or short story, her draft of a novel "was clearly not the work of an amateur or a tyro," Hohoff decided.[15] In fact, it was hard to believe that Nelle was in her early thirties and had waited until now to approach a publisher. "[B]ut as I grew to know her better," Hohoff said later, "I came to believe the cause lay in an innate humility and a deep respect for the art of writing. To put it another way, what she wanted with all her being was to *write*—not merely to 'be a writer.' "[16]

At the end of the summer, Nelle resubmitted her manuscript to Hohoff, who had volunteered to work with her. "It was better. It wasn't *right*," Hohoff realized. "Obviously, a keen and witty and even wise mind had been at work; but was the mind that of a professional novelist? There were dangling threads of plot, there was a lack of unity—a beginning, a middle, an end that was inherent in the beginning."[17] Nevertheless, Hohoff was convinced that Nelle's willingness to accept criticism and her demonstrated work ethic meant that the book could be molded into shape. In October, Lippincott offered Nelle a contract with an advance of a few thousand dollars.[18] Elated and feeling flush with cash, Nelle offered to begin paying back the Browns' Christmas "loan," as she insisted on calling it. But Michael Brown, more experienced in the ways of publishing, recommended that she wait.

As editor and author got down to the business of working together, and as Nelle, said Hohoff, "found out that editors' teeth were made more for talking than biting and that we could be friends, I began to discover a vivid and original personality hiding behind her intense reserve."[19] The younger woman's speaking and writing voices were very similar—wry, subtle, and engaging, perfectly suited for the regional southern novel she wanted to write. Hohoff encouraged Nelle to keep writing in that vein about Monroeville and its people. But as the Lippincott editors had tried to explain, a short story—even a series of short stories with the same setting and main character— was different in scope from a novel. A short story usually hangs by one incident or revelation. A novel, however, needs an overarching story, deep and big enough to encompass everything else, especially the ongoing development over time of related characters and themes. The engine of this unifying story had to include continuing tension arising from a major conflict, too, enough to keep the reader turning the novel's pages. What story could Nelle write about, Hohoff wanted to know, that could pull everything else together?

Readers, teachers, and scholars alike tend to assume that in writing

To Kill a Mockingbird, Nelle was choosing to tell a version of the Scottsboro Boys trials in 1931–1937. The Scottsboro "boys"—teenagers, with none older than nineteen—were nine Negroes accused of raping two white girls in boxcars on the Southern Railroad freight run from Chattanooga to Memphis, as the train crossed the Alabama border on March 25, 1931. The public was fascinated by the story because of its sheer ugliness. During the boys' first trial, in Scottsboro, Alabama, their legal counsel was an alcoholic real estate attorney and his doddering assistant. Newspapers boosted their circulations by blaring the prurient and racist angles of testimony with headlines such as "All Negroes Positively Identified by Girls and One White Boy Who Was Held Prisoner with Pistol and Knives While Nine Black Fiends Committed Revolting Crime." The jury found all of the accused guilty; the judge sentenced eight of the nine defendants to death, with the exception of a twelve-year-old who was, mercifully, considered too young to die.

During a second trial, ordered by the United States Supreme Court, champions for the boys rode into the fray from an unlikely quarter: the Communist Party. Hoping to expose the inequities of the U.S. justice system, the Communists appointed attorneys Samuel Liebowitz and Joseph Brodsky, who mounted an aggressive and combative defense of the accused. Four of the boys were released after all charges against them were dropped. Eventually, all of the Scottsboro Boys were paroled, freed, or pardoned, except for one, who was tried and convicted of rape and given the death penalty four times. He escaped from prison in Alabama and fled to Detroit. After his arrest by the FBI in the 1950s, the governor of Michigan would not permit him to be extradited.

These events, most of which occurred when Nelle was about the age of her child-narrator, Scout, would seem to be the historical foundation of *To Kill a Mockingbird*: the racial injustice of the Scottsboro trials is blatant; the white jurors' fear of miscegenation is on display; and the courageous efforts of two attorneys can be grafted onto Atticus Finch.

The trouble is, the scope of those trials was too big, too excessive for Nelle's purposes. She wanted "to leave some record of the kind of life that existed in a very small world."[20] The courtroom scene of Atticus defending Tom Robinson from a false charge of rape, for example, compresses a history of racial injustice into a hot afternoon. Much of its power comes from the classical unities for drama—unity of action, place, and time. By comparison, the Scottsboro Boys case—a protracted national scandal involving nine young men and two women (one of them a prostitute, it later turned out)—was huge in its implications, and too far removed from Nelle's experience.

Nelle later said as much, years after writing *To Kill a Mockingbird*. In a letter written in 1999 to Hazel Rowley, author of *Richard Wright: The Life and Times*, Lee said that she did not have so sensational a case as the Scottsboro Boys in mind, "but it will more than do as an example (albeit a lurid one) of deep-South attitudes on race vs. justice that prevailed at the time."[21]

Instead, she chose a crime that shocked the readers of the *Monroe Journal* when she was a child and her father was editor and publisher of the newspaper. A Negro living near Monroeville was accused, falsely probably, of raping a white woman.

ON THURSDAY, NOVEMBER 9, 1933, the *Monroe Journal* reported that Naomi Lowery told authorities that Walter Lett had raped her the previous Thursday near a brick factory south of Monroeville. According to the newspaper, Lett "was captured on Saturday afternoon and taken into custody. Fearing that an attempt would be made to lynch the Negro by a mob following the news of the attack, Sheriff Sawyer took the Negro to the jail in Greenville for safekeeping."[22]

Both Lett and Lowery were luckless types, human flotsam on the surface of economic hard times. Lett, in his early thirties, had done time in the state prison farm in Tunnel Springs, Alabama, draining swamps and cutting roads through wooded areas. The length of his sentence, less than ten years, suggests that he was convicted of drunkenness or fighting. Naomi Lowery, twenty-five, had drifted into Monroe County with her husband, Ira, after living for several years in a fifteen-dollars-a-month rented house in Memphis, Tennessee. She and Ira were too poor to afford even a radio.[23]

Regardless, she was white, and her word mattered more than a Negro's. Lett desperately protested that he didn't know his accuser, and that he was working elsewhere during the time of the assault. It may have been that he and Lowery were lovers, or that she was involved with another Negro man. If a white woman became pregnant under those circumstances, it was not uncommon for her to claim rape, or accuse someone other than her lover. John N. Maxwell, who grew up in nearby Beatrice in the late 1930s, remembered his father "remarking about a local case in which a black man was accused of molesting a white woman. He said he had the feeling the man wasn't guilty, but later, when the suspect tried to escape, my father said that proved it, the man was guilty. Any educated person today knows that that man was running for his life."[24]

Likewise, Lett was cornered in a deadly trap. For six months, he awaited trial until the circuit court's spring term commenced in the Monroeville County Courthouse.

He was arraigned on March 16, 1934, on a grand jury indictment on a capital crime of rape, which carried the death penalty. He pled "not guilty." Ten days later, circuit court judge F. W. Hare—who would later jump-start Alice Lee's career—and a jury of twelve white men heard Lett's testimony. Through his attorney, Lett repeated that he did not know Lowery, and that he had been working at another location when the alleged rape occurred. The case took an unusually long time to be heard and decided. It was not until 9:00 P.M. that the jury returned to the courtroom with its verdict: "We, the jury, find the defendant guilty of rape as charged in the indictment and fix the punishment at death by electrocution."[25]

On March 30, Lett appeared a final time before Judge Hare and was asked if "he had anything to say why the judgment of the law should not now be passed upon him." Lett stood manacled before the judge, head down, and remained silent. Judge Hare set the date of execution for Friday, May 11, 1934.[26]

The verdict, however, didn't sit well with some of the leading citizens of Monroeville and the county at large. Apparently, there was more about the affair than had come out at the trial. Objections reached the statehouse in Montgomery, and on May 8, the Alabama Board of Pardons and Governor B. M. Miller granted a stay of execution to allow Lett's attorney to file a brief of testimony. Miller reset the date of execution for June 20. A second reprieve moved the date again, to July 20. The reason for the stays, Miller told the *Montgomery Advertiser,* was that "many leading citizens of Monroe County" had written to him stating, as he expressed it, "I am of the opinion and conviction that there is much doubt as to the man being guilty."[27]

One of the petitioners may well have been A. C. Lee. He was the editor and publisher of the *Monroe Journal,* a director of the Monroe County Bank, an attorney, and an elected representative from Monroeville. If his name hadn't been among the "many leading citizens of Monroe County" calling for clemency, Lett's cause might have suffered. In response, Governor Miller split the baby Solomon-like, commuting Lett's sentence from death in the electric chair to life imprisonment.

But it was too late. Lett had been incarcerated four miles north of Montgomery, on Kilby Prison's death row. Two months before his arrival, six prisoners, all Negroes, had been electrocuted in the chamber down the hall. The room had no soundproofing, and the inmates heard nightmarish sounds of agony. While Lett waited his turn on three different dates, he suffered a mental breakdown. The prison physician wrote to the governor on July 20, "Shortly before his commutation, we began to notice symptoms of schizophrenia in him. . . . He, now, lies in an assumed state of catalepsy and demonstrates fairly definite features of schizophrenia. It is our opinion that he is a mental patient and that his place is not here."[28] Miller asked the state physician inspector to examine Lett personally. "It is my opinion that the above named prisoner," the inspector replied a few days later, "the man whose sentence you recently commuted, is insane."[29]

On July 30, Lett arrived at Searcy Hospital for the Insane, in Mt. Vernon, Alabama. He remained confined to the state mental hospital until he died of tuberculosis in August 1937. Then a truck carried his body to Atmore where his mother, Lula Brown, was waiting for him.

THE POTENTIAL OF WALTER Lett's trial to inspire sympathy, and its power to cast light on a racist judicial system in a small, manageable setting, made it the better choice in Nelle's mind for her novel's foundation than the Scottsboro Boys trials. Moreover, she knew the details of the Lett case well, as do many older people who still live in Monroeville. And in her mind's eye, too, she could see the hero, the attorney in charge of a fictionalized version of Lett's defense, fitting inside the Monroe County Courthouse with ease, because she had seen him there many times—he was her own father, A. C. Lee.

In fact, in November 1919, Mr. Lee had defended two Negroes accused of murder. In those days, an inexperienced twenty-nine-year-old attorney with only four years of practice under his belt, he was appointed by the court to argue his first criminal case. He did his utmost, but lost, as he was destined to do, given the times.[30] Both his clients were hanged and afterward mutilated, with pieces of their bloody scalps mailed in a gruesome Christmas package to their victim's son in Irvington, New York, as proof that "justice" had been done.[31] Using the remedial power of fiction, however, Nelle had a free hand to retell this macabre episode in her father's life, which he always referred to in vague terms, no doubt because of the pain it caused him. (He never accepted another criminal case.) This time, under his daughter's sensitive hand, A. C. Lee, in the character of Atticus Finch, could be made to argue in defense of Walter Lett, and his virtues as a humane, fair-minded man would be honored.

Worth pointing out, however, is that Mr. Lee himself only gradually rose to the moral standards of Atticus. Though more enlightened than most, A.C. was no saint, no prophet crying in the wilderness with regard to racial matters. In many ways, he was typical of his generation, especially about issues surrounding integration. Like most of his generation, he believed that the current social order, segregation, was natural and created harmony between the races. It was a point not even worth discussing that blacks and whites were different. As the Bible said, "In my Father's house are many mansions." That divine structure's great roof covered all humanity. Hence, blacks deserved consideration and charity as fellow creatures of God; and the law should protect them. But they were not the same as white people; and for that simple reason—to continue the biblical metaphor—they did not need to be in the same room with whites.

It may also surprise admirers of Atticus Finch that the man he was modeled after did not believe that a church pulpit was the proper place for preaching about racial equity. He insisted that the mission of the Methodist church where his family had worshipped for generations was to bring people to salvation, *not* to promote social justice. In a speech delivered in 1952, probably to church laity, entitled "This Is My Father's World," A. C. Lee described the only place where the church and the world intersected:

> It is in and through the church that we study and inform ourselves
> about God's way for us, and fortify ourselves with the necessary
> faith and courage to go forth into our other relationships of life and

there apply the rules and regulations God would have us recognize at all times and in all situations. If we have learned well what it is our privilege to learn in the church, it will not be so difficult for us to deal with all the problems of life, including our governmental problems, and to dispose of them as God would have us do.[32]

On this point he was in agreement with Methodist pastor G. Stanley Frazier, an outspoken segregationist in Montgomery who believed that the church should bring souls to God, and not ensnare them in transient social problems.

A.C. made his viewpoints abundantly clear in a confrontation with the Reverend Ray Whatley, minister of the First United Methodist Church in Monroeville, who was preaching too much, in Lee's opinion, about racial and social justice.

One of the first times A.C. heard Reverend Whatley preach was at the funeral of his son, Edwin, in July 1951. Starting not long after that, the relationship between the two men began going downhill. For Labor Day, Whatley penned a sermon called "The Laborer." After pointing out that control of the church was often in the hands of the wealthy, he warned, "If we lose the common man from our church, it will spell doom for us, for there are always labor unions and other organizations to welcome him in."[33] There were whispers afterward that the sermon had "created some feeling."

Six months later, in February 1952, Whatley tread lightly as he composed "A Brotherhood of Love," a sermon about race relations. "There are many mistaken assumptions about Negroes in America," he told the congregation. He disputed impressions about Negroes' desiring to intermarry with whites and about Negroes being intellectually inferior, which tests had shown not to be true. He called for equal economic opportunity, too, saying that it was the purpose of the federal Fair Employment Practices Committee (FEPC), for example, to try to end discrimination in hiring practices.[34]

At that instant, if Whatley had touched A. C. Lee, seated near the front, with the frayed end of an electrical cord, he couldn't have sent a stronger jolt through him. Lee was adamantly opposed to the FEPC, as were many businessmen. Federal hiring guidelines, A.C. maintained, would "take away from every employer in this United States the right to choose his employees."[35]

He'd heard enough. He decided on the spot he was going to have to speak to Whatley privately after the service ended. The young reverend needed to be taken in hand and firmly. As chairman of the Official Church Board, chairman of Pastoral Relations, and a lay member of the Annual Conference, A.C. had cast the most important vote in the church's decision to hire Whatley in the first place.

After the last of the congregants had exited, A.C. told Reverend Whatley that he needed to see him in his office at the back of the sanctuary. Even in that small room, A.C.'s lifetime of involvement in the Methodist church was visible everywhere, from the pictures on the walls to the books on the shelves. Not long after he and his family arrived in Monroeville, in 1912, he had volunteered to serve on the building committee to erect the first new Methodist church in the area since 1835. But scarcely had the debt been paid on the new brick church when it caught fire, in 1929. The building committee reconvened and resurrected it. So A.C. could rightfully claim—though he would never have done so—that he had *twice* built the Methodist church in Monroeville.

Now, he barely waited for Whatley to close the door before getting to the point.

"Get off the 'social justice' and get back on the gospel," he said sharply.[36]

Whatley was shocked. He explained that he believed it was within his responsibilities as minister to speak about issues that touched on all moral questions that Christians should be concerned about, especially brotherhood. And hadn't Jesus set the example?

A.C. cut him off. He wasn't interested in a theological debate: the day's sermon was inappropriate and had upset people. They felt lectured to, and that's not what they came to church for. If anything, Whatley had alienated people. Was that his purpose?

Whatley admitted that it wasn't, of course. A.C. became more conciliatory and urged the young man, in the future, to keep the church's mission foremost in his mind. That was important.

The meeting ended uneasily.

Whatley waited exactly a year to return again to the theme of brotherhood between Negroes and whites. Under the title "My Brother's Keeper," he cited as his text Genesis 4:1-10, where Cain asks God if he should be expected to take care of his brother, Abel.

The congregation knew the story well and could have taken no of-
fense from Reverend Whatley's initial observations about the challenges
of interacting with people. But they reacted angrily when he pointed
to Alabama as setting a poor example for the rest of the world. "No
longer can we isolate ourselves and our actions," Whatley said, because of the impact of mass communication. "They are heard and seen
literally around the world. Any act of injustice, unfair discrimination,
or intimidation occurring in the United States—whether in Alabama,
New York, or any other state—may make headlines all over America.
But that is not all. These incidents make splendid propaganda materials on the other side of the globe."

Some in the congregation would later say that this was a taunting
remark.

"Who then are our brothers?" Whatley continued. "Surely we
would not say that God does not love a yellow man, or a brown man,
or a red man, or a black man just as he does a white man. He is the
God and Father of us all. If that is true, then we are all brothers."[37]

The remainder of the sermon was anecdotal, but the die was cast.
The board of First Methodist met, and in the spring of 1953 they informed Reverend Whatley that the members were seeking a "more
evangelistic" preacher; they would be requesting that he be assigned
to another post.

It was the usual ploy. "When they initially opposed you, they
would try not to oppose you on the issue of race," said former Methodist
minister Don Collins, author of *When the Church Bell Rang Racist*.
"They would always try to find something else, if they could. If they
couldn't be successful at that, then they would attack you on race."[38]
For years afterward, Whatley wondered why a person couldn't be both
evangelistic in the traditional sense and also preach a social gospel. But
"concerns for racial justice and brotherhood were apparently part of
my problem," he decided.[39]

Sent to the six-hundred-member St. Mark's in Montgomery, Alabama, Whatley became active in issues of race and equity. In 1955,
he was elected president of the Montgomery chapter of the Alabama
Council on Human Relations. His vice president was twenty-six-year-
old Dr. Martin Luther King, Jr., pastor of Dexter Avenue Baptist
Church.

* * *

BUT A. C. LEE CHANGED his views about race relations during the remainder of the 1950s. And Nelle watched as her father, formerly a conservative on matters of race and social progress, became an advocate for the rights of Negroes. Part of the reason for his change of mind was the influence of events that no thoughtful American in the 1950s could ignore. In 1954, two white men murdered Emmett Till, a fourteen-year-old Negro visiting Alabama from his home in Chicago, for whistling at a white woman. The killers were acquitted, and then bragged about their crime to the media. Two years later, Autherine Lucy, a black student, attempted to enroll at Nelle's alma mater, the University of Alabama, but violence on the campus for three days forced her to flee. Despite a court order to readmit her, the Board of Trustees barred her from campus. Former Alabama state senator J. M. Bonner, whom A. C. Lee probably knew from his own career in the statehouse, wrote to the *Tuscaloosa News,* "I call now on every Southern White man to join in this fight. I proudly take my stand with those students who resisted, and who will continue to resist the admission of a negress named Lucy."[40]

A contest of warring principles was gearing up in the South, and a civic-minded man like A. C. Lee could not fail to recognize it happening in his own backyard. In 1959, the Ku Klux Klan forced the cancellation of the annual Monroeville Christmas parade by threatening to kill any members of the all-Negro Union High School band who participated. The morning after the parade was cancelled, A.C. walked into the store owned by A. B. Blass, noting that the store's façade had been vandalized with racist graffiti. As president of Kiwanis, Blass had made the decision to call off the parade for safety's sake. "Mr. Lee came down to our store from his office and knowing what we had done put his hand on my shoulder," said Blass, "looked me in the eye and said, 'Son, you did the right thing.' "[41]

By the time *To Kill a Mockingbird* was published, A.C. counted himself an activist in defending the civil rights of Negroes. In 1962, while a reporter was interviewing Nelle at her home in Monroeville, Alice and A.C. stopped by on their way to the offices of Bugg, Barnett & Lee. The eighty-one-year-old A.C. interrupted to speak earnestly about the importance of reapportioning voting districts to provide fairer representation for Negro voters. "It's got to be done," he said.[42]

Though this was not a reversal in so many words of his stand a decade earlier on the importance of keeping the church out of secular affairs, it was clear that racial equity had become a matter of conscience for A.C.; and so a religious man, such as he was, had to confront his convictions about justice and humanity.

Influencing him too, it must be pointed out, was Alice, more progressive in outlook in matters concerning race than her father. At a critical moment in the reorganization of the Methodist church, for instance, her beliefs about integration, honed over the decades, electrified an audience of hundreds of fellow worshippers.

During a meeting in the mid-1960s of the Alabama-West Florida Conference—one of the few regional holdouts against integrating Negro Methodists with whites—a "committee report concerning the problems of our racially divided church and society had come to the floor," said Reverend Thomas Lane Butts of Monroeville. "Amendments had been made, and debate had started. The advocates of continued racism were poised and ready to try to drag the church deeper into institutional racism, but before their titular leader could get the floor, a wee woman from Monroeville got the attention of the presiding officer of the conference."

For years, Alice had been impatiently waiting for such a moment. Taking the floor microphone, recalled Reverend Butts, she made "her maiden speech to the Alabama-West Florida Conference of the Methodist Church. Her speech electrified the seven or eight hundred delegates. It consisted of five words. She said: 'I move the previous question,' and sat down. The conference applauded enthusiastically and voted overwhelmingly to support her motion, and then proceeded to adopt the committee report without further debate. The advocates of racism were left holding their long prepared speeches. Miss Alice became the hero of the conference and from that day the enemy of the racists."[43]

WITH THE CORE COMPONENTS of her novel in place, Nelle set to work revising *Atticus* in the winter of 1957. As any successful novelist must do, she needed to create a fictional reality, a unique landscape for her reader to enter. So the setting of *To Kill a Mockingbird* is Maycomb, Alabama, a town similar to Monroeville. The time is the Depression, and Maycomb County is so poor that the energy of life itself seems to be on hold. "People moved slowly then," Lee writes. "They ambled across the square, shuffled in and out of stores around it, took their time about everything. A day was twenty-four hours long but seemed longer. There was no hurry, for there was nowhere to go, nothing to buy and no money to buy it with, nothing to see outside the boundaries of Maycomb County."[44]

Lee's time frame is a three-year period in Maycomb between the summer of 1932 and Halloween night 1935. Capote later said that the first two-thirds of the book, the portion about Scout, Dill, and Jem (Nelle, Truman, and Nelle's brother, Edwin, probably) trying to coax Boo Radley out of his house, "are quite literal and true."[45] Supporting this is the way actual incidents reported by the *Monroe Journal* during those years became part of the fabric of the story. For instance, in February 1933, when Nelle was six years old, a Mr. Dees fired a shotgun at somebody prowling in his collard patch, which parallels Nathan Radley firing a load of buckshot in Jem Finch's direction while he was retrieving his pants from the Radley's backyard.[46] In May 1934, a rabid dog bit two adults and two children, prefiguring the scene in the novel of Atticus shooting a mad dog.[47]

To populate the streets of Maycomb, Lee thought back on the inhabitants of Monroeville in the early 1930s: its officials, merchants, churchgoers, and even the local ne'er-do-wells. After the novel was published, some Monroeville folks believed they recognized themselves and neighbors. Capote made no bones about telling friends, "Most of the people in Nelle's book are drawn from life."[48]

An interesting twist about the novel is that there are two first-person narrative voices: the first is Jean Louise Finch, nicknamed "Scout." She talks, thinks, and acts like a six- to nine-year-old girl—albeit a very bright one—who perceives her world and the people in it as only an insatiably curious (and garrulous) child could. The second narrator is Scout, too, now an adult known as Jean Louise Finch, looking back on events with the benefit of hindsight. Sometimes the voices will alternate. For example, the adult Jean will set the stage:

> When I was almost six and Jem was nearly ten, our summertime
> boundaries (within calling distance of Calpurnia) were Mrs. Henry
> Lafayette Dubose's house two doors to the north of us, and the
> Radley Place three doors to the south. We were never tempted to

break them. The Radley Place was inhabited by an entity the mere description of whom was enough to make us behave for days on end; Mrs. Dubose was plain hell.

That was the summer Dill came to us.[49]

Then six-year-old Scout describes the actual moment Dill appeared, and drama replaces exposition. In a cinematic sense, the narration provided by the adult Jean Louise is like a voice-over.

A few critics later found fault with this technique. Phoebe Adams in the *Atlantic* dismissed the story as "frankly and completely impossible, being told in the first person by a six-year-old girl with the prose style of a well-educated adult."[50] Granville Hicks wrote in the *Saturday Review* that "Lee's problem has been to tell the story she wants to tell and yet to stay within the consciousness of a child, and she hasn't consistently solved it." W. J. Stuckey, in *The Pulitzer Prize Novels: A Critical Backward Look,* attributed Lee's "rhetorical trick" to a failure to solve "the technical problems raised by her story and whenever she gets into difficulties with one point of view, she switches to the other."[51]

It might be that Lee floundered when she was trying to settle on a point of view. She rewrote the novel three times: the original draft was in the third person, then she changed to the first person and later rewrote the final draft, which blended the two narrators, Janus-like, looking forward and back at the same time.[52] She later called this a "hopeless period" of writing the novel over and over.

Aside from what Nelle's intention might have been, the effort involved was more frustrating than she imagined it would be. The writing went at a glacial pace. A perfectionist, Nelle was more of a "rewriter" than a writer, she admitted later.[53] She "spent her days and nights in the most intense efforts to set down what she wanted to say in the way which would best say it to the reader," said Hohoff.[54] While working out of her apartment in New York, she lived on pennies, according to friends, still typing at the makeshift desk on York Avenue she had hammered together years earlier. No one "inquired too closely into what she ate," although now and then, Sue Philipp from Monroeville, another of Miss Watson's protégés from the old days who was living in New York at the time, invited Nelle over for a square meal and the chance to talk about how things were going on the book.[55] Then, for months at a time, Nelle returned to Monroeville.

She did so reluctantly, because it was no treat returning home to a humdrum existence for long stretches, sometimes four to six months. She was bored to tears. Having lived a cosmopolitan life, it was hard being without bookstores, museums, better restaurants, and so on. Why did she do it, and continue to do it, year after year?

Conceivably, Alice could argue that she had always been the one to step into the breach for the family—joining the law firm, supervising her mother's care, and now caring for A.C. For thirty years, Alice had "kept the home fires burning," as she liked to say, while her other siblings had moved away or married. Now, Nelle was a bohemian in New York and jobless while she lived on her advance for the book. She had no responsibilities other than to herself, while Alice had put her life on hold. It didn't seem fair, to put it simply. Moreover, Nelle could write in Monroeville or New York; which, in fact, she did when she took the train to Monroeville. She found a room at the country club and wrote without interruption.

Regardless, it was a return under duress to the life she had wanted to leave behind. Sometimes, just to get away, she would go into the country to Truman's aunt Mary Ida Carter's house, along with her favorite brand of scotch or gin, and just hang out there for long afternoons, reading and sipping. "Mr. Lee and Alice didn't want to see it or know about it," said Mary Ida's sister, Marie Faulk Rudisill.[56] It was Nelle's quiet way of rebelling.

When she returned to New York after a long hiatus down South, she and Hohoff met to discuss the book's progress. Hohoff remembered, "we talked it out, sometimes for hours. And sometimes she came around to my way of thinking, sometimes I to hers, sometimes the discussion would open up an entirely new line of country."[57] (She concurred with Nelle about changing the title to *To Kill a Mockingbird*, from *Atticus*, and about Nelle calling herself Harper Lee. Nelle never liked it when people mispronounced her name "Nellie.")[58] Hohoff's main concern was the structure of *To Kill a Mockingbird*, having recognized that the "editorial call to duty was plain." In her view, Nelle needed "professional help in organizing her material and developing a sound plot structure. After a couple of false starts, the story line, interplay of characters, and fall of emphasis grew clearer, and with each revision—there were many minor changes as the story grew in strength and in Nelle's own vision of it—the true stature of the novel became evident."[59]

Hohoff "was a terrific editor," said Wayne Greenhaw, who worked with her a few years later on his novel *The Golfer.* "She would go through the manuscript and jot down little questions in the margins. From those questions, you would start questioning your own work."[60]

For Nelle, it was like assembling puzzle pieces of scenes and short stories into a narrative whole. "As I understand it from what I've heard," said Greenhaw, "those 'pieces' fit together very nicely, but they weren't in novelistic order. Tay started her thinking about the arrangement of events. Now when I read the book, I don't see the seams. But as a writer, I can see how many of the stories in the book could have been fragments. It's like a piece of iron sculpture. It starts out as pieces of metal, and then through arranging and rearranging becomes a melded work of art."[61]

Undercutting Nelle's achievement has been a persistent rumor since the book's publication that Truman Capote wrote portions or all of it. "I've heard they were up there at the old Hibbert place, which is right north of Monroeville—out there in the woods," said a former classmate of Nelle's, Claude Nunnelly. "They just went out there, there's an old farmhouse, and they went out there and wrote and wrote and wrote."[62]

Tay Hohoff's son-in-law, Dr. Grady H. Nunn, said that such a deception wouldn't have occurred to Nelle.

I am satisfied that the relationship between Nelle and Tay over those three years while *Mockingbird* was in the making developed into a warmer and closer association than is usual between author and editor. I believe that special association came about at least in part because they worked, together, over every word in the manuscript. Tay and [her husband] Arthur became Nelle's close friends, sort of family, and that friendship continued beyond the publication of the book. I doubt that the special closeness could possibly have happened had there been an alien ghostwriter, Capote, involved.[63]

Also, given Truman's inability to keep anybody's secrets, it's highly unlikely that he wouldn't have claimed right of authorship after the novel became famous. He did say, which Nelle never denied, that he read the manuscript and recommended some edits because it was too long in places.

Without question, however, the hard work of creating *To Kill a Mockingbird* fell squarely on Nelle, though "she always knew I was in her corner," said Hohoff, "even when I was most critical"; and Hohoff was never one to suffer fools gladly, recalled Nicholas Delbanco, another of her young authors.[64] One winter night Nelle was seated at her desk in her apartment on York Avenue, rereading a page in her typewriter over and over. Suddenly she gathered up everything she'd written, walked over to a window, and threw the entire draft outside into the snow. Then she called Hohoff and tearfully explained what she'd done. Tay told her to march outside immediately and pick up the pages. Feeling exhausted, she bundled up and went out into the darkness, "since I knew I could never be happy being anything but a writer . . . I kept at it because I knew it had to be my first novel, for better or for worse."[65]

Nor did the coveted status of being a writer-under-contract change her "intense reserve," as Hohoff called it. She was still shy around strangers, though she could easily have taken out bragging rights on the novel she was writing. "I first met Nelle Lee in 1958," said Dr. Nunn.

> We were living in Tuscaloosa, and Tay visited us in connection with a Lippincott-sponsored search for promising authors in the writing program there. There were several such visits during our tenure there. As usual a New York–style cocktail party for Tay was included. Nelle was in Monroeville at the time and was invited up for the party. She arrived, was introduced around, and promptly disappeared. I discovered her later sitting on the back steps with our daughter, who was then five. They were there until Nelle left at the party's end. Definitely Nelle was no party lover.[66]

Besides Hohoff, there were others in her corner, of course. Her second family in Manhattan gathered around her, giving her creative and emotional support. Michael and Joy Brown continued to depend on Nelle as an aunt to their children, and Joy's best friend. Annie

Laurie Williams and Maurice Crain began inviting Nelle to their summer place, the Old Stone House, in West Hartland, Connecticut, for long weekends. Nelle wrote them long, chatty letters from Monroeville during her visits home, catching them up on family news and local events. One Christmas, she mailed Williams a cowbell as a present, confirming their sisterhood as southern rural people.[67] Another New York agent might have read this gentle overture as a hallmark of someone who was almost embarrassingly unsophisticated. But Williams understood that Nelle was inviting her to become part of her southern family. Then the following year, boughs of fresh-cut Alabama evergreens arrived for the office; Williams reciprocated by sending to Monroeville a box of hard candies because "I remembered you told me that your father loved [them]"; in addition, she promised she was having "some of the farm pictures [of the house in Connecticut] you loved made up for you and they will be along for you to enjoy them with Alice and your father before you leave."[68]

Finally, in the spring of 1959, right before the final draft of the manuscript was ready for delivery to Lippincott, Nelle reached out to a seminal figure in her dream of becoming a writer. She presented her novel to her former English teacher, Miss Gladys Watson, now Mrs. Watson-Burkett, and asked her to critique it. At night, Mrs. Watson-Burkett would take it out of her sewing basket, write notes in the margins, and discuss it with her husband.[69] One day after school, she asked a student, Cecil Ryland, to come up to her desk. According to Ryland, she said she had finished proofreading a novel by a former student, and asked would he please run it over to her house. "And so, I gathered up the manuscript in an old stationery box, and took it and went knocking on her door. Nelle Harper Lee came to the door, and I said, 'Here's your book.' And she said 'Thank you.' Little did I realize that I held a little bit of history in my hands."[70]

THAT FALL, IN MID-NOVEMBER, Nelle was biding her time waiting for galleys of the book to arrive when Truman called. An item in the *New York Times* had caught his attention, headlined "Wealthy Farmer, 3 of Family Slain." It read, in part:

Holcomb, Kan., Nov. 15 (UPI)—A wealthy wheat farmer, his wife and their two young children were found shot to death today in their home. They had been killed by shotgun blasts at close range after being bound and gagged.

The father, 48-year-old Herbert W. Clutter, was found in the basement with his son, Kenyon, 15. His wife Bonnie, 45, and a daughter, Nancy, 16, were in their beds.

There were no signs of a struggle, and nothing had been stolen. The telephone lines had been cut.

"This is apparently the case of a psychopathic killer," Sheriff Earl Robinson said.[71]

William Shawn, editor of the *New Yorker* magazine, had assigned Capote to use the item as a springboard for writing about the impact of a quadruple murder on a small town. It was going to be a tough assignment, vastly different from researching "The Muses Are Heard," a long article Truman had written three years earlier about a mainly black theatrical troupe touring the Soviet Union with George Gershwin's opera, *Porgy and Bess.* The Kansas story involved murder, and the killer or killers were still on the loose. Truman, slight, blond, and bespectacled, was looking for someone to go with him. His first choice was Andrew Lyndon, a former roommate who dabbled in writing, but Lyndon was unavailable. Now he turned to Nelle.

His idea was to explore, by interviewing dozens of residents of Garden City, the nearest big town to Holcomb, and create a composite of the town's traumatized psyche. It sounded like an adventure that was poles apart from the drudgery of writing, and Nelle accepted instantly. "He said it would be a tremendously involved job and would take two people," she said. "The crime intrigued him, and I'm intrigued with crime—and, boy, I wanted to go. It was deep calling to deep."[72]

Before they could go, however, they needed a contact in Kansas who was influential, someone who could open doors. Bennett Cerf, Capote's publisher at Random House, happened to know the president of Kansas State University, James McCain. McCain offered that if Capote would speak to the English faculty, he would provide letters of introduction to key people in Garden City.

So, on the strength of this slim connection, Nelle and Truman prepared to travel by train to Kansas during the second week of December 1959.

They met at Grand Central Terminal, the most convenient location for both of them, and at about 5:30 P.M. passed through a pair of bronze doors set in marble. With a porter wheeling their luggage in front of them—Truman's excited gait more of a skip than a walk—they followed the red carpet that led to the gleaming 20th Century Limited, one of the finest passenger trains in the country. Alfred Hitchcock had used it the year before, to film scenes for *North by Northwest*. Truman liked nice things—beautiful paperweights, expensive clothes, and sports cars. An attendant handed Nelle perfume and flowers, and Truman a carnation, which he put through the buttonhole in his lapel. They had a pair of roomettes reserved for the eight-hundred-mile run to Chicago, where they would catch the Santa Fe Super Chief going west. At 6:00 P.M. sharp, with approximately one hundred passengers aboard, the train pulled out, heading north along the Hudson River and west to Buffalo. Sometime during the night it would turn southwest, along the southern shore of Lake Erie, and head straight for Chicago.

The next day, they arrived at the LaSalle Street Station shortly before lunch. Since they had the entire afternoon to spend before the Super Chief left, they decided to explore the Loop. Nelle had been to Chicago for a journalism convention in college, and Truman had some recommendations on a few good places to eat, so they hailed a cab. Half a dozen museums and the lakefront were within a fifteen-minute ride, too. They were two friends having a lark, just like when they were children, only now they were not barefoot behind the Faulks' smokehouse puffing on rabbit tobacco tamped into catalpa pods, or cradling on their tongues chips of ice swiped from the ice wagon. They were adults, crossing the continent like travelers on the Orient Express. And tonight on the train they would choose between oyster pan roast, rock Cornish hen, or tournedos of beef tenderloin, in a dining car decorated with mirrors, golden draperies, and turquoise carpeting. Then they might go to the observation car, with its huge glass dome, lie back in one of the swivel chairs, and watch the moon sail overhead as they crossed the Mississippi.

At St. Louis, they changed trains and continued on to Manhattan, Kansas, and Kansas State University. Capote spoke to the English faculty at Kansas State University, after which the instructors threw him a small party. Then Nelle and Truman rented a Chevrolet and prepared to drive the four hundred miles to Garden City.

The route they took, US-83—past beet fields, slaughter yards, and meatpacking plants—follows the one hundredth meridian from Canada to Mexico. The "gently rolling prairie is serrated by the scraggy cottonwood, that rises awkwardly by some sandbarred stream, oozing over the moundy land," wrote Kansas native and newspaperman William Allen White, while "around some sinkhole in the great flat floor of the prairie, droops a desolate willow."[73] Experienced travelers call this route, where the eye and the imagination are starved for anything interesting, the Road to Nowhere.

"See NL's Notes"

THEY ARRIVED AT TWILIGHT IN GARDEN CITY, A TOWN OF eleven thousand on the high western Kansas wheat plain, as the sky was turning a deep icy green. The radio kept repeating the same bulletin at intervals: "Police authorities, continuing their investigation of the tragic Clutter slaying, have requested that anyone with pertinent information please contact the sheriff's office."[1] Driving down North Main Street, Truman and Nelle glanced expectantly left and right for the Warren Hotel. It was supposed to be the best and closest accommodation to the Clutter farm in Holcomb, a village of 270 residents seven miles west on US-50. Nelle noticed that street signs and even traffic lights were hard to see because everything was festooned with Christmas decorations—strings of lights, wreaths of evergreen, and red cardboard bells.[2]

The hotel was small but pleasant-looking, nothing on the scale of the 1887 four-story Windsor, just down the street. Once called the "Waldorf of the Prairies," this edifice for rich cattlemen had been ruined by the Dustbowl years in the 1930s and was teetering toward bankruptcy. At the Warren, they registered for adjoining rooms and then took the elevator upstairs to rest. The drive from Manhattan, Kansas, had taken eight hours, the last one hundred miles of it across country flat and featureless ("level," Kansans preferred to call it).

The next day, December 16, they walked a block to the Finney County Courthouse, the headquarters of the murder investigation. The courthouse, built to the same proportions as a gigantic lump of sugar and faced with whitish-gray limestone, was separated from the street by a half acre of lawn, in the middle of which was a bronze replica of the Statue of Liberty. The person they needed to see was Kansas Bureau of Investigation (KBI) detective Alvin Dewey, who had been appointed to coordinate the investigation by KBI chief Logan Sanford. Dewey was both a former Finney County sheriff and a former FBI agent. Chief Sanford had given him the additional responsibility of handling the press because he was not easily ruffled. In the field, a team of investigators was combing western Kansas for leads.

Nelle and Truman consulted a hand-painted directory on a dun-colored wall of the courthouse's first floor and took the stairs to the second. A secretary greeted them and escorted them to Mr. Dewey's office.

Alvin Dewey was "just plain handsome," Nelle decided on the spot, and made a point of saying so in her notes.[3] Dark-haired and dressed in a blue suit, he was seated at a large mahogany desk positioned catty-corner in a cramped room. His mission seemed defined by two prominent items in the room: a large Santa Fe Railroad map of the United States on the wall, and a thick criminal statute book on the desk. Dewey's brown eyes sized Nelle up—"a tall brunette, a good looker," he thought, an observation that suggests that Nelle had put aside the frumpiness of her college years to help Truman make a favorable impression.[4] Dewey invited them to sit down. His curiosity was piqued: he hadn't seen either of them among the reporters who had been hanging around during the past three weeks.

Truman, about five foot four and wearing a sheepskin coat, a long scarf that reached the floor, and moccasins—his version of Western wear, apparently—acted as if he thought he was pretty important. Nelle took her cue from Truman and waited for him to begin a carefully rehearsed introduction. The forty-seven-year-old Dewey concealed a smile behind a drag on his Winston cigarette when he heard the sound of his visitor's contralto voice.

"Mr. Dewey, I am Truman Capote and this is my friend, Nelle Harper Lee. She's a writer, too." The *New Yorker* magazine, he explained, had assigned him to write an article about the Clutter case. Miss Lee was his assistant. His friend, Bennett Cerf, the publisher of Random House books, had contacted Dr. James McClain, the president of Mr. Clutter's alma mater, Kansas State University, who had been very helpful. But now they needed to get down to *business*. They were here to find out the facts about the murder, the family, and how the town was reacting.

Dewey listened noncommittally. Except for the name-dropping, they sounded like your average reporters trying to get the inside scoop. "You're free to attend press conferences," he said. "I hold them about once a day."

"But I'm not a newspaperman," Capote insisted. "I need to talk to *you* in depth. . . . What I'm going to write will take months. What I am here for is to do a very special story on the family up to and including the murders."

Dewey indicated that he hadn't heard anything to make him change his original offer: they could attend press conferences with the rest of their kind.

"Look," Capote said, struggling to separate himself from newspaper men with daily deadlines, "it really doesn't make any difference to me if the case is ever solved or not."[5]

Dewey's face darkened, and Nelle suspected immediately that Truman had just torpedoed the mission. In fact, privately Dewey had been worrying for three weeks about the trail growing cold, and the dread of defeat was starting to gnaw at him: "In homicide, if you don't come up with some answers in twenty-four to forty-eight hours, you get a feeling in your gut that the thing may never be solved. . . . 'Anything new on the Clutter case?' folks would be asking me on the post office steps for months to come. And then it would be, 'Never did find out who killed the Clutters, did you?' for the rest of my life."[6]

Anger suddenly got the better of him. "I'd like to see your press card, Mr. Cappuchi," he snapped.[7]

Truman let the mispronunciation pass, seeing that they were off on the wrong foot. "I don't have one," he said mildly.

The get-to-know-you meeting had turned into a showdown. Exercising the better part of valor, Nelle rose. Both men got to their feet.

Dewey bid them a stiff goodbye and, after they had gone, returned to his work.

The next day, Nelle and Truman appeared in Dewey's office again. "I just wanted to establish my identity," Truman said in a friendly voice, and presented his passport. Perhaps Nelle, witnessing the earlier confrontation, had reminded Truman that honey catches more flies than vinegar. The detective glanced at Capote's passport and repeated that they could attend press conferences. Truman thanked him as though they had been granted a special favor.

"From then on," Alvin Dewey said later of the pair,

he and his friend joined the news people at every conference. They were quiet, attentive, asked few questions, and, as far as I could tell, caused no commotion. I did hear they were hard at work, interviewing everyone, people said . . . in Holcomb, up and down Garden City's Main Street, in farm homes, in the coffee-drinking places, in the schools, everywhere. The New Yorker was getting his story together.

I could see that Miss Lee would be a great help. If Capote came on as something of a shocker, she was there to absorb the shock. She had a down-home style, a friendly smile, and a knack for saying the right things. Once the ice was broken, I was told, Capote could get people to talking about the subject closest to their hearts, themselves.[8]

Nelle had accompanied Truman to Kansas as his salaried "assistant researchist"—a term he invented for her. Their assignment was to take a six-inch news item in the *New York Times* about the murder of the farm family in Holcomb—just a pinprick on the map—and find the humanity buried beneath the crime. They would have to find out everything about the family—Herb and Bonnie Clutter, and their children, teenagers Nancy and Kenyon—so the Clutters would be real. Truman wanted to accomplish all this without the benefit of taking notes or tape-recording during interviews. He was convinced people were more guarded when they could see they were going on the record. He would just talk to people instead—conduct interviews as conversations.

Nelle's job was to listen and observe subtleties that Truman might be too busy to notice. Then they would return to the hotel and separately write down everything they could recall. Nelle's gift for creating character sketches turned out to complement Truman's ability to recall remarks. Many times over the next month, Capote's telegraphic descriptions of a conversation would end with "See NL's notes" to remind him to use her insights later.

The hotel's Trail Room coffee shop became their unofficial office during the day for reviewing notes, or for keeping appointments with folks who could spare only enough time for a chat and a cup of coffee. If either Nelle or Truman drew a blank about a fact or a remark that had been made, they would prod each other's memories. In instances when key information was missing or unclear, they would have to go back and visit a person a second or a third time. "Together we would get it right," Nelle said.[9]

That was the plan. Unfortunately, obstacles existed everywhere, it seemed.

To begin with, residents in both Garden City and Holcomb were afraid. With the killer or killers still at large, interviews were hard to get. When Capote went alone to the home of Mrs. Hideo Ashida, a neighbor of the Clutters, she refused to open the door until he could provide her with the name of someone to verify his identity.[10] The Plains states were still reeling from the rampage the year before when two Nebraska teenagers, nineteen-year-old Charles Starkweather and his fourteen-year-old girlfriend, Caril Fugate, had killed ten people in five states. News of the Clutter murders had sent people in Garden City and Holcomb into a paranoid frenzy: farmers padlocked their gates and put combination locks on their sheds; homeowners installed deadbolt locks on doors; apartment dwellers added chain locks to their bedrooms. Some took the added precaution of fixing all the windows with ten-penny nails. Even though most folks said that the authorities should be looking for an outsider—a native would have known that Herb Clutter never had any cash on hand—neighbors kept an eye on one another, and porch lights burned until dawn. The KBI received three hundred letters with tips from anonymous sources, many of them postmarked Garden City, accusing local people by name.[11]

But Nelle and Truman were determined to get this story, and Truman was notoriously persistent. Sometimes, a little cash would buy an interview. Mrs. Ashida's son Robert and other residents said that Capote willingly paid, if necessary.[12] In his list of expenses, written on the inside cover of a handsome gold-colored journal he had purchased in Italy, Truman itemized his Kansas expenses: car rental, meals on the train, and "farewell gifts," but left one amount unidentified: "spent cash $1400."[13]

Once invited into someone's home, however, he found a further stumbling block, a mundane problem that he and Nelle never anticipated, which was trying to keep the person's attention turned away from the TV. NBC had begun broadcasting from Garden City the year before, and the clear black-and-white picture on the screen seemed to hypnotize bored farming families trapped inside during the long winter. The nuisance of manic commercials in the background tested Nelle's and Truman's patience—neither of whom owned a television set—especially when the whole point of an interview was to try to talk intimately with someone.

Also interfering with getting good interviews was Truman himself—he just wasn't going over very well with people. "Nelle looked like normal folk. She was just a fantastic lady," said Harold Nye, one of the principal KBI detectives running down leads on the Clutter case, "but Truman was an absolute flake."[14] Nye, who at one point went five days and nights without sleep during the week after the murders, had no patience for fancy Johnny-come-latelies showing up on the scene.

Neither did postmistress Myrtle T. Clare: "Capote came walking around here real uppity and superior-like and acting so strange that I think people was scared of him. He was real foreign-like, and nobody would open their doors for him, afraid he'd knock them in the head."[15]

"I thought Capote was queero," said Gerald Van Vleet, Clutter's business partner. "He was nosy as hell and very, very rude. He came out to my farm on a few occasions to talk to me, and I tried to avoid him."[16]

How they were going over was obvious to Nelle. "We were given the cold shoulder. Those people had never seen anyone like Truman—he was like someone coming off the moon."[17]

In the end, there were key people who refused to be interviewed under any circumstances; they'd had their fill of reporters snooping around, hoping to sniff out the gory details of a crime that had hit close to home in the tight-knit town. The first to find Nancy Clutter's body had been teenagers Nancy Ewalt and Sue Kidwell, who had run screaming from the Clutters' house. When Nelle and Truman approached Nancy Ewalt's father, Clarence, and asked for a moment of his time, he fixed them with his watery blue eyes, framed in a red weather-beaten face, and said evenly three times to their questions, "I'm a busy man," and finally turned away.[18]

Fortunately, one resource available to them—and to everyone else—was the legwork being done by Kansas journalists on the scene. The *Garden City Telegram,* the *Hutchinson News,* the *Kansas City Star,* and other papers were following the manhunt closely. Dr. Mc-Clain, the president of Kansas State University, had recommended to Nelle and Truman that when they arrived in Garden City they introduce themselves to Bill Brown, the managing editor of the *Garden City Telegram.* They tried, but he brushed them off. The crime had taken place in his backyard, and he wasn't dealing in out-of-towners. The lights in the newspaper office burned late most nights: "I was busy putting out a newspaper," he later said flatly.[19] In her notes, Nelle dismissed him as a "Catonahottinroof."[20]

Even if they had been able to enlist Brown's help, weaving a pastiche primarily from newspaper stories and secondhand reporting would have been unacceptable to *New Yorker* editor William Shawn. He was expecting art, not paraphrased remarks, hearsay, and canned statements from press conferences. Nelle and Capote understood that, of course, but after a week in Kansas the truth was their spadework hadn't turned up anything beyond what reporters on the scene had already unearthed. The dozen or so interviews they had conducted yielded predictable responses: people were shocked by the murders; congregation members at the church the Clutters attended eulogized them as a fine family; and so on. Herb Clutter, everyone said, was a go-getter, always smiling. Nelle knew enough about Bonnie Clutter, the mother, and daughter Nancy to form sympathetic composite portraits of them. Kenyon was a bit of a mystery—a loner, more absorbed by projects that would appeal to an engineer than to a farmer. But these were just sketches in the corner of a canvas that needed to be much larger and more original.

They didn't have much time to get the formula right. The Christmas and New Year's holidays were not far off, and then businesses would be closed and people would be occupied with family celebrations. No one would be interested in picking at the wound caused by the blow of the Clutter killings.

Capote began to believe that coming out to Kansas had been a mistake all around. "I cannot get any rapport with these people," he told Nelle. "I can't get a handle on them." Except for two high school English teachers who had read some of his work, no one knew him from the man in the moon. How many more times was he going to be called "Mr. Cappuchi" or "Ka-poat"?

"Hang on," Nelle said. "You *will* penetrate this place."[21] A few days later they got their big break.

ON SUNDAY, DECEMBER 20, Nelle and Truman were waiting to be picked up in the lobby of the Warren Hotel by Herb Clutter's former estate attorney, Cliff Hope. Hope was on Dr. McClain's list of people to get to know, and Truman had been pestering him for several days. Finally, he had agreed to drive the pair out to the Clutter farm. The KBI had placed the farm off-limits, but Hope agreed to intercede with the family's executor, Kenneth Lyon, explaining that Nelle and Truman were friends of Dr. McClain's. Lyon acquiesced, but insisted on being present, driving the two hundred miles from Wichita to meet them there.[22]

When Detective Nye found out later about the visit, he wasn't pleased: "I was in charge of securing the house. [Detective] Roy Church was helping me. We examined the entire house for evidence, during which all was secured. And how they got in later, I don't know."[23]

Cliff Hope turned out to be a lean, blond man who smoked a briar pipe (his favorite tobacco's "foul smell" offended Nelle's nose); Kenneth Lyon was a "slim, dark" man and seemed to Nelle to have an "open honest face."[24] As Hope escorted them to the waiting car he mentioned that the trip out to the farm would take only about fifteen minutes. As they left downtown Garden City behind, the pavement ended with a thump and the road turned to gravel and gray dirt. Gray seemed to be the predominant color everywhere, bleeding into the sky, the leafless trees, and the frost-killed silvery grass. About a half mile south of Holcomb, they came to a lane leading off from the road. A ROAD CLOSED sign nailed to a sawhorse marked the entrance to the Clutters' River Valley Farm. Tacked to one end of the sawhorse, a limp red rag flapped disconsolately in the cold wind. Kenneth Lyon got out and turned the sawhorse aside to allow the car to pass.

The lane leading to the house was bordered on both sides by tall Chinese elms, their branches creating a spidery archway. The effect was graceful, but their aesthetic appeal was secondary to their practical purpose—they served as windbreaks for slowing the rate of dust or snow that whipped over the prairie during windy spells. Two years before, in 1957, a blizzard had buried Holcomb in snowdrifts twenty-seven feet deep in some places. A farmer lost in a snowstorm, or a motorist stopped on the road because the earth and sky were both a blur of white, could freeze to death within hailing distance of a house without a friendly landmark such as a row of trees to mark the way to shelter.

Isolation was always something to be on guard against in the vast, beguiling openness of the prairies. The night the Clutters were murdered, no one had heard the shots because the wind was blowing; not even employee Alfred Stoecklein, who lived with his wife and three children in a small house on the other side of the Clutters' enormous barn; and no one had seen anything suspicious in the utter darkness. The feeling of naked vulnerability translated into the dislike of strangers that had plagued Truman and Nelle thus far. As one old man had said in Mrs. Hartman's café on the day of the Clutter murders, "All we've got out here are our friends. There isn't anything else."[25]

Reaching the end of the quarter-mile lane, Cliff Hope parked near the front door. The yellow brick and white clapboard home with fourteen rooms, three baths, and two wood fireplaces had been built in the late 1940s, a time when many homes in the county went without running water. Surrounded by a lawn landscaped with pointed jade green arborvitae, the big house had been the diadem of Herb's four-thousand-acre farm.

At forty-eight, Clutter had been justifiably proud of his twenty-year rise from 1939, when his financial records indicated he was worth "$1000 I hope," to his position as one of the wealthiest farmers in the state.[26] With the help of half a dozen employees, sometimes as many as twenty, he had raised sorghum, milo grain, and certified grass seed. That day on the Clutter farm, Nelle noticed that hundreds of red-and-white Hereford cattle were still grazing peacefully in the pasture.[27]

Even as his wealth expanded, Herb Clutter could be stubborn

about taking advice concerning his financial affairs, and he had foot-dragged about estate planning, despite dogged reminders from Cliff Hope. "Herb would come into my office with some Saturday errands written on the back of an envelope. He gave me a few minutes, checked me off, and [went] on his way."[28] Clutter had died without a will to protect his Kansas fiefdom; and in a few months, River Valley Farm would be auctioned off by sheriff's order.

From around the barn, Alfred Stoecklein came out to meet the group. Stoecklein had been the Clutters' odd-job man ("spectacles and yellow rotting teeth," Capote noted; Nelle got the impression he drank, despite Herb Clutter's iron rule that he wouldn't abide drinkers).[29] Emerging from a car nearby was Gerald Van Vleet, Clutter's business partner. He was a big man in khaki work clothes and heavy boots who seemed more interested in twisting the engine belt in his rough hands than in making conversation. When Kenneth Lyon signaled from the house that he'd unlocked the front door, everyone started up the hedge-lined walk. The heat in the house was off, but the scent of lemon furniture polish hung in the chilly air. Van Vleet crossed the living room to Clutter's office and promptly sat down in his former partner's wooden swivel chair, rotating slowly back and forth. To every question Nelle put to him about the murder, he answered, "I wasn't here."[30]

Evidently, when it came to interpreting what this farm had to say about its former inhabitants, Nelle and Truman were on their own. They decided to examine the house separately: each would make maps of the floor plan and take notes on the contents of the rooms. In a sense, they would be interviewing the house the way they did people, and then, afterward, they could compare their impressions.

"Apparently [Hope] saw nothing evil in our explorations," Nelle noted, though he was "alert as a fox."[31] He and Lyon stepped away for a whispered conversation while Nelle and Truman oriented themselves to the layout of the house.

In a way, they had come full circle from their childhoods in Monroeville. They were figuratively once again on South Alabama Avenue, where they had lived next door to each other and fantasized that a madman lived down the street in the tumbledown house owned by the Boleware family. They had spied on that house, speculated about the goings-on inside, and dared each other to sneak inside that lair.

Nelle had used the house, with some embellishments, as the home of Boo Radley in *To Kill a Mockingbird*. By contrast, this successful Kansas farmer's house, perched in a breezy, sunny spot, didn't have creaking hinges, broken shutters, and flickering shadows, or any of the lurid conventions associated with horror. But by exploring it, they were embarking once again on a hunt for something monstrous.

Nelle excused herself and walked past Van Vleet, who it seemed was permanently ensconced in his late partner's chair, to examine Herb Clutter's office.

Herb and his wife, Bonnie, forty-five, had been one of the most admired and active couples in Holcomb and Garden City. On the walls of Herb's dark veneer–paneled office were framed certificates and labeled notebooks covering his career. "If something happened in Holcomb, you pretty much knew Herb or Bonnie had something to do with it," said Merl Wilson, who, with his wife, Argybell, alternated with the Clutters in leading the local 4-H.[32] Herb had been president of the National Association of Wheat Growers and directed the Farm Credit Administration for the district covering Kansas, New Mexico, Oklahoma, and Colorado. The books in the floor-to-ceiling shelves in his office reflected his singular interests—*Crops in Peace and War, Beef Cattle in Kansas,* and *Farmers at the Crossroads.* In Garden City, Clutter had also served on half a dozen committees for the First Methodist Church. In many ways, he was to western Kansas what Nelle's father, A. C. Lee, was to southern Alabama: a pillar of the small-town community determined to preserve its sanctity.

Nelle headed upstairs next, out from under the quietly watchful eyes of Hope, Van Vleet, and Lyon. At the top of the stairs she looked briefly into a small bathroom with pink tile and towel rods before moving on to the bedrooms. Room by room, she began to take inventory in her notes, of everything she saw.

The first bedroom she came to had belonged to Eveanna, who was, by this time, married and living in Mt. Carroll, Illinois. (She was one of the two older daughters who no longer lived at home.) Bonnie Clutter had been sleeping in Eveanna's bedroom, and that was where her body had been discovered. Mrs. Clutter, a pretty wraith of a woman, taught Sunday school and belonged to the Women's Society of Christian Service. She was said to suffer from debilitating bouts of depression that kept her crying in bed for days. One night, she had been found wandering distractedly in Garden City and taken home. (Truman, rummaging downstairs in the basement bathroom, had found vials of prescription tranquilizers labeled "Bonnie Clutter, Wesley Hospital, take four a day.")[33]

Nelle glanced at the old-fashioned dresser of heavy oaklike wood with a big mirror, the throw rugs, and an "atrocious table lamp on the table beside the bed."[34] It was a stuffy room to be cooped up in. Then she moved on to Beverly's room, but since Beverly was away at Kansas University Medical Center studying nursing, and nothing about the crime involved her room, Nelle only took note of the dark, heavy furniture.

Around the corner was Kenyon Clutter's pale gray-green bedroom. Solitary and studious, according to classmates, Kenyon had been fifteen when he died. His bedroom was the largest, stretching nearly half the length of the house, suggesting that he was the intended heir of River Valley Farm. On the bookshelf above his bed were titles of boys' books—the complete *Hardy Boys* series—and a handful of sanitized bestsellers, including Junior Literary Guild selections. Framed pictures of his two eldest sisters, Eveanna and Beverly, held pride of place on one of the shelves above his desk. "Kenyon Always be Good," Nelle read in the corner of Eveanna's picture. There were also several completed plastic cars from model kits, three figurines of Kenyon's favorite breeds of dogs, two snapshots of his prizewinning sheep, and four horse figurines. Against the opposite wall stood an antique wind-up Victrola, a symbol of Kenyon's fascination with mechanical things.

Down the hall was the smaller bedroom belonging to Kenyon's sixteen-year-old sister, Nancy. Dark-eyed, creamy-complexioned, smart in school, active in school clubs, and the recent star of her school play, Nancy was any parent's ideal of a middle-class teenager. On the day before her death, she taught a neighbor girl how to bake cherry pie "her special way."[35] The walls of her bedroom were pink, and the ceiling painted light blue. She had created a vanity for herself by adding a skirt to an old table. On a cork bulletin board were photos of classmates and clippings from the school newspaper. Near the window was a print of Jesus Christ; and above the bed where Nancy's body had been found were pictures of three kittens. In an overstuffed chair sat a button-eyed teddy bear that Nancy's steady, Bobby Rupp, had won for her at a county fair. Missing, though, and in the hands of the KBI as evidence, was a diary that Nancy had kept for three years with daily entries. "Damnation. We've got to see them," Nelle wrote in notes when she found out about the diary's existence.[36]

She returned downstairs where Lyon, Van Vleet, and Hope were making small talk. Truman was outside drawing a map of the property.

Having seen Herb Clutter's office already, Nelle walked around the living room. A light green sectional sofa matched the walls; the carpet was pink. Mounted above a console record player was another print of Jesus Christ. Christian books and magazines such as *A Man Called Peter* and *Guideposts* lay on shelves within reach of Herb's favorite easy chair—"modern religious crap," in Nelle's opinion.[37] Off the living room by an adjoining hallway was a large bathroom with pink tiles on the walls, white and chocolate-colored ones alternating on the floor, and a door to the master bedroom, where Herb slept alone. The walls of Herb's bedroom were light blue, the bed large enough for two; above it was a print of Jesus Christ, this time gazing down on biblical Jerusalem. (By now Nelle was beginning to see humor in the pronounced household themes; later she asked Truman if there was a print of Jesus by the washer and dryer she might have missed.)[38]

Going back out into the hallway, Nelle turned left toward the dining room, which was the same banal green as the living room. The dining table and chairs were blond and matched a breakfront. Continuing on through the dining room, she came to the white-and-blue kitchen Herb had designed with an eye toward good organization. The cabinets, featuring a built-in dishwasher and stove—unusual for the times—were all at a convenient height, and in a few places the kickboards turned down to provide steps for the children to reach things. There was an ingenious swinging door by the baseboard for sweeping refuse from the floor and sending it down a chute to a garbage can in the basement. One side of the kitchen was devoted to a breakfast nook with a table that would have been large enough to accommodate all six members of the family for a big farm-style breakfast.

Around the corner from the kitchen was a utility room. On the morning the murders were discovered, two boys doing chores on the farm had placed fresh milk inside the utility room at dawn and gone out again, unaware of why the Clutters weren't up and about.

That was all there was to see on the main and upper floors. Nelle went down into the basement.

At the bottom of the stairs was a third bathroom—very up to date, Nelle thought, and done in blue and white tile. The center room in the basement was the playroom, scene of church parties for the United Methodist Youth Fellowship. "They were typical 1950s church youth parties, probably on Sunday night, with refreshments, chatting and Ping-Pong. No dancing or music as I remember," said one of Eveanna's friends, Ted Hall. "Drinking, smoking and profanity was not a part of that crowd and most parents trusted their daughters with young men that they knew. Usually with good reason."[39] Kenyon's body had been found on the sofa, and Nelle made a dark blotch on her basement map to indicate that. She reached for the bookshelf and flipped through Nancy's 4-H notebook. The girl had written that her father had helped her decorate the basement by drilling holes over the fireplace for an eight-pointed star clock. In a corner of the playroom was a small vending machine that Kenyon had taken apart out of curiosity.

One room over, at the farthest end of the basement, was the furnace where Herb's body had been found lying on a cardboard mattress box. Nelle stood near a red stain on the wall and drew another gout of blood on her map to indicate the location of Herb Clutter's murder. She made no remark about the hellishness of the place, only listed what she saw: low ceiling, unfinished walls, cement floor, three water heaters. Then she went back upstairs to wait for Truman.

It had taken about an hour for Nelle and Truman to go through the house and walk around the property. They thanked Hope and Lyon for making the house available to them—especially in light of how far Mr. Lyon had driven—and bid taciturn Mr. Van Vleet goodbye. They had two more interviews scheduled that day: a second one with Mrs. Ashida, and one with Mrs. Clarence Katz, whose daughter Jolene was the girl Nancy taught to bake a pie on the last day of her life. Afterward, they returned to the Warren Hotel to go over their notes.

The inside of the house had been an eye-opener. For some time, Nelle had been wondering about the peculiar mix of behaviors in the Clutter family: Herb's hail-fellow-well-met conduct evident everywhere, Bonnie Clutter's debilitating emotional problems, Nancy's perkiness, and Kenyon's reputation as a loner. The interior of the big house provided a clue to the emotional atmosphere of River Valley Farm: it was cold and repressive. A small brass door knocker identified the occupant behind each bedroom door. It was as if the rooms were private offices belonging to individuals instead of one home embracing a family. Truman marveled at the implication: "quite impersonal," he jotted down.[40] But it suited Herb Clutter's need for control. Said a neighbor, Herb never did anything that didn't benefit Herb Clutter. He was a driven man—"spare, quick, and dynamic in appearance"—wrote a *New York Times* reporter sent to interview him in 1954 as a paradigm of the modern farmer.[41] The only way he'd permit a natural gas company to drill on his land, for instance, was if he received a one-eighth share of the profits. He used some of the gas money to pump underground water for the farm. But since his royalty receipts paid to run the water pump, he was getting both gas and water for nothing. His home operated along the same lines: tight, efficient, and well-managed.

The two surviving Clutter daughters, Eveanna and Beverly, were the embodiments of women who grew up in such an environment. Arriving at the farm the day after the murders, they informed KBI investigators that they would like them to leave because there were things in the house they wanted. Detective Harold Nye, thinking about the shock they must have suffered, permitted them to enter certain rooms only. Once inside, they argued over furniture, knick-knacks, kitchen utensils—everything in sight—like magpies. "I mean, good Lord," said Nye, "here we had the murder of the entire family, and we're working this thing up and they were in the house fighting over the merchandise that was there."[42] Once, he stopped to listen when they had fallen silent. They were taking a break to play the piano and sing.

Four days after the murders, neither young woman showed much emotion during the funeral. Nelle overheard a mourner speculate later whether they were under sedation.[43] (By contrast, Bobby Rupp, Nancy's steady, who had sneaked into the funeral home to hold his girlfriend's hand one last time, sobbed for months whenever he heard the song "Teen Angel" on the radio.)[44] After the service, Eveanna promptly went to the high school to collect Kenyon's and Nancy's belongings, completely cool and collected, said Nancy's English teacher,

Mrs. Polly Stringer. Mrs. Stringer, fighting back tears because Eveanna looked so much like Nancy, was hoping Eveanna would let her keep the ribbon Nancy had worn in her hair the night she starred in the school play. But no, Nancy's sisters had to have that, too.[45] Hearing this, Nelle dubbed Eveanna "Miss Iceberg of 1959."[46]

The whole community was aghast when Beverly went ahead with her wedding the week after the murders. Invited guests who attended the ceremony at the First Methodist Church in Garden City were there out of a sense of loyalty to the family, but most had also been among the one thousand mourners at the four Clutters' memorial service. On the spot where just a few days earlier the caskets of her parents and brother and sister had been placed on biers, Beverly took her vows. The leftover funeral meats could truly have furnished the wedding feast. The sisters departed shortly thereafter with a vanload of furniture and clothing. In addition, they were each forty thousand dollars richer because Herb Clutter, by an eerie coincidence, had taken out a double-indemnity insurance policy on the day of his death.

For Nelle, it all added up with the material she had collected from the interviews—the house's interior, careful as a window display; the showy sanctimony of religious materials on view; and Mrs. Clutter, still an attractive woman in her midforties, sleeping apart from her husband and medicated for depression. Then there was Nancy, in her officelike bedroom, channeling sexual feelings into love objects such as stuffed toys appropriate for younger children. (The week of her death, her father had ordered her to break up with Bobby because Herb had caught the two petting, Nelle learned.)[47] And in the room next door to his sister's, Kenyon burrowed into his textbooks. No friends could link him to a girl. In school photographs, his face is completely without expression. In Herb Clutter's household, emotions were screwed down tight.

On one rare occasion Nancy had cracked. Mrs. Stringer told Nelle it had happened when she was giving the Clutter girl a ride home after school. As they were about to turn up the River Valley Farm's tree-lined lane, Nancy asked if they could please stop for a moment. Mrs. Stringer pulled over and waited. Groping for words, Nancy broke down: "If you only knew about Mother," she said, gasping between shuddering sobs.[48]

Nancy's mother was a casualty, but no one inside the family seemed to want to acknowledge it. "I can't worry about her," Herb snapped when someone in the community suggested they try the doctors at the Mayo Clinic.[49] Bonnie Clutter's emotional illness had left Nancy feeling utterly alone, deprived of female reassurance. Nelle spoke to a number of people who had known Nancy and her mother well, but she couldn't find "anything resembling a normal mother-daughter relationship. . . . Nancy was one of the lonely ones, not made any the less lonely by the fact that her days were spent in almost unceasing activity. . . ."[50]

Yet she was expected to carry on energetically, competently, like one of her father's employees. The normal concerns and feelings of a teenage girl had no place or outlet. She was a child, Nelle wrote sympathetically, "who had been trained by an expert to make every second and every penny count, bear her private sorrows in private and present a cheerful aspect to the public; she was taught early in life to take everything to God in prayer. . . . How did she maintain the outward semblance of a wholesome, extremely bright and popular sweet teenager without cracking at the seams? Her family life was ghastly."[51] In that light, Beverly and Eveanna's diamond-hard reserve offered its own explanation.

Bonnie Clutter was also victim of the pressure that had caused Nancy to burst into tears, Nelle believed. But she suffered the additional pain of being tormented by guilt by what she saw as her failure to measure up to Herb's expectations on every count. As if arguing for the deceased, Nelle characterized Bonnie as

> stomped into the ground by her husband's Christ-like efforts to regulate her existence. . . . She was probably one of the world's most wretched women: highly creative in instinct but with the creative will in her stifled over the years by a dominating husband. . . . She seems totally to lack a sense of achievement in any relationship; and truly so, for there's no indication that she was successful as a wife, a lover, a mother, a homemaker; or that she was successful as an effective personality in her own right or as Clutter's helpmate.[52]

The Clutters were an emotionally troubled family, and Nelle wrote pages of notes providing evidence of it. But in the end, Capote barely used her insights in the final version of what would become *In Cold Blood.* One reason was simple: a harsh view of a murdered family would have been unacceptable. Feeling sympathy for the innocent was natural, and Capote, who wanted literary fame and a bestseller, knew better than to alienate readers. But another reason why it was necessary to paint the Clutters in flattering hues emerged later. Originally, Truman had arrived in Kansas to write about the impact of multiple murders on a small town. After he got to know the killers, however—two unexpectedly intelligent men but without moral restraint—Capote saw possibilities for a story about the nature of evil. To tell it in the strongest dramatic terms, he needed a foil for evil that was unblemished—an idealized Clutter family. He was aware, of course, that Herb Clutter, the "master of River Valley farm," could be a hard man and not always the benevolent neighbor and paterfamilias that Herb himself wanted to be seen as. Local authorities, in fact, seriously entertained the theory at first that Clutter's inflexible attitude might have led to the murders. "Clutter prohibited hunters from hunting on his land," one deputy said. "Maybe one of them overrode Clutter's objections and ran into an argument that got out of hand."[53]

But in order to keep the Clutters consistent with his vision, Capote took the hunting scenario and turned it around. Early in *In Cold Blood,* he has Herb Clutter encounter some hunters trespassing on his land. In life, Herb would have sent them packing. The fictionalized Herb, on the other hand, is a model of Christian charity. When the trespassers "offered to hire hunting rights, Mr. Clutter was amused. 'I'm not as poor as I look. Go ahead, get all you can,' he said. Then, touching the brim of his cap, he headed for home and the day's work, unaware that it would be his last."[54]

It's a Hollywood fade-out by a writer with screenwriting experience who knew the importance of keeping the good guys separate from the bad guys.

THE DAY FOLLOWING THE visit to the farm, Monday, began the workweek leading up to Christmas on Friday, which would mean an enforced break in Nelle and Truman's research. The courthouse, library, and post office would be closed; even local law enforcement authorities would be hard to reach. To celebrate Christmas Day, the two would probably have to fall back on a holiday dinner special in the

Warren Hotel coffee shop—turkey, gravy, instant potatoes, and canned cranberry sauce.

The holidays were unavoidable; but it was also isolation, the inimical feature of the prairies, that was still interfering with their making steady progress. Truman had arrived in Kansas with no friends, and still he hadn't made any. Like a child going to camp for the first time, he had boarded the train in New York with a suitcase loaded with food, afraid there wouldn't be any he liked where he was going. On the other hand, he was aware of Nelle's ability to get along with people and tolerate his need for attention. "She is a gifted woman, courageous, and with a warmth that instantly kindles most people, however suspicious or dour," he later told his friend George Plimpton, for a 1966 *New York Times* interview, "The Story Behind a Nonfiction Novel."[55] But under the terms of their partnership in Garden City, she was only following his lead. So far, they hadn't been in a friendly social situation where she could model, in a sense, how to take Truman "Cappuchi"—which was indulgently, and with a big grain of salt.

On Christmas Eve, Nelle spent part of the day assembling a description of the Clutters' last evening, based on several interviews with Nancy's boyfriend, Bobby Rupp, who had stayed at their house watching television until 10:00 P.M. on November 14. Sometime after that, police estimated, the killers had arrived.

The phone rang in Nelle's room. It was Cliff Hope. "You and Truman going to be in town tomorrow?" he asked.

Nelle said they were.

"Any plans?"

None that she knew of.

"How about coming over for Christmas dinner?" He mentioned that he and his wife, Dolores, were having another couple over: Detective Alvin Dewey and his wife, Marie.[56]

She and Truman accepted.

THE HOPES LIVED IN a cream-colored, two-story house built in 1908 in Garden City—an old house by western standards—on Gillespie Place, a block-long street with a sign at either end announcing PRIVATE DRIVE: "an attempt to establish a small-town aristocracy at one time, I suppose," remarked one of the Hopes' daughters, Holly.[57] There were eleven houses on Gillespie Place: eight across from the

Hopes, and only three on their side. On Sundays, people tended to drive slowly past and stare.

Truman and Nelle arrived half an hour late because first he had to locate a gift bottle of J&B scotch, his favorite brand. During the introductions, Detective Al Dewey's wife, Marie, an attractive raven-haired woman, explained her southern accent by saying she was Kansan by marriage but Deep South by birth and upbringing—from New Orleans, in fact; to which Truman replied that he had been born in New Orleans and Nelle was from Alabama. "It was instant old home week," said Al Dewey.[58] Nelle, shaking hands, insisted everyone call her by her first name.

"Can I help in the kitchen?" she asked Dolores Hope.

"This way," Dolores replied happily. As the two women took twice-baked potatoes from the oven and put condiments in bowls to go with roast duck, the main course, Dolores found herself liking Nelle right away. "After you talked to her for three minutes, you felt like you'd known her for years. She was 'just folks'—interested in others, kind, and humorous."[59]

Dolores announced that dinner was ready, and the adults seated themselves in the dining room. The Hopes' four children—Christine, Nancy, Quentin, and Holly—sat at a miniature version of the grownups' table.

Looking around the scene, Truman realized it was a breakthrough in eliminating the town's suspicions about them, and he also knew Nelle deserved the thanks: "She was extremely helpful in the beginning when we weren't making much headway with the townspeople, by making friends with the wives of the people I wanted to meet," he later told Plimpton.[60] Here he was sharing a meal with Alvin Dewey, the coordinator of the Clutter investigation, who had completely stonewalled him just two weeks earlier. And as dinner got under way, Truman further learned that both couples, the Deweys and the Hopes, were bright, well-informed people, interested in him, Nelle, and books. "Reading was an unqualified good" in the Hope family, said Holly Hope, "a quiet pleasure, not requiring special equipment or adult supervision. The glass doors of the built-in china cabinet in the dining room were removed to make room for more books; magazines and newspapers accumulated on coffee tables and chairs until my mother took a stack to a neighbor or to a doctor's office. Even the rest of the household hesitated to interrupt a member of the family who was embarked on a story."[61] Al Dewey was a book lover, too; his ability to read deeply had helped him breeze through law enforcement training. Marie Dewey was secretary to Cliff Hope's father, former U.S. congressman Clifford R. Hope. Cliff, Jr., was a Harvard graduate; and Dolores wrote for the *Garden City Telegram.*

At last Truman was in his element with an audience; and the irrepressible raconteur leaned forward to signal that he was about to launch into one of his best tales. "Capote was the center," Al remembered. "What he had to say and the way he said it was usually intelligent and always interesting. His friend (she asked us to call her 'Nelle') was unaffected and charming. She joined everyone else in listening to Capote, never attempting to upstage or interrupt him. Capote talked about himself mostly . . . what he had written, who was suing him."[62]

Through it all, everyone took their cue from Nelle, who rocked back and forth with laughter at Truman's gossip and love of attention, and winked confidentially at the others when it was obvious Truman was stretching the truth. Dolores Hope said Nelle's motherly attitude was "almost like if you have a child who doesn't behave well" and begs people's indulgence.[63]

One of the Hopes' daughters, Holly, later author of *Garden City: Dreams in a Kansas Town,* said Christmas dinner that night brought together six people who became lifetime friends because they met on an intellectual level. "My experience in a small town is that there are always some people who have been involved in the arts and they like to keep up, but they might not have much opportunity. So when someone like Lee and Capote come through, it's a big deal. You just have to tap into it."[64]

By the end of the evening, Marie Dewey had invited Truman and Nelle to dinner at their house for red beans and rice—a real southern dinner. It was music to their ears. And Truman felt emboldened to ask a favor of Al. He and Nelle were going over to see Dr. Fenton, the coroner, the next day—would Al meet them there to smooth the way? Sure he would, Dewey said. Truman took to calling Al "Foxy"; and Dewey called him "pardner" in return.

"Harper Lee had a way of smiling as she explained in her soft drawl, 'Well, Truman is a genius, you know. He really is. He's a genius,'" said Dewey. "I don't know a lot about geniuses, but I could buy that."[65]

In retrospect, KBI detective Harold Nye, who by now was logging thousands of miles chasing down leads, saw the pattern developing. "Truman didn't fit in, and nobody was talking to him. But Nelle got out there and laid some foundations with people. She worked her way around and finally got some contacts with the locals and was able to bring Truman in."[66]

DR. ROBERT M. FENTON, the Finney County coroner, stammered the next day during introductions. And because Detective Dewey's presence implied that the visit had some official importance, Fenton was anxious to impress his visitors. He produced a report he'd written, drawn from firsthand observations made at the Clutter crime scene, which he had dictated at the time into a Dictaphone. At first, he tried reading important sections of the report aloud, but his stammer grew worse. Nelle and Truman said they were really more interested in getting answers to specific questions. Fenton relaxed and, with the help of gestures to aid him in descriptions, such as forming a circle with his thumb to indicate the size and shape of a wound, the interview went smoother.

At one point, Nelle got up to admire photographs of Dr. Fenton's three children on a wall. He switched on the office light so she could get a better look.[67] As Nelle kept him busy, Truman slipped around the desk and read Fenton's Dictaphone transcript for himself. Hurriedly, he memorized as much as he could, and scribbled down a passage about Mrs. Clutter in particular: "The bed covers are thrown back as though the patient had been in bed and awakened, put the robe on; lying on a stool in front of the dresser is a heating pad and a small bottle of Vicks nose drops. No sign of struggle seen."[68] Returning to his seat, he joined Nelle in asking Fenton a few more questions; finally, they thanked him for his time.

During the whole cloak-and-dagger episode with the transcript, Detective Dewey said nothing.[69]

NELLE AND TRUMAN ARRIVED at the Deweys' the following Wednesday night, December 30, at about 6:30 P.M. Marie Dewey had planned quite a spread: a shrimp-and-avocado salad (her mother had sent the avocados from New Orleans), red beans and rice cooked with bacon, cornbread, country-fried steak, and a bottle of sweet white wine. Al introduced the guests to the rest of the family: Alvin Dewey III, twelve; and Paul Dewey, nine.

Marie offered to get drinks for everyone—scotch and soda for Al, vodka and tonic for Nelle and Truman. Nelle invited little Alvin to sit beside her at the spinet piano and learn the bottom half of "Chopsticks," which he picked up immediately. Paul, not to be outdone, played "Auld Lang Syne" and "The Yellow Rose of Texas," one of his father's favorites.

For about an hour, the adults sat in the living room, getting better acquainted. (Two days earlier, Nelle and Marie had met for lunch at the Trail Room coffee shop and traded "girl talk" about how Marie and Al courted during World War II.) Al tried to play the role of good host, getting up from his easy chair to refresh drinks, but clearly the strain of seven weeks of relentless investigation was getting to him. His clothes hung loose; he drank three scotches, one right after the other. There was hardly a moment when a cigarette wasn't between his lips. Since the murders in mid-November, the KBI had received 700 tips; of those, he'd followed up on 205 on his own. Ninety-nine percent were worthless.

At about 8:00 P.M., dinner was ready. As everyone pulled up to the table, the phone rang for the sixth or seventh time since Nelle and Truman had arrived. Marie said it rang at all hours ever since the murders—always a call for Al about some aspect of the case. He got up to answer while they waited to begin eating. From his office down the hall, they could hear him talking louder and louder. When he returned a few minutes later, his voice crackled with excitement.

"Well, if you can keep a secret, this is *it*: our agent out in Las Vegas said they just nabbed those two guys . . . Smith and Hickock."

Marie started to cry. "Oh, honey . . . honey, I can't believe it."[70]

For Nelle and Truman, the news squared with what they had deduced on their own. A rumor had been percolating among the reporters at the Finney County Courthouse about a prisoner, Floyd Wells, in Lansing State Penitentiary, in Kansas, who read in the newspapers about the Clutter murders. Hoping to win a break from the prison authorities and claim the thousand-dollar reward offered by the *Hutchinson News*, Wells had told the warden about a former cellmate of his, Richard Hickock, who had planned to hook up with another guy, Perry Smith, and rob the Clutters. Hickock was convinced that Clutter must have plenty of cash because Wells, a former farm-hand on the Clutter place, had told him that there was a safe in the house. After Truman had found out as many details as he could about the rumor, he had written them up as incontrovertible fact, and carefully read a statement to Dewey one day at the courthouse to test his reaction. "Say, Dewey, I hear you've got a good lead going. . . . What do you think of this story out of the state prison?"[71] The bluff worked. Dewey shot Nelle a sharp look, lit a fresh cigarette, and refused to confirm or deny anything. But it was plain that they had hit the mark.

But now, in his euphoria, Dewey threw caution to the wind and put the pieces together for them. The call he had just received was from Detective Nye. The Las Vegas Police had taken into custody Smith, thirty-one, and Hickock, twenty-eight, for a minor traffic violation. Nye had been doing "setups" in several states, alerting the police to be on the lookout for them. As soon as Nye, Dewey, and a third KBI detective, Clarence Duntz, could get to Vegas, they would begin interrogating the suspects, who had been leaving a tantalizing trail of bad checks like bread crumbs all over the country. Dewey got up from the table to retrieve photographs of Smith and Hickock taken during previous arrests.

"I've been carrying those faces around in my head for weeks," Marie said.[72] One night she dreamed she saw Hickock and Smith at a booth in the Trail Room coffee shop. But she was so frightened she couldn't move.

Al handed around the black-and-white jailhouse portraits—front and side views.

Nelle thought Richard Hickock had a "ghastly face," due to a disfiguration that made one eye off-center and larger than the other. He was tall and well built. Perry Smith's face, on the other hand, struck Nelle as having eyes that showed a "certain shrewdness and intelligent cunning."[73] The floor-to-ceiling ruler behind him indicated that he was five foot four—exactly Truman's height.

Once everyone had studied the pictures, Al laid out the next steps. Smith and Hickock had been arrested with pairs of boots that matched prints on the Clutters' basement floor—a "Cats' paw" sole and a diamond-tread heel—an early break in the investigation that had been kept secret. (Marie opened a hall closet to retrieve a rubber boot belonging to one of the children to show what Al meant about tread patterns.) The evidence of the boots, plus the Lansing State Penitentiary convict's story, formed a pretty good circumstantial case. But the gold standard in court was signed confessions; Al would have to get out to Las Vegas as quickly as possible to assist in the interrogations. He got out a map and estimated that it would take about a day and a half to drive to Las Vegas if he, Clarence Duntz, and Roy Church left at 7:00 A.M. Nye had said he could fly there.

"There's a lot of desert between here and Las Vegas," Dewey said, tapping the map with his finger. "On the way back, I don't care if we only make sixteen miles a day. We'll just drive around and around until we've made them talk. One or the other, whichever's the weaker, we'll kill him with kindness. We've already got them separated . . . it shouldn't be long before we get them hating each other."

"Can I go with you?" Truman asked.

"Not this time, pardner."

From one of the pine cabinets in the kitchen, Dewey got out a bottle of crème de menthe, Marie's "special treasure," he said, and poured everyone a shot.[74]

Years later, Dewey insisted, "Capote got the official word on developments at the press conferences along with everyone else. Some people thought then, and probably still do, that he got next to me and got in on every move of the law. That was not so. He was on his own to get the material for his story or book. . . . That's the way things were when the good news finally came on December 30."[75]

Marie backed him up: "Alvin refused to talk about the case. We just visited, that's all. Our friendship developed in that way, but the investigation wasn't talked about."[76]

But Nelle's notes about everything that was said and done that night in the Deweys' home tell a different story.

THE ASSOCIATED PRESS AND United Press International broke the news of the arrests the next day. KBI director Logan Sanford had been struggling to keep the investigation under wraps until the last possible moment. A few days earlier, he had met privately with a reporter whose hunches about the suspects' names and motives were correct. Sanford asked the reporter to hold his story until Smith and Hickock were in custody; otherwise, they would be tipped off before the KBI agents could nab them. In exchange for the favor, Sanford promised he would later share everything the bureau had on the case. The reporter said he would wait. When his gentlemen's agreement with Sanford came to light, his newspaper fired him.[77]

Nelle and Truman, however, continued to receive updates about the case through their friendship with the Deweys. Marie kept them posted on Al's progress as he crawled over the plains through heavy snowstorms, calling on New Year's Eve while she kept busy taking down the Christmas tree. The travel situation was precarious, she told Nelle—timing was everything. The KBI detectives had to reach Smith and Hickock before they read about themselves in newspapers. The plan was to blindside them about the Clutter murders, then ratchet up the tension by mentioning the existence of an unnamed "living witness"—actually the convict who had bunked with Hickock in the Lansing State Penitentiary. Under pressure, Smith and Hickock might confess to the murders, figuring there was no use holding out. The day after New Year's, Marie felt so stressed she told Nelle she'd driven to the post office, realized she had forgotten the special air mail stamp she needed, and then run out of gas returning to get it.

While they waited for more news from Al, relayed by Marie, Nelle and Truman followed a routine they'd developed that was a far cry from their shaky start a little more than three weeks earlier. Usually they started the day by walking two blocks to radio station KIUL. The news director, Tony Jewell, didn't mind them sifting through the AP or UPI wire services stories that spooled through the clattering teletype machines. Eavesdropping on informal messages between reporters in Garden City and editors on faraway city desks sometimes provided leads for interviews. "Dave," began one note, "Tell the New York Times man that the undertaker, whose name I'm no longer sure of but I rather believe it's Palmer, loves the sound of his own voice and obviously would like all the publicity he can get. I suggest he try to keep the undertaker's wife out of the picture—she tries to shush her husband all the time."[78] The loquacious mortician would end up on their list of people to see. Next, a stop at the courthouse was always mandatory, in case a press conference was scheduled. But as a result of their pipeline through the Deweys, they knew more than any of the reporters did. These preliminaries out of the way, they went out into the field like anthropologists to continue with their interviews.

By now, they could paint Garden City in broad strokes as a community, even its social hierarchy of respected old families ("determined by the amount of land their ancestors homesteaded," Nelle noted).[79] Next they needed to focus in particular on the Clutters' network of friends to re-create Herb, Bonnie, Nancy, and Kenyon, in order to flesh out the portraits Nelle had created after the visit to River Valley Farm. It was the only way to see them alive—through the eyes of those who had known them well.

On January 2, while Dewey, Duntz, and Church were still plowing their way through snowstorms and toward Las Vegas, Nelle and Truman interviewed Nancy Clutter's best friend, Susan Kidwell. Susan shared a tiny pink-and-yellow apartment with her mother, made more cramped by a huge Hammond organ against one wall.

As Nelle listened quietly to Susan and Truman talk, a vision of what Nancy Clutter valued in a friend became clear. Susan was

completely against the grain of the majority of her contemporaries and life in Holcomb and G. C. [Garden City]," Nelle realized. "Pathetically sensitive and lonely; stands out on landscape like a fine and well-wrought thumb. Girl of remarkable sensibility for 15. . . . Every cut, every pleasure, everything shows in her eyes. . . . Loved Nancy as she loved no other person.[80]

Truman used a more cinematic eye to describe Susan, thinking perhaps he would use details to complement Nelle's insights:

Susan is very thin and extremely tall for her age." "[S]he has a broad-boned but thin and very expressive face, and a poor complection [sic]; nevertheless, she is an attractive girl with a good-speaking voice (low, and with rather elegant inflections) and a nice sense of humor. . . . She has long sensitive fingers; her hair is long, a sort of greenish/brownish blonde, and rolled up at the bottom. She has had an unhappy life; her father deserted Mrs. Kidwell some years ago etc. She and her mother live in a kind of genteel poverty (Mrs. Kidwell, "Of course, it's easy for you to see that we once had money").[81]

Occasionally, Nelle and Truman went their separate ways in Garden City, particularly when Nelle wanted to act as a listening post. "She

became friendly with all the churchgoers," Truman said.[82] The minu-
tiae she heard from the gossipers in Garden City that he might not
have heard contributed to the murmuring subtext that he later channeled into his narrative. "Nelle provided a number of insights and descriptions that Capote would have missed," said Dolores Hope.[83] For
instance, Nelle found out that Nancy Clutter bit her nails when she
was under stress; that the night of her starring role in the school play
she held hands backstage with someone besides her boyfriend, Bobby
Rupp (she liked to flirt, one of her teachers said); and afterward, she and
Rupp went to a scary midnight movie because it was Friday the thir-
teenth. Truman later combined these details into a simulated phone
conversation between Nancy and her best friend, Susan Kidwell:

"Tell," said Susan, who invariably launched a telephone session with
this command. "And, to begin, tell why you were flirting with Jerry
Roth." Like Bobby, Jerry Roth was a school basketball star.

"Last night? Good grief, I wasn't flirting. You mean because we
were holding hands? He just came backstage during the show. And
I was so nervous. So he held my hand. To give me courage."

"Very sweet. Then what?"

"Bobby took me to the spook movie. And *we* held hands."

"Was it scary? Not Bobby. The movie."

"He didn't think so; he just laughed. But you know me. Boo!—
and I fall off the seat."

"What are you eating?"

"Nothing."

"I know—your fingernails," said Susan, guessing correctly.[84]

It was the synergy of two writers at work in Garden City that
gave *In Cold Blood* such verisimilitude. Later, George Steiner, a re-
viewer for the *Manchester Guardian,* called the book "uncanny" when
it was published in 1965. "Looked at minutely enough, filtered
through the lens of a highly professional recorder, caught by the tape
recording ear in its every inflection and background noise, the most
sordid, shapeless of incidents, take on a compelling truth."[85]

Nelle scoured the town for information that might be useful to Truman, applied the eye of a novelist to identify elements of drama, and
opened doors of homes for him that otherwise might have remained

closed. And now, in early January 1960, with the killers caught and soon to be returned to Garden City, Truman was about to come into a windfall of privileged information, as a result of the friendship that Nelle had nurtured with the Deweys. If KBI director Logan Sanford had known the extent of the clandestine breach in bureau protocol that was opening wider and wider, the entire investigation would have been compromised.

ON SUNDAY MORNING, JANUARY 3, Marie Dewey phoned Nelle at the Warren Hotel to tell her, "Al made it."[86] Dewey had arrived in Las Vegas after midnight; Smith and Hickock had already signed waivers of extradition to Kansas, unaware that they were about to be questioned about the Clutter murders. Dewey expected to arrive back in Garden City late Tuesday or early Wednesday with both men in custody and, he hoped, a pair of confessions in hand.

The phantoms who had terrorized the community would be coming back. Until then, Nelle and Truman would just have to stay busy, biding their time. This being a Sunday just three days after New Year's Day, it was hard to overcome a feeling of lethargy. They spent most of the afternoon interviewing one person—the Clutters' housekeeper, Mrs. Helm—trying to get a better sense of how the family had lived. Despite his claims later that he never took notes, Truman either jotted down a few things in Mrs. Helm's presence or made notes afterward in a palm-size spiral pad he carried: "Mrs. Helm—did all laundry[.] Nancy did own housework. Saturday [the day of the murders]—had a large dinner. Steak—in sink soup bowls—3."[87]

That evening, while Nelle and Truman were having dinner at the Warren Hotel with a long-winded foreign correspondent, a waiter interrupted to say that there was a call at the front desk. It was Marie. Hickock had confessed—why didn't they come over right away for a celebration? Abruptly they extended apologies to their surprised dinner partner and made a quick getaway to the Deweys'.

Marie, Nelle, and Truman stayed up late discussing the case. Marie was feeling light as a feather and in the mood to talk about Al and his career in law enforcement. Around 10:45, Dewey called from Vegas to speak to Truman. Hickock's confession was Nancy Clutter's birthday present, Al said, she would have turned seventeen that day. Now Smith, hearing that Hickock had confessed, would likely crack, too. All four KBI detectives—Dewey, Nye, Church, and Duntz—were about to go out on the town and have some fun. Truman recommended the Sands Hotel Casino in the center of the Las Vegas Strip. Marie, proud to bursting about Al's work, brought out Christmas cards from convicts as proof that he cared about the men he had helped put away.

The next day, Nelle filled three single-spaced, typewritten pages with everything she and Truman had heard. "Truman and Nelle were pretty damn good interrogators themselves," commented Nye later. "And they played Al and Marie both—it was obvious."[88]

On Monday morning, KBI director Logan Sanford, standing in for Al Dewey, held a press conference at the courthouse and announced to reporters that the suspects were on their way from Las Vegas and would get in sometime late Tuesday afternoon. Nelle met Marie at the Trail Room coffee shop for lunch after the press conference. A highway patrolman stopped by their table and asked Marie to call him when Al was about fifty miles away from Garden City, so his men could prepare for the big crowd expected outside the courthouse. After he left, Marie promised to call Nelle, too, the moment she heard anything.[89]

There was an anxious sense in the air of the curtain about to rise on the second act. Nelle and Truman, feeling too fidgety to start anything fresh, spent the rest of the afternoon just wandering around. With no particular purpose in mind, they walked the few blocks to the courthouse. In a hallway, they bumped into six-foot-four Duane West. West, twenty-eight, was just beginning a second two-year term as Finney County prosecutor, and was excited about the prospect of grilling Hickock and Smith in the courtroom. He was talkative in the glare of television lights, but when Nelle and Truman wanted a word with him, he wouldn't give them the time of day. From his suit pocket he produced an envelope, which, he showed them with a flourish, was addressed to "Mr. Duane (Sherlock Holmes) West." Nelle held her tongue, but jotted in her notes, "D.W. a slob."[90]

They climbed the stairs to Undersheriff Wendle Meier's office. Just deposited in the undersheriff's office as prime evidence was the shotgun used in the murders, which the KBI had found in plain sight at the home of Hickock's parents. The Savage 300 model twelve-gauge looked practically brand-new. Examining it, Nelle noticed someone had scratched *M* or maybe *H* near the trigger. It was an unexceptional weapon, the kind that any hunter, proud of his new purchase from a sporting goods store, might take into the fields on an autumn day.

With two hours of winter daylight remaining, the pair decided to drive the mile or so out on North Third Street to Valley View Cemetery, where the Clutters had been laid to rest. They hadn't visited the graves yet, but now, with the killers in custody, it seemed fitting that they should.

The sun was going down when they arrived, and it was cold. The cemetery was eighty-three acres, half of it unused. In the 1890s, a group of settler women had tried to beautify the prairie burial ground with trees and bushes, hauling barrels filled with water twice a day to nourish the plantings. But the long, brutal droughts of the Dust Bowl years in the 1930s had wiped out their efforts. Truman and Nelle walked the rows until finally—in Zone A, Lot 470, spaces 1–4—they came upon the mounded graves of Nancy, Kenyon, Herb, and Bonnie Clutter. The upturned earth was marked with the names of the interred, but there were no headstones yet or any signs of remembrance. Nelle found the scene "desolate and lonely in the extreme."[91]

Late that night, Al Dewey called Marie with a message for Truman: "I killed him with kindness." In the car during the ride across the desert, Smith had confessed.[92]

HUNDREDS OF GARDEN CITY and Holcomb residents prepared to brave the blustery weather, with a temperature cold enough to bring on snow, on Tuesday, January 5, the day scheduled for Smith and Hickock's arrival. At the Deweys' house, Nelle and Truman had deposited a fresh bottle of J&B scotch with a note attached:

Dear Foxy,

After your long and heroic journey, we are certain you will appreciate a long swig of this.
So: welcome home!

From your ever faithful historians
Truman
Nelle[93]

KBI chief Logan Sanford had said only that the suspects were due "late Tuesday afternoon," so Nelle and Truman showed up at the courthouse at around 3:00 P.M. to wait for word from Sheriff Earl Robinson's office. The hallway was filled with bored newsmen smoking and waiting. Nelle found a Coors beer ashtray to crush out her cigarette butts, and settled in. Out of the corner of her eye, she caught a glimpse of *Garden City Telegram* editor Bill Brown, who had figured out that she and Truman had some kind of pull with Dewey. He wasn't the only one, he said later. "I was busy talking to other KBI agents and local sheriff's officers who moaned about Dewey paying more attention to Truman than the case at hand."[94] A little after four, the radio dispatcher announced to everyone that Finney County prosecutor Duane West would have to delay a press conference until 5:00 P.M. A highway patrol captain appeared, champing on a cigar, and gave instructions to the press to keep the sidewalk clear. Nelle assumed that a crowd must be gathering, and she went outside to see it. The overcast sky was cold enough to snow, but bystanders in twos and threes were beginning to fill the square.

> The thermometer was dropping and T's ears (good barometer) were red; my feet numb. We had stood for perhaps twenty minutes when we were aware that a few teenagers grouped under a tree nearby was now a definite crowd. Two Holcomb High basketball jackets in the midst. As they waited, the teenagers squirmed, wriggled, fought mock battles; the girls giggled and flirted with the photographers—two ran over to the press line and asked to be photographed. . . .
>
> At first the photographers were professionally eager & avid to get their work done, but as time passed and the afternoon grew colder, fingers became rigid, feet stamped, jokes turned bluer.[95]

A reporter asked a middle-aged man standing near the sidewalk if death would be sufficient punishment for the killers. "Like in the Bible," he replied. "An eye for an eye. And even then, we're two short." Truman overhead the comment and included it in *In Cold Blood*.[96] A photographer asked a gum-chewing little boy named Johnny Shobe to blow a big bubble, but the air was so cold that the trick worked only after several tries.

By 6:00 P.M., the crowd was four or five deep and had never stopped murmuring. Newsmen stamped their feet and blew on their hands. Then suddenly someone shouted, "They're coming!"

At the curb, two dark mud-splashed sedans rolled to a halt. Al Dewey got out of the backseat of the first car; then, quickly, a handful of other men exited both cars, as if on cue. The figures strode quickly up the sidewalk and toward the courthouse. It had grown so dark that the photographers' flashbulbs acted like strobe lights and caught them in midstep. There were no jeers, no catcalls from the crowd. Everyone seemed strangely struck dumb. Dewey had the arm of Perry Smith, who was a head shorter than Al and wearing dungarees and a black leather jacket. Hickock came next, also accompanied by a detective, but Nelle couldn't get a good look because a broad-backed policeman had stepped in front of her. When the platoon of suspects and detectives sprinted up the courthouse steps, Nelle, Truman, and the reporters surged after them.

They went up to the second floor where a large room had been set aside for a press conference. A few seats were still open in the front row before a table with four microphones. TV lights were switched on and lit up the place like day. Dewey sat down behind a mike and said, "Hello, Bill," to Bill Brown, and then smiled down at Nelle and Truman.

Questions came pell-mell from the reporters, but Dewey seemed to enjoy playing poker with everyone. Yes, the suspects had confessed, but no reporters would be allowed to listen to their taped interrogations or statements. Right now, Smith and Hickock were being held upstairs in the fourth-floor jail. They would be arraigned tomorrow morning.

"What time did you get in?" someone shouted.

"About five o'clock," Dewey said cryptically. It was 6:30 P.M. (The entourage had stopped to look unsuccessfully for evidence that Smith and Hickock claimed they had buried by a roadside.)

Duane West tried to direct some attention his way, but no one was interested. The press conference sputtered to an end.

Outside the courthouse, the crowd had dispersed, leaving a few pop bottles and candy wrappers in the grass. Truman was disgusted. He expected the return of the killers to be dramatic. Why had everyone just stood there gawking? And that press conference! The whole thing, he complained to Nelle as they walked back toward the hotel, was "a debacle."[97]

THE NEXT MORNING, THE sound of a heavy iron door clanking shut overhead signaled that Smith and Hickock were coming down for their arraignment. Nelle, Truman, and about thirty-five members of the press had been waiting for an hour in the wood-paneled Finney County Courtroom since 10:00 A.M. Probate judge M. C. Schrader, a formal-looking, white-haired man in a dark suit, entered the courtroom and took his place behind the bench. ("Central casting judge," Nelle noted.)[98] She also noticed that the U.S. flag above him had forty-eight stars, although Alaska and Hawaii had become the forty-ninth and fiftieth states the previous year.

Hickock entered the courtroom first, without handcuffs, but flanked by sheriff's deputies, who directed him to sit in a chair at the very front. The glare of floodlights set up for television cameras enabled Nelle to see him as if he were an actor under stage lights. He was about five foot ten, she estimated, blue-eyed and clean-shaven with his dark blond hair in a crew cut. His clothes were drab: gray khaki trousers, blue denim prisoner's workshirt, brown shoes, and white socks. He rubbed his chin thoughtfully to reveal a large cat tattoo on his left hand. His face, misshapen as a result of a car accident, intrigued Nelle: "as if someone cut it down the middle, then put it back together not quite in place," a description Truman later changed to "It was as though his head had been halved like an apple, then put together a fraction off center."[99] As the judge read the charges against Hickock—four counts of first-degree murder—the defendant listened, eyes downcast and hands clasped. Nelle noticed that a muscle in his jaw twitched at the mention of Nancy Clutter's name.

"Would you like to have a preliminary hearing?" Judge Schrader asked.

"I'd like to waive a preliminary hearing," replied Hickock, in a Kansas rural-accented voice that most people would associate with the way cowboys talk. With that, and a few additional perfunctory remarks from the judge, Hickock returned upstairs.

Smith entered moments later. A short man with a ginger complexion and coal black hair, indicating his heritage as the son of a Native American mother, he wore clothes similar to Hickock's, except that

Smith's jeans were rolled at the cuffs, and his black shoes had a high polish. Heavy sideburns seemed to be an attempt to add seriousness to a face that was feminine and winsome. His dark brown eyes under long lashes glanced around at the reporters.

"Look," Truman whispered to Nelle as Smith sat back in the chair near the judge, "his feet don't touch the floor!"[100] It was an admiring remark that surprised her, but she understood its meaning: Truman was infatuated. Smith's size and demeanor seemed weirdly familiar. His dark coloring was a complement to Truman's fair skin and blond hair. Capote thought he was seeing his doppelganger. "I think every time Truman looked at Perry he saw his own childhood," Nelle told *Newsweek* later.[101] Composer and author Ned Rorem went further. Over dinner in 1963, Truman talked about his progress on *In Cold Blood*. To Rorem, he "seemed clearly in love" with Smith.[102]

Judge Schrader followed the same ponderous but necessary procedural reading of the charges against Smith. Nelle got the impression that Smith was pressing his lips together, trying not to cry. At the mention of Nancy Clutter's name, Hickock had reacted almost imperceptibly. Smith, on the other hand, sighed and squinted at the bright lights when the judge charged him with the murder of Herb Clutter. The last thing he had said to Clutter before killing him, Smith confessed to Dewey, was that "it wasn't long till morning, and how in the morning somebody would find them and then all of it, me and Dick and all, would seem like something they'd dreamed."[103]

"I wish to waive my rights to a preliminary hearing," Smith replied to Judge Schrader. Then, his appearance over, he pulled "himself up to his full minute height," in Nelle's words, and walked briskly from the room.[104] A reporter burst from his seat with the other newspeople and hurried after Smith, shooting photos. Prosecutor Duane West, watching the spectacle, angrily threw down a sheaf of papers.

Despite Al Dewey's announcement to the press that no one would be allowed to interview the suspects or listen to their tape-recorded confessions, all it took was a pair of fifty-dollar checks drawn on a New York bank and made out separately to Perry Smith and Richard Hickock for Nelle and Truman to talk to them on Monday, January 11. Dewey arranged for the meeting to take place in his office, with Smith's and Hickock's lawyers present.

Resting up at home the previous Saturday, Dewey had recounted for Nelle and Truman, step by step, what Smith had said during his interrogation. He "went into extraordinary detail about the crime," Dewey said, paraphrasing as much of Smith's confession as he could recall. Hickock was in another room, being questioned, but Smith's descriptions re-created the night of the murders so thoroughly that Hickock was nailed, too.[105] Thinking about what they would ask the killers, Nelle and Truman decided to skip over the crime, since that would become a matter of record anyway, and get them to talk about themselves instead.

On Monday morning, Dewey scooted a couple of extra chairs into his office. Smith came in first. Seeing that Nelle was standing, he waited for her to be seated. He acted as solemn as a "small deacon," Nelle thought, "feet together, back straight, hands together: could almost see a celluloid collar and black narrow tie, so prim he was."[106] Truman was ready with handwritten questions. Reflecting the fashionable interest in Freudian psychology at the time, he wanted to launch into a series of prepared questions about Smith's attitudes toward marriage, his father, and other introspective topics.[107]

Gently, Smith waved aside the questions after he heard the first few. His attorney hadn't briefed him about this meeting. "What's the purpose of your story?" he wanted to know. Nelle was taken aback by his condescending tone. Its purpose, they assured him, was to give him a chance to tell his side of the story. Nelle smiled at him several times, but his large eyes kept flicking away from hers.[108] He clearly felt "cornered and suspicious," Truman realized. To everything they asked over the next twenty minutes, Smith countered with "I decline," "I do not care to," or "I will think it over." Some kind of cat-and-mouse game was under way. After he returned to his cell, Nelle commented in her notes, "Rough going."[109]

Hickock, on the other hand, breezed in, ready for a good bull session. He plunked down in a chair before Nelle was seated. "Never seen anyone so poised, relaxed, free & easy in the face of four 1st-degree murder charges," Nelle marveled. "He gave the impression of being completely in the moment, with no concern about tomorrow's troubles."[110]

Nelle and Truman expressed admiration for Hickock's tattoos, which worked like a charm in unlocking his affability. Soon, he was talking about his favorite reading subject matter (motors or engineering); his vision of the good life (well-done steaks, gin rickeys, screwdrivers, dance music, and Camel cigarettes—he bummed five smokes from Nelle's pack); how often he liked to eat (three times a day, but in jail it was only two); how he'd like to get a good job in an auto shop and pay off the bad checks he'd written and live in the country. Then he segued to describing the high times he and Smith had had traveling around Mexico before they got caught in Las Vegas. It was practically more than Nelle and Truman could absorb. Truman said Hickock was "like someone you meet on a train, immensely garrulous, who starts up a conversation and is only too obliged to tell you *everything.*"[111] Nelle tried to get questions in edgeways, to which Hickock would reply, "Yes, ma'am," and then commence spinning another yarn. "No trace of the Smith syndrome," Nelle commented dryly in her notes.[112]

Hickock would have extended his stay, except that Dewey had something he wanted to share with Nelle and Truman, so the suspect was shut off like a valve and taken back to his cell.

AFTER HICKOCK HAD GONE, Dewey reassured Nelle and Truman, telling them not to worry if Smith wanted to play it cagey. Reaching into the Clutter case file in his desk, he produced for them the pièce de résistance: the transcripts of Smith's interrogations. Like dialogue from a play, the pages of transcribed conversation between Smith and the two KBI detectives, Dewey and Clarence Duntz, contained everything said in the nine-by-ten interrogation room during the three and a half hours that Smith was questioned in Las Vegas. The transcript couldn't leave the courthouse, and was too much for Nelle to copy, so she targeted key passages. As she worked, Dewey added visual descriptions that weren't evident on the tape.

> AL: Perry, you have been lying to us, you haven't been telling the truth. We know where you were on that weekend—you were out at Holcomb, Kansas, seven miles west of Garden City, murdering the Clutter family.
>
> (Perry white; swallowed a couple of times. Long pause.)
>
> PERRY: I don't know anybody named Clutter, I don't know where Garden City or Holcomb is—
>
> AL: You'd better get straightened out on this deal and tell us the truth—

PERRY: I don't know what you're talking about . . . I don't know what you're talking about.

(Al & Duntz rise to go.)

AL: We're talking to you sometime tomorrow. You'd better think this over tonight. Do you know what today is? Nancy's Clutter's birthday. She would have been seventeen.[113]

When Nelle had finished copying as much as she could, Dewey let them see another piece of evidence: Nancy Clutter's diary, containing three years' worth of entries. Since the age of fourteen, Nancy had recorded, in three or four sentences every night, the day's events and her thoughts about family, friends, pets, and, later, her adolescent love affair with Bobby Rupp. Different colored ink identified the years. Nelle and Truman riffled through the pages. The final entry was made approximately an hour before Nancy's death. Nelle copied it down.[114]

With the seal on the KBI investigation broken, any pretense that Al Dewey was protecting the case from Nelle and Truman's prying eyes was dropped. They spent most of the rest of the week working out of his office. Harold Nye, shortly before his death in 2003, complained that Dewey was only supposed to "take care of the press, the news media, take our reports in, send them to the office, and be the office boy. But he was playing footsie with Truman and Nelle." Apparently, however, Nye, too, was brought into the loop. He later said, "Nelle and I would just stand in the corner or sit down on a chair and casually talk. But she was good, she was good."[115]

On Wednesday, January 13, Nye provided her with all the information he'd gleaned along the way while he pursued Hickock and Smith through the Plains and the Southwest, including his stop at the home of Smith's sister in San Francisco—disguised, he later wrote to Truman, as a local policeman pretending to be following up on Smith's parole violation. ("She was such a nice lady, and I always felt like a dirty dog for pulling that trick.")[116] In addition, he gave Nelle the inventory of items found in Smith and Hickock's stolen car; and finally, as Nelle copied Hickock's interrogation, or listened to a tape of it—it isn't clear which—Nye interrupted to add background or clarify the suspect's remarks. On Friday, Truman paid another fifty dollars each to Smith and Hickock to interview them, and this time Smith was much more forthcoming. He had decided, he said—once again exhibiting his strange sense of self-importance—to tell his story as a cautionary tale to others. Fortunately for those others, Nelle and Truman evidently resorted to hiding a tape recorder in the room, having been overwhelmed by Hickock's talkativeness. In her notes on Smith, Nelle says parenthetically, "I can hardly hear a word he says."[117]

No one else outside the investigation was granted anything close to the access Nelle and Truman had. The *Hutchinson News,* for example, was the first newspaper permitted to interview the killers, and that was more than a week after Nelle and Truman had talked to them. Had it not been for their friendship with Al Dewey—brought about by Nelle's making a favorable impression with people when Truman was perceived as "an absolute flake" and "uppity"—they would have been stopped cold.

In fairness, they were not like the journalists on the scene, either. As Bill Brown of the *Garden City Telegram* pointed out, "My deadline was immediate; Capote's was years away."[118] (Actually, at that time, Capote was still thinking in terms of a magazine article.) Capote may have given Dewey and Nye his word that he would be working on his article for months, at least—well beyond the date of a trial. There would be no leaks. And in those days of speedier justice, Smith and Hickock went to trial in late March, only three months after being captured. Still, the risk Dewey took was enormous. Looking back, Harold Nye, who became director of the KBI in 1969, thought better about the extent of his involvement, too. Dusting over his tracks, he said later, "I really get upset when I know that Al gave them a full set of the reports. That was like committing the largest sin there was, because the bureau absolutely would not stand for that at all. If it would have been found out, he would have been discharged immediately from the bureau."[119]

Dewey would never admit he'd let the cat out of the bag. "I never treated Truman any differently than I did any of the other news media after the case was solved. He kept coming back, and we naturally got better acquainted. But as far as showing him any favoritism or giving him any information, absolutely not. He went out on his own and dug it up. Of course, he got much of it when he bought the transcript of record, which was the whole court proceedings, and if you had that, you had the whole story."[120]

*   *   *

LOADED WITH NOTES FROM interviews, transcribed interrogations, newspaper clippings, some photos Truman had snapped, sketches of the Clutter farmhouse, and any copies Dewey had given them, Nelle and Truman boarded the luxury Santa Fe Super Chief on January 16 in Garden City. It was snowing hard, and they settled in for the forty-hour ride to Dearborn Street Station in Chicago. Over the course of approximately a month, they had gathered enough to lay the foundation of a solid magazine article for the *New Yorker*. They would have to return for Smith and Hickock's trial in March. If the two men were sentenced to death, should their execution be part of the story? It was a grisly thought. Before his ideas escaped him, Truman wrote some notes on a Santa Fe cocktail napkin.

Nelle, of course, had plenty of other things to think about. As soon as she returned to New York, she would have to go over the galleys of *To Kill a Mockingbird*—a painstaking but nevertheless thrilling task for a first-time novelist. There was a small change she was thinking of making. The Kansas state motto, "Ad astra per aspera"—To the stars through difficulties—struck her as the right theme for the agricultural pageant that takes place in the fictional town of Maycomb at the end of the book. It sounded hopeful.

As she watched Truman in the seat opposite hers, musing out the window of the train, it probably seemed incredible that her novel would be in bookstores in a few months. Then she would have the right to call herself a writer, though not in Truman's league by any means. All she hoped for was a "quick and merciful death at the hands of reviewers."[121]

The Super Chief was delayed for six hours along the route, and when they arrived in Chicago, they had already missed their New York Central connection. They stayed in the city overnight and departed the next day, arriving in New York on Wednesday, January 20.

"Returned yesterday—after nearly 2 months in Kansas: an extraordinary experience, in many ways the most interesting thing that's ever happened to me," Truman wrote to his friend the photographer Cecil Beaton. "But I will let you read about it—it may amount to a small book."[122]

WHILE SHE WAS WAITING to return with Truman to Kansas, Nelle had the bittersweet experience of reading the galleys of her first novel.

This is how it would look, for better or worse. Although she was cautioned not to make significant changes, she kept seeing places she wanted to change.[123]

Two months later, she and Truman were back in Kansas for the trial, scheduled to begin the third week of March. By coincidence, the Clutters' farm was going up for auction the same week.

They left behind a late snowy season in New York. A wet, warm spring had come to western Kansas. Nelle and Truman drove out to River Valley Farm on Sunday, March 21, to witness the sale. Bumper-to-bumper traffic met them at the entrance to the lane lined with elms, which were just beginning to cast a hint of shade. After crawling toward the house at a speed slower than a walk, they were waved into a muddy parking area strewn with hay. The sunny weather in the low seventies had brought out more than four thousand people for the largest farm auction in western Kansas history. There were cars and trucks from Colorado, Nebraska, and Oklahoma, and practically every county in Kansas west of Newton and Wichita. Auctioneer John Collins, his white shirt shining in the sun, sold everything of value to a swarm of men in coats and Stetsons—tools, tractors, and farm implements. "Herb had a lot of good stuff," Clutter's brother, Arthur, commented.[124] Two weeks earlier, the Clutter sisters, Eveanna and Beverly, had leased the land, the house, and all the buildings to a businessman from Oklahoma. Inside a big Quonset hut forty yards from the house, the Ladies Circle of Holcomb Community Church sold $500 worth of hamburgers, ham sandwiches, and pieces of pie.

On Tuesday, jury selection began. For the first time since the courthouse was erected in 1929, the varnished church-type pews were slid to the sides and rear to leave room at the front for a special press table and thirteen chairs. Bill Brown of the *Garden City Telegram* handed out press passes, including one apiece for Truman and Nelle identifying them as representatives of the the *New Yorker*. Truman had brought along photographer Richard Avedon, who had to be content to sit on the side. The men at the press table, pleased to see Nelle back, had taken to calling her "Little Nelle."[125] Someone asked, tongue-in-cheek, if Nelle and Truman would be coming back for the trial of the screwball that was poisoning dogs in Garden City—a total of twelve, according to the front page of the day's *Telegram*.

A little before ten o'clock, district judge Roland Tate entered—a changed man, most folks noticed, since the death of his small son several years before—and took his seat on the bench. Courthouse custodian Louis Mendoza had spent most of Monday unsuccessfully trying to locate a U.S. flag with fifty stars on it, until Judge Tate instructed him to put the one with forty-eight back up. While Nelle and Truman had been out of town, Tate had weighed the youth and lack of experience of Finney County prosecutor Duane West and appointed a special prosecutor to assist him: Logan Green, who "looks like a mottled tough old piece of steak and has the voice to go with it," Nelle wrote. "He is going to be hell on the defense witnesses. Has a remarkable ease of delivery, of forming questions, of saying exactly what he wants to say exactly how he wants to say it."[126] The court-appointed counsel for Richard Hickock's defense, Arthur Fleming, nodded to Logan Green and said, "Cool morning." Perry Smith's attorney, Harrison Smith (no relation), also court-appointed, pulled a chair up to the defense table, dressed like a "symphony in blue-gray," in Nelle's estimation.[127] Overhead, the telltale metallic clunk of the jail door announced that Perry and Dick were coming down.

The effects of sitting in jail for two months told on the two men. Nelle noticed Smith was softly rounder. "His thighs are like Lillian Russell's." Dick Hickock: "fatter, greener, and more gruesome."[128] Outwardly, the two men seemed bored, covering perhaps for being stared at by the forty-four prospective jurors who had assembled in the courtroom to be sworn in and questioned. District court clerk Mae Purdy called the jurors' names in a droning voice. Only four were women.

By day's end, the jury was composed entirely of men, including the reserve of alternates. Half were farmers. Smith, an amateur artist, had passed the time sketching on a legal pad. Hickock chomped relentlessly on a wad of gum, his chin resting on his hand now and then. The two men had implicated each other in their confessions, but there seemed to be no visible rupture in their relationship. Nelle saw Hickock glance at Perry Smith just once, "the briefest exchanges of glances, and the old eye rolled coldly. . . . Perry looked at him—gave Hickock one of his melting glances—really melting in its intensity— Hickcock felt eyes upon him, looked around and smiled the shadow of a smile."[129]

As expected, the turnout for the trial exceeded the courtroom's capacity of 160 persons. "Our trial was more like a circus than anything else," Dick Hickcock complained to reporter Mack Nations of *Male* magazine. "It took only one day to choose the jury. . . . The courtroom overflowed with spectators and the halls were lined with photographers and newspaper reporters. Every exit was covered by a pair of highway patrolmen. Extra deputy sheriffs were brought in from neighboring counties. . . . I never did think much of the Finney County Attorney and I sure liked him less after our first day in court. He kept pointing his finger at me and telling the jury how no good I was. I resented it."[130]

At the press table, Associated Press reporter Elon Torrence noticed that Truman, dressed in a blue sports jacket, khaki trousers, white shirt, and a bow tie, spent most of his time listening, while Nelle, bringing to bear her incomplete law school training, "took notes and did most of the work during the trial."[131]

There were no surprises. "How cheap!" exclaimed special prosecutor Logan Green in his closing argument to the jury. "The loot was only about eighty dollars, or twenty dollars a life." Harrison Smith and Arthur Fleming, attorneys for the accused, did not contest the state's evidence but pleaded for life imprisonment. Smith argued that capital punishment is "a miserable failure." The jury deliberated less than two hours.

On Tuesday, March 29, Judge Roland Tate sentenced both men to hang. "When the judge was telling the jury what a good job they had done," Hickcock told *Male* magazine,

> I thought that these pompous old ginks were the lousiest looking specimens of manhood I had ever seen; old cronies that acted like they were God or somebody. Right then I wished every one of them had been at the Clutter house that night and that included the Judge. I would have found out how much God they had in them! If they had been there and had any God in them I would have let it run out on the floor. I thought, boy, I'd like to do it right here. Now there was something that would have really stirred them up!
>
> When the jury filed out of the courtroom not one of them would look at me. I looked each one in the face and I kept thinking, Look at me, look at me, look at me!
>
> But none of them would.[132]

Street Scene, looking South,
Monroeville, Ala.

Nelle Harper Lee's street in Monroeville, Alabama, when she was a child.
Her house was about where the car is parked.

A. C. Lee, the model for Atticus
Finch: civic leader, politician, and
title lawyer in the late 1930s.

Frances Cunningham Lee: a sensitive
woman whose "nervous disorder"
bewildered her youngest child, Nelle.

A cabin outside Monroeville during the Great Depression, like one Lee would have imagined belonged to her characters Tom Robinson or Bob Ewell. *(Library of Congress)*

The sophomore class of Monroe County High School. Nelle (second row from top, farthest right) adored her English teacher, Gladys Watson (top row, center).

Nelle (far right) poses stiffly with two classmates at Huntingdon College in Montgomery, Alabama, on a Sunday afternoon during her freshman year.

A happier Nelle (second from left) found her niche at the University of Alabama writing for campus publications. Here she appears in the 1948 yearbook as a "Campus Personality."

A snapshot of Nelle in downtown Garden City, Kansas, during the winter of 1959–60. *(Garden City Telegram)*

"Just plain handsome" is how Detective Alvin Dewey impressed Nelle the first time she met him while accompanying Truman Capote as his "assistant researchist" during the Clutter murders investigation in Kansas. *(AP Photo)*

A beaming Truman, with copies of *In Cold Blood* under his arm in 1966, being filmed by Albert and David Maysles for the National Educational Television program *U.S.A.: The Novel. (Bruce Davidson/Magnum Photo)*

Nelle (far left) with Dutch and Fern Hafner, brother- and sister-in-law of her agent, Maurice Crain. The occasion is a publication party for *To Kill a Mockingbird*, due out the next day, July 12, 1960. The sheet cake resembles the cover of the novel. Nelle was just hoping for a "quick and merciful death at the hands of the reviewers." *(Photograph courtesy of Joy Hafner Bailey)*

Lee and producer Alan Pakula watch the filming of *To Kill a Mockingbird* in 1962. Nelle endured a punishing promotional tour after the film's release, using her teasing wit to charm reporters. *(AP Photo)*

Lee and Gregory Peck as Atticus Finch on the production set. Lee doubted his suitability for the role at first— she had Spencer Tracy in mind. *(Corbis)*

Alice Lee, Nelle's elder sister, an attorney and editor of the local newspaper like her father. Though petite, her nickname in the family is Bear. *(The United Methodist Church)*

During a meeting of the National Council of the Arts in Tarrytown, New York, 1966, some of the members take a break. (Back to front) Nelle Lee; Roger Stevens, Broadway impresario; R. Philip Hanes, business executive; Agnes de Mille, dancer and choreographer. *(Photograph courtesy of R. Philip Hanes)*

Nelle Lee attends Celebration of a Decade, a Los Angeles Public Library Awards Dinner held in her honor in 2005. *(Corbis)*

This jury was no different from others in not looking at the defendants, Nelle wrote. "Why they never look at people they've sentenced to death, I'll never know, but they don't."[133]

Back in his cell, Perry Smith slipped a note with his signature on it between two bricks in the wall: "To the gallows . . . May 13, 1960."[134]

Mockingbird Takes Off

IN SPRING 1960, NELLE PRESENTED TRUMAN WITH 150 PAGES of typed notes, organized by topics including the Landscape, the Crime, Other Members of the Clutter Family, and so on. Truman, feeling expansive as he rested in Spain after several months of working on the outline for *In Cold Blood,* was suddenly in the mood to make one of his gossipy pronouncements, for it was immensely satisfying to him that his protégé—which is how he now regarded Nelle— had written a publishable novel in which he was an important character. Obviously, he loved the idea of being mythologized. To his society friends, film producer David O. Selznick and Selznick's wife, Jennifer Jones, he wrote, "On July 11th [1960], Lippincott is publishing a delightful book: TO KILL A MOCKINGBIRD by Harper Lee. Get it. It's going to be a great success. In it, I am the character called 'Dill'—the author being a childhood friend."[1]

On the evening before *To Kill a Mockingbird*'s publication, Maurice Crain and Annie Laurie Williams threw Nelle a cozy party in an apartment at 240 First Avenue in New York City. As guests began arriving, some of the small talk was about politics. The latest issue of *Time* magazine, just out that day, featured a cover photo of Democratic hopeful for the presidency John Kennedy, his wife Jacqueline, and Kennedy's parents. In just two days, the Democratic convention would get under way in Los Angeles. Hold-out liberals were hoping that efforts to draft moderate Adlai Stevenson from Illinois would bump Kennedy at the last minute. But JFK was already drafting a convention acceptance speech that included the words "We stand today on the edge of a new frontier—the frontier of the 1960s—a frontier of unknown opportunities and perils—a frontier of unfulfilled hopes and threats."

The hosts circulated around the apartment—actually the residence of Williams's sister Fern and her husband, "Dutch" Hafner—refreshing drinks and trying to make Nelle as comfortable as possible in her debut as an author. Their interest in showing her the ropes of the literary life was more than just professional; they felt genuinely affectionate toward the young woman. Williams often began her letters to Nelle, "Nelle Darlin'." Even Crain found his reserve pierced by Nelle's disarming frankness, humor, and sincerity. For this evening, Nelle had prepared a presentation copy of *To Kill a Mockingbird* to express her gratitude to them for guiding the book from manuscript to publication, inscribing in it, "Maurice and A.L.: this is the charming result of your encouragement, faith and love—Nelle."[2]

When talk in the apartment began to wind down, a big sheet cake arrived in the dining room, created by the Town Rose Bake Shop, a few blocks away, and frosted to look like the novel's cover: a leafy tree stood against a light brown background; the title was set in white letters in a black band across the top. The spare design had a classic look, yet suggested a kind of loss because of the absence of any of the novel's characters. Everyone gathered at the table as Nelle cut the first piece. They toasted her and the book, which already felt like a success.[3]

CAPOTE, WHO LIKED TO say he was "as big as a shotgun and just as noisy," was eager to broadcast among the bicoastal jet set that he was a character in a new novel, but his prediction that *To Kill a Mockingbird* would be popular was hardly pure prescience. During March and April, well before the book reached bookstores, responses from early readers had outstripped all Nelle's expectations. "I sort of hoped that maybe someone would like it enough to give me encouragement. Public encouragement. I hoped for a little."⁴ So far, early signs promised far more than that: the Literary Guild had chosen *To Kill a Mockingbird* as one of its selections, and Reader's Digest as one of its Condensed Books.

In Monroeville, the news of a local girl making good led to an exuberant item in the *Monroe Journal*: "Everybody, but everybody, is looking forward to publication . . . of Nell [*sic*] Harper Lee's book, *To Kill a Mockingbird. . . .* It's wonderful. The characters are so well defined, it's crammed and jammed with chuckles, and then there are some scenes that will really choke you up."⁵ Ernestine's Gift Shop, on the town square, scored a coup when the owner announced that Nelle would be holding a book signing there just as soon as she was back in town.

Within a few weeks after the publication party in New York in July, *To Kill a Mockingbird* hit both the *New York Times* and the *Chicago Tribune* lists of top ten bestsellers. Reviewers for major publications—who would generally cast a skeptical eye on tales about virtue standing up to evil and peppered with homespun verities about life—found themselves enchanted by *To Kill a Mockingbird*. "[I]t is pleasing to recommend a book that shows what a novelist can do with familiar situations," wrote Herbert Mitgang in the *New York Times*. "Here is a storyteller justifying the novel as a form that transcends time and place." Frank Lyell, in another *New York Times* piece, breathed a sigh of relief that "Maycomb has its share of eccentrics and evil-doers, but Miss Lee has not tried to satisfy the current lust for morbid, grotesque tales of Southern depravity." The *New York World Telegram* predicted "a bright future beckoning" the author, and the *Tennessee Commercial Appeal* announced the addition of "another new writer to the growing galaxy of Southern novelists." The *Washington Post* began its review by praising the novel's power to carry a moral theme: "A hundred pounds of sermons on tolerance, or an equal measure of invective deploring the lack of it, will weigh far less in the scale of enlightenment than a mere 18 ounces of new fiction bearing the title *To Kill a Mockingbird*."⁶

Such praise brought Nelle unbroken, dizzying joy. Part of her delirium stemmed from vindication. Positive reviews meant that she had talent; she had been right to leave Alabama ten years earlier and go to New York with the dreamy notion of becoming an author, right to seek out the publishing world, right to quit a subsistence-level job so she could write full-time. And she had proved that she could withstand the rigors of first drafts, criticism, and rewriting without becoming discouraged.

Williams, who had been dumped by Capote as his agent for film and drama rights, couldn't resist gloating to him, "We are so *proud* of Nelle and what is happening to her book is thrilling."[7]

What was happening was that the book had not been dealt a "quick and merciful death," as Nelle had imagined. In fact, it seemed to have tapped into the important concerns of the era—the burgeoning interest in civil rights for blacks, the appeal of life set in simpler, pre–cold war times, and the need on the part of Americans to see themselves as justice-loving in the face of communism. *To Kill a Mockingbird* struck a resonant chord. Alden Todd, another one of Williams's young author-clients, strolled into the Francis Scott Key Book Shop in Washington, D.C., and learned that the owner had hand-sold two hundred copies of *Mockingbird* in less than a week because "of all the novels I have read in my years in the book business, Harper Lee has written the one I would be proudest to have done myself."[8]

But the novel's blastoff in the realm of bestsellerdom was not solely the result of penning the right book at the right time. There was another novel published about the South that summer: Leon Odell Griffith's *Seed in the Wind,* about racial tensions in a small southern town. Dismissed as a "dismal book, full of hackneyed situations and characters," it proposed that integration was retribution for the white man's sins against Negro women.[9] The book dropped from sight like a stone, demonstrating that a plotline revolving around race, with overtones about justice and civil rights, was hardly enough to guarantee readers, even given the tenor of the times.

NELLE RECEIVED A TORRENT of requests for interviews and book signings, rendering the novice author breathless. Sacks of fan mail arrived at Lippincott. Capote wrote to friends: "Poor thing—she is nearly demented: says she gave up trying to answer her 'fan mail' when she recieved [*sic*] 62 letters in one day. I wish she could relax and enjoy it more: in this profession it's a long walk between drinks."[10] Most of the letters lauded the book, but a few were angry. "In this day of mass rape of white women who are not morons, why is it that you young Jewish authors seek to whitewash the situation?" complained a reader. Nelle was tempted to reply, "Dear Sir or Madam, somebody is using your name to write dirty letters. You should notify the F.B.I." And she planned to sign it, "Harper Levy."[11] Typical was another outraged letter that read, "Regarding your successful book, *To Kill a Mockingbird,* you picked the kind of plot the Yankee element literally read.... You picked the same counterpart of Uncle Tom—the kind, harmless Negro accused/abused falsely by the arrogant whites.... You could write a book describing Southern whites killing Negroes and stacking them up like cordwood. It would make you another bestseller.... I've lived in the North five years. There are many good ones who mind their own business. Whenever you find the wiseacre who is going to remake the South—and never been here, they are filth and poison."[12]

But as sales of the book rose into the hundreds of thousands during the fall of 1960, there was also the enjoyment of receiving congratulations from people Nelle knew or admired from a distance. Composer Alec Wilder, whose melodies were favorites of Frank Sinatra, Zoot Sims, Peggy Lee, and Stan Getz, wrote to say he "loved" the novel. Hudson Strode, her Shakespeare professor from her undergraduate days at the University of Alabama, sent her "felicitations. I enjoyed the book very much indeed. It is fresh, and skillfully done, with delightful characters and the best possible ending.... I think part of your success lies in the shock of recognition—or as the Japanese might say, 'the unexpected recognition of the faithful "suchness" of very ordinary things.' You have a wide, warm audience waiting for Number Two."[13] (Privately, Strode "wished she had taken his class," said one of his students, Wayne Greenhaw. "He wanted to take credit for her, and he did tell us that she learned a lot from him through Shakespeare.")[14]

One day, to escape the attention for a few hours, Nelle used the excuse that Tay Hohoff was mad about cats to deliver to her an abandoned kitten with six toes on its forefeet. Nelle had found the kitten in the basement of her building, cuddled up to the furnace. She named it Shadrach, after the biblical character who endured Nebuchadnezzar's fiery furnace. After delivering it safely to the Hohoff sanctuary, a "beehive of books" scented with aromas of good tobacco and whiskey, Nelle sank into a big comfortable chair and muttered, despite the early morning hour, "I *need* a drink. I'm supposed to be at an interview right now."[15] After she left, Hohoff and her husband, Arthur, had a good laugh about how their young friend was finding out that literary success was not all it was cracked up to be.

In September 1960, Nelle retreated to Monroeville for a breather, squeezing in a book signing at Capitol Book and News Company, in Montgomery. Seated at a table next to a vase of white carnations and wearing a fresh-cut corsage pinned to her dress, she was the center of attention. Less a literary event than a combination celebration and reunion, the book signing was an occasion where people "crowded into the bookstore because they saw her picture in the paper, wondered if she were kin to so and so, heard that her book was good, knew her at the University of Alabama, knew someone who used to know her somewhere or had read the book and enjoyed it and came to say so."[16]

Nearby was her father, eighty-one-year-old A. C. Lee, looking very old as he watched quietly with his large owlish eyes through big glasses. His wife, Nelle's mother, Frances, had been dead for almost a decade. (A.C. himself would die in two years, still in the harness at the law office.) His suit vests, once buttoned tightly over a healthy paunch, now hung loose. The knuckles of his right hand turned white when he pressed hard on the crook of his cane to rise from his chair and shake someone's hand, perhaps an old acquaintance from his days as a state legislator. Nelle was grateful that her father had lived to witness this triumph. A perceptive newspaper reporter had remarked that *To Kill a Mockingbird* "is written out of Harper Lee's love for the South and Monroeville, but it is also the story of a father's love for his children, and the love they gave in return."[17] This came nearest to Nelle's true reason for writing the novel: it was a tribute to her father. The book's hero, the courageous but humble attorney Atticus Finch, was a portrait of A. C. Lee done in generous, loving strokes.

After a month's respite in Monroeville, Nelle returned to New York, hoping in vain that she could meet the demands that the book was creating. But then, seeing there was no respite in sight, she rushed off for Williams and Crain's vacation house in rural Connecticut instead. Capote, hearing of the effects of celebrity overtaking his friend, noted, "poor darling, she seems to be having some sort of happy nervous-breakdown."[18]

FOR SOMEONE LIKE NELLE, who preferred solitude over parties, observing instead of participating, the onrush of instant celebrity resulting from *To Kill a Mockingbird* imposed a tremendous strain she hadn't expected. Somehow, in the space of a very short time, just a few months, she had gone from having a private self that she could control to a public persona that she could not. Unlike Capote, for instance, who said, "I always knew that I wanted to be a writer and that I wanted to be rich and famous," Nelle didn't regard herself as an important person, and the attention being paid to her almost seemed to be happening to someone else.[19] (A revealing moment about her self-perception occurred during an interview with *Newsweek* in the lounge of New York's Algonquin Hotel. Catching sight of Irish playwright Brendan Behan walking by, she confessed, "I've always wanted to meet an author.")[20]

Just as long as the intense attention stayed primarily on the book, she could cope with it. Usually, her quick, folksy wit stood her in good stead during interviews. She was the first to poke fun at her heavy Alabama accent. ("If I hear a consonant, I look around.")[21] She deflected seriousness by claiming to be a Whig and believing "in Catholic emancipation and repeal of the Corn Laws."[22] Asked about how she wrote, she cracked, "I sit down before a typewriter with my feet fixed firmly on the floor."[23] Not even her appearance was off-limits, within reason; she admitted to being a little heavier than she would like to be (according to a friend, she put herself on a thousand-calorie-a-day diet of "unpalatable goop").[24] Generally, interviewers, such as Joseph Deitch for the *Christian Science Monitor,* found her "instantly good company . . . a tall, robust woman with a winsome manner, a neighborly handshake, and a liking for good, sensitive talk about people and books and places like Monroeville, Alabama, her home town."[25]

But for reasons she could not fathom, success gave strangers license to write reviews, letters, and opinion pieces not only about the book, but also about her. A sly column appeared in the *Alabama Jour-*

nal, "This Mockingbird Is a Happy Singer," written by her former classmate at the University of Alabama, John T. Hamner. Hamner expressed surprise that Nelle could have written such a novel, in light of how fellow students knew her in college.[26]

"If you knew Nelle like I know Nelle, you'd be as surprised as I was at what a delightful book she's written," began managing editor Hamner. ". . . It's a lot of other things, too, almost all of which amaze me when I think of the author." Pretending he had only known Nelle by sight at the University of Alabama, he set out to verify what he could recall about her by polling people in the newsroom who also knew her then. "They're pretty well universal in their surprise that Nelle, or Harper Lee, could write such a book," he reported. "I even found a couple who were shocked to find that, having written it, Nelle would allow it to be printed under her name."

Hamner, along with his colleagues, he said, were puzzled over why in the novel she "thought back with such fondness to what must have been her own childhood." In college, she was no sentimentalist. He remembered her as a "beatnik before anyone else thought of being one." He recalled her delight at satirizing campus life in her columns for the *Crimson White* and the *Rammer Jammer.* To account for the change in Nelle's outlook between those days and the publication of the book, he hinted broadly that there was something disingenuous about her: "Nelle was a carefully developed campus character. . . . Many, like me, whom she did not know, knew her. . . . Those differences, I would have thought, would lead her almost anywhere except to *To Kill a Mockingbird.*"

A few days later, the editor and publisher of the *Brewton Standard,* in Brewton, Alabama, Tom Gardner, fired back in defense of his hometown and his friend: "As a former resident of Monroeville, it is no surprise to those of us who 'grew up' with Nelle that she would someday write a book or do something equally as brilliant. . . . And that Nelle would own up to the contents of her books is a foregone conclusion. It is inconceivable that she wouldn't." Regarding Monroeville in the 1930s, Gardner said, "those of us who were reared there along with Nelle could never think with anything but fondness of the place." And beatnik? He remembered her as "about as much of a beatnik as Eleanor Roosevelt . . . and not half as contentious in her philosophical belief."[27]

To witness the exchange in local papers must have been annoying for Nelle. To be summarized by journalists as "impish" or someone with "a faint touch of gray in her Italian boy haircut" was mere shorthand for being labeled a character. But this was a public debate over whether she was genuine. ("Nelle's grown skillful, though," Hamner wrote, concluding his column. "She doesn't overly debunk now. She paints the picture, tells the story, and leaves it to the reader to supply his own interpretation.")[28] Nelle took matters into her own hands and fired back a letter to the *Alabama Journal* that began, "Who the hell is John T. Hamner?"[29]

To avoid becoming fodder for this kind of thing, Nelle found the temptation to hide out at Crain and Williams's home in Connecticut, or in her hometown of Monroeville, hard to resist. And of the two, Monroeville, the little town of 3,600, offered the safest harbor. Not too many years earlier, Monroeville's remoteness had been one of Nelle's chief reasons for wanting to stay away; now it guaranteed some peace of mind. Most reporters and interviewers, after studying maps of Alabama where two-lane roads meandered like blue and black threads, opted to telephone the Lee residence instead. When the phone rang, often it was Alice who negotiated with the press. ("She wouldn't even let Nelle take a call about the book," said Charles Ray Skinner, a friend of the family.)[30] The world and its demands could wait on the Lees' doorstep. Inside, Nelle liked to curl up with a book. Alice wouldn't even permit a television in the house lest it disturb the quiet.

In December 1960, reviewers' year-end roundups of the big books of year ranked Harper Lee's first-ever novel with Updike's *Rabbit, Run,* John O'Hara's *Sermons and Soda-water,* Michener's *Hawaii, The Rise and Fall of the Third Reich* by William Shirer, Allen Drury's *Advise and Consent, Born Free* by Joy Adamson, John Hersey's *The Child Buyer,* and John Knowles's *A Separate Peace.*

HUNKERED DOWN IN MONROEVILLE for the winter, Nelle went hunting with friends for whitetail deer near the Christmas holidays. Equipped with a rifle, she slipped into the woods, pretending she was a settler competing with Creek Indians for game in the wilderness. She wrote a vivid letter to Leone Dehn, a secretary in Williams's office, describing her pioneer adventures. Mrs. Dehn had no trouble picturing her "in old timey clothes and wearing a gingham bonnet, sighting down the barrel of a rifle." But when a deer timidly stepped out into a clearing, Nelle lowered her rifle and watched silently until the animal skipped away. Unlike her forebears who hunted for food in these woods, she had no reason to shoot.[31]

Maurice Crain, picking up on the spirit of Nelle's hunting experience, composed an appropriate invitation to his and Annie Laurie's Old Stone House in Connecticut:

> I write on behalf of the remnant of a small tribe of Indians living in the Berkshire Mountains. We would like to adopt you into the tribe, on an honorary basis, in view of our admiration for your work, and because the mockingbird happens to be our totem. . . . You may remember me. I am Eats No Fat. . . . At the time of initiation into the tribe, it is customary to choose a tribal name. The names Sleeps Late, Girl With the Ringing Laugh, and Picks Up Live Coals have occurred to us, but we await your suggestions.[32]

Her friends' entreaties to return to New York arrived regularly. "We will go early on a Saturday [to Connecticut] and stay all afternoon and evening and eat and talk and play and sing. Now you know what is in store for you when you return to your New York home," wrote Williams. "Yesterday we grabbed a copy of *Newsweek* off the stands and raced through the pages until we saw your smiling face and then read what we think is a good piece." She couldn't resist teasing Nelle about the constant references to the author's imagined ancestry circulating over and over: "As a relative of General Lee, we must remember to bow a little lower next time we see you."[33]

But Nelle stayed pinned down in Monroeville, as much to satisfy Alice's wishes that she help to "keep the home fires burning," as to avoid the demands of bestsellerdom that awaited her in New York. At least in this corner of the world the attention was friendly and uncritical. (Although the Boleware family was making noises about suing over the likeness between Son Boleware and Boo Radley, Nelle had adopted a policy of brushing aside comparisons between characters in the novel and real people by saying, "It's only fiction.")[34]

By and large, authorship down home had brought a type of congratulations that would be offered to any neighbor who had accomplished something exciting. When word went round in Eufaula that
Nelle Harper Lee was coming to visit her sister Louise, a line of
dessert-bearing ladies got busy. One woman, Solita Parker, with a reputation in the neighborhood for being a wit, pretended to be jealous
that Monroeville had been chosen for the novel's setting. She firmly
announced that Eufaula ought to chip in and rent Nelle an apartment, because there were so many peculiar characters in Eufaula to
write about.

"Oh, you want a kick-back on stock in the publishing company,"
Nelle teased back.

"No," said the woman, "I just want to *read* the book."[35]

That kind of pleasantry and the feelings of gratification it inspired
were exactly what Nelle had expected from publishing a novel. Here
in these familiar surroundings, with people who spoke, thought, and
joked as she did, she could be what she wanted—a Southerner satisfied with joining the tradition of regionalist writers south of the
Mason-Dixon Line. Here she could give free rein to her personality.
To a cookbook editor's request for a recipe that would "demonstrate
food as a mean of communication," Nelle provided one for crackling
bread—a backwoods staple—couched in the style of tongue-in-cheek
southern humor that mixed formal talk with nonsense.[36]

"First, catch your pig," she instructed. "Then ship him to the abat-
toir nearest you. Bake what they send you back. Remove the solid fat
and throw the rest away." Having wasted most of the pig, the cook
was then supposed to add the fat to meal, milk, baking powder, and
an egg, and bake the dough in a "very hot oven." The result, Nelle
promised, would be an authentic dish: "one pan crackling bread serving 6. Total cost: about $250, depending upon size of pig. Some histo-
rians say by this recipe alone fell the Confederacy." To the editor, she
concluded, "I trust that you will find the above of sufficient artistic
and social significance to include in the Cookbook."

It was a response that friends would recognize as "typical
Nelle"—offbeat, skeptical, thought-provoking. Friends from her days
at the University of Alabama described her to the *Montgomery Advertiser* as "a warm though independent-minded girl who took great delight in deflating phoniness wherever it appeared."[36]

To requests for more information about herself, she responded coyly. At Huntingdon College, librarian Leo R. Roberts tried to compile a profile of the former freshman in response to journalists, alumnae, and Nelle's admirers who were clamoring to know more about the author whose book had sold more than half a million copies in six months. Roberts, probably a little nonplussed by the lack of information about Nelle in Huntingdon's archives, finally wrote to her in January of 1961 requesting some facts about her background.

"I'm afraid a biographical sketch of me will be sketchy indeed; with the exception of M'bird, nothing of any particular interest to anyone has happened to me in my thirty-four years," she replied. After supplying a few details about her family, she deadpanned, "I was exposed to seventeen years of formal education in Monroeville schools, Huntingdon College, and the University of Alabama. If I ever learned anything, I've forgotten it."[37]

THE EVENING AFTER NELLE replied to Roberts at Huntingdon, Williams called from New York to say she had sold the movie rights to *To Kill a Mockingbird.*

The novel's skyrocketing sales had caught the attention of Hollywood almost immediately, and Williams, as Nelle's agent for dramatic rights, had been reviewing proposals from filmmakers. She was in her element brokering deals between studios or production companies hunting for literary properties. Sifting through the proposals on her desk for *To Kill a Mockingbird,* however, she found too much of the usual overheated language about turning it into a Hollywood hit.

Producer Robert P. Richards, for instance, wrote on behalf of himself and his partner, James Yarbrough. Yarbrough's credits included television dramas such as *Robert Montgomery Presents* and two Western series, *Rawhide* and *Bonanza.* Richards felt strongly about the need to shoot on location and use "as many natives as possible for extras and bits." For the roles of Aunt Alexandra and Miss Maudie, he suggested Bette Davis and Ann Sheridan. "Atticus is a problem," Richards admitted; among the biggest leading men of the day— Marlon Brando, John Wayne, Burt Lancaster, Gregory Peck, and a few others—"the only one who might be right is [Gary] Cooper, but I'm afraid that his public image is wrong. The public is unwilling to think of Cooper as an intelectual [sic]." Yarbrough had an idea, though: "to ask John Huston to play the part, he is Atticus, in thought, body and personality, a little wilder, a little crazier."[38] Williams politely turned down their offer of twenty-five thousand dollars for the rights.

Most offers were from small outfits and partnerships. Major studios were conspicuously absent because *To Kill a Mockingbird* lacked the tried-and-true ingredients that attracted movie audiences: shoot-'em-up action, a love story, danger, or a clear-cut "bad guy." In addition, the press had likened *To Kill a Mockingbird*'s nine-year-old narrator Scout to preadolescent Frankie in Carson McCullers's *The Member of the Wedding,* and the film version of McCullers's novel had flopped. (The surface similarities of the two novels were not lost on McCullers, either, who commented acidly about Lee to a cousin, "Well, honey, one thing we know is that she's been poaching on my literary preserves.")[39]

It was just as well that the big studios weren't sniffing around, anyway. In thirty years of working with Hollywood, Williams had learned to adhere to a basic principle: try to get for authors and playwrights what they need to feel appreciated or satisfied. Some required top-dollar deals to feel validated; others would work only with directors or playwrights they admired. In Nelle's case, Williams had an author who did not put emphasis on conventional marks of prestige. But she would be reluctant to let go of the story unless she could be assured that a film version would not be undignified or hurt people she loved. That was her price; and other considerations—the money paid for screen rights, percentage agreements, and so on—were of much less concern to her.

A second reality about doing business with Nelle was that the locus of control for the book was slipping from her hands alone and into her father's and Alice's, too. Williams knew she could close a film deal for the novel only if Alice and A.C. approved of the people involved as much as Nelle did. Whoever was chosen to turn the novel into a film had to come across as decent and trustworthy.

The Lee family had come to the *To Kill a Mockingbird* party late, so to speak, but once it was clear that Nelle had achieved something grand, A.C. and Alice—increasingly Alice as A.C.'s health declined—were taking over her affairs. Previously, when Nelle was working full-time in New York as an airline reservationist during the 1950s and was down at the heels, the Lees had allowed her to scrape along, probably figuring she would come to her senses eventually. Then, against all odds, this long run-up to what should have ended in a sorry admission that A.C. had been right all along, resulted in Nelle's producing a novel that was becoming famous. Suddenly, the family was receiving calls from reporters, and with no choice except to acquit themselves well, they were undertaking the responsibility of managing their prodigy.

While happy for Nelle's success, A.C. and Alice put little stock in overnight riches. That wasn't how honest people made their way in the world. The Lees lived simply, heeding the New Testament injunction, "Do not hoard treasures on earth where moths and rust corrupt, and where thieves break in and steal." Nelle was on her way to becoming rich, but her financial ascendancy was a fluke—there was no other way to explain it. "I never dreamed of what was going to happen. It was somewhat of a surprise and it's very rare indeed when a thing like this happens to a country girl going to New York," A.C. said when his daughter's novel simultaneously landed on the *New York Times* and *Chicago Tribune* lists of bestsellers. "She will have to do a good job next time if she goes on up," he continued, inadvertently issuing a mandate that might certainly have chilled the creative spirit, however it was intended.[40] And then, still marveling, apparently, that Nelle had strayed from the narrow but dependable path of a nine-to-five job, he added, "I feel what I think is a justifiable measure of pride in her accomplishment, and I must say she has displayed much determination, confidence and ambition to give up a good job in New York and take a chance at writing a book."[41] Nelle's sister Louise was the least impressed by all the hoopla surrounding her sister's novel and didn't think much of Nelle's talent, either. She told her son's teacher that *To Kill a Mockingbird* was just "ridiculous."[42]

So it was that when Williams sent a follow-up letter to the Lee home in Monroeville the day after her phone call about closing the deal on the motion picture rights, she acknowledged that Alice, as family spokesperson and Nelle's self-appointed manager, would have to be reckoned with every step of the way. "Dear Alice and Nelle," the letter began,

> [I tried] to keep in mind everything you said[,] Alice[,] about not getting any *cash* money for Nelle this year and not too much each succeeding year. . . . The sale is to Alan Pakula and Robert Mulligan,

who are forming their own company to produce together, with Bob Mulligan also directing. This is the real "prize" having him direct the Mockingbird picture. Alan is a good producer but he knew when he first talked to Nelle in our office, that he must have a sensitive director to work with him. We think that Bob Mulligan is just right for this picture.[43]

She was not overstating their good luck in closing with Pakula and Mulligan, and she had held off a major studio until the pair could make their bid. As filmmakers, they were drawn to stories about character, life's tragic quality, and situations that were ripe for strong dramatization.

At first glance, Pakula would not give the impression of being the right man for the job of making a film about racial prejudice in a small southern town in the 1930s. Darkly handsome, the son of Polish immigrants, and a Yale graduate who dressed like a 1960s IBM salesman, Pakula was fastidious in ways that extended even to his film crews, insisting they pick up their cigarette butts after shooting on location. But he was also personable, warm, and conscientious. At twenty-two, he had turned away from the family printing business in New York, and become a production assistant at Paramount. His father underwrote his first film as producer, *Fear Strikes Out* (1957), the story of baseball player Jimmy Piersall's mental illness caused by his obsessively critical father, for which Pakula teamed with Robert Mulligan as director. The film was well received, and it not only launched the careers of Mulligan and Pakula, but also earned praise for newcomer Anthony Perkins in the role of Piersall. A publicist at Lippincott had urged Pakula to read *To Kill a Mockingbird,* and Pakula in turn had made Mulligan read it.

Bob Mulligan did not have Pakula's exterior polish, nor was he as reserved. Sandy-haired, informal, and impulsive, Mulligan was born in the Bronx and studied briefly for the priesthood before enrolling at Fordham University, where he majored in radio communication, receiving training that made him a specialist in the Marines during World War II. After the war, he started at the bottom at CBS as a messenger, but rose during the popularly nicknamed Golden Age of Television to become a director of live dramas aired on *The Philco Television Playhouse, Studio One,* and *Suspense.* Mulligan was part of a new wave of postwar directors learning their craft on television— men such as John Frankenheimer, Sidney Lumet, Arthur Penn, George Roy Hill, and Martin Ritt. Unlike Pakula, however, who later moved into directing films with a social-political agenda such as *Klute* (1971), *The Parallax View* (1974), and *All the President's Men* (1976), Mulligan would remain attracted to telling human interest stories: *Love with a Proper Stranger* (1963), *Up the Down Staircase* (1967), *Summer of '42* (1971), and *The Man in the Moon* (1991).

Overall, the fit was good between the content of *To Kill a Mockingbird* and what Pakula and Mulligan wanted to do artistically. Even better, the relationship between Nelle and Pakula had gotten off to a good start in Williams's office the previous autumn, during a meeting that Williams had presided over like an old-fashioned matchmaker. Well before the deal was closed, in January 1961, she had sent Pakula a letter lecturing him about not trifling with Nelle or her book: "From the very beginning, everybody who had anything to do with the book has felt that it was *special,* deserving the most thoughtful handling. Now if you can find exactly the right Atticus and exactly the right children, especially the little girl to play Scout, we will feel confident that you can produce the kind of picture you promised Harper Lee you would make when you first met her in our office."[44]

In the meantime, because Mulligan was still working on *The Spiral Road* (1962), a big-picture drama with Rock Hudson and Burl Ives about colonialism in the tropics, Pakula made arrangements to visit Monroeville and "see Nelle about the 'creative side,'" as Williams put it—though he knew in advance he was auditioning for Alice and A.C.'s approval, too. When he arrived in Monroeville in February 1961, the weather was overcast and rainy. But even if he had seen the town under the best conditions, it wouldn't have changed his mind about using it as a possible location: "There is no Monroeville," Pakula wrote glumly to Mulligan, meaning that modernization over the last thirty years had rendered the town characterless. Except for the courthouse, which the citizenry was considering tearing down because a new, flat-roof, cinder-block version was on the drawing board, Monroeville was a mishmash of old and new. A façade for Scout's neighborhood would have to be built on a studio back lot, and the interior of the old courthouse, which was not in good repair, would have to be measured and reconstructed on a Hollywood soundstage.

After spending several days getting to know the Lees, Pakula left for California, apparently having secured their approval about the ideas he and Mulligan had in mind for the film: "They want to give the movie the same approach that the book had," Alice said approvingly.[45] Nelle, trying to assuage Pakula's disappointment about Monroeville with a dose of lightheartedness, sent him a few photographs with a note: "Here is the courthouse, some rain-rotted lumber, and two sprigs of Spanish moss to keep you company. If you'll believe me, that's the sun, not a flashbulb, shining on the side of the house."[46] He thanked her for the pictures, betraying no sense of concern about the crimp in his plans, and saying he was looking forward to meeting up with her in New York soon to introduce her to Bob Mulligan— "Affectionately, Alan."

THE SETTING FOR FICTIONAL Maycomb that Pakula had expected to find had seemingly vanished. Where Capote's house had stood— the one belonging to Dill's aunt in the novel—was an empty lot. The streets in town that emanated sour red dust on a hot day in the 1930s were smooth with blacktop. Now, teenagers crowded into the Wee Diner for cokes and hamburgers, a hot spot for dates made from two buses joined together with flower boxes and brightly painted booths. A visitor resting on one of the benches on the courthouse square might conclude, just looking around, that a film with a story like *To Kill a Mockingbird* was passé. How different times seemed from the days of lynch mobs and racist trials. On the other hand, if anyone in Monroeville cared to notice—but it was so much a part of life that no one consciously would—Negroes were not allowed to use the park or recreation facilities owned by the Vanity Fair underwear factory, the largest industry in town, and there were separate water fountains marked WHITE and COLORED.

That era was indeed dying—not gone, but dying—and *To Kill a Mockingbird* would help hasten its death. Some labeled the book just another of many traitorous blows falling on the South. A few days after newspapers announced the sale of the movie rights to the novel in February 1961, an unsigned squib headed "Spreading Poison" appeared on the letters-to-the-editor page of the *Atlanta Journal-Constitution*: "That book 'To Kill a Mockingbird' is to be filmed. Thus another cruel, untrue libel upon the South is to be spread all over the nation. Another Alabama writer joins the ranks of traducers of their homeland for pelf and infamous fame."[47]

Yet the novel, and the issues it treated, was a harbinger of change that had been on the horizon for years. Perhaps that's why it wasn't vilified more often: because it was part of a crescendo of ever-more-important events. The National Association for the Advancement of Colored People (NAACP) and the NAACP Legal Defense and Educational Fund had won *Brown v. Board of Education* of Topeka in 1954 before the U.S. Supreme Court, which ruled that segregation in the public schools was in itself unequal and thus unconstitutional. The following year, Rosa Parks, a seamstress and civil rights activist in Montgomery, Alabama, was arrested for disobeying a city law that required Negroes to give up their bus seats to whites. The resulting Montgomery bus boycott by Negro riders lasted 382 days, ending only when the city abolished the bus law. It was the first organized mass protest by Negroes in southern history, and it thrust Martin Luther King, Jr., onto the national stage. The year *To Kill a Mockingbird* was published, 1960, Negro and white college students formed the Student Nonviolent Coordinating Committee to assist the civil rights movement with sit-ins, marches, boycotts, and demonstrations.

On May 4, 1961, the Freedom Ride—sponsored by the Congress for Racial Equality—had left Washington, D.C., intending to test the Supreme Court's 1946 act that declared segregated seating of interstate passengers unconstitutional. Buses loaded with white passengers in the back and Negroes in the front set off for the South, planning to arrive in New Orleans on May 17, the seventh anniversary of the *Brown v. Board of Education* decision. The buses encountered little resistance in the upper South. Then, on May 14, the buses split into two groups for the trip through Alabama, anticipating trouble ahead. When the first bus arrived in Anniston, a rock-throwing mob of about two hundred descended on it and slashed its tires. The driver managed to pull away and continue six miles out of town before stopping to change the tires. As the vehicle sat by the side of the road, carloads of pursuers firebombed it. In Birmingham, Freedom Riders on the second bus were severely beaten at the bus depot. Birmingham's public safety commissioner, Bull Conner, claimed he had assigned no officers for protection because it was Mother's Day, a holiday. Alabama governor John Patterson offered no apologies, either.

"When you go somewhere looking for trouble," he said, "you usually find it."

And there was yet much trouble ahead. Still, the days of flagrant social and legal inequities directed at Negroes seemed numbered. In American culture, *To Kill a Mockingbird* would become like *Catch-22, One Flew Over the Cuckoo's Nest, Portnoy's Complaint, On the Road, The Bell Jar, Soul on Ice,* and *The Feminine Mystique*—books that seized the imagination of the post–World War II generation—a novel that figured in changing "the system."

THERE WAS A LULL in late spring 1961 with plans surrounding the movie. Pakula and Mulligan were anxious to, in casting parlance, "set the star"—get a commitment for the leading man—so they could move on to making a distribution deal. The previous fall, Nelle had engaged in some star hunting on her own, thinking that a direct approach might entice a leading man with a reputation for integrity suitable for him to play Atticus. Through the William Morris Agency, she sent a note to Spencer Tracy. "Frankly, I can't see anybody but Spencer Tracy in the part of 'Atticus.' "[48] The actor replied via an agent, George Wood, that he "could not read the book till he has finished his picture 'The Devil at Four O'clock.' He must study and concentrate at present." Instead, Wood suggested Robert Wagner who "would love to hear from you and any ideas that you might have for him." In March 1961, Maurice Crain wrote to Alice: "The latest development is that Bing Crosby very much wants to play Atticus. . . . He should be made to promise not to reverse his collar, not to mumble a single Latin prayer, not to burble a single note. . . . As for the Southern accent, he has been married for several years to a Texas girl and the accent is 'catching.' "[49]

Aside from the movie, things were continuing to percolate on the literary front. By mid-April, *To Kill a Mockingbird* was approaching its thirty-fifth week on the bestseller lists. Yet Nelle apparently couldn't shake the feeling that she was still an amateur who could learn from her betters. After having lunch with Crain, she went back to his office and happened to see the manuscript for a new novel by Fred Gipson, author of *Old Yeller*. "She picked up the first page, just to see how Fred Gipson began a story," Crain wrote to Gipson. "Under protest she was dragged away from it 111 pages later to keep another date, but took a copy of *Old Yeller* with her. You have another fan."[50]

Back home in Monroeville by the end of the month, Nelle was invited to attend a luncheon of the Alabama Library Association. At the table of honored guests was her former professor Hudson Strode, with one of his former creative writing students, Mississippi regionalist writer Borden Deal, who had just published his sixth novel, *Dragon's Wine*. At the conclusion of the luncheon, Nelle received the association's literary award.

ON MONDAY, MAY 2, when *To Kill a Mockingbird* was in its forty-first week as a bestseller and had sold nearly half a million copies, the phone rang in Annie Laurie Williams and Maurice Crain's offices. It was a friend of Williams at a publishing house who wanted to speak to Nelle about hearsay from a reporter.

In California, Pakula had already heard the same rumor and was excitedly calling his partner, Bob Mulligan.

When Mulligan answered, Pakula shouted, "We got it! We got it!"

"We got what?" asked Mulligan.

"The Pulitzer Prize. Our book won it!"[51]

Nelle hardly dared believe it until she received an official call: "A friend from a publishing company called and had gotten the word from a newspaper. I haven't heard from the Pulitzer committee yet, but I haven't been back to my apartment since I heard the news."[52] When she finally did hear from a spokesperson for the Pulitzer Prize Committee, she called Alice several times, who by now was becoming adept in the role of her sister's spokesperson and at fielding phone calls from reporters. "Nelle was anxious to find out the local reaction," she said in response to questions. "She still claims Monroeville as her home, and when she leaves, it is usually for business purposes" (a hint that Alice was not reconciled to Nelle's living months at a time in New York). "The whole town of Monroeville is amazed about the Pulitzer prize."[53]

The annual Pulitzer prizes in drama, letters, and music, created by newspaper publisher Joseph Pulitzer in a bequest to Columbia University, were worth only five hundred dollars at that time, but their cachet, in terms of bringing artists' names to the public, was enormous. Hudson Strode immediately tapped out a letter of congratulations to

Nelle: "I announced the good news to my writing class last night and there was a response of cheers. The University and the State, and the whole South are proud of you. But no one more than myself."[54]

Besieged by phone interviews that kept her pinned inside Williams's office for hours, Nelle resorted to modesty and humor as ways of modulating questions about herself. "I am as lucky as I can be. I don't know anyone who has been luckier."[55] She claimed that the effort to write the book had worn out three pairs of dungarees. And about whether a movie was forthcoming based on the book, all she would say was that production was slated to begin in the fall.

Almost immediately, a second avalanche of fan letters began. "Snowed under with fan letters," wrote *Newsweek*, "Harper Lee is stealing time from a new novel-in-progress to write careful answers."[56]

It was the proverbial Cinderella story: from nowhere comes a young writer, without benefit of grants, fellowships, or even an apprenticeship at a major newspaper or magazine, who produces, on her first try, a novel snapped up by three American book clubs: Reader's Digest Condensed Books, the Literary Guild, and the Book-of-the-Month Club. In addition, the British Book Society had selected it for its readers, and by the spring of 1961, translations were under way in France, Germany, Italy, Spain, Holland, Denmark, Norway, Sweden, Finland, and Czechoslovakia.

Truman Capote, who craved winning the Pulitzer or the National Book Award, and hoped he would with *In Cold Blood,* wrote to friends in Kansas: "Well, and wasn't it fine about our dear little Nelle winning the Pulitzer Prize? She has swept the boards."[57]

Despite Capote's casual tone, he no doubt resented this turn of fortune in his friend's life. After all, when they were children, he had been the one to urge her to write stories (he later revised the nature of their partnership, telling the *Washington Post,* "I got Harper interested in writing because she typed my manuscripts on my typewriter. It was a nice gesture for her, and highly convenient for me"). Moreover, Lee tended not to put the emphasis on winning the Pulitzer Prize that Capote would have. "The Pulitzer is one thing; the approval of my own people is the only literary reward I covet," she wrote to a friend.[58] It was gall that Truman had to swallow, as gracefully as he could, but his cousin Jennings Faulk Carter recalled, "The only time I've ever heard him say anything about Nelle's book was that he remarked, 'She got the Pulitzer, and I've never, never done that.' I forget how he put it, but you could tell he was hurt badly. That as much writing as he had done, he had never won it, but Nelle had."[59]

In mid-May, the Alabama legislature attempted to pass a resolution honoring Nelle when segregationist senator E. O. Eddins stepped in to stop it. The senator had been at the head of the charge to ban Garth Williams's 1958 book *The Rabbits' Wedding,* which featured the wedding of two rabbits, one black and one white. The White Citizens' Council in Alabama, with Eddins's support, had attacked the Williams book as "communistic" and promoting racial integration. Eddins and other legislators tried but failed to remove the state's director of the Alabama Public Library Service, Emily Wheelock Reed, for refusing to remove the book from library shelves. But this time, Eddins sensed that a similar backlash might build if he lambasted Lee and *To Kill a Mockingbird,* so he finally withdrew his protest "lest it make a martyr of the author."[60] A joint resolution passed on May 26 offering "homage and special praise to this outstanding Alabamian who has gained such prominence for herself and so much prestige for her native state."

And there was surely more to come from an author so promising. She had written an essay, "Love—In Other Words," which appeared in the April issue of *Vogue* magazine. She told reporters that she had several short stories under way. She seemed to have talent and a work ethic that indicated that a long career was just beginning. As James B. McMillan, chairman of the English Department at the University of Alabama, pointed out shortly after *To Kill a Mockingbird* won the Pulitzer, the novel was a "mixture of ingredients that ought to guarantee a bad novel. The story is told from the point of view of an eight-year-old child; it is set in the kind of Southern small town that has been described in fiction a thousand times; the characters are exactly the types that a correspondence-school course in fiction would prescribe for a Southern small-town novel. . . . The denouement is pure Gothic fiction." But, said McMillan, what puts the book head and shoulders over others of its type is that "Miss Lee remembers much of what she has seen, heard, and felt; she has discriminating feelings and judgments about what she has seen and heard; she knows what to tell and what to leave out; and she must have worked hard at the craft of putting words to paper. *To Kill a Mockingbird* is a superior book because it was written by a superior person who became a professional writer without inflicting her apprenticeship on the public in a trial book."[61]

In its first year, *To Kill a Mockingbird* sold more than 2.5 million copies. W. S. Hoole, director of the University of Alabama libraries, "nearly fell over his size thirteens asking for the manuscript!" Nelle wrote to friends in Mobile, but she thought better of giving it to him.[62]

Maurice Crain, Annie Laurie Williams, and certainly Tay Hohoff, couldn't wait for Nelle's second novel. In July 1961, a teasing note arrived at Nelle's apartment on the Upper East Side, where she had just moved with a friend, Marcia Van Meter: "Dear Nelle: TOMORROW IS MY FIRST BIRTHDAY AND MY AGENTS THINKS THERE SHOULD BE ANOTHER BOOK WRITTEN SOON TO KEEP ME COMPANY. DO YOU THINK YOU CAN START ONE BEFORE I AM ANOTHER YEAR OLD? We would be so happy if you would. (signed) THE MOCKINGBIRD AND ANNIE LAURIE AND MAURICE CRAIN."[63]

To reporters asking the same question—What are your plans for a second book?—Nelle replied, "I guess I will have to quote Scarlett O'Hara on that. I'll think about that tomorrow."[64]

The remark was more than apt. Like the heroine from *Gone With the Wind,* for whom unpleasantness and hard decisions could always be put off until an eternal tomorrow, "tomorrow" would never come for Nelle Harper Lee as an author. With her first novel, which became the most popular novel in American literature in the twentieth century, and which readers rank in surveys as the most influential in their lives after the Bible, Nelle seemed poised to begin a writing career that would launch her into the annals of illustrious American writers. Instead, almost from the day of its publication, *To Kill a Mockingbird* took off, but gradually left its author behind.

"Oh, Mr. Peck!"

ONE COLD NIGHT IN EARLY JANUARY 1962, WEDNESDAY night services had just ended at the imposing First Baptist Church on Monroeville's town square when a stranger made his way up the front steps through the trickle of worshippers exiting the sanctuary. By his downcast and rough appearance, he appeared to be homeless.[1]

"May we help you?" asked one of the ushers.

"I'd like to see the reverend," came the gruff reply.

The usher assured the man that if he needed a meal or a place to stay, then that could be taken care of. No, that wasn't the problem, said the stranger. He needed to see the reverend. The usher, beckoning over a couple of gentleman who were busy returning hymnals to the backs of pews, explained the situation. They agreed to accompany the visitor to Dr. L. Reed Polk's office.

Reverend Polk was just hanging up his vestments when the little group appeared on the threshold of his office. He thanked the ushers, invited the tall and rather well built man in, and shut the door so they could have some privacy.

"What can I do for you?" asked Reverend Polk.

Looking up suddenly and extending his hand, the stranger said, "How do you, sir—I'm Gregory Peck."

Peck was in town to meet the Lee family and to soak up some of the setting for the character he was going to play in the film version of *To Kill a Mockingbird*. The reason he had stopped at the First Baptist Church, he told Dr. Polk, was that he wanted to speak to someone who knew the town and its people. Polk had been the minister at First Baptist for more than fifteen years. Peck apologized for the disguise, but he didn't want word to get around that he was visiting before he'd gotten a chance to get his bearings and meet the reverend. Dr. Polk was amused and flattered that Peck had come directly to him.

For the next hour, the two men talked about the town and about the man Peck was going to play. The actor asked for particulars about Mr. Lee's standing in the community, his thoughts and behaviors— anything that "set Mr. Lee apart" would be helpful. Polk stood up and demonstrated how Lee had a tendency to fumble with his pocket watch as he talked and how he paced back and forth. Peck watched intently, making mental notes about how he was going embody Atticus Finch on the screen.

GREGORY PECK HAD NOT been Universal Studios' first choice for the role. Rock Hudson was offered the part, and he was prepared to do it when the project entered what is now sometimes called "development hell" in Hollywood—the period of massaging the screenplay and wrangling over creative control. But, in a nutshell, Pakula didn't want Hudson for the part; he wanted Peck. The studio agreed that if the latter would sign on, then they would provide the financing. Pakula sent the actor a copy of the novel. "I got started on it," said Peck, "and of course I sat up all night and read straight through it. I understood that they wanted me to play Atticus and I called them at about eight o'clock in the morning and said, 'If you want me to play Atticus, when do I start? I'd love to play it.' "[2] Peck formed a production company called Brentwood Productions, which would be a three-way partnership with Pakula and Nelle Lee, who, with the assistance of Alice and Annie Laurie Williams, had formed her own company, Atticus Productions, as a tax shelter. Peck, however, would have input into the film's casting, the development of the screenplay, and other creative decisions.

With Peck on board, the next piece of business was turning the novel into a screenplay. Pakula deferred to Nelle before approaching anyone else, but she wasn't interested in the difficult work of adaptation. First, she was busy with a new novel, also set in the South. Working on it, she told a journalist, was like "building a house with matches."[3] The second reason was that she didn't mind if someone else pruned the book to fit a feature-length movie. She felt "indifference. After all, I don't write deathless prose." So Pakula turned to playwright Horton Foote instead. "I was asked to write the script," said Foote, "because the actor, producer, and Miss Lee were familiar with my writings."[4]

A stocky, soft-spoken Texan with blue eyes, Foote actually had very little experience as a film writer. The only other screenplay he'd written was a film-noir piece, *Storm Fear* (1955), the adaptation of a novel by Clinton Seeley, starring Cornel Wilde. A former actor, Foote had begun his career with the American Actors Theater, a small repertory group founded in the early 1940s. The theater's members at that time included Agnes de Mille, Jerome Robbins, and Mildred Dunnock. But he soon realized he was a so-so actor and started listening to friends who advised him to write plays about the town of Wharton, in southeast Texas, where he was raised.

When he was given the job of adapting *To Kill a Mockingbird,* he recognized a historical kinship with Nelle. His forebears had come from Alabama and Georgia in the early 1800s. Nevertheless, he worried about "despoiling the quality of the story" because "it's agonizing to try to get into someone else's psyche and to catch the essence of the work, yet knowing you can't be just literal about it. There has to be a point where you say, 'Well, the hell with it—I've got to do this job for another medium, and I've got to cut out this over-responsible feeling and roll my sleeves up and get to work.' "[5]

At Pakula's urging, Foote ratcheted up the drama by compressing the novel's three years into one. He added a touch of backstory, too. "Harper never mentions the mother, and I was wondering how I could sneak in that emotional element. I remember as a boy my bedroom was right off the gallery on the porch and when I was supposed to be asleep I would hear things I was not supposed to hear from the adults. This was something I invented for the two children."[6]

Most important, he heightened the intensity of the novel's social criticism. Social protest, particularly about racial conditions in the South, receives more emphasis in Foote's screenplay than it does in Nelle's novel, a reflection of the civil rights movement's gaining momentum. To underscore this theme's seriousness, Foote removed some of Nelle's satire, probably thinking that too many caricatures of southern types would diminish the courageousness of Atticus's moral stance against the town. Gone are Aunt Alexandra and her racist church ladies; Colonel Maycomb, admirer of Stonewall Jackson; Miss Fischer, the barely competent first-grade teacher from northern Alabama who behaves like a carpetbagger of education; and Mrs. Meriwether, the long-winded speaker at the Halloween pageant. Foote added a dab of love interest to the story by having Miss Maudie from across the street appear at Atticus's breakfast table one morning, hinting that a relationship might be in the offing. Nelle, on the other hand, preferred her hero to be absolutely asexual—deaf, in fact, according to a political cartoon described in the novel, to the siren call of ladies in Montgomery who find the eligible attorney-legislator attractive.

In spite of the significant changes, Nelle later hailed Foote's screenplay: "If the integrity of a film adaptation is measured by the degree to which the novelist's intent is preserved, Mr. Foote's screenplay should be studied as a classic."[7]

Director Bob Mulligan wasn't so sure. "You know what your problem is," he told Pakula, after reading Foote's work, "too often you lose the point of the view of the children."[8] It was true, but Foote had chosen to thrust Atticus onto center stage at the expense of the children's coming-of-age story, believing the adult character could carry drama that would appeal to moviegoers.

A still more drastic change was contemplated. Before Peck had even read the screenplay, he wanted to drop the title *To Kill a Mockingbird*. Annie Laurie Williams, who had assured Nelle that the novel's artistic integrity would be respected, was furious. "Don't believe any items you may see in the newspapers saying that Gregory Peck wants to change the title of *To Kill a Mockingbird*," she wrote to George Stevens, managing editor at J. B. Lippincott. "He has been signed to play the part of Atticus, but has no right to say what the title of the picture will be. The change of title has been denied by Mulligan and Pakula in a column story in the *New York Times*."[9]

Nevertheless, Peck was the star of the film, and had a considerable financial stake it. Moreover, he had the support of Universal Studios in his back pocket. In ways that mattered, the film was more his than anybody else's.

AFTER SPEAKING TO THE Reverend Polk in his church office, Peck and his wife, Veronique Passani, checked in at the ranch-style LaSalle Hotel in Monroeville. Working the hotel desk that night was Miriam Katz. Not recognizing the stranger signing the register, she quietly repeated, "Gregory P-e-c-k . . . Oh, Mr. Peck!" Startled, she turned to the hotel's only bellhop and mustered all the decorum she could. " 'D.J! This is Mr. Peck. See that he gets anything he wants.'

Peck smiled. 'Thank you very kindly, Mrs. Katz, but I don't want any special favors.' "[10]

Accompanying Peck was a small production crew, sent to photograph period details, and director Bob Mulligan and his wife. But Monroeville only cared that Gregory Peck was in town. The next day, when the word spread—broadcast by the fact that the actor drove around in a convertible—a legion of dessert-bearing ladies got busy. The presence of a movie star led to some strange contretemps. Peck strolled into the Western Auto Store owned by A. B. Blass and asked for a soft drink from the cooler. When Blass presented him with a Dr. Pepper, Peck fished around in his pockets and then sheepishly admitted he didn't have any money with him. Blass gallantly replied that the drink was on him so that he could tell his grandchildren that Gregory Peck owed him six cents. Peck thanked Blass for his largesse, but next he went to the Monroe County Bank for some cash. The girl in the teller window primly informed him that she needed to see some ID. Behind her, the manager, feeling mortified, said evenly, "I think we can take Mr. Peck's check." Finally, it was time to attend to the primary reason Peck was in town: to meet the Lees and study, as unobtrusively as possible, the gentleman he was going to play.

The Lees no longer lived on South Alabama Avenue, having moved to a brick ranch house across from the elementary school not long after the deaths of Mrs. Lee and Edwin in 1951. Alice, no doubt, had felt her father needed a small change of scene, away from painful memories. Mr. Lee was looking forward to meeting Gregory Peck, although he was feeling tired as a result of a mild heart attack. He'd never met a film star. For that matter, he'd never seen Gregory Peck in a movie. The two men sat in the living room getting to know each other, while Nelle and Alice shooed away neighbors trying to peek in through the picture window. Peck got the impression that the elderly lawyer "was much amused by the invasion of these Hollywood types. He looked on us with benign amusement." For his part, the actor found Mr. Lee "a fine old gentleman of eighty-two, and truly sophisticated although he had never traveled farther than a few miles from that small Southern town."[11] They got along together well.

After an hour or so of conversation, Nelle offered to take Peck on a short tour of the square and a stop-off for lunch. The weather was brisk and overcast, but Peck, dressed only in a lightweight suit, gamely followed Nelle, who was wearing a parka, jeans, white socks, and sneakers, around town until they arrived at the Wee Diner.

The Wee Diner was built from two Montgomery buses joined at a forty-five-degree angle, creating a triangular courtyard effect. The intersection served as the entrance. To rustle up customers, owner Frank Meigs put a chopped onion on the grill and turned on the exhaust fan, a welcome smell to Lee and Peck on such a chilly January day. They slid into one of the booths and ordered.

Then, suddenly, through the door came Wanda Biggs, the official hostess for the Welcome Wagon. She had been tracking them all over town, she said, out of breath. On behalf of the Chamber of Commerce, she presented Gregory Peck with a basket of gifts and coupons for newcomers. "He was as polite and kind a man as I had ever met," Biggs later told everyone. "He asked if I would mind taking [the basket] to his wife across the street at the hotel. That he would like for me to meet her. I did and found her to be equally as warm and friendly. They were just our kind of folks."[12]

Nelle and Peck's final stop after the Wee Diner was the home of Charles Ray Skinner. The production crew had arranged to meet them there because they wanted to photograph what servants' quarters looked like in an older home. While flashbulbs popped, Peck made small talk with Skinner about his spacious kitchen, including that he'd never had a real down-home southern meal.

Probably as a result, by seven thirty that evening, the lobby of the LaSalle Hotel was jammed with not only dessert-bearing ladies but also other well-wishers bringing covered dishes. Peck left a message at the front desk expressing his thanks and asked that the items be left for him to pick up. Not to be denied, teenager Martha Jones and a friend pushed through to the receptionist and asked which room Mr. and Mrs. Peck were staying in. Miriam Katz told them huffily that the Pecks were not in at present. The two girls got in their car and drove around town on a scavenger hunt until they spotted Nelle's car outside the Monroe Motor Court. Door by door they listened. Finally, hearing voices, they knocked on one, and were confronted by Nelle, who was obviously not amused.

"Martha Louise Jones, what are you doing here?"

"I was just hoping I could get Mr. Peck's autograph."

Beyond Nelle, intrepid Martha could see Peck, Mr. Lee, and Peck's wife, Veronique.

"Well, we're busy now. You just go on home," ordered Nelle, and began to shut the door.

"Hold on, Nelle," Peck interrupted, "I'll be glad to give the young ladies my autograph." Star-struck, the two adolescents offered Peck damp scraps of paper. He signed both and then bid the girls a gracious good night.[13]

The following morning, until it was time to leave, Mr. and Mrs. Peck didn't venture outside the LaSalle Hotel lest they send the town into a second uproar. Frank Meigs sent over breakfast from the Wee Diner, and later Peck sent him a handwritten note expressing his gratitude.

PRODUCTION ON THE FILM was scheduled to begin in early February in Hollywood, and Nelle had been invited to attend. But she had also promised Truman that she would go with him to Kansas again after Christmas. So the middle of January—two weeks after Peck had left Monroeville—found her back in Garden City, Kansas, once again as Capote's "assistant researchist," though by now her profile in the town was higher than his. "It was pretty dicey for Nelle, as she was known by local people who had come to like her very much," said Dolores Hope.

> She was always very protective of Capote and made sure the limelight was on him most of the time. She was quick to divert mention of the Pulitzer prize back to Capote. She also gave him credit for his help and encouragement. My impression of the Pulitzer time is that

people who had come to know Truman here in Kansas just had a gut feeling that he would have his nose out of joint about it. Nelle knew him so well and she was anything but an attention-getter herself. In fact, she shunned it. She was the exact opposite of Truman, being more interested in others than she was in herself.[14]

For her Kansas friends, she brought an armload of complimentary, autographed copies of *To Kill a Mockingbird*. Her stay was necessarily brief, however, because filming was slated to begin in a few weeks. (Her notes for Truman don't mention this second trip to Kansas, or a third one she made a year later. But indications are that she forged a closer relationship with Perry Smith and Dick Hickock while they were on death row because Truman let them know to expect a letter from her now and then.) Consequently, at the end of the first week of February, she boarded the Super Chief in Garden City, having finished helping Truman, and continued on to Los Angeles. Total sales of her book, hardback and paperback, were approaching 4.5 million. In an unusual move at the time for a publisher, J. B. Lippincott took out eighteen radio ads in major markets to announce that production was beginning on *To Kill a Mockingbird,* starring Gregory Peck.

Casting had been completed just in the nick of time, with some of the roles being settled on just weeks before shooting began. Pakula and Mulligan preferred faces audiences wouldn't recognize "to retain the sense of discovery, which is so important in the novel," Pakula said.[15] They turned to character actors from films, Broadway professionals—unfamiliar then to most film-going audiences—and, for the roles of the children, complete unknowns.

Frank Overton, as Sheriff Heck Tate; Paul Fix, as the judge; Richard Hale, as Mr. Nathan Radley; and Crahan Denton as Walter Cunningham, Sr.—all four were fixtures in Westerns, playing ordinary folk, and could be depended on to render solid performances. Alice Ghostley, who played Dill's aunt Stephanie Crawford; William Windom, who became prosecutor Horace Gilmer; Estelle Evans, who transformed herself into the Finches' housekeeper, Calpurnia; and Rosemary Murphy, who took the role of Miss Maudie Atkinson—all were stage and Broadway performers. Newcomers to film were Collin Wilcox Paxton as Mayella Violet Ewell, and Robert Duvall, who had impressed Horton Foote when he gave a first-rate performance in Foote's drama *The Midnight Caller* at the Neighborhood Playhouse in New York. To prepare for the role of Boo Radley, Duvall stayed out of the sun for six weeks and dyed his hair blonde, thinking it would give him an angelic look.

The competition for the role of Tom Robinson was down to two actors: Brock Peters and James Earl Jones. Peters badly wanted the part because his career seemed to be slipping into a rut of playing heavies and villains. "Well, of course, I was scared out of my wits," he remembered. "I didn't know how to present myself in order to get this coveted prize. I went into the meeting—it was in a building at Park Avenue and 57th Street and I tried not to appear frightened but I wanted to look cool and calm and still suggest the character of Tom Robinson, and do that dressed in a suit."[16] He got the part, and a few days before filming began, Peck called to congratulate him. Peters was so surprised, he didn't know what to say at first. "I worked over the years in many, many productions, but no one ever again called me to welcome me aboard, except perhaps the director and the producer, but not my fellow actor-to-be."[17]

The part of Bob Ewell, the impoverished white man who accuses Tom Robinson of having raped his daughter, was still open when actor James Anderson met with Mulligan. Raised in Alabama, Anderson told Mulligan with conviction, "I know this man." Mulligan believed he did, but he also had to confront Anderson with his reputation for drinking, fighting, and not showing up on sets. He told Anderson to come back in three days (probably to see whether he would be on time and sober). When Anderson arrived, Mulligan laid it on the line. "I want you to be in this movie but you and I are going to have to have a clear understanding. And you're going to have to take my hand and shake it. If you do, you have to promise me that you will be sober, that you will be on time, that you will not cause trouble for me or for anyone. And that you will do honor to this script. He said, 'I understand.' He put out his hand and shook mine, and he kept his word. Boy, did he know that man."[18]

The role of Jem went to thirteen-year-old Philip Alford, a child with practically no acting experience who auditioned only because his parents promised him a day off from school. Hundreds of children competed for the roles of the Finch children, including nine-year-old Mary Badham, who was selected for the part of Scout. Previously, she had appeared in a *Twilight Zone* episode. She was feisty and frank, a good match for her character. When a reporter commented, "You're a very little girl for your age," she replied, "You'd be little, too, if you drank as much coffee as I do."[19] By coincidence, Alford and Badham were Birmingham natives who lived four blocks apart. Alford's parents were, however, working-class people, while Badham's could afford a Negro nanny to help raise her. The part of the Finches' next-door neighbor Dill went to nine-year-old John Megna, brother of actress Connie Stevens, who had recently appeared in the Broadway hit *All the Way Home,* based on James Agee's Pulitzer Prize–winning novel, *A Death in the Family.* "John looked up to me like a big brother," Alford said, and the two boys formed a childish pact to hate Badham.[20] (The threesome banded together when they were bored, however. One day, Alan Pakula was handed a note from studio security saying that they must stop fishing in the pond on a back lot. It was a freshwater reservoir and placed off-limits by the California Fish and Game Commission.)

Pakula and Mulligan had already arranged to shoot many of the scenes on soundstages at the Revue Studios, but that still left the question of what do to for exterior scenes, since Monroeville no longer resembled a Depression-era southern town. Alexander Golitzen, a former architect and the film's co–art director, studied sketches and photographs of Monroeville until he came up with an idea. Some of the houses in old Monroeville resembled clapboard cottages that were disappearing from the outskirts of Los Angeles. Golitzen suggested to his colleague, Henry Bumstead, that they get from wrecking companies leads on houses slated for demolition. Near Chavez Ravine, where a new baseball park for the Los Angeles Dodgers was nearing completion, they found a dozen condemned cottage-style houses. For a total of five thousand dollars, they hauled the frames to the set. Sometimes known as "shotgun hall" houses because they have a center hall with all the rooms off to the left or right, the houses were popular everywhere in the United States during the first thirty years or so of the twentieth century. For a quarter of the cost of building them from scratch on the set, the relocated houses were placed on either side of a re-created Alabama street, with porches, shutters, and gliders (seat swings) added for a touch of southern flair.[21]

When Nelle arrived on the set, she was dazzled not only by the illusion but also by the attitude of the crew making the film. "I know that authors are supposed to knock Hollywood and complain about how their works are treated here," she said, "but I just can't manage it. Everybody has been so darn nice to me and everything is being done with such care that I can't find anything to complain about."[22]

On February 12, principal photography began. Until now, Nelle had been harboring some doubts about Peck's suitability for the role. "The first time I met him was at my home in Alabama. . . . I'd never seen Mr. Peck, except in films, and when I saw him at my home I wondered if he'd be quite right for the part." But that was without seeing him in character. "[T]he first glimpse I had of him was when he came out of his dressing room in his Atticus suit. It was the most amazing transformation I had ever seen. A middle-aged man came out. He looked bigger, he looked thicker through the middle. He didn't have an ounce of makeup, just a 1933-type suit with a collar and a vest and a watch and chain. The minute I saw him I knew everything was going to be all right because he *was* Atticus."[23]

Since her arrival in Los Angeles, Nelle had been "getting the royal treatment from the studios," according to novelist Fred Gipson's wife, Tommie, who kept Maurice Crain informed of his favorite client's activities. "I saw Nelle Lee's picture in the *L.A. Times* the other day. The story said she was visiting the Universal International lot. I was hoping we could buy her a dinner or a drink or something. She was only here for the weekend, it turned out, and was booked solid."[24]

The reason Nelle had to leave so abruptly was that her family needed her. Crain replied to Tommie, "She has a nephew in the Air Force, stationed at Lowry Field, Denver. His little pregnant wife developed pneumonia and landed in a hospital soon after she arrived in California. He couldn't get off the base often, and was worried sick. Nelle was the only member of his or her family within a thousand miles, so she went to Denver and took charge until the girl was out of danger. She finally made it home yesterday [February 19] and called us."[25]

It was too bad she couldn't have stayed to see the courtroom scenes. To film them, scenarists constructed a soundstage set built to look exactly like the interior of the courthouse in Monroeville, based on painstaking measurements. Ironically, one of the novel's major themes is tolerance, but a production assistant kept reassembling the extras for the trial by shouting, "All the colored atmosphere upstairs; all the white atmosphere downstairs." Brock Peters, the film's Tom Robinson, had a word with him, and the call was changed to, "Downstairs atmosphere in, please; balcony atmosphere upstairs, please." Because of the mores of the times, Alford, Badham, and Megna were not allowed to attend the filming of the courtroom scenes, even though they appear to be watching from the courtroom gallery. For children that age, listening to a trial about rape and incest, even a fictional one, was deemed inappropriate.

During the trial, Brock Peters delivered one of the most memorable performances in the entire film. For two weeks of rehearsals and filming, Peters was required to break down on the stand, begin to weep, and then make a dignified attempt to try to stifle his sobs. By the end of this slow disintegration, his self-respect has to gain hold again and turn into barely suppressed rage at being falsely accused. Mulligan coached him until "Once we were on track I needed to go only to the places of pain, remembered pain, experienced pain and the tears would come, really at will." Peters later called those two intense weeks "my veil of tears."[26] Peck found it difficult to watch Peters because the actor's performance was so affecting.

Between Peck and James Anderson, the actor playing Bob Ewell, however, there was no love lost. To begin with, for some reason Anderson would only speak to Mulligan. Peck tried to make a suggestion about one of their scenes, and Anderson snarled back, "You don't show me *shit!*"[27] Second, he was a Method actor, meaning that he tried to remain in character at all times, which in this case was a violent man. In the struggle with Jem Finch, near the end of the film, Anderson yanked Philip Alford out of the frame by his hair.[28]

IN APRIL, AFTER A month of filming, word reached the set that Nelle had returned to Monroeville because her family needed her again. At age eighty-two, A. C. Lee had died early in the morning on Palm Sunday, April 15, 1962.

Of his daughter Nelle, A.C. had said, "It was my plans for her to become a member of our law firm—but it just wasn't meant to be. She went to New York to become a writer."[29] It was typical of him that he tended to think the best of others, including his headstrong daughter who had proven him wrong about her choice to drop out of law school and write fiction instead. He believed that people are basically good, capable of improving, and as eager as the next person for a better future. Change was necessary.

It was true that in his private life, rigorous and traditional Methodism defined his religious convictions rather narrowly. But when, during the 1950s, for example, it became increasingly clear to him that issues of race and fairness overlapped with Christian morality, he enlarged his view of his responsibilities as a religious man.

On Easter Sunday, a week after his death, the *Montgomery Advertiser* wished for more men like Lee to come to the aid of the South, and help pour oil on the roiling waters of the civil rights movement and its nemeses: white supremacists.

Harper Lee, as is the case with most writers of fiction, says that the father in her book, Atticus Finch, isn't exactly *her* father. But she told John K. Hutchens of the *New York Herald Tribune* book section the other day that Atticus Finch was very like her father "in character and—the South has a good word for this—in 'disposition.' "

What makes Atticus Finch or Amasa Coleman Lee, thus a remarkable man? He was a teacher of his own children, a small-town citizen who thought about things and tried to be a decent Christian human being. He succeeded.

. . . Many Southern individuals and families with the Lee-Finch family principles have not asserted themselves and offset another image of the Deep South.

This may be an appropriate thought for this Easter Day. But if it is appropriate, let the individual say. The Lee family, and the Finch, is one of great independence. Amasa Coleman Lee, so evidently a great man, voted Democratic until the mid-30s, then independently. Said a daughter, "We have a great tendency to vote for individuals, instead of parties. We got it from him."

Indeed, was and is the Lee-Finch family so unusual? Could Amasa Coleman Lee, in his care, responsibility and sense of justice, have been so unusual and served so long in the Alabama Legislature, or so long edited a county newspaper in the deep south of this Deep South state?

There are many "likenesses" of Atticus Finch. They are far too silent.[30]

* * *

AFTER HER FATHER'S DEATH, Nelle buried herself in writing. "Not a word from Nelle," Capote wrote to Alvin and Marie Dewey on May 5, "though I read in a magazine that she'd 'gone into hiding; and was hard at work on her second novel.'"[31]

She may have retreated to Maurice Crain and Annie Laurie Williams's Old Stone House in West Hartland, Connecticut, which was becoming one of her favorite places to work. Located on a winding dirt road surrounded by woods and constructed in 1749 from stones and hand-hewn timbers, the house was as solid as a colonial outpost and ideal for solitude. In the backyard, Crain had planted gardens and built a pool for his nieces, Penny and Joy Hafner. "He wasn't afraid of work. He was often out there in a pair of overalls and mixing cement or laying stones and so forth," said Douglas Roberts, who dated one of the Hafner girls. Near to Crain and Williams lived fellow Texan Ruth Cross, author of *The Golden Cocoon,* who labored with her husband to restore forty run-down acres and a crumbling house. When they were finished, they dubbed it Edendale. Because the Old Stone House was conducive to writing without distractions, Williams and Crain regularly offered it to authors, such as Kathleen Windsor and Alan Paton.

Nelle found the Old Stone House congenial, and not just because she was so fond of Crain, Williams, and their relatives Fern and Hans "Dutch" Hafner, who were frequent guests. Nelle didn't own a car, but many times she drove her hosts in theirs, and the threesome enjoyed the two-and-a-half-hour ride up to Connecticut, bringing them to the Old Stone House before nine o'clock on a Friday night after dinner at the nearby Riverton Inn. If the Hafners or other in-laws were there, a few hands of bridge or games of Scrabble by the fireplace were favorite ways to spend an evening. "You had to be careful playing against Nelle or Maurice," said Joy Hafner-Bailey, "they were both so bright—minds like cameras."[32] Sometimes, Nelle stayed behind on Sunday, when the others had left, and worked the entire week alone. A hired man, Roy Law, brought groceries from town, took care of the property, and delivered wood for the fire when the weather was cold.

It was an idyllic setting, but even there she found no magic charm for turning out publishable material. In fact, the previous November she had received what probably was her first rejection letter—from *Esquire* magazine. Commissioned to write a short nonfiction piece on the South—an easy assignment it would seem for the winner of the Pulitzer Prize—she submitted an article so far off the mark that editor Harold Hayes was a little embarrassed about how to respond.

> I feel lousy about returning this to you—on several counts: 1) I asked you to do it; 2) you knocked yourself out to make our deadline; 3) it's something, I know, of great significance to you and the other principals involved.
>
> What seemed to go wrong—from our point of view—is that the piece is working too hard to carry a lot of weight—humor, characterization, the barbarity of the Klan, the goodness of a brave man and so on. A novel's worth, in fact, with the result that it never quite makes it on either of these levels as a short feature.
>
> I'm sympathetic to your decision to change it to a fictional form, and I really don't think that is a factor against it.

Hayes paid her two hundred dollars for her "willingness to be pursued relentlessly by us for a piece that was our idea for you to do."[33]

The fact that she had submitted a piece of fiction with *To Kill a Mockingbird* overtones again, when a nonfiction piece was requested, suggests a certain lack of versatility.

PRINCIPAL SHOOTING ON *To Kill a Mockingbird* had ended May 3, and the picture wrapped in early June 1962. During the five months of production, Alford had grown from four foot eleven to five foot three, and his costumes had to be altered several times. Also, his voice was beginning to change. The final scene to be filmed was outside the jail, when Atticus is protecting his client from a lynch mob and the children unexpectedly intervene. Badham, who didn't want the film to end, kept deliberately flubbing her lines over and over, until her mother pulled her aside and told her that L.A. traffic would be a nightmare if she made everybody stay any longer. Chastened, she said her lines correctly, then Peck, whom the children loved to spray with squirt guns, stepped back. From overhead, the lighting crew poured buckets of water on them.

Peck said he felt good about how the shooting went. "It seemed to just fall into place without stress or strain."[34] He was not pleased, however, when he saw the rough cut of the picture. In a memo to his agent, George Chasin, and Universal executive Mel Tucker dated June 18, 1962, he itemized forty-four objections to the way his character was presented. In sum, the children appeared too often, in his opinion, and their point of view diminished the importance of Atticus. "Atticus has no chance to emerge as courageous or strong. Cutting generally seems completely antiheroic where Atticus is concerned, to the point where he is made to be wishy-washy. Don't understand this approach."[35] But Pakula and Mulligan had taken the precaution of stipulating that they would make the final cut, which kept them, and not the studio, in control of the editing. "Universal did not like the picture very much," said Foote, "and if they had got their hands on it, God knows what they would have done, but they couldn't."[36]

After reviewing Peck's memo, Mulligan and Pakula made another pass at reediting the film, but the star still wasn't satisfied. In a second memo to Universal's Tucker, on July 6, Peck wrote, "I believe we have a good character in Atticus, with some humor and warmth in the early stages, and some good emotion and conflict in the trial and later on. . . . In my opinion, the picture will begin to look better as Atticus' story line emerges, and the children's scenes are cut down to proportion."[37] More footage fell to the cutting room floor, including whole scenes of the children. Pakula said later, "It just tore my heart out to lose the sequence [where Jem reads aloud to Mrs. Dubose, who is dying]."[38]

In the end, Peck positioned himself firmly and prominently at the center of the film. Only about 15 percent of the novel is devoted to Robinson's rape trial, whereas in the film, the running time is more than 30 percent of a two-hour film.

MEANWHILE, NELLE CONTINUED TO work on her follow-up to *To Kill a Mockingbird*; the pressure was on her for a repeat performance. In August, Capote wrote to the Deweys, "As for Nelle—what a rascal! Actually, I know she is trying very hard to get a new book going. But she loves you dearly, so I'm sure you will be the first to hear from her when she *does* reappear."[39]

The success of her first novel had given her something like the corner on the market for popular fiction about growing up in the Deep South. Other authors who wrote about the same region discovered that reviewers held up *To Kill a Mockingbird* as the standard. Elise Sanguinetti, Nelle's friend from the *Rammer Jammer* days, complained about comparison because her novel *The Last of the Whitfields* (1962) seemed to be getting scant attention. A coming-of-age novel told from the perspective of an adolescent, it describes how two upper-middle-class white children in Georgia cope with the new social order welling up around them. "The book is running into some difficulties with this MOCKINGBIRD rage that is going about," Sanguinetti wrote to her mentor, Hudson Strode. "The early reviewers seem to think they are very similar. I didn't think so, and ironically I wasn't very taken with that book. The Negro-white situation there was much too melodramatic for my taste and somewhat unbelievable (as was a nine-year-old daughter of a lawyer going around saying 'ain't' all the time etc.). But one can't argue with success, can you?"[40]

Success was an understatement. By now, Nelle's novel had completed an eighty-eight-week run on bestseller lists, and she was wealthy. In September 1962, the First United Methodist Church of Monroeville broke ground on a new educational building and chapel, helped by an annual percentage of royalties which Nelle had earmarked for it. In addition, she purchased furnishings for the chapel in memory of her parents and her brother, and commissioned a statue of Methodist founder John Wesley. Nevertheless, she was uncomfortable with the assumption that she was rich, which she tried to undercut with rough humor. On the day of the dedication ceremony for the chapel, Nelle rose to use the ladies' room before events got under way. Reverend A. F. Howington cautioned her not to leave her purse on the pew. "Goodness, don't do that—someone might take something," he said.

"Take something!" Nelle replied. "I spent my damn money on this church. There's nothing in it."[41]

ALTHOUGH *TO KILL A Mockingbird* was no longer on the bestseller lists, it continued to sell thousands of copies weekly, both in the United States and abroad, buoyed along not only by its appeal to readers but by a wave of concern about race and justice that was gaining strength.

On September 25, 1962, James Meredith, a twenty-eight-year-old Negro Air Force veteran, attempted to enroll at the University of Mississippi, at Oxford, where he had been accepted. Surrounded by white

United States marshals, Meredith approached the offices of the Board of Trustees. Blocking the doorway was Governor Ross Barnett.

"Which one of you is Meredith?" asked Barnett. The fifty state legislators flanking the governor erupted in laughter. Barnett then read a prepared statement: "I, Ross R. Barnett, governor of the State of Mississippi, having heretofore by proclamation, acting under the police powers of the state of Mississippi . . . do hereby deny you admission to the University of Mississippi."

Five days later, on a Sunday afternoon, Meredith, this time accompanied by 536 deputy U.S. marshals wearing white helmets and carrying billy clubs, arrived at his assigned dormitory and was placed under protective guard. Then a contingent of marshals walked a half-mile to the Lyceum building to prepare the way for Meredith to register for classes. But the registrar was nowhere to be found. Outside the Lyceum building, students tore down the United States flag and ran up the Confederate Stars and Bars. By nightfall, thousands of students and townspeople were battling with the marshals. Rocks, Molotov cocktails, and occasionally bullets spattered the streets. President John F. Kennedy went on national television to announce the federalizing of fifteen thousand National Guard troops to maintain law and order in Mississippi. During the riot in Oxford, two men were killed and hundreds injured. Of the 536 marshals, 166 were injured, and 30 suffered gunshot wounds. Said one military police officer, "I can't believe this is America."

On October 1, Meredith walked to his first class, a seminar on colonial American history, again escorted by U.S. marshals past a crowd of hundreds of jeering students.

AGAINST THIS BACKDROP, IN November, Nelle received her first honorary doctorate of letters, from Mount Holyoke College in Massachusetts. Along with Senator Margaret Chase Smith from Maine, she had been chosen, said Mount Holyoke authorities, because the two women had "won the kind of recognition in their own fields that is customarily accorded to men." At the Founder's Day ceremony, college president Richard Glenn Gettell said, To Kill a Mockingbird had "made possible in us a deeper perception of the forces at work in our society. Without sensationalism, without cynicism, without bitterness, but with delicacy and strength, compassion and sternness, you have humanly treated the great themes of justice and suffering and the growth of understanding, and have formed them into a memorable work of art."[42]

Her appearance at Mount Holyoke was the start of a long period of standing before audiences. The film *To Kill a Mockingbird* was slated for release at Christmas in order for it to qualify for the 1962 Academy Awards, and Nelle had agreed to pitch in with publicity. Alice claimed that her sister "would be terrified to speak" to groups, but it was not so, judging from how cleverly she handled herself before a roomful of newsmen in Chicago shortly after the film's release. After a local press agent muffed her introduction by calling her "Miss Hunter," Nelle stepped up to take questions. "She is 36-years-old, tall, and a few pounds on the wrong side of Metrecal [a diet drink]," wrote a reporter for the Chicago Press Club's newsletter, *Overpress*. "She has dark, short-cut, uncurled hair; bright, twinkling eyes; a gracious manner; and Mint Julep diction." The rapid repartee between Nelle and the reporters comes off best as it is reproduced in the newsletter:[43]

REPORTER: Have you seen the movie?

MISS LEE: Yes. Six times. (It was soon learned that she feels the film did justice to the book, and though she did not have script approval, she enjoyed the celluloid treatment with "unbridled pleasure.")

REPORTER: What's going to happen when it's shown in the South?

MISS LEE: I don't know. But I wondered the same thing when the book was published. But the publisher said not to worry, because no one can read down there. . . .

REPORTER: One of your sisters is a lawyer. Is she a criminal lawyer?

MISS LEE (deadpan): She's not a criminal, no.

REPORTER: You studied law, too, didn't you?

MISS LEE: Yes. For three years. I had to study something in college, and I grew up in a legal household. (Her father, like the hero of *Mockingbird,* is also a lawyer—ed.) The minute, though, that I started to study law, I loathed it. I always wanted to be a writer.

REPORTER: How did the lawyers you know like the book?

MISS LEE: Southern lawyers don't read novels much.

REPORTER: I understand that Gregory Peck, after seeing his straight dramatic performance in *Mockingbird,* says he will no longer do romantic leads.

MISS LEE: Maybe he liked himself in glasses.

REPORTER: When you wrote the book, did you hold yourself back?

MISS LEE (patiently): Well, sir, in the book I tried to give a sense of proportion to life in the South, that there isn't a lynching before every breakfast. I think that Southerners react with the same kind of horror as other people do about the injustice in their land. In Mississippi, people were so revolted by what happened, they were so stunned, I don't think it will happen again.

REPORTER: If you wanted to be a writer, why did you study law?

MISS LEE: I think you should always do the opposite thing from what you want to do. If you have a job writing during the day, I think it's too hard to try and write four hours when you go home. So dig ditches for a living, anything. A change of pace is good.

REPORTER: Do you find it difficult to write?

MISS LEE: I've found it difficult in terms of time. A lot of people like to drop around and visit now. I'm drinking more coffee than ever.

REPORTER: Do you find your second novel coming slow?

MISS LEE: Well, I hope to live to see it published.

REPORTER: How long have you been working on it?

MISS LEE: I've spent one and a half years on it now. *Mockingbird* took two and a half years of writing. . . .

REPORTER: What do you think of the Freedom Riders?

MISS LEE: I don't think this business of getting on buses and flaunting state laws does much of anything. Except getting a lot of publicity, and violence. I think Reverend King and the NAACP are going about it in exactly the right way. The people in the South may not like it, but they respect it.

REPORTER (cub variety): I came in late, so maybe you've already been asked this question, but I'd like to know if your book is an indictment against a group in society.

MISS LEE (nonplused [*sic*]): The book is not an indictment so much as a plea for something, a reminder to people at home. . . .

REPORTER: Were the characters in the book based on real people?

MISS LEE: No, but the people at home think so. The beauty of it, though, is that no two people come up with the same identification. They never think of themselves as being portrayed in the book. They try to identify others whom they know as characters.

REPORTER (grinning slyly): What with royalties and a sale to the movies, you must be getting awfully rich.

MISS LEE: No, not rich. You know that program we have at Cape Canaveral? I'm paying for it. Ninety-five percent of the earnings disappeared in taxes.

REPORTER: What is your opinion of Governor Barnett's failure to obey a federal directive?

MISS LEE: I have no opinion. That's for the court to decide. I presume the gentleman is innocent until proven guilty. But I presume he'll be proven guilty. I think he was wrong. . . .

REPORTER: Will success spoil Harper Lee?

MISS LEE: She's too old.

REPORTER: How do you feel about your second novel?

MISS LEE: I'm scared.

REPORTER: Don't some people presume the name "Harper Lee" belongs to a man?

MISS LEE: Yes. Recently I received an invitation to speak at Yale University, and was told I could stay in the men's dormitory. But I declined that part of the invitation. (She smiled.) With reluctance.

TRUMAN INTIMATED TO OTHERS that he knew how Nelle was coming along with her new book, but apparently she didn't confide in him about it. "I can't tell you much about Nelle's new book," he wrote to Donald Cullivan, a former army buddy of Perry Smith's. "It's a novel, and quite short. But she is *so* secretive."[44] In any case, she couldn't have been devoting much time to it, because publicity demands having to do with the upcoming release of the film were keeping her busy.

For instance, amid all the other scheduled appearances, she received an invitation to visit the Texas home of Vice President Lyndon Baines Johnson and his wife, Lady Bird.

"Texas and Alabama girls attending schools in Washington had a holiday party with an English lesson Saturday afternoon when they were the guests of Mrs. Lyndon B. Johnson, wife of the Vice President, at the Elms in Spring Valley, Texas," reported the *Washington Post.*

> Mrs. Johnson had an array of distinguished Alabamans and Texans there to meet the girls who are boarding at the schools and colleges in the Washington area. Two of the special guests, novelists Harper Lee of Alabama and Allen Drury of Texas, were called on to speak to the students. They answered questions ranging from "How can you prepare yourself to become a novelist?" ("Read your head off," suggested Miss Lee) and "Do novelists make exceptional grades in high school English?" ("Those were the only good grades I ever did get," she replied).[45]

Writing a novel wouldn't make an author automatically famous, either, Nelle cautioned, judging from reactions she got even in her home state. One afternoon she visited a country school near Monroeville. A blond boy of ten or twelve emerged from the building with a teacher, who recognized her.

> "Herbert," said the teacher, "do you know who she is?"
> "No, ma'am."

"She has written a very famous book," the teacher hinted.

"She has," Herbert said flatly.

"This is our own Miss Harper Lee, who has written a wonderful book," explained the teacher. "If I hadn't kept you in after school, you would have missed seeing her. Aren't you glad, Herbert?"

"No, ma'am."[46]

On Christmas Day 1962, two days after J. B. Lippincott had donated three hundred books in A. C. Lee's memory to the Monroe County Library, *To Kill a Mockingbird* premiered in Hollywood. At a buffet supper afterward, film celebrities who had attended the screening—Rock Hudson, Gregory Peck, Natalie Wood, and Paul Newman, among others—offered Nelle their congratulations. "It's a fantastically good motion picture," she said happily to the press. "And it remained faithful to the spirit of the book. It is unpretentious. Nothing phony about it."[47] Annie Laurie Williams wrote to Truman: "You will be happy to know that Nelle's picture 'To Kill a Mockingbird' is getting rave reactions from everyone who has seen the previews."

Alabama cities and towns vied to be the first to premiere the film in the state. The prize had gone to Mobile for the third week of March; Monroeville, which had submitted a petition of citizens' signatures, would get it at the end of March, even before Birmingham— a plum for a small town. In the meantime, First Lady Jackie Kennedy arranged for a private showing in Washington, D.C., in early January for one of her charities. Alan Pakula proudly showed the film to several senators and Supreme Court justices, but he ended up with the wrong print, "a study in grays—no black and white resonance. It was one of the worst nights of my life."[48]

On Valentine's Day 1963, the film opened in New York City. Nelle soldiered on through another public appearance, having given her word that she would. "I must quote to you from a letter I received from a Mr. John Casey, the man who is in charge of the preview room at Universal-International at 445 Park Avenue," Annie Laurie Williams wrote to Alice Lee. "'Miss Harper Lee has been in many times helping on the promotion of the picture and I have had occasion to speak with her. My personal opinion is that Harper Lee is such a wonderfully warm and friendly woman that I have had all I could do to keep from giving her a big hug right in public. Oh Susanna, do not cry for me, 'cause I met a real fine woman and her name is Harper Lee.'"[49]

Audiences for the New York premiere lined up around the block.

Despite the film's subject matter, racism and intolerance, the first few minutes of the movie run against audiences' expectations by showing images of innocence. Credits appear over a child's collection of miniature toys contained in an old cigar box. An unseen child hums, picks up small objects, and draws with crayons on construction paper, a sequence that title designer Stephen Frankfurt shot on his kitchen table on East Fifty-eighth Street in New York. Frankfurt enlisted a neighbor girl to play at the table. Each of the objects in the box has a real or symbolic meaning, including a white marble, which starts to roll via a concealed magnet until it gently bumps into a black one. The *click!,* when the marbles touch, cues the music, a simple melody played on a piano with one hand, as if a child were picking out a tune. Composer Elmer Bernstein, a former concert pianist who had studied under Aaron Copland, suggested the theme music for Mulligan by placing the phone next to his piano one morning and playing it for him. Mulligan was delighted. The effect of the plaintive but sentimental music, which swells into an orchestral treatment, combined with the tiny world inside the cigar box, is charming and, as Mulligan said, "put us directly into the movie."[50]

At the time, the film was considered politically liberal because of the attention paid in the screenplay to social justice. Looking back, however, Peck's insistence that Atticus's character occupy more of the film's center injects a heavy dose of white patriarchal values. In a word, Atticus, an educated white male, appears to be the most important person in the film. Everyone else defers to him, humors him, reacts to him, or disagrees with him. As one critic recently noted, the elimination of Scout's voice-over from most of the film means that the viewer doesn't see small-town southern society from the perspective of a young female growing up in it.[51] Instead, *To Kill a Mockingbird* is largely Atticus's story, even to the point that Tom's fate, which means death, seems less important than Atticus's losing the case—a critical failure in making the audience "walk in Tom's shoes," as Atticus would have put it.

After the New York premiere, reviewers by and large praised the film as entertainment, though some of the more perceptive identified aesthetic problems.

"The trial weighed upon the novel, and in the film, where it is heavier, it is unsupportable. The narrator's voice returns at the end, full of warmth and love . . . but we do not pay her the same kind of attention any more. We have seen that outrageous trial, and we can no longer share the warmth of her love," wrote *Newsweek*.[52] Bosley Crowther in the *New York Times* pointed out, "It is, in short, on the level of adult awareness of right and wrong, of good and evil, that most of the action in the picture occurs. And this detracts from the camera's observation of the point of view of the child. . . . [*I*]t leaves the viewer wondering precisely how the children feel. How have they really reacted to the things that affect our grown-up minds?"[53]

Brendan Gill, writing for the *New Yorker,* disliked that the film's resolution, Bob Ewell's death, was no more defensible than it was in the novel: "In the last few minutes of the picture, whatever intellectual and moral content it may be said to have contained is crudely tossed away in order to provide a 'happy' ending. . . . The moral of this can only be that while ignorant rednecks mustn't take the law into their own hands, it's all right for *nice* people to do so."[54]

Andrew Sarris for the *Village Voice* wrote the most critical review of all: " 'To Kill a Mockingbird' relates the Cult of Childhood to the Negro Problem with disastrous results. Before the intellectual confusion of the project is considered, it should be noted that this is not much of a movie even by purely formal standards."[55]

Nelle was unfazed. "For me, Maycomb is there, its people are there: in two short hours one lives a childhood and lives it with Atticus Finch, whose view of life was the heart of the novel."[56]

THE JUGGERNAUT OF PUBLICITY rolled on into the early winter of 1963. Nelle had promised Truman she would accompany him to Garden City again, but he was clearly becoming peeved at having to play second fiddle to her success. "I think our friend Nelle will meet me in G.C.," Capote wrote to the Deweys in February. "However, she is so involved in the publicity for her film (she owns a percentage, that's why; even so, I think it very undignified for any serious artist to allow themselves to be exploited in this fashion)."[57]

Annie Laurie Williams, on the other hand, couldn't have been more pleased with Nelle. Writing to Alice Lee on February 16, Williams lavished praise on her:

When Nelle came in yesterday with the enclosed clippings, she was so tired she could hardly sit. She had been with the Universal people being interviewed by Hal Boyle of the Associated Press and the hours on hours of public appearances, plus sitting and being asked questions, was about all she could take. Phil Gerard [a press agent] says she talks so well before little or big audiences and never stops or is halting in what she is saying but "performs" like a real professional lecturer, but when she gets through, she always thinks she didn't do so well and gets real surprised when you tell her how good she is.

I have never seen a picture receive so much love and tender affection as To Kill a Mockingbird. . . . And I want to end by saying Nelle will carry on with her two next out of town engagements, as she is what we call a "good trooper." I love her dearly and think she has come off in every way with not only deserved honors but with many new friends and admirers.[58]

Nelle had opened up with Hal Boyle more than she had with most interviewers, or perhaps she was becoming more relaxed. She admitted, tongue in cheek, "Success has had a very bad effect on me. I've gotten fat—but extremely uncomplacent. I'm running just as scared as before." Then, apropos of nothing, but perhaps speaking of herself and the pressures on her, she said, "Self-pity is a sin. It is a form of living suicide. . . ."[59] Williams wrote to Alice, "It was a good interview and I'm glad Nelle 'spoke her mind.' "[60]

The Alabama premiere took place on March 15, with many shows sold out in advance. Two weeks later, the film arrived in Monroeville, and Nelle was in town to witness the reaction. A full-page ad in the *Monroe Journal,* paid for by businesses, trumpeted, "We Are Proud of Harper Lee . . . and Her Masterpiece! We Would Like to Share with Her These Moments of Artistic Triumph!" Reserved-seat tickets were on sale by March 17 at the theater box office or by mail order: one dollar for adults and fifty cents for children. The first five customers who brought in a live mockingbird would receive ten dollars apiece.

Dorothy and Taylor Faircloth drove over from Atmore on a starry, cool night to see the movie: "You were really fortunate to get tickets. It was a fantastic event for a small town like Monroeville."[61] Also in the audience was Joseph Blass who, as a teenager, had caddied for Mr.

Lee. "Mr. Lee did not look much like Peck in the movie, although Peck, who had spent time with Mr. Lee, copied some of his mannerisms in a way that was almost eerie to those of us who knew him."[62]

When the film ended, remembered Taylor, there was no applause. Few people said anything until they reached the lobby. "At that time in the South, everybody seemed to be divided. You were either a liberal or a racist. And when the movie ended, the discussion afterwards went along those lines."[63] The film was held over a week. Nelle posed for a photo under the marquee with some Monroeville dignitaries, squinting in the springtime daylight, but obviously beaming.

The film was the object of enjoyment and praise, but judging from its premiere in Birmingham at least, it didn't seem to prick people's consciences. When the film opened in Birmingham, on April 3 at the Melba Theater, "huge crowds jammed the street . . . to catch a glimpse of the movie's two child stars: Birmingham natives Mary Badham and Philip Alford," writes Jonathan S. Bass in *Blessed Are the Peacemakers*. "Ironically, the story line depicted white bigotry and black injustice in Alabama during the 1930s and illustrated the meaningful role a paternalistic, decent, and moderate white southerner could play during a racial crisis. Regardless, the movie apparently had little impact on the racial outlook of Birmingham's white community during the spring of 1963."[64]

At the same time that the Melba Theater was filled with appreciative audiences, the Southern Christian Leadership Conference had organized thousands of Negro children to march in Birmingham. Police carried them off in buses to jail. When there was no more room, "Bull" Connor ordered that police dogs and fire hoses be turned on the demonstrators. The pressurized water was powerful enough to rip the bark off trees and sent children skidding down the pavement. After weeks of violent acts by the Birmingham police, Attorney General Robert Kennedy successfully lobbied white business leaders to desegregate public facilities. The whole country, he pointed out to them, even parts of the Western world, was watching the city of Birmingham become a spectacle of brutality.

By spring of 1963, *To Kill a Mockingbird* had been nominated for eight Academy Awards, including Best Picture, Best Director, Best Supporting Actress (Mary Badham), Best Black-and-White Cinematography, and Best Music Score—Substantially Original.

As a year in film history, 1962 was remarkable for the number of high-quality films released, many of which became classics. John Frankenheimer had directed three of those films: *All Fall Down,* adapted from James Leo Herlihy's novel about a dysfunctional family, starring Warren Beatty, Eva Marie Saint, Karl Malden, Angela Lansbury, and Brandon De Wilde; *Birdman of Alcatraz,* with Burt Lancaster, making a plea for prison reform; and *The Manchurian Candidate,* a political thriller about right-wing zealots taking over the government.

Blake Edwards released two films: a stylish thriller, *Experiment in Terror,* and an uncompromising look at alcoholism, *The Days of Wine and Roses,* which was Jack Lemmon's breakout role as a dramatic actor.

Arthur Penn directed the film version of his Broadway hit *The Miracle Worker,* starring Anne Bancroft and Patty Duke. Also from Broadway came the screen version of *The Music Man,* starring Robert Preston. Stanley Kubrick adapted Vladimir Nabokov's *Lolita.*

In the Western genre, Sam Peckinpah's *Ride the High Country* put a rousing moral dilemma in the hands of two cowpokes, veteran actors Joel McCrea and Randolph Scott, each in one of his best roles. John Ford directed *The Man Who Shot Liberty Valance,* and Kirk Douglas starred in *Lonely Are the Brave,* a modern-day Western.

Two horror films that year depended on psychological twists: *Whatever Happened to Baby Jane?* featured Bette Davis and Joan Crawford in roles that destroyed their images as femme fatales; and Robert Mitchum was alternately charming and frightening as he stalked a family in *Cape Fear.* For the epic re-creation of D-day, *The Longest Day,* Darryl F. Zanuck engaged the talents of so many actors that audiences became preoccupied with whom they could recognize.

From abroad came two François Truffaut masterpieces, *Shoot the Piano Player* and *Jules and Jim.* David Lean's epic *Lawrence of Arabia* probed the masochism and megalomania of its hero, T. E. Lawrence, played by Peter O'Toole in his first major role. Marcello Mastroianni was nominated for an Oscar in Pietro Germi's satire of infidelity and male arrogance, *Divorce Italian Style.* Tony Richardson released *The Loneliness of the Long-Distance Runner.* Finally, Alain Resnais puzzled audiences with his enigmatic *Last Year at Marienbad.*

On awards night, April 8, Nelle went to a friend's house in Monroeville to watch the presentations. She didn't own a television because "it interferes with my work." Horton Foote won the Best Adapted Screenplay Oscar, and the team of Art Directors/Set Decorators for *To Kill a Mockingbird* also received the top honor. Some days before the ceremony, Nelle had sent Gregory Peck her father's pocket watch, engraved, "To Gregory from Harper." Now, as he sat in the Hollywood audience waiting for the envelope to be opened and the announcement made of who had been voted Best Actor, Peck clutched the watch. When Sophia Loren read his name as the winner, he strode onto the stage with A.C.'s watch still in his hand. One of the first people he thanked was Harper Lee.

She cried "tears of joy."[65]

A few days later, Truman returned to Monroeville from Switzerland to visit his aunt Ida Carter. About forty people attended a little party at the Carter home for both Truman and Nelle. But most of the attention, Truman couldn't help but notice, went to Nelle.[66]

The Second Novel

IN MID-1963, AFTER THE END OF THE PUBLICITY CONNECTED with the film *To Kill a Mockingbird,* Nelle was free now to work as much as she liked on her next novel. Alice was handling her finances, and income from *To Kill a Mockingbird* and the Academy Award–winning film adaptation were like two springs of a stream flowing to Monroeville. "My advice would be for you to work out just how much money Nelle can take in the coming years," Annie Laurie Williams suggested to Alice, "without causing too much to be paid to the Government, and then when we know what her tax situation is, we can then make arrangement with the Atticus Company to let her have so much a year."[1]

Williams, Crain, and Nelle were practically inseparable. When Nelle was in New York, the three saw each other almost daily during the summer of 1963. On weekends, she often went up to their home in Connecticut. "Nelle is looking fine again, we are glad to report," Williams reassured Alice, referring to the young author's fatigued state after the grind of her public appearances earlier that year. "She will be with us again this weekend at the Old Stone House. Last weekend it rained all day Saturday, but Sunday was a nice day. My sister Fern said, 'Nelle, do you think your sister Alice will ever come up here to see us?' "[2]

Williams, no doubt, recognized the importance of staying in Alice's good graces. Nelle discussed everything with her older sister. Alice scrutinized contracts and percentages, and weighed in on negotiations that affected Williams's bottom line. So keeping on the best of terms with the Lee clan was good business. In addition, Alice seemed able to snap her fingers and make Nelle scamper back to Monroeville, interrupting her sister's work and potentially delaying the second novel still more—another financial consideration from an agent's point of view. As it turned out, Alice jumped at the invitation and made arrangements for both herself and middle sister Louise Connor to visit in the fall and get to know these important friends of Nelle's.

Meanwhile, the civil rights movement reached a watershed that summer. In June, George Wallace, the governor of Alabama, stood in front of a schoolhouse door at Nelle's alma mater, the University of Alabama, in a symbolic attempt to oppose the enrollment of Vivian Malone and James Hood, two Negro students. When federal marshals confronted Wallace, he stepped aside, but segregationists cheered his protest. At her home near the campus of the University of Alabama, Hudson Strode's wife, Therese, not sympathetic to the civil rights cause, felt dread about the course of events and voiced the sentiments of many white Southerners. "I have given up completely," she wrote to a friend.

> The white race is lost. The U.S. has become not only the champion but leader of the colored races. Now I understand why Plato rejected democracy, regarding it as little more than rule by the mob. And Greek mobs were neither black nor "mixed."
>
> Hudson walks in and out among it all like Daniel in the lion's den. We pay as little attention to it as possible. . . . Do not worry about us, darling Peggy. We live five miles from town in the midst of twenty acres of trees. Negroes are urban people. If these green, gentle woods were the Wilds of Africa, they could not regard them with more terror.[3]

In August, a quarter of a million people participated in the March on Washington, which was climaxed by Reverend Martin Luther

King, Jr.'s "I have a dream" speech, delivered from the steps of the Lincoln Memorial.

But privately Nelle was wary of forcing too much, too soon. As she had said to reporters in Chicago during her promotional tour for the film, in answer to a question regarding the Freedom Riders, "I don't think this business of getting on buses and flaunting state laws does much of anything. Except getting a lot of publicity, and violence."[4]

She was right about the South's having a culture that was sensitive to northern coercion. According to Alabama historian Virginia Van der Veer Hamilton,

> Plain folk sensed that it was *they,* not the most prosperous whites, who were to ride buses, live in neighborhoods, and compete for jobs with blacks; *their* children who were to be seated alongside black children in schools. But the sight of white demonstrators from the North goaded them to even greater fury. Here came another wave of outsiders retracing the steps of all those old abolitionists, Yankee soldiers, school teachers, missionaries, and federal judges who had meddled in the affairs of their state. They were concerned that they would count for even less.[5]

"Nelle didn't agree with the tactics being used to integrate the South," said Kay Wells, a friend from Kansas who visited Nelle in New York. "She thought sending troops was only going to cause more trouble and anger people."[6]

In her private opinion, Lee was not speaking as the author of a "novel of man's conscience," as she described it, "universal in the sense it could have happened to anybody, anywhere people live together."[7] But as a Southerner, hers was "not an uncommon position for even progressive people to take," according to Donald Collins, author of *When the Church Bells Rang Racist,* a history of segregation in the Methodist church. "They didn't object to the goals being sought, but rather the methodology that was being used. It was a way of not fighting the real issue."[8]

Meanwhile, national concern over law and order and civil rights was adding to *To Kill a Mockingbird*'s foothold in public schools. Eight percent of public junior high schools and high schools nationwide had added the novel to their reading lists only three years after its publication.[9] Nelle marveled at the book's appeal to youngsters: "I find that hard to understand. The novel is about a former generation, and I don't see how this younger generation can like it." Informed that she had done a wonderful job of writing for children, she replied, tongue in check, "But I hate children. I can't stand them."[10]

In September, the exchange of letters between Annie Laurie Williams and Alice Lee became more animated with excitement over their getting together at the Old Stone House. "It will soon be time for you and Louise to start on your trip," Williams wrote to Alice. "We are all standing on tiptoe waiting to see you. Last weekend Nelle got a Hertz car and drove my sister Lee, her husband, Maurice and me to the farm. She is an excellent driver. Today my brother-in-law, Dutch [Fern's husband], Maurice and Nelle and I are going up for a quiet weekend."[11]

Alice replied, "I do hope that the leaves are beginning to turn so they will put on a spectacle for us in October. . . . Don't worry about feeding us, just being at the farm with you is going to be exciting enough to keep us going, and we will start N.H. [Nelle Harper] on a reducing diet when we arrive!"[12]

If Williams felt any trepidation about meeting Alice, now the head of the Lee family, and Louise, her anxieties were put to rest only moments after the sisters arrived. Alice presented Williams with a gift: a handmade apron sewn by her aunt Alice McKinley, her mother's sister in Atmore, Alabama. Williams wore it every moment she was in the kitchen. The New England weather was perfect for autumn, and the trees surrounded the colonial Old Stone House with a panorama of fall colors. The sisters stayed for a week and then attended to some business in Manhattan. In the city, they lunched with Jonas Silverstone, an attorney whom Williams had retained to handle the income from films and plays. He informed Alice to expect a check for Nelle in the neighborhood of fifty-eight thousand dollars—the equivalent of ten times the average annual salary of a wage earner in 1963. "He liked the three Lee girls very much and you have a real friend 'at court' if you feel you ever need to ask Jonas anything about the returns from the Mockingbird picture," Williams told Alice.[13]

Finally, though, it was time for the Lee sisters, including Nelle, to head back to Alabama. She was eager to get back to her new book. "You know that we always talk on the phone on Sunday night just to report on our weekend and find out 'how you feel,'" Williams wrote to Nelle, "and this letter is just to say we are glad you are with Bear [Alice] but we sure *do miss you.*"[14]

Even though A.C. was long gone, and Alice by now was a single woman living on her own with a well-established career in the offices of Bugg, Barnett & Lee, she still gave a tug to her youngest sister, when it was time, in Alice's judgment, for Nelle to come home. To an interviewer, Nelle said with a hint of defeat, "Well, I don't live here, actually. I see it about two months out of every year. I enjoy New York—theaters, movies, concerts, all that—and I have many friends here. But I always go home again."[15] She was rich, almost forty, and a regular Manhattanite for fifteen years, but she had to return to a town without so much as a bookstore for stretches of six months or longer every year. Both her parents were dead; her former sister-in-law, Sara, had remarried and moved away after Edwin Lee's death; and Louise lived two hours from Monroeville, yet Alice insisted that Nelle "come home."

BACK IN MONROEVILLE, NELLE bent to the task of trying to write regularly. Requests for personal appearances and speeches were still pouring in, but she decided that since "I'm in no way a lecturer or philosopher, my usefulness there is limited." At a dinner given in her honor at the University of Alabama, she warned her hosts to expect a "two-word speech," and that if she felt talkative, she might add, "very much."[16]

Even in Monroeville, however, demands on her time were hard to escape. "I've found I can't write on my home grounds. I have about 300 personal friends who keep dropping in for a cup of coffee. I've tried getting up at 6, but then all the 6 o'clock risers congregate."[17] To get away by herself, she went to the golf course, forgiving her neighbors for their trespasses on her privacy. "Well, they're Southern people, and if they know you are working at home they think nothing of walking right in for a cup of coffee. But they wouldn't dream of interrupting you at golf."[18] She liked to spend the hours on the golf course thinking about her novel. "Playing golf is the best way I know to be alone and still be doing something. You hit a ball, think, take a walk. I do my best thinking walking. I do my dialog, talking it out to myself."[19]

She had to know at least two chapters ahead what characters were going to do and say before she could make any progress. Even so, she was a slow writer. Her method was to "finish a page or two, put them aside, look at them with a fresh eye, work on them some more, then rewrite them all over again."[20]

As 1963 neared an end, Alice did a rough estimate of her sister's income and taxes. Nelle "nearly flipped," Alice wrote Williams, about the tax implications of her income, "and she worried terribly for a short while, then she took off to the golf course and had a good time."[21] Worrying about money, her second novel, and dieting—Williams congratulated her "on losing all those pounds"—was making her a little snappish. Truman wrote soothingly to Marie Dewey after Nelle groused that she was too busy to get together with her. "Don't be upset about Nelle. That's just the way she is. And always will be. It doesn't mean a thing. She *adores* you both."[22]

Before she had published anything, Nelle imagined the writer's life as the best possible for someone like her who loved independence and shunned conformity. Now she was discovering that expectations of success could be a ball and chain.

Come spring, Nelle returned to New York. She was eager to continue her stays at the Old Stone House, where she could be with friends but also left alone when she needed to work. "I have a place where I don't know anybody and nobody knows me. I'm not going to tell, because somebody would know."[23] In Connecticut, her pattern was to write steadily for six days, then stop and take a break for two, which suggests that she worked approximately Monday through Friday, then let her pen rest when Crain, Williams, and a few of their in-laws arrived on weekends. Although writing "has its own rhythm," she said, it was "the loneliest work there is."[24]

She also had to be back in New York because Truman needed her help with the final phases of *In Cold Blood*. For more than four years, he had been laboring on the manuscript. His childish handwriting filled more than a dozen school notebooks, every paragraph double-spaced and written in pencil. To keep from looking back at what he'd finished, he turned the notebook upside down for the next blank page. The work continued while he made return trips to Garden City, sometimes accompanied by Nelle, and to the Kansas State Penitentiary to interview Perry Smith and Dick Hickock on Death Row. Most of the book was finished by 1964, but appeals by the killers' attorneys forced the case upward through the legal system, even to the U.S. Supreme

Court. Truman wrote to his publisher, Bennett Cerf at Random House, "please bear in mind that I *cannot* really finish the book until the case has reached its legal termination, either with the execution of Perry and Dick (the probable ending) or a commutation of sentence (highly *un*likely). . . . Nevertheless, it is the most difficult writing I've ever done (my God!) and an excruciating thing to live with day in and day out on and on—but it *will* be worth it: I *know*."[25]

Of the two possible outcomes, Truman knew that the most satisfactory dramatic denouement would be execution. KBI detective Harold Nye, who had pursued Hickock and Smith all over the West, wouldn't settle for anything less. "I'm not really bloodthirsty," he wrote to Truman, "but I will never feel the case is closed until I see that pair drip [*sic*] through the hole."[26] Truman was not so blunt, but he had taken the precaution to ask permission to attend Smith and Hickock's hanging. On Truman's behalf, Cliff Hope wrote to Robert J. Kaiser, director of Penal Institutions, requesting that Capote be allowed to serve as a witness. Kaiser replied, "I can tell you quite frankly that I would not recommend to the Warden such permission. Numerous people have made a similar request, and I can anticipate many more in the event an execution date becomes imminent."[27]

Until the book was in print, it was important that Truman remain in good standing with the folks of Garden City and Holcomb. He would need some of them to sign legal agreements. In the spirit of reciprocating their hospitality, for instance, Truman let it be known that he would welcome a visit from anyone who happened to be in New York. But he was surprised when Duane West, the Finney County prosecutor, took him up on the offer. West had never acted friendly to Truman and Nelle, and Capote had already whittled down his role in the book to a nub. West wrote to say that he and his wife would be attending a Red Cross convention in Manhattan in May 1964. Inwardly, Truman groaned. He called Nelle and asked her to please help him by playing hostess. She agreed, which meant getting gussied up, one of her least favorite things to do.

They fêted the out-of-towners by pulling out all the stops. First, they escorted them to a performance of *Hello, Dolly!* Then, after the curtain, Truman played his trump card by escorting everyone backstage to meet the show's star, Carol Channing. Next it was off to Sardi's for a late dinner, during which the author pointed out a caricature of himself hanging on the restaurant's wall of celebrities. When the two couples finally parted, Truman breathed a sigh of relief. "I spent all of last week in the city—where [I] was caught by Mr. Duane West," Truman wrote to the Deweys. "Nelle and I (for our sins) took them to see 'Hello, Dolly'—ugh. I thought he was bad, but *the wife is worse!* The End. What a pair! Never again."[28] A few weeks later, he followed up with a letter to West, recounting their good time together and asking him to sign a release. The release stated that West would never write about the Clutter murders.

But West was a "good ol' boy" who could tell when he was being had, Nye said, and he didn't take the bait. "Now I know why we were treated so royally in New York," West said later, apparently convinced Nelle was in on it, too. Capote was angry, but tried to conceal his frustration in a chilly reply. "If you do not care to sign the release, that is of course your privelege [*sic*]. But please do not think, as I am told you do, that this matter of the release was why I tried to be hospitable during your New York visit. My motive was much simpler: I liked and respected you—and because you wrote to advise me of your impending trip, assumed you have some regard for me."[29]

Things went better a few months later when Harrison Smith, Perry Smith's attorney, arrived with his children for a visit. Again, Nelle and Truman rolled out the red carpet. They guided the Smith family to the 21 Club for dinner, where Bennett Cerf and his wife were waiting. (The attorney recognized Cerf as the "guy from 'What's My Line?' ") And the top-drawer treatment had its intended effect. "It was the thrill of a lifetime for my kids," said Smith. Capote also mentioned that his apartment was available for months at a time—why didn't Harrison keep that in mind for the family's next trip? "You know," said Smith, "he must have thought I was somewhat of a good Joe if he'd invite me to use his apartment."[30]

Whether Nelle had any second thoughts about helping Truman manipulate the people he needed for his book isn't clear. All she would say about her role in assisting him was, "It was the sort of obligation I was proud to pay back."[31] The irony is Capote was using her, too. It seemed as if the process of reporting and writing the book had transformed him into a person who was, more than ever, completely self-centered and willing to exploit any of his friends in his own self-aggrandizing quest for fame and fortune. About the time he had written all but the final chapter of *In Cold Blood,* Capote stopped off in Topeka to see KBI detective Harold Nye at his home. While they were talking about the case and the final stages of the book, Nye remarked. "Well, Nelle will certainly play a part in all this."

"No," Capote said emphatically, "she was just there."

That response never sat well with Nye. "As well as they knew each other," he said, looking back, "there is no reason not to give some credit to her."[32]

SHORTLY BEFORE THE VISITS of the Wests and Smiths to New York, Nelle gave one of her last interviews, in March 1964, which also happened to be her best. She appeared on Roy Newquist's evening radio show, *Counterpoint,* on WQXR in New York. Newquist, a Midwesterner, loved everything about books and writers. He had studied creative writing under Sinclair Lewis and Mari Sandoz; then, bowing to the exigencies of having to make a living, he went into advertising. But his syndicated book reviews and radio program eventually became a second career. Once a month, he commuted from his home in Park Forest, Illinois, for his broadcast in New York. A genial and engaging man, he had the ability to put people at ease. And Nelle, normally given to bantering with reporters and deflecting personal questions, opened up as she never had about her work and her aims as a writer.

She described herself to Newquist as someone who *"must* write. . . . I like to write. Sometimes I'm afraid that I like it too much because when I get into work I don't want to leave it. As a result I'll go for days and days without leaving the house or wherever I happen to be. I'll go out long enough to get papers and pick up some food and that's it. It's strange, but instead of hating writing I love it too much." Newquist asked her to name the contemporary writers she admired most. At the top of her list she put her friend Capote.

"There's probably no better writer in this country today than Truman Capote. He is growing all the time. The next thing coming from Capote is not a novel—it's a long piece of reportage, and I think it is going to make him bust loose as a novelist. He's going to have even deeper dimension to his work. Capote, I think, is the greatest craftsman we have going."

About her own ambition as a writer, she expressed a desire to write more and better novels in the vein of *To Kill a Mockingbird.*

I hope to goodness that every novel I do gets better and better, not worse and worse. I would like, however, to do one thing, and I've never spoken much about it because it's such a personal thing. I would like to leave some record of the kind of life that existed in a very small world. I hope to do this in several novels—to chronicle something that seems to be very quickly going down the drain. This is small-town middle-class southern life as opposed to the Gothic, as opposed to *Tobacco Road,* as opposed to plantation life.

As you know, the South is still made up of thousands of tiny towns. There is a very definite social pattern in these towns that fascinates me. I think it is a rich social pattern. I would simply like to put down all I know about this because I believe that there is something universal in this little world, something decent to be said for it, and something to lament in its passing.

And then she added a remark that set the bar high for herself—perhaps too high, in hindsight—but one that seemed plausible for a writer who had already written one of the most popular books since World War II.

"In other words," she said, "all I want to be is the Jane Austen of south Alabama."[33]

IN THE SUMMER OF 1964, with her second novel still unfinished, she opted for a vacation on Fire Island, hoping for a salutary effect on her imagination by combining work and play. The Browns were staying on the island for several months and invited her as their guest. Michael had written and produced a musical revue called the *Wonderful World of Chemistry* for the Du Pont pavilion at the 1964 New York World's Fair. A dozen times a day, performers clad in space-age tights of white and orange, and white bowlers with sprays of Styrofoam molecules, sang and danced the development of chemistry from ancient Greece to modern times. The show would run for a year, and as Michael and Joy liked to do with financial windfalls, they were celebrating.

Nelle's accumulating fortune, on the other hand, continued to worry her, because her income had catapulted her into a tax bracket associated with the rich. The situation was at odds with the simple lifestyle she preferred. "We know that Nelle Harper wishes these checks would not come in every few months, but I'm sure we understand that there's no way of stopping them," Annie Laurie Williams wrote to Alice in August, enclosing another check.[34] The original J. B. Lippincott edition of *To Kill a Mockingbird* was still selling, and the Popular Library paperback had sold about five million copies. *Reader's Digest* magazine continued to distribute two million copies of the novel's abridged version. There were six hardbound editions in German, an Italian version, and the Swiss book club Ex Libris had chosen it as a selection. The novel continued to sell vigorously in England, in both the Heinemann and Penguin editions. British Reader's Digest Condensed Books and its branches in Australia, New Zealand, and South Africa distributed the novel as a bonus to new members. During the summer Nelle was on the island, translations in Hungary, Romania, and Greece appeared. The U.S. Information Agency was looking into publishing editions in a number of Indian and Middle Eastern languages. Nelle had received invitations to speak all over the world. Even in the Soviet Union, beyond the reach of copyright, audiences packed a playhouse to see an unauthorized adaptation of the novel for the stage.

TO CHECK IN WITH his bestselling client, Maurice Crain took the thirty-minute ferry ride to Fire Island. It was obvious to him from a glance that Nelle wasn't going to get much done on her new book. Joy Brown was nine months pregnant, and the couple's two little boys were at the age when they raced between the cottage and the beach all day. Not long after Crain departed for the mainland, Joy ignored her doctor's advice to go home to Manhattan because she was due. One night, after the last ferry from the island had left, "Mike had to get a patrol boat and hire an ambulance to rush her to the hospital," Williams wrote Alice Lee. "She got there just in time as the baby was born only 15 minutes after she got there."[35] In circumstances suitable for a romantic comedy, Nelle pitched in, putting her work aside, and helping the Browns get a handle on the pandemonium.

She stayed on all through September, being a good sport, while Crain and Williams went up to the Old Stone House without her. Perhaps in a bid to induce Nelle to return to Connecticut, where she could enjoy peace and quiet, Williams wrote Alice, "We talk to Harper Lee on the phone almost every day, but we go to Connecticut on the weekends, so do not get to see her. I have not been out to Fire Island yet, and feel sure that I won't get around to making the trip this season. . . . Wish we were greeting the Lee sisters. I can realize [sic] it has been a year since you all were here."[36]

Nelle stopped off only briefly in the city before taking the train to Monroeville for the holidays. But then, the third week of January 1965, she was involved in a terrible kitchen accident. She "burned herself very badly, especially her right hand. It seems some sort of pan caught fire and exploded," Capote wrote to Perry Smith. Friends called and sent cards from New York and Kansas as word spread that the accident was serious and Nelle was in the hospital.

With her hand wrapped in white gauze from her fingers to her forearm, she was limited to reading and answering correspondence with Alice's help. It would be months before a doctor could fully determine whether or not she would need plastic surgery. Perhaps because she was out of action at the typewriter, Nelle accepted an invitation of the sort that she would normally have refused on the grounds that she was "in no way a lecturer or philosopher."

Colonel Edwin Van Valkenberg Sutherland, Ph.D., chairman of the English department at the United States Military Academy at West Point, asked Lee to speak to the freshman cadets. Sutherland, tall, angular, lean, pleasant, with a Lord Kitchener handlebar mustache, had assigned Nelle's novel to the "plebes," along with several "tortuous interpretive writs" (or essays), as cadet Gus Lee remembered them.[37] Nelle accepted.

In March, the thirty-nine-year-old writer arrived on the campus, located fifty miles north of New York City on a promontory overlooking the Hudson River. The talk was scheduled for the auditorium, and until Nelle took her seat on the stage, the seven hundred young men in gray uniforms remained standing. Once seated, they studied their speaker. She was "conservatively garbed in a simple dark dress," according to Gus Lee, who later wrote *Honor and Duty* about his experiences at West Point, "her hair wrapped in a conservative bun atop her head. Her voice was softly Southern, with high musical notes, and crystal clear in a hall that was utterly silent."[38]

"This is very exciting," she said slowly, "because I do not speak at colleges. The prospect of it is too intimidating. Surely, it's obvious— rows of bright, intense, focused students, some even of the sciences, all of them analyzing my every word and staring fixedly at me—this would terrify a person such as myself. So I wisely agreed to come here, where the atmosphere would be far more relaxing and welcoming than on a rigid, strict, rule-bound, and severely disciplined college campus."

For the first time since becoming a class, the young men laughed together, and followed their laughter with a roar of applause.

Knowing that the young men were away from home, many for the first time, she made a subtle comparison between aspects of *To Kill a Mockingbird* and the cadets' future mission as soldiers:

> When we seek to replace family in new environs, we seek to reestab-lish trust, and love, and comfort. But too often we end up establish-ing difference instead of love. We like to have all our comforts and familiars about us, and tend to push away that which is different, and worrisome. That is what happened to Boo Radley, and to Tom Robinson. They were not set apart by evil men, or evil women, or evil thoughts. They were set apart by an evil past, which good peo-ple in the present were ill equipped to change. The irony is, if we di-vide ourselves for our own comfort, *no one* will have comfort. It means we must bury our pasts by seeing them, and destroy our dif-ferences through learning another way.

Regarding people who were difficult to accept or respect, Nelle said, "Our response to these people represents our earthly test. And I think, that these people enrich the wonder of our lives. It is they who most need our kindness, *because* they seem less deserving. After all, *anyone* can love people who are lovely."

Then she reflected on how writing *To Kill a Mockingbird* had influ-enced her life. "People in the press have asked me if this book is de-scriptive of my own childhood, or of my own family. Is this very important? I am simply one who had time and chance to write. I was that person before, and no one in the press much cared about the details of my life. I am yet that same person now, who only misses her former anonymity."[39]

A few weeks after speaking at West Point, Nelle received another request for her presence, one that couldn't be further away in spirit from speaking to an audience of hopeful, forward-looking young men. Perry Smith and Dick Hickock asked her to attend their executions.

They had the right to choose witnesses and they had both named Nelle and Truman.

"Truman tracked down Nelle to the Old Stone House and called her there," Joy Hafner-Bailey, Maurice's niece, remembered. "He said the killers had asked for her and he needed her besides for this final episode that would close the book. But she didn't want to go. She refused." Nelle formally replied to Warden Charles McAtee that she would not attend.[40]

The killers' appeals had been heard and denied, twice, by the U.S. Supreme Court. Finally, five years after their conviction in Garden City, they were sentenced to hang on April 14, 1965, between midnight and 2:00 A.M. The scaffold was a simple structure made of rough, unfinished lumber located in a jumbled warehouse at Kansas State Penitentiary, in Leavenworth. Inmates called the spot "The Corner." Thirteen steps led to the platform, where a noose dangled over a trapdoor. Fifteen men had been hanged there.

On the night of the fourteenth, the executioner, an anonymous paid volunteer from Missouri, sped through the rain in a black Cadillac. He wore a long, dingy coat and a large felt hat to hide his face. Smith, assuming both Nelle and Truman had denied his request, wrote a hasty note at 11:45 P.M.: "I want you to know that I cannot condemn you for it & understand. Not much time left but want you both to know that I've been sincerely grateful for your friend[ship] through the years and everything else. I'm not very good at these things—I want you both to know that I have become very affectionate toward you. But harness time. Adios Amigos. Best of everything. Your friend always, Perry."[41]

In a hotel nearby, Truman agonized and wept in his room, trying to decide whether he should go or not. Finally, he hurried to the prison in time to say good-bye. A handful of reporters and KBI agents were waiting in the warehouse. Hickock arrived first, trussed in a leather harness that held his arms to his sides. "Nice to see you," he said pleasantly, smiling at faces he recognized. He was pronounced dead at 12:41 A.M. When it was Smith's turn on the gallows, twenty minutes later, Capote became sick to his stomach.

On April 17, Al Dewey submitted the final report on the Clutter murders, ending it with the statement that it was a "joint report of

Special Agents Roy Church, C. C. Duntz, Harold Nye and the writer. The executions were witnessed by above four mentioned agents." An unidentified hand wrote "Closed" on the outside of the folder.[42]

Capote flew home to New York immediately. "Perry and Dick were executed last Tuesday," he wrote to his friend Cecil Beaton. "I was there because they wanted me to be. It was a terrible experience. Something that I will never really get over. One day I will tell you about it—if you can bear it."[43]

To mark the killers' side-by-side graves in row twenty-nine of Mount Muncie Cemetery, Truman paid $70.50 apiece for basic granite headstones.

WITH SUCH A MACABRE event behind her, Nelle could look forward to Maurice Crain accompanying her on a visit to her hometown in May. "Nelle Harper and Maurice are leaving Sunday for their trip to Alabama," Annie Laurie Williams wrote to James Mitchell, a British mystery author who wrote under the name James Munro. "Maurice will spend about a week visiting her family and then will fly back to New York. She will stay in Monroeville, Alabama (that is her home as you know) until late August when she comes back to New York to see her plastic surgeon."[44]

Nelle's friends in New York, including Tay Hohoff, her editor at Lippincott, were fascinated by the aura around Monroeville created by the novel. "Nelle would come home while she was writing the book and sit on that porch of theirs [the Lees'])," remembered Nelle's friend Riley Kelly, "and tell us about the editors in New York. They couldn't believe the stories and situations in the book were really the way things were—and are—down here. She would have them call Alice or A.C. to verify that something she wrote really could have happened that way down here."[45]

Maurice Crain had grown up in small Texas towns, but he wanted to take a gander and compare for himself Nelle's description of Monroeville with fictional Maycomb. A lot had changed, of course. "I don't know what you'd really care to see in Monroeville, except maybe a new courthouse standing beside an old one, or an underwear factory," Nelle said apologetically to another visitor later that summer.[46] But Crain was not disappointed, especially because Alice and Nelle, both history buffs, arranged for a tour of famous southern battlefields.

Returning from his journey to the Deep South, Crain raved to his wife about the wonderful time he'd had. "Maurice has never expressed to you folks what he felt about the memorable trip," Annie Laurie wrote to Alice.

> He still talks to us about it and says how much it meant to him to [be] with the Lee family. I enjoyed seeing the pictures in case Maurice forgot to tell you he received them. I am sorry you didn't get a film of the battlegrounds, as that really is an important chapter of that visit. Just being away from the office for awhile helped Maurice and he has been much calmer since he got back. You all were so good to him and he did appreciate it. . . . It is almost seven o'clock and Maurice gets hungry around this time (we used to eat at eight) so I will stop talking and go along to Stouffers with him.[47]

Lately Crain had been getting hungrier earlier. And Williams noticed that even though he scooped up the cake and cookies she put out for teatime at 4:00 P.M., he wasn't gaining any weight. Although no one knew it yet, he was showing early symptoms of cancer from years of heavy smoking.

FOR THE REST OF the summer of 1965 in Monroeville, Nelle buckled down again to work. It had been five years since the publication of *To Kill a Mockingbird*. Although novelists often go years between books, she had been trading on her first novel for quite some time. But now she shunned interviews, first, because questions about *To Kill a Mockingbird* had become redundant; second, because she had gone on record a number of times that a second novel was in the offing. So far, it was a promise she hadn't made good on. What she needed was "paper, pen, and privacy," the formula that had produced her first success.

She made one exception to turning down interviews, however. A young Mississippian, Don Keith, approached her about granting one for a small quarterly, the *Delta Review*.[48] She consented to a "visit," not an interview, perhaps because she saw in the earnest young writer a glimpse of herself from her *Rammer Jammer* days.

Keith, who would go on to become a first-rate journalist in New Orleans, provided a remarkably fresh portrait of Nelle, placing her in the context of a writer at work. "When I met her that Sunday afternoon in Monroeville, Alabama, she was the same as I knew she would be. We had spoken twice briefly over the telephone. I had written her two letters; she had written me one. But regardless of the long distance acquaintance, we exchanged hello kisses in that familiar manner characteristic of Southerners. Once inside the modest but comfortable brick house," they settled down to a "long talk over coffee and cigarettes. She consumes both in abundance."

The young visitor was the first to use the term *recluse* in connection with Nelle, but he did so for the sake of denying she was one. "Harper Lee is no recluse," he said. "She is no McCullers or Salinger whose veneer of notoriety cannot be punctured to reveal, after all, another individual. She is real and down-to-earth as is the woman next door who puts up fig preserves in the spring and covers her chrysanthemums in winter.

"During most of our afternoon together, she sat at a card table placed in front of an armchair in the living room. On the table was a typewriter, not new, and an abundance of paper. A stack of finished manuscript lay nearby, work on a new novel." Nelle explained that she hadn't set a deadline for it, and that her publisher, Lippincott, didn't know the entire plot yet. But she hinted that it was set in a southern town again, perhaps Maycomb. Whether Jem, Scout, and Atticus would figure in the story, she wouldn't say.

Also piled near the table were new books, sent by publishers in the hope that she might pen a blurb for their back covers, or even write a review. Alfred A. Knopf had sent her four such requests, for instance, but she never replied.

The conversation turned to another literary project that needed her attention. She was scheduled to leave the next week for New York, where she was to read, before publication, Capote's finished manuscript.

"It must seem a chore," Keith said.

"But one I'm looking forward to," replied Nelle. As always, she was Truman's friend and advocate.

IT WAS A PIVOTAL interview, this final "visit" that Lee consented to. Despite Keith's avowal that "Harper Lee is no recluse," she was in fact becoming one. Granted, she disliked publicity, but unlike most writers she also evinced a continual lack of interest in participating in the literary scene. She didn't accept a post as a writer-in-residence at a college, or speak at a writer's conference, or participate in the Iowa Writers' Workshop, for example, although she knew the director, Paul Engle, well. When friends from Alabama called her and expressed an interest in meeting certain authors during a visit to New York, Lee replied, "I don't know them myself."[49] Once *To Kill a Mockingbird* was launched and sailing on its own, Nelle turned back to being "the woman next door who puts up fig preserves in the spring and covers her chrysanthemums in winter." She was withdrawing into an ordinary life and writing, as she once described Jane Austen, "cameo-like, in that little corner of the world of hers." Perhaps her temperament and interests weren't as suited to the arena of literature as she had once dreamed. Reentering the difficult and demanding fray of public literary life was a sacrifice and, apparently, she was unwilling to make it.

Besides needing to be in New York to read Truman's typewritten manuscript of *In Cold Blood,* it was time for Nelle to let a doctor examine her injured hand and see if surgery would be required. Everyone hoped for a good prognosis. "We were all looking at her hand and were pleased and surprised how beautifully it has healed. We hope when she sees Dr. Stark on the 19th [of September] that he will tell her she doesn't have to have the operation," Williams wrote to Alice.[50]

Nelle could hold a pen or pencil again, but her fingers' movement was slightly constricted and her handwriting—normally open and highly legible—looked compressed. Perhaps because of this, she jotted only succinct comments on Truman's pages. Regarding a piece of dialogue, for instance, she noted, "Everybody talks in short sentences. Mannered."[51]

In August, however, *McCall's* magazine published her first piece—"When Children Discover America"—since *Vogue* had carried "Love—In Other Words" in 1961. But the new article, just like the *Vogue* essay, showed none of Nelle's hallmark humor or vividness. In fact, a strong whiff of sanctimony replaced the exuberance that readers would have expected from *To Kill a Mockingbird.* It was as if her high spirits and insouciant wit were being tamped down by too much self-consciousness, perhaps a result of her being in the public eye.

I do not think the youngest or even the most jaded citizen could go to Washington and through the Capitol or the Smithsonian Institution without having the feeling of yes, we *are* something; yes, we *do* have a history. . . . Younger children may not respond in words, but they will drink everything in with their eyes, and fill their minds with awareness and wonder. It's an experience they will enjoy and remember all their lives; and it will give them greater pride in their own country.[52]

She finished reviewing *In Cold Blood* and then hurried off to Fire Island again to spend time with the Browns, who had returned for another season. She was almost done with a draft of her second novel and hoped to polish it up before showing it to Hohoff.

Truman, meanwhile, was certain he was on the verge of volcanic fame, and he was feeling ecstatic about it. The *New Yorker* would begin serializing *In Cold Blood* at the end of September in four consecutive issues. Anticipating that this would be his best book yet, he had a huge party in mind, the Black and White Ball, which would set high society on its ear. Even though the date for the ball was more than a year off, he was already dropping tantalizing hints about the exclusive guest list, and promising invitations to those with whom he wanted to curry favor.

So he was stunned when Harold Nye threatened to throw a wrench into everything.

As a perfunctory last piece of business, Truman had mailed Nye a copy of the manuscript. He asked Nye to give it a final read-through for accuracy. But Nye, reading it from beginning to end for the first time, saw that Alvin Dewey, the KBI's "office boy" as he later bitterly characterized him, had been cast as the book's hero. When Truman arrived in Kansas City, right before the first magazine installment was scheduled to run, the disgruntled detective abruptly dug in his heels.

"Truman and I, we got into a heck of a fight," said Nye. "That happened in the Muehlebach Hotel on 12th and Baltimore Avenue when we got together. He brought down, I can't remember—he was an editor of the *New Yorker,* who was also a 'piccolo player'—and my wife and I went over to the hotel and had dinner with them. Well, this came up after our dinner and we went through the manuscript and I had told him I would not approve it, because it wasn't true."

Truman was aghast, and went in a rage reminiscent of one of his boyhood tantrums.

"And we got into a hell of a fight right in the Muehlebach Hotel," said Nye. "He marched me outside and he was screaming. He called me a tyrant and told my wife I was a tyrant. Now, I had been invited to the Black and White Ball and he told me that night, 'Cancel your invitation!' and that I'd never get another one. Never did, of course."[53]

Capote threw aside Nye's objections, and on the strength of his own word and the *New Yorker*'s exhaustive fact-checking, the 135,000-word serial began anyway, on September 25, 1965, beginning with the oft-quoted sentence "The village of Holcomb stands on the high wheat plains of western Kansas, a lonesome area that other Kansans call 'out there.' "

The *New Yorker*'s circulation went through the roof, and sight-seers poured down the elm-lined road to the Clutters' old house.[54]

NELLE'S PHYSICIAN DECIDED that an operation would be necessary after all, otherwise scar tissue would permanently impair her hand. "Just a wee note to tell you that Maurice and I will take Nelle Harper to St. Lukes on Sunday," Annie Laurie Williams wrote Alice Lee in September.

> We are not going to the Old Stone House as we want to be with her when she is admitted to the hospital. . . . We will see that she gets settled in her room and is comfortable and we will leave her. Monday Maurice will go up alone to be with Nelle Harper when she comes out from under and opens her eyes. He will then telephone you. And when the doctor says she can be released Maurice will take her back to her apartment and see that she is fed and taken care of until she feels well enough to let him leave. Nelle Harper thinks this is a lot of nonsense, but we don't pay any attention to what she says, as we want to be with her.[55]

The operation was a success: "We are so thrilled that Nelle had such a good report from Dr. Stark yesterday. She sounds like a different person on the phone because now she knows her hand is going to be all right. She will be able to use it for writing and playing golf."[56] And the timing was perfect, because Nelle's high school English teacher Gladys Watson was coming to New York at Nelle's invitation. Unmarried until she was in her forties, Gladys had wed Ralph Burkett, "one of the most handsome bachelors in Monroeville." The teacher and former student were about to embark on a memorable month-long trip to England on October 8, and Nelle had insisted on paying for the excursion. "It was a thank-you for editing her manuscript," said Sarah Countryman, Gladys's daughter.[57]

"Harper Lee and Gladys got away on schedule yesterday," Williams informed Alice. "Maurice went with them and saw that they got aboard the *Queen Elizabeth* with all their baggage. The day before Nelle Harper brought Gladys in to meet us and we enjoyed our brief visit with her."[58]

A completed second novel had not materialized before Nelle left, and Tay Hohoff was getting tired of the delay. Williams sprang to Nelle's defense: "I told her that I thought it was better the way things turned out about her second book, as she was under pressure and thought she had to write it this summer," she assured Alice.

It doesn't have to be written according [to] her publisher's schedule and I think she should take her time and not try to work on the book until she gets back down to Alabama with her folks. . . . Too many people up here ask too many questions and she seems to feel that she is expected to turn in another manuscript, because everybody says, "Are you working on another novel." I always say "Of course, she is going to write another book but she is not *going to be hurried.*" It is difficult, as you know to follow Mockingbird as this book was such an all-around success that measuring up to that book is almost impossible. *But she is a writer* and her next book will be a success too, and will have some of the flavor of the first one. I am saying all of this to you, because I want you to know that she was depressed when she didn't come back from Fire Island with a finished manuscript. *She doesn't have to be driven by her* publisher to turn in another script, as she is in the driver's seat and can be independent. Maurice would never prod her, and as you must know is always standing by when she needs him.

We love that sister of yours and appreciate what a difficult time she had this summer helping take care of Joy Brown and her children and having the neighbors running in and out.[59]

Nelle returned from England in November. As a parting gift for her favorite teacher, she took Watson-Burkett, Crain, and Williams as her guests to a performance of Beatrice Lilly in Hugh Martin and Timothy Gray's musical *High Spirits.* Watson-Burkett had never seen a Broadway show before, and it was a fitting send-off. Then, a few weeks later, Nelle followed her to Monroeville.

Nelle knew, as everyone did, that *In Cold Blood* would be out soon. The magazine serialization had served as a drum roll leading up to publication. For Nelle, it would be the end to a long experience. More than five years earlier, she had bucked Truman up in Garden City when he was convinced that they would never get past people's suspicions about them. Then, for two months, she had served as his listening post in town and made friends with the folks he needed to interview. Later, she had accompanied him on return trips: once to attend the trial, and two more times just to go over the territory—sifting, sifting for more information. "Without her deep probing of the people of that little town," Capote told Alabama author Wayne Greenhaw, "I could never have done the job I did with it."[60] And finally, she had tightened up his manuscript while she was supposed to be working on her second novel.

So when, in January 1966, she opened the first edition of *In Cold Blood,* she was shocked to find the book dedicated to her, a patronizing gesture in light of her contribution—"With Love and Gratitude," it said. And, out of the blue, she found she had to share Capote's thanks with his longtime lover, Jack Dunphy.

Nelle was not a woman who was quick to anger or demanding of attention. Still, "Nelle was very hurt that she didn't get more credit because she wrote half that book. Harper was really pissed about that. She told me several times," recalled R. Philip Hanes, who became friends with her later that year.[61] She was "written out of that book at the last minute," maintained Claudia Durst Johnson, a scholar who has published extensively about *To Kill a Mockingbird.* Not even the perfunctory acknowledgment page paid tribute to Nelle's large and important contribution.[62]

Truman's failure to appreciate her was more than an oversight or a letdown. It was a betrayal. Since childhood, Truman had been testing their friendship, because perhaps, deep down, he believed that no one, including Nelle, really liked him—not since his parents had withdrawn their love. He was constantly showing off to get people's attention and approval, all the while gauging their response. But hurting her so gratuitously, perhaps to see what she would do, spoke volumes about whether she could trust him. She would remain his friend, but their relationship had suffered its first permanent crack.

If Truman suspected the amount of damage he had done to their lifelong friendship, he doesn't seem to have taken special steps to repair it. For instance, he could have counteracted rumors that he had written all or part of *To Kill a Mockingbird,* but he never went to any strenuous lengths to deny it.[63] And later, when *In Cold Blood* didn't win a National Book Award or a Pulitzer Prize, he used a little trick of backhanding his friend's success by asking interviewers if they'd ever heard of her book. What he did to Nelle was the beginning of his deliquescing into the sad person he became at the end of his life.

Nelle's pain over the *In Cold Blood* affair was soon to be compounded by another incident. In 1966, the Hanover County School Board in Richmond, Virginia, ordered all copies of *To Kill a Mockingbird* removed from the county's school library shelves. In the board's opinion, the novel was "immoral literature."[64]

The episode began when a prominent local physician, W. C. Bosher, the father of a Hanover County student and a county Board of Education trustee, protested that a novel about rape was "improper for our children to read." On the strength of his criticism, the board voted to ban *To Kill a Mockingbird* from the county schools. The next day, the *Richmond News-Leader* editorialized about the board's "asinine performance" and created a Bumble Beadle Fund, named for the famous character in *Oliver Twist,* "also an immoral novel." The first fifty students of the local high school who requested a copy of *To Kill a Mockingbird* would receive one gratis, courtesy of the newspaper.

For almost two weeks, the controversy went back and forth on the letters-to-the-editor page, until the *News-Leader* called a halt by allowing Nelle to have the last word. She fired with both barrels.

> Recently I have received echoes down this way of the Hanover County School Board's activities, and what I've heard makes me wonder if any of its members can read.
>
> Surely it is plain to the simplest intelligence that "To Kill a Mockingbird" spells out in words of seldom more than two syllables a code of honor and conduct, Christian in its ethic, that is the heritage of all Southerners. To hear that the novel is "immoral" has

made me count the years between now and 1984, for I have yet to come across a better example of doublethink.

I feel, however, that the problem is one of illiteracy, not Marxism. Therefore I enclose a small contribution to the Beadle Bumble Fund that I hope will be used to enroll the Hanover County School Board in any first grade of its choice.[65]

Eventually, *To Kill a Mockingbird* was restored to Hanover County school libraries because of a technicality in board policy. But the Richmond debate over the book's suitability for young readers was the first of many in the ensuing years. As more schools added *To Kill a Mockingbird* to their reading lists, the book also joined the list of the one hundred novels most often targeted for banning.

DESPITE INDICATIONS THAT NELLE was close to finishing her second book, the spring of 1966 found her accepting another responsibility. President Lyndon Baines Johnson had appointed her to the National Council on the Arts. It was going to be a long commitment, six years, which would cut into her writing time when she was already far behind in delivering a second manuscript to Hohoff. But it's likely that she accepted the appointment because Gregory Peck had urged her to say yes.

The council had been established through the National Arts and Cultural Development Act of 1964. Its responsibility, in a nutshell, was to advise the National Endowment for the Arts. Johnson selected a galaxy of appointees to make sure the council got off to a strong start. The original members included Marian Anderson, Leonard Bernstein, Agnes de Mille, Helen Hayes, Gregory Peck, Sidney Poitier, Richard Rogers, Rosalind Russell, Ralph Ellison, Elizabeth Ashley, John Steinbeck, and Isaac Stern. Roger Stevens, a real estate magnate and cultural impresario, would chair the council. In addition to reviewing and recommending proposals for encouraging the arts, the council would also nominate individuals and organizations for the National Medal of Arts, a presidential award in recognition of outstanding contributions to the arts in America.

The members were each given a thick notebook filled with grant proposals, and a modest budget. How the council would function was left in Roger Stevens's hands. One morning, during the council's first meeting, Stevens went for a walk with fellow member R. Philip Hanes.

" 'We can't be all going off the council at the same time,' Stevens told Hanes, 'so we're going to have two-year terms, four-year-terms, and six-year terms. I'll draw names out of a hat and see what happens. Your number's going to be six! And Gregory Peck—he's a hack actor—he's going to be a number two.' "

"Well," recalled Hanes, "Gregory hadn't been on there a year before he took off for several months and he went to every single repertory theater in America: to Providence, to Cleveland, to San Francisco, to Houston. He went to every single one and saw at least one play, sometimes two. And he came back to the council and produced a huge written report. Roger was stunned!"[66] As a result of Peck's research, repertory theater companies and the training of young actors occupied an equal place beside larger initiatives on the council's agenda. Then, probably because Peck was now in a position to pull some strings, the number of members on the council increased from twenty-four to twenty-six, to make room for abstract painter Richard Diebenkorn and for Harper Lee.

"Gregory just worshipped her," said Hanes. "Often he would be seated studying his papers," said Hanes, "and when Harper would walk in, he would jump up like a bolt of lightning and pull out her chair."[67]

During the meetings, which were spread over two or three days, usually in Tarrytown, New York, the council would review proposals one at a time, discuss, and vote on them. Requests varied from asking for funds for a citywide art exhibit, to producing a play, to providing a research grant to find out why the Stradivarius had such a unique sound. Although the nation had more pressing needs than putting money behind the arts—particularly with the Vietnam war claiming American lives everyday—"If anything," said council member and sculptor Jimilu Mason, "we felt we had to do more in the arts to counteract the effects of the war."[68]

Nelle reserved her comments at council meetings for times when she believed she needed to speak up. Said Hanes, "She was quiet, unassuming—concise, terse, powerful, and gained the love and respect of all. She only spoke when she had something to say. It was always something important and always heeded. And often her remarks were wry. She would seldom say more than just a sentence, but they would drop down like a small bomb.

"She had the total respect of Roger Stevens."[69]

When she couldn't be found during a social hour before dinner, she could often be spotted with John Steinbeck, standing in a corner discussing favorite books.[70]

IN HER CAPACITY AS a well-known author, Nelle would do favors for friends such as Peck, ideally if there was no fanfare directed at her. And she was always good for an annual appearance at Monroe County High School in Monroeville, a few blocks from her home. Students in Marjorie Nichols's English class became accustomed to seeing the Pulitzer Prize–winning author poke her head in the classroom when they read *To Kill a Mockingbird*. Unfortunately, they were usually so awed by her that they didn't know what to say.

"She was very frazzled, she was matronly, she was kind of disheveled," said Darryl Pebbles, who saw Nelle in 1968. (Pebbles later became a novelist himself, under the name Hutton Hayes.) "She was a person who didn't seem to care about appearances. She wore a beige skirt with the blouse tucked in unevenly. She dressed like a woman who seemed much older, not like a woman who spent time in New York. She had a loud voice and she was rather brusque. She just took over the class. After talking a little bit about the writing of the book, she asked if there were any questions, but of course there weren't any because we were too intimidated. So, with a remark like, 'See you next week at bridge, Marj!' she left."[71]

Interestingly, the novel was not taught throughout the Monroe County school system. Although it was on the approved reading list, few teachers used it in their classrooms. Sarah Dyess, a Monroeville resident and former teacher, said that there was a "certain reluctance to get into the controversial issues of race relations, rape accusations, and so on. Some also felt that perhaps some local folks did not at that time regard the book as great literature. Plus, there may have been more people in the 1960s and '70s who would have thought they recognized their family members as characters in the novel and been offended."[72]

In addition to speaking at the local high school, Nelle also accepted an invitation from another close friend, Anne Gary Panell, president of Sweet Briar College, to speak to Professor William Smart's creative writing classes. Smart had only recently joined the faculty as a young instructor, and was nervous about squiring Nelle around the campus for several days. When the train pulled into the station with Nelle aboard in late October, Smart studied the passengers as they descended to the platform.

"Are you Harper Lee?" he said cautiously to a stout woman with salt-and-pepper hair.

"I sure am!" she said and handed him her suitcase.[73]

The eighty students who attended her talks received never-to-be-repeated insights into her experience about the craft of writing.[74]

"It's absolutely essential that a writer know himself," Nelle began, "for until he knows his abilities and limitations, his talents and problems, he will be unable to produce anything of real value. Secondly, you must be able to look coldly at what you do. The writer must know for whom he writes, why he writes, and if his writing says what he means for it to say. Writing is, in a way, a contest of knowing, of seeing the dream, of getting there, and of achieving what you set out to do. The simplest way to reach this goal is to simply say what you mean as clearly and precisely as you know how."

In answer to a student's question about her typical workday, Nelle described a regime that must have made some of the young listeners quail. She said she stayed at her desk six to twelve hours a day and ended up with, perhaps, one page of finished manuscript. "To be a serious writer requires discipline that is iron fisted. It's sitting down and doing it whether you think you have it in you or not. Everyday. Alone. Without interruption. Contrary to what most people think, there is no glamour to writing. In fact, it's heartbreak most of the time."

And to disabuse the novice writers listening to her of the notion that merely completing a novel would guarantee its publication, she added, "it's just as hard to write a bad novel as it is to write a good one. And if a writer does come up with a manuscript worthy of publication, it is assured that many pages of unpublished material have preceded it."

Given the tone of her remarks, and her description of the demands she made on herself, perhaps she was venting her frustration over failing to complete the second novel she had been working on for almost six years.

ON NOVEMBER 28, 1966, all of New York society was agog with Truman Capote's "Black and White Ball," held at the Plaza Hotel. It was, Truman told the press, a "little masked ball for Kay Graham [president of the *Washington Post* and *Newsweek* magazine] and all my friends."[75] Five hundred and forty of his friends had received invitations, but the red-and-white admission tickets were printed only the week before to prevent forgeries. Stairways and elevators were blocked, except for one elevator going up to the ballroom. From its doors emerged the glitteratti of the times: politicians, scientists, painters, writers, composers, actors, producers, dress designers, social figures, and tycoons—including Frank Sinatra; William F. Buckley; poet Marianne Moore; Countess Agnelli, wife of Henry Ford II; Mr. and Mrs. Norman Mailer; and Rose Kennedy. Truman invited ten guests from Kansas, too, including Alvin and Marie Dewey and the widow of Judge Roland Tate. Secret Service agents made a mental note of everyone getting off the elevator, and the guests were announced as they entered the ballroom.

Nelle received an invitation, but she didn't attend, an indication of how much she wanted to distance herself from *In Cold Blood* and everything associated with it.

IN JANUARY 1968, MAURICE Crain's cancer had progressed to a point that "I have been urged by my doctors to curtail my activities somewhat in the future," he wrote to a writer who had submitted a manuscript for review. "I do not feel it would be fair to you or to my present clients to undertake any new projects at this time."[76]

Nelle was in limbo about what to do. Her novel was still unfinished, and Crain, who was not only her agent but also one of her dearest friends, was ill. He had been her bulwark against pressure from Lippincott to hurry up. He was the first one she saw when she opened her eyes after the surgery on her hand, and now he needed that kind of support. Naturally, however, Annie Laurie Williams wanted to spend more private time with her husband, and the two went for long weekends alone to the Old Stone House as often as they could.

Turning to another old friend to ease her worries, Nelle temporarily patched up things with Truman, and the two of them went on a sentimental trip through Alabama. "Capote showed up in Monroeville driving a Jaguar convertible," said Wayne Greenhaw. "I saw a picture of him and Nelle that his cousin John Byron Carter had. Truman was leaning against the front fender. Nelle was standing to the side with a smile on her face. I think she was amused at his putting on the ritz. It wasn't a long road trip. They just rode through the south Alabama countryside and down to Destin, where they enjoyed the white sand beaches and the seafood restaurants."[77]

Despite the pleasure excursion, thoughts of death weren't far from Nelle's mind. Later in 1968, a colleague on the National Council of the Arts, René D'Harnoncourt, director of the Museum of Modern Art, was hit while walking and killed by a drunk driver. "The news of René's death has no doubt reached you," Nelle wrote to fellow council member Paul Engle, director of the Iowa Writers' Workshop. "A sad cruel thing. I for one shall miss him sorely. There is nothing of the slightest interest to report from Alabama."[78]

In spite of his illness, Maurice Crain continued to go into the office. He enjoyed his work and wouldn't hear of taking it easy. Characteristically, he put up a front of gruffness, even as his cancer treatments were taking their toll on his energy. An agent sent him a proposal for a book about deserters from the war in Vietnam. Crain, a former War World II bomber crewman and prisoner of war, sent back a reply that crackled with contempt: "It would be hard to find a subject which would interest me less or which I think less deserving of treatment at book length than the confused and bewildered Army deserters who have inflicted themselves upon the Swiss. Has it occurred to you that the younger generation has produced an extraordinary high proportion of jerks—a much higher proportion than our own? The material is returned herewith."[79]

Six months later, Maurice was too ill to go into the office any longer. Because there were still commitments with authors and publishers that had to be shepherded to completion, Annie Laurie ran both her dramatic rights agency and Maurice's literary agency by herself. While she did that, Nelle took care of Maurice. There were hospital visits to make, errands to run, and appointments to keep with doctors. "Nelle was there for him," said his niece, Joy Hafner-Bailey. "There was no choice—Annie Laurie had to keep the business running."[80] When he became bedridden, Nelle stayed with him most of the day until Annie Laurie could arrive in the evening.

On April 23, 1970, Maurice Crain died.

"I DON'T KNOW WHETHER you know my sad news. My husband M Crain died last April of cancer, so I have been 'going it alone' now for the past sad months," Annie Laurie Williams wrote to a friend in barely decipherable handwriting that suggests she was still emotionally distraught.[81]

Nelle disappeared from view. The death of her older friend had robbed her of her most valuable advocate and upset the balance of her relationship with Williams. The two women stopped seeing each other very often, probably because being together conjured up too many painful memories. Not long after Crain's death, Williams received a request asking if Horton Foote's screenplay of *To Kill a Mockingbird* could be adapted for the professional theater market. After not hearing an answer from Nelle for months, Williams wrote her a testy note, "Will you please tell me what I should say to Lucy Kroll? I hope that sometime soon you will have dinner with me."[82]

It's conceivable that the relationship between Nelle and Crain was something more than deep friendship. The description "platonic" sounds too cerebral; perhaps "chaste affair" comes closer to the mark. Because although Crain was a thoughtful man, it's hard to limit his role to agent in light of what he did for Nelle. He was the first person she saw when she awoke from surgery; he was the one who cared for her at home while she was recuperating; he made a special trip out to Fire Island for the purpose of paying her a visit; he called her regularly, perhaps as often as once a week; he waved her off on the *Queen Elizabeth* for her celebratory trip to Britain; and, finally, he went to Alabama to meet her extended family. Despite all this, among his papers at Columbia University, there is not a single piece of correspondence from Nelle. It's as if the collection was scoured clean of the relationship. Yet, in the papers of Fred Gipson, another of Crain's clients, which are housed at the University of Texas at Austin, there are half a dozen letters from Crain, a few of which have Nelle as their main subject. The clues about the relationship are suggestive, but inconclusive. Even Truman was intrigued. In December 1961, he wrote to Alvin and Marie Dewey, "About Nelle. I am rather worried about her. *Just between us,* I have good reason to believe that she is unhappily in love with a man impossible to marry etc."[83] What's certain is that in Nelle's life, Crain's death "left a hole in the world," in the words of a Japanese proverb.

IN HER OWN GRIEF, Annie Laurie began to suffer health problems and she lost interest in the agency. In September 1971, her sister Pamela

Barnes informed Erskine Caldwell's wife, Virginia, "Annie Laurie intended writing you a personal letter but unfortunately she fell and fractured a rib and has been in the hospital. However, she asked me to write you and tell you that we are giving up our office but you can reach her at the Bedford Hotel, 118 East 40th Street. . . . We are vacating the office as of tomorrow and have been trying to return books and scripts to authors."[84]

Nelle's surrogate family, the community that had sustained her through the creation of her first novel and whom she had relied upon for guidance when she was a beginning writer, was growing smaller. She continued to see the Browns regularly whenever she was in New York, but their friendship was unrelated—except for the unforgettable Christmas loan she repaid—to her career as a writer. Maurice Crain was dead and Annie Laurie Williams living sadly with relatives, having turned over her beloved Old Stone House to her sister Fern; Truman's place in Nelle's life was uncertain because he was drinking and using drugs heavily, a result of strain caused by *In Cold Blood,* he said. Nelle was prepared to stand by him, but he was difficult, even to people who genuinely cared about him.

Getting a manuscript to Tay Hohoff no longer mattered, either, because Hohoff had retired from Lippincott in the early 1970s. Besides, the bloom was off the rose as far as bringing out another novel from Nelle Harper Lee was concerned. It had been more than ten years since *To Kill a Mockingbird.*

Hohoff was on her own since the death of her husband, Arthur, several years earlier. On the evening of January 4, 1974, her son-in-law, Dr. Grady Nunn, daughter Torrey, and granddaughter, also named Tay, went to her apartment in New York to urge her to move in with them in Tuscaloosa, Alabama. "It was hardly an ideal solution," Dr. Nunn remembered. "Tay loved Manhattan, and the Deep South was a far cry from what she was accustomed to. But it would have worked. She had the heartfelt assurances of our affection and welcoming embrace. And she knew from visits with us in Tuscaloosa over the years that we attracted and were attracted to the kind of people with whom she was comfortable. Tay accepted our invitation, and it was settled."

The next morning, the Nunn family came to talk more about the arrangements. "There was no response when we knocked on Tay's door. Torrey used a key Tay had given her, went immediately to the bedroom and found her mother still in bed, lifeless. In the next few days we were gratefully kept busy doing all the things that had to be done and calling all the people who had to be notified. It fell to me to call Nelle Lee with the news. Also, sadly, I took Shadrach uptown to Tay's veterinarian, for his last taxi ride. Shadrach, the six-toed cat, was Nelle's gift to Tay and Arthur."

And so Nelle was deprived of the editor she trusted, too. "I think it's fair to say that Nelle owes her immediate success to her relationship with Tay," said Wayne Greenhaw. "They were very close and it just devastated Nelle when she died."[85]

About the same time, a strange thing happened. Peter Griffiths, a film producer visiting Monroeville for the BBC, asked Alice Lee whatever happened to the second novel her sister was supposed to have been working on. According to Alice, just as Nelle was finishing the novel, a burglar broke into her apartment and stole the manuscript. It was something about hunting a deer, Griffiths seem to recall.[86] Apparently, she didn't have the heart to start over. And that was the last ever said by the Lee family about a second novel by Harper Lee being almost done.

Quiet Time

GLIMPSES OF HARPER LEE DURING MOST OF THE 1970S AND '80s were as infrequent as spotting a rare bird native to the South in New York's Central Park. In 1967 she moved to a new apartment, still on the Upper East Side, only her third address since arriving in the city almost twenty years earlier. All of the apartments where she had lived were within a fifteen-minute walk of one another, and none was particularly luxurious. She wasn't living like a rich person; that wasn't her style. The new place—a four-story brick building—would have looked quite ordinary to most passersby. "I couldn't pick it out from a hundred others," said a visiting friend.[1] It seemed the perfect camouflage for someone who wanted to go unnoticed. Lining her side of the street were a dozen stunted trees, more identifiers of where residents should put their garbage cans once a week than adornments for the neighborhood. The usual spate of commercial properties interrupted the eye's sweep of the block where there was a dry cleaner's, a travel agent, and a restaurant that served wild game. The only hint of community was a storefront church.

Inside her apartment, 1E, the décor was unexceptional, too. There were no indications that she was the author of a book that had sold nearly ten million copies by the late 1970s. A visitor couldn't recall anything particular about it years later.

Slowly, her world was becoming more circumscribed. Although she continued her migratory pattern of returning to Monroeville every October and staying until spring, she stayed close to familiar haunts while in New York. "I honestly, *truly* have not the slightest idea *why* she lives in New York," said Capote in an interview. "I don't think she ever goes *out*."[2] When a friend visiting from Alabama suggested that they meet downtown for dinner, Nelle objected, "My God, I wouldn't go into downtown Manhattan for the world!"[3] Any new venture seemed to make her hesitate. Several times over the years she phoned Louise Sims, an acquaintance from her earliest days in New York, to set up a lunch date. But if Louise said, "I'll have to call you back," Nelle would reply "Okay, I'll get back to you," and hang up without giving a phone number where she could be reached. Horton Foote marveled that for years Nelle lived within blocks of mutual friends of theirs without ever contacting them.[4]

Instead, she preferred friends from long ago. She corresponded regularly with Ralph Hammond, a writer from her days on the *Rammer Jammer* at the University of Alabama. ("I've got a whole drawerful of letters from Nelle," he liked to boast, "she's my best friend in all of Alabama.")[5] And Joy Brown could always be relied on for shopping trips and jaunts to secondhand bookstores. Nelle's oldest friend, however, Truman, whose ties spanned both Monroeville and New York, seemed to be undergoing a slow-motion breakdown she was unable to stop. Fears and regrets assailed him. When *People* magazine requested an interview in 1976, he brought Nelle along for comfort. As he was describing his unhappy childhood, she interjected that a kindergarten teacher in Monroeville had smacked his palm with a ruler because he knew how to read.

"It's true!" Capote wailed.

Glancing protectively at him, Nelle explained, "It was traumatic."[6]

Truman's deterioration became newsworthy in July 1978 when he appeared as a guest on *The Stanley Siegel Show* radio program in New York.[7] During the first few minutes of the program, he seemed all right, but gradually his speech became slurred and hesitant. Clearly, there were problems.

"What's going to happen unless you lick this problem of drugs and alcohol?" Siegel asked.

Seconds of dead air followed while Truman tried to rally himself. Finally, he replied in a croaky voice, "The obvious answer is that eventually I'll kill myself."

Thoughts of suicide preoccupied him because of an emotionally disastrous situation he'd gotten himself into. Between 1975 and 1976, *Esquire* magazine ran installments of *Answered Prayers,* the title taken from Saint Teresa of Avila, who said answered prayers cause more tears than those that remain unanswered. Truman claimed he had been working on the book for years, but other times said he'd tossed it off as a lark. It was a public shellacking of many of his friends from the glittering social world—the Duchess of Windsor, Montgomery Clift, and Tallulah Bankhead—who had once embraced him.

Revenge was swift. Knowing how much Truman cherished his role as raconteur to the rich and famous, they simply turned their backs on him. He was no longer included in their lives. Perversely, he proved it was true that no one really liked him by making himself persona non grata.

He hung on for eight more years, washing up now and then like driftwood in hospital emergency rooms, until he died in 1984 in the home of Joanna Carson, Johnny Carson's ex-wife. His last words were for his mother.

Nelle, along with Al and Marie Dewey, attended Capote's memorial service in Los Angeles, where the first chapter of *In Cold Blood* was read aloud as a tribute. Afterward, they went to the home of one of Truman's friends from happier times, novelist Donald Windham. When Windham asked Nelle during dinner when the last time she'd spoken to Truman was, she had to say she hadn't heard from him in a very long while.

"In my opinion," said Dolores Hope, "the strain in her friendship with Capote came with his continuing debauchery—alcohol and drugs—and with his sordid treatment of longtime friends, associates and celebrities in his book, never completed, *Answered Prayers.*"[8]

TRUMAN'S DEATH ENDED A long chapter in Nelle's life. But it also spun her thoughts back twenty-five years to those Kansas days when she'd been the most creative. In 1960, she had been his "assistant researchist," contributing to one of the most sensational and highly regarded books in American literature, while simultaneously her first novel, *To Kill a Mockingbird,* was just months away from publication. That brief period had been the apogee of her writing life thus far.

And so in the mid-1980s, retracing her steps over familiar ground, Nelle embarked on a book project that resembled *In Cold Blood.* It would be a nonfiction novel based on a serial murder case in Alabama she'd read about involving a man accused of killing relatives for their insurance money. And this time, unlike *In Cold Blood,* the book and the credit would belong wholly to her. The working title she chose was *The Reverend.*[9]

The story revolves around W. M. "Willie Jo" Maxwell, a veteran of World War II, born and raised in east Alabama. During the mid-1970s, in addition to working in the wood pulp business, he did some preaching on the side in black churches in Alexander City and became known as the Reverend Maxwell. One night, Tom Radney, Sr., an attorney and former state senator, received a call from Maxwell. "You've got to come out here to my home," Maxwell pleaded, "the police are saying I killed my wife." Mrs. Maxwell had been found tied to a tree about a mile outside of town and murdered.

Radney agreed to take the case. Fortunately for the reverend, the woman next door provided him with an alibi, and he was found not guilty. From a portion of his late wife's insurance policy Maxwell paid Radney's fees. Later, he married the woman next door.

"A year or so passed," said Radney, "and then the new wife showed up dead."

Again, Maxwell asked Radney to defend him. During the trial, the jury was persuaded that there was no evidence linking Maxwell to the murder. He was acquitted and paid Radney from his second wife's insurance policy.

The third time Maxwell was charged with murder was in connection with his brother, who was found dead by the side of a road. The district attorney argued that Maxwell, either by himself or with someone's help, had poured liquor down his brother's throat until he died of alcohol poisoning. But the jury wasn't convinced and returned another verdict of not guilty. Maxwell was his brother's beneficiary and had another lump sum due him. The Alexander City Police Department began referring to Radney's law offices as the "Maxwell Building."

The fourth death involved Maxwell's nephew, discovered dead behind the wheel of his car. Apparently, he had run into a tree. The following day, Radney, retained again as Maxwell's attorney, inspected the crash site. "Not even the largest trees were more than two inches around," he said. "It was obvious that hitting those little trees didn't kill the reverend's nephew. However, the state could not prove the cause of death. I remember having a pathologist on the witness stand. I asked him, 'C'mon, what did he die of?' And the reply was, 'Judge, I hate to tell you, but we don't know what he died of.'" Maxwell left the courtroom a free man and settled with Radney with proceeds from his nephew's insurance policy.

The fifth death touching the reverend appeared on the front page of the *Alexander City Outlook* on June 15, 1977. Police reported that Shirley Ellington, Maxwell's teenage niece, had been changing a flat tire when her car fell off the jack and killed her. After reading the news story, Radney decided, "I've had enough." When Maxwell showed up at his offices, his erstwhile attorney turned him down.

"Mr. Radney, you're not being fair to me," Maxwell protested. "I have done nothing wrong. You've got to defend me."

Radney later recalled the next few minutes clearly. "I said, 'Reverend, enough's enough. Maybe you're innocent, you never told me anything differently, and I'll never say a word against you, but I will not defend you anymore.' In the meantime, the area behind my office building was filled with cameras and reporters from Birmingham, Montgomery, and Columbus, Georgia. A newswoman was standing behind his car, and the last thing I heard the reverend say as he got into his big Chrysler was, 'Ma'am, if you don't move, I'm going to run over you.'"

The police waited to arrest Maxwell, hoping he might do or say something during his niece's funeral service that would incriminate him. Instead, a scene took place that Nelle decided was the perfect beginning to *The Reverend,* one that was both awful and comic in one stroke.

A week after Shirley Ellington's death from being crushed underneath a car, three hundred people gathered for her memorial service in the chapel of the House of Hutcheson funeral home. One of the teenager's uncles, Robert Burns from Chicago, took a seat in the pew behind Maxwell. As the organist was playing and the choir singing in the loft, Burns took out a .45 from his suit jacket and shot Maxwell point blank in the back. For a moment, Maxwell dabbed at his forehead with a handkerchief while blood spilled from his mouth. Then he fell to the floor, dead. Suddenly, all the mourners made for the doors, but finding police blocking the exits, they pushed back inside.

"Two or three ladies, little heavy ones," said Radney, "tried to get out the windows and got stuck. The preacher didn't stop preaching, he just got under the pulpit. The organist got under the organ and kept playing, and the choir in the choir loft kept singing—nothing stopped. The next day, police found more than a dozen guns and twice as many knives scattered under the pews."

That's where Nelle would end her first chapter.[10]

Radney defended Burns, after first checking with the Alabama Bar Association to determine that it wouldn't be a conflict of interest. But since Maxwell was dead, there was none. The jury was out twenty minutes and came back with a verdict of not guilty. The judge sent Burns on his way. As court adjourned, the district attorney mused aloud that he must be the only prosecutor in the United States to have lost a first-degree murder case when there were three hundred witnesses.

The Maxwell killings were tailor-made for someone with Nelle's experience. Moreover, Radney was "really excited about the possibility of a book or movie" when she contacted him about giving the story an *In Cold Blood* treatment. He agreed to share all his files going back to the beginning, when he first met the reverend. For the movie version, she said she wanted him to play the defense counsel. Gregory Peck would probably get the lead. (Peck, who had kept up his friendship over the years, was bewildered when she said she had a really good part for him if he could play an old woman! "I'm not sure she was kidding," he mused.)[11]

For about a year she made her writing headquarters the Horseshoe Bend Motel in Alexander City, the same way Truman had closeted himself at the Wheatlands Motel outside Garden City, where she pored over the records of the trials and took notes on the setting. Then she shifted to her sister Louise's house in Eufaula for three months.[12] Louise, though never especially interested in her sister's writing, was glad for company, since her husband, Herschel, was in poor health.

During the next few years, Nelle would call Radney with updates on how the book was progressing, sometimes saying that it was practically done. "The galleys are at the publishers; it should be published in about a week," she would say.

But nothing materialized. According to Jack Dunphy, Capote's former lover, Nelle couldn't find a satisfactory structure for the material. About 1984, Radney finally concluded, "she's fighting a battle between the book and a bottle of Scotch. And the Scotch is winning."[13] It may have been so. Shortly before his death that year, Capote remarked about Lee's drinking. It "was a problem in that she would drink and then tell somebody off—that's what it amounted to. She was really a somebody. People were really quite frightened of her."[14]

Impatient with being put off about the book any longer, Radney went to New York to retrieve his files. After that, he gradually stopped hearing from Nelle. "Don't bring up writing," a friend of hers cautioned William Smart, the Sweet Briar College professor whose creative-writing classes Nelle had addressed years earlier. He, too, was going to meet her in the city. "She's very sensitive about that."[15]

Nelle's conflicted feelings about writing, the past, and the invasiveness of publicity came to a head in 1988 with the publication of Gerald Clarke's bestselling *Capote: A Biography*. Reminiscing to Clarke about growing up next door to the Lees, Capote claimed that Mrs. Lee had twice tried to drown two-year-old Nelle in the bathtub. " 'Both times Nelle was saved by one of her older sisters,' said Truman. 'When they talk about Southern grotesque, they're not kidding!' "[16]

Nelle was outraged. There was no more vulnerable or painful side of her life he could have touched on.

She wrote to Caldwell Delaney, an old friend and former director of the Museum of Mobile,

> Truman's vicious lie—that my mother was mentally unbalanced and tried twice to kill me (that gentle soul's reward for having loved him)—was the first example of his legacy to his friends. Truman left, in the book, something hateful and untrue about every one of them, which more than anything should tell you what was plain to us for more than the last fifteen years of his life—he was paranoid to a terrifying degree. Drugs and alcohol did not cause his insanity, they were the result of it.[17]

Unfortunately for the Lee family, newscaster Paul Harvey repeated the story of Mrs. Lee on his program in 1997, this time invok-
ing a public broadside from Alice. "It was a fabrication of a fabrication,"
Alice told the *Mobile Register,* a "pack of lies. My mother was the gen-
tlest of people. According to the broadcast, I was one of the ones who
saved Nelle from drowning. It is false. How would you feel if someone
told a story that in essence accused your deceased mother of being an
attempted murderer?"[18]

Clarke's rejoinder was that "Everything Capote told me is in the
book as closely as I could relate it." He declined to say whether he had
verified the drowning incident.

PROTECTING HER LEGACY BECAME important to Nelle as the
chances of her publishing again seemed more and more unlikely. At
one point, her cousin Dickie Williams asked her, " 'When are you going to come out with another book?' And she said, 'Richard, when
you're at the top there's only one way to go.' "[19]

Meanwhile, her hometown, Monroeville, had realized its singular
advantage as the birthplace of the author who had written one of the
most popular and perhaps truly influential novels of the twentieth
century. By 1988, the National Council of Teachers of English reported that *To Kill a Mockingbird* was taught in 74 percent of the
nation's public schools. Only *Romeo and Juliet, Macbeth,* and *Huckle-
berry Finn* were assigned more often. In addition, as the lightly fictionalized setting for Nelle's novel—her *only* novel—Monroeville enjoyed
a second distinction that no other town could claim.

So, in 1990, on the thirtieth anniversary of the publication of *To Kill
a Mockingbird,* Monroeville staged its first production of the play based
on the novel, adapted and licensed for amateur theatrical use by Christopher Sergel, owner of Dramatic Publishing, in Woodstock, Illinois. As
far back as 1965, Sergel had tried to persuade Annie Laurie Williams to
allow an adaptation, saying that "Schools all across the country continue to write to us with requests for a dramatization of *To Kill a
Mockingbird*—it is much more requested than *any* other book."[20] Thus
Monroeville was tardy in embracing its literary heritage by twenty-five
years, but eager to see what the local response would be.

The Monroeville staging of *To Kill a Mockingbird* had charms
that no other production could have matched. Audience members sat

in chairs and risers placed outside the courthouse, next to sidewalks where Nelle had roller-skated as a child. Huge pecan trees provided a natural canopy above the sets representing porches on the street where the Finches live. The cast, consisting of residents—businesspeople, farmers, students—rehearsed for weeks in the evenings, trying to re-capture the Depression in Alabama, though few could personally recall it. Some hoped that Nelle might make an encouraging appearance at their inaugural opening night, but they were destined to be disap-pointed. "She sort of hates publicity," said Julie Fallowfield, Nelle's agent at McIntosh and Otis, an understatement for those who were unfamiliar with Nelle's ways by 1990. "The book stands. Which in a way is wonderful."[21]

The first act unfolded under trees by the side of the courthouse, where mockingbirds can be heard singing cascades of brilliant notes in the branches. When Atticus raised a rifle to shoot an imaginary mad dog in the distance, the children in the audience gleefully covered their ears. *Bang!* echoed off the storefronts on the square. For the scene in which Atticus defies a lynch mob bent on kidnapping his client, the courthouse's side door doubled as the entrance to the jailhouse. Across the street was the actual jail Nelle had in mind.

During intermission, the actor playing the sheriff called the names of twelve white males in the audience for jury duty—the only citizens eligible to serve under the laws of Alabama in the 1930s. Coolers heaped with ice, a welcome anachronism, provided drinks and snacks during the break to combat the weather, which, as early as May, was already muggy.

Once inside the courthouse for the start of the second act, the au-dience settled into the pewlike benches. Up in the "colored" gallery members of a local black church sat and watched, a poignant re-minder of how things once were. In the jury box, a dozen white men prepared to hear the case.

Everyone knew the trial's outcome, although in the stuffy court-room built in 1903 with one ceiling fan turning tiredly high above, there was a sense that the sins of history could be reversed if only the jury would find Tom Robinson not guilty. But while the jury was se-questered in a hot, dark stairway to "deliberate," the sheriff informed them that no verdict except the "right one" would be tolerated.[22] The foreman then led the jury back into the courtroom and Robinson was again convicted for a crime he hadn't committed.

The play was such a success—both in attendance and for the boost it gave civic pride—that the following year, 1991, the Monroe County Heritage Museums—a consortium of local history museums—hired a director to further capitalize on Monroeville's link with *To Kill a Mockingbird*. In light of such a tribute to the novel and its creator, few could have anticipated that it would be the start of an uneasy relationship between Nelle and the town.

AS THE ANNUAL THEATRICAL performances of *To Kill a Mockingbird* in Monroeville became more popular, and the Monroe County Heritage Museums tended to put more emphasis on Monroeville's link to Harper Lee, the author was not pleased to see that her birthplace was getting on the bandwagon, so to speak. It augured more requests for autographs, more fan mail, and more occasions when strangers would quiz her about the book. At a Christmas party one year in Monroeville, an out-of-towner began chatting her up about *To Kill a Mockingbird*. She turned on her heel and walked away.[23]

By now Nelle was in her seventies and weary of any attention connected with *To Kill a Mockingbird*. She had put that far behind her, along with the film. Rarely could invitations to receive honors induce her to depart from her well-worn paths. Twice, Huntingdon College invited her in the 1990s to attend graduation. She never replied.[24] The University of Alabama succeeded in awarding her an honorary degree in 1993—perhaps the appeal for Nelle was closure after never having graduated—but all she would say to the audience was, "Thank you."

The distance she felt from her only novel was unmistakable in a foreword to the thirty-fifth anniversary edition in 1993:

> "Please spare *Mockingbird* an Introduction," she wrote.
>
> As a reader I loathe Introductions. To novels, I associate Introductions with long-gone authors and works that are being brought back into print after decades of internment. Although *Mockingbird* will be 33 this year, it has never been out of print and I am still alive, although very quiet. Introductions inhibit pleasure, they kill the joy of anticipation, they frustrate curiosity. The only good thing about

Introductions is that in some cases they delay the dose to come. *Mockingbird* still says what it has to say; it has managed to survive without preamble.[25]

With dismay, she watched the transformation of Monroeville into the "Literary Capital of Alabama." After volunteers had finished painting twelve-foot-high outdoor murals of scenes from the novel, Nelle pronounced them "graffiti." When a television crew asked to film portions of the play and interview the actors, Nelle responded through her agent, "Not just no, but *hell* no."[26]

A lengthy article in the *Chicago Tribune* contended that, according to Reverend Thomas Lane Butts, one of Nelle's closest friends and the retired minister for Monroeville's First United Methodist Church, "She isn't too happy about any of it." Apparently, her friend and counselor was referring to the rise of *To Kill a Mockingbird* tourism in Monroeville, which, as of 2005, brings in about twenty-five thousand visitors annually. Said Butts, her attitude is a combination of wanting privacy and resenting people looking to profit, without permission, from her or her book.

"She would give you the shirt off her back," added the reverend's wife, Hilda, "but do not try to take it without permission."[27]

In fact, someone's going ahead once without permission brought about the most serious showdown between Nelle and the Monroe Heritage Museums. It was over a cookbook.

Calpurnia's Cookbook, named for the Finches' cook and housekeeper, was the kind of recipe collection assembled by churches to raise money. Only, in this case, the idea was that profits from the sale would support the museums. When Nelle got wind that one of her characters' names would soon be appearing beside *To Kill a Mockingbird* pens, coffee mugs, and T-shirts in the courthouse museum gift shop, she threatened to sue. The entire print run of the cookbook, several thousand copies, was pulped.

"I think it is an attempt to keep the characters from being exploited, as well as herself," Reverend Butts said. "When people start using the characters from the book, it sort of fragments the book. They're using it to promote their hamburgers or their automobiles or their own [things]. She wants the characters from *To Kill a Mockingbird* to stay back in the

'30s where they belong. To drag them by the hair on their head into the 21st Century is to do the characters an injustice."[28]

In the town's defense, the late twentieth century hadn't been kind to Monroeville. The only major industry, Vanity Fair, an underwear factory, shut down some years ago, laying off hundreds of workers and pulling the plug on one of Monroe County's main sources of tax revenue. Today, in many ways, Monroeville fits Nelle's description of its alter ego, Maycomb, in the 1930s. It's "a tired old town." Except for the money spent by tourists on meals, gas, trinkets in the museum gift shop, and tickets to the annual play, Monroeville's hope for a better day partly depends on promoting its most famous resident, Harper Lee—the "golden goose," some residents call her.[29]

To prevent any future misunderstandings on the order of *Calpurnia's Cookbook,* now all journalists must run the gauntlet past probate judge Otha Lee Biggs. Judge Biggs, who has been a political boss in Monroe County for more than thirty years, is a slender gentleman about seventy, who smiles easily and wears a cordovan-colored toupee. Through the grapevine he finds out in a matter of hours that someone is writing about Harper Lee, or at least asking a lot of questions. Judge Biggs has the person fetched and brought to his office in the "new courthouse," as everyone calls it—a flat-roofed building of aluminum, painted cinder block, linoleum, and glass erected in the early 1960s.

Every surface of the judge's office is stacked with file folders and paper as if he hasn't done a lick of work in years. But those who know him say he can root around in his papers and find what he needs in an instant. He will talk about anything, as if passing the time in a leisurely southern way: the Civil War, local history, the town (his favorite), and a little about Harper Lee. He likes to ask a trick question to see if his listener is honest—"Say, you're from the South, that correct?" He knows the answer in advance. At the end of the pleasantries, he really only wants to get one message across: "Now, don't quote me. If you do, I'll find out about it and I'll get you."[30]

The Monroe County Heritage Museums has a second line of defense, too. A cadre of retired gentlemen who have spent most of their lives in Monroeville act as docents and, in a sense, "official residents." Journalists who go through videotapes and articles about Monroeville going back ten years will find the same men quoted over and over and the same folksy stories told.

When it seems likely that a reporter and Harper Lee might meet by accident in Monroeville—she and Alice tend to frequent Dave's Catfish Cabin on Saturdays, for instance, for a child's plate of catfish fillet, sweet tea, and hush puppies—then the "official residents" go into action, all the while acting as if they don't know Nelle is a stone's throw away.

In 2003, for instance, John Humphrey, a commentator for the BBC, arrived in Monroeville with a camera crew to do a story on *To Kill a Mockingbird*.[31] Nelle was aware that they were in town, and Judge Biggs had taken the precaution of calling her agent to find out what would and wouldn't be allowed. Two Monroeville docents met Humphrey and his crew at the local country club for lunch. One of them, George Thomas Jones, said, "We had gotten there before the BBC crew and had fixed our plates since we both eat so slowly. I spotted Nelle first and thankfully she was sitting in the furthest corner in the dining room."

It wasn't so much keeping a straight face as it was holding our breath, since Nelle and her sister had finished and were working their way out when they stopped to speak to several people at a table en route. I really do not believe that Nelle spotted them, since the BBC people were going down the serving line fixing their plates. Nelle and her sister walked right by them so close that they could have reached out and touched her.

Thankfully, their backs were to Nelle and their attention was on serving their plates. Anyway, after they had exited the building and were headed to their car, A. B. [Blass] leaned over and asked Humphrey if he knew who the lady was using the walker. He said no, and then A.B. told him that it was Nelle's sister Alice.

Then after the Lee sisters had left the parking lot, I asked Humphrey if he had seen the lady walking beside Alice. Again, he said he hadn't paid any attention. That's when we lowered the boom by telling him that it was Harper, in person, and that she had walked past them earlier. I thought he was going to choke, but he took it good-naturally. He said. "Now I know firsthand how you folks protect her down here."

Great fun!

Yet, Nelle's secluded life and decades-long anonymity continue to exert a fascination for newspaper editors and other media people looking for a good story. Features headlined "What Ever Happened to Harper Lee?" crop up several times a year. As Reverend Butts rightly observed, "Whether she intended to or not, she created a mystique when she withdrew from the public eye like that."[32]

Mostly the reporters who visit Monroeville get a feel for the town and interview a handful of people who know Nelle. Phone interviews with her are impossible because Alice, still in the role of her sister's manager, politely turns down requests. A few reporters and writers have tried sheer rudeness. A case in point were the antics of Jay C. Grelen, a columnist for the *Mobile Register,* who gloated in his headline, "Freaking Out the Talented Harper Lee."[33]

Since I had come to work in her home state, I decided I was going to be the one to land the Harper Lee interview. Never mind that literary luminaries as bright as George Plimpton, founding editor of *Paris Review,* had failed.

My strategy was simple if not subtle: I would visit her town as often as possible, write columns about my visits and mention her name every time.

Within my first month on the job, I drove the two hours to Monroeville and went to the historic courthouse whose courtroom was the model for the courtroom in the movie. I had a videotape of the movie, and with the help of the keeper of the courthouse, I moved a video player into the courtroom and watched the movie. I wrote a column about it.

Another year, I was a juror in the stage version of the novel, which local actors produce in the courthouse every spring. I wrote a column about it.

Then there was the time I actually met Miss Nelle. I had been told her favorite spot for coffee is the Hardee's, of all places, in Monroeville. So I stopped in one Saturday morning.

At one table I saw a man and two women, one of whom I thought might be Miss Nelle. I waited for them to finish.

When they stood, the woman I thought might be the author looked like any senior citizen. I followed the trio out of the restaurant, and the woman I thought was Miss Nelle broke off from the other two, who entered a car. I noticed a "clergy" placard on the driver's side of the dashboard and figured that if the man was a preacher, there was a 50-50 chance he'd tell me the truth.

"Is that Harper Lee?" I asked.

"Yes," he said.

So I rapped my knuckles against the window of Miss Nelle's car, and she rolled it down. "I enjoyed your book," I said with all the cleverness I could muster, and extended my hand, which she graciously took and replied with equal wit: "Thank you."

Knowing how she feels about reporters, I didn't tell her I was one. A year later, true to my strategy, I wrote a column about the day I met Harper Lee.

The obvious question for me, though, was whether my strategy was working. This is how I learned the answer:

A friend of mine was invited to his aunt's in Monroeville for lunch with Miss Nelle and her sister Miss Alice, a sneaker-clad lawyer still practicing in her 80s.

He brought three hardbound copies of *To Kill a Mockingbird*, one of which was for me.

After lunch the next day, Miss Nelle signed the first two with no fanfare. When he handed her the third and told her it was for me, she set the book in her lap and said, "That's the man who's been stalking me."

The *Columbia Journalism Review*, noting Grelen's column, pointed out that he "says he has written a series of peculiar columns about Lee, sent her unsolicited gifts and letters, ferreted out her former residences in New York City and even waylaid her in her home town of Monroeville, Ala. Yet he seems surprised that Lee thinks of him as a potentially dangerous stalker."[34]

On the other hand, some encounters with her have been memorable when pilgrims to Monroeville have behaved with a modicum of respect. Reporter Kathy Kemp took a chance one evening in 1997 and rang the doorbell of Nelle's home.[35] Nelle opened the door.

She was not expecting company. Barefoot, white hair uncombed, the seventy-one-year-old woman answered the doorbell wearing a long white pajama top and a scowl.

"What is it?" Harper Lee wanted to know.

Staring at her through the storm door were a reporter and a photographer from Birmingham. Miss Lee has a famous dislike for reporters and photographers. We'd been warned, repeatedly, by folks all over town, "Don't even think of trying to do an interview."

Instead, we thrust forth a copy of "To Kill A Mockingbird" and asked for her autograph.

"Good gosh," Miss Lee exclaimed, a look of disgust on her face. "It's a little late for this sort of thing, isn't it?"

It wasn't yet 6 P.M. on a balmy Tuesday. Folks on her street in the small southeastern Alabama town of Monroeville were just coming home from work. Televisions blared through open windows. Schoolchildren played in front yards.

We apologized.

"Just a minute then," she snapped before disappearing into the house. Seconds later, she was back with her fine-point pen and an even more pointed lecture. "I hope you're more polite to other people," she said as she opened the book to the title page.

"Best wishes, Harper Lee," she wrote in a neat, modest script.

She handed back the volume. "Next time try to be more thoughtful."

"Thank you," we said, frankly terrified. And for the first time since opening the door, Harper Lee smiled. In a voice full of warmth and good cheer, she replied, "You're quite welcome."

As reporter Kemp knew in advance, one sure way to get Nelle riled was to ask for an interview. Some years ago, Mark Childress, author of *Crazy in Alabama* and a former native of Monroeville, wrote

what I thought was a very nice letter, asking if she'd grant me a few minutes on the phone or submit to an interview in writing. In a few weeks my letter came back with "Hell No" printed in green ink across the top. Some years later, though, when I wrote a novel of my own, I mailed a copy to Miss Alice Lee, Nelle's older sister. . . . One day a white envelope landed in my mailbox, addressed in the same open, feminine hand I remembered from the autographed copy at Miss Wanda's house [a neighbor friend]. A four-page handwritten letter from Nelle Harper Lee, it brought kind words about my own work. Her voice, clear and warm and familiar, rose up like lovely perfume from the pages.[36]

The best kind of interaction tends to occur when Nelle is free to be spontaneous. Then her warmth and generosity, known mainly to close friends and family, become evident.

"One day many years ago when she was signing books at The Magnolia Cottage, a specialty shop in Monroeville," said Mary Tomlinson,

I was walking in as she was walking out. I told her who I was and that I played volleyball with her at Huntingdon. I told her my name, knowing that she would probably not remember this fledgling freshman. I told her I hoped I could get an autographed copy of her book for my granddaughter. She smiled, patted my hand and said, "Mary, I'm sorry, I actually do not remember you." Then she added, "But I'll be happy to sign your granddaughter's book." She waited until I could go inside and purchase it for her signature and a short note. She couldn't have been more tactful or genuine.[37]

Likewise, in 2000, Richard Chalfin, owner of the Better Book Getter, in Manhattan, received a call from an elderly-sounding woman:[38]

She had a delightful Southern accent and was looking for a novel called *When Rain Clouds Gather.* I found it on the Internet and had them pack and send it. When I called to tell her it had been shipped, I noticed the name on her credit card.

"Any relation to Harper Lee?" I asked.

"That's my best friend," she said, and laughed.

"Oh, God," I said, "what an honor. I love your book." This was true. *To Kill a Mockingbird* was one of the Big Seven, my favorite among them, and I had seen the movie for about the 20th time the night before. "You never know a man till you walk in his shoes," I added, like a slobbering imbecile.

"Bless your heart," she said.

"How come you never wrote another?"

"I said what I had to say." She paused. "You are so sweet. If you ever need me to sign a copy of my book, I'll be glad to."

It was a gesture of uncalled-for charity. I thanked her again and again.

"My book must be going for quite a price nowadays," she said.

This was just plain coy. She almost never signs books; her signature would multiply by ten the worth of a *Mockingbird* first edition, and she knew this well. I began to sweat when I remembered a signed copy had just been sold for $12,000 at auction. Now I only had to find an unsigned one. I high-fived Albert [my assistant].

Almost immediately I found a first British edition for $400, and picked it up. But the first Americans were seldom listed, and expensive. It was another year before a Georgia dealer, for reasons known only to him, listed one for $10. I assumed it was the charred remains of a first edition, until it arrived—jacketless but in good condition, and real. A bizarre quirk of fate. I now had two first editions—an O.K. if not great first American and a fine first British, with a nice watercolor on the jacket and Harper Lee's 1960 photograph on the back (it is a lovely picture; her hand on her hip, short hair, an adorable thin-lipped smile). But I had lost her address. I didn't find it for another year.

I thought I had missed my chance, even after I'd found, when cleaning my apartment, the scrap of paper with her name and a P.O. box in Alabama. I sent the books anyway—by now it was late 1999. I had sent two rare books to a P.O. box in Alabama. After two weeks, I was resigned to a like-minded postal worker having had the books signed by "Miss Lee" himself. I thought of him driving around in his new truck. Then spring came and she called.

"I'm in New York but the books are in Alabama with my sister," she said. "When she sends them up, I'll sign them," she said.

"I'll pick them up," I said. "I'll take care of it," she said. Another week went by. Then the call. "What's your address?" she asked.

I told her.

"I'll see ya!" she said.

The intercom buzzed. She was waiting in the lobby—maybe 5-foot-2, in sneakers and a pantsuit, in her 70s but still with the same bright, present smile of her photograph. My assistants and I lined up at attention.

"It's an honor to meet—" I said. It was becoming like Tourette's.

"Here's your books signed." She put them in my hands, then put her arms around me and hugged me as I hugged them.

She had taken a bus over from the East Side. She said she was about to walk up to Columbia.

"You know, I'm a fourth-generation bookseller," I said.

"I guess I found the right person," she answered.

"If you ever need a book, it's on me."

"I know," she said.

Of course, I sold the American first edition, to Bauman's. That was a given, was it not? I made four figures on it. Had there been a jacket, God only knows.

I keep the British on the shelf above my desk, turned around. I love her picture, the smile. Her signature is also surprisingly youthful and unpretentious, like her. Later in the spring she wrote me a letter; I have that staring down at me too. It's a windowless office. I need the light.

Nelle still evinces a special affection for young readers, sometimes responding positively to requests to visit local high schools for book signings or unpublicized appearances. "I was in the National Honor Society at Monroe County High School," said Amanda McMillan,

and every year we induct an honorary member at our induction ceremony. My sophomore year it was Alice, Harper Lee's sister, because she's the oldest practicing female attorney in Alabama.

[The adviser] didn't tell us because they didn't think she would say yes. But since she went to high school there, she thought it was super-cool and agreed to it. Our president was there, but he had a leg cast, so I had to hand her the plaque. I was sitting next to Miss Alice, and Harper Lee was on the other side of her.

I heard her talking to Miss Alice (who is partially deaf, so she was talking pretty loudly), and she said, "I don't get nervous at these things anymore. You want to know why?" Miss Alice asked why, and Harper Lee said, " 'Cause you and I are the oldest ones here!"[39]

According to Don Collins, a former Methodist minister in Alabama, Nelle has funded scholarships over the years. "Many have attended college without knowing she was their benefactor."[40]

Aside from unexpected personal encounters with Harper Lee, one of the strangest happened to Jim Gilbert, managing editor of River City Publishing, in Montgomery, Alabama. In a piece headlined "Cold, Cold Mockingbird" for the *Mobile Register* in 2001, Gilbert explained that he had decided to investigate the decades-old rumor that Truman Capote had written *To Kill a Mockingbird*. Gilbert's methods weren't scientific: he simply compared a close reading of *In Cold Blood* to one of *To Kill a Mockingbird*. "I firmly believe, in my amateur 'forensic linguist' view," Gilbert concluded, "(and also in my heart, where it matters most anyway) that Harper Lee wrote *To Kill a Mockingbird*— just like it says on the cover. Even if you want to insist that she didn't write it—that at some stage in the game a different hand tinkered with or restructured or rewrote the initial drafts—I think you'd still have to admit it was written by someone other than Capote. The styles simply differ too much, according to my reading."[41]

Four days after the article appeared, Gilbert received a call.

"Is this Mr. Jim Gilbert? The same Jim Gilbert whose article ran in the Sunday paper?"

Yes, he assured the female voice.

"Well, I just want to let you know, I think that's a very nice article you wrote."

Thank you, he said.

"And I want you to know, you're right. I *did* write that book."

"I'm speaking to *Harper Lee*?" The woman laughed, and Gilbert was convinced that she was indeed Miss Lee.

Gilbert "proceeded to thank her for calling, to thank her for writing her book, and to prattle other witty things which I'm sure she never heard before—I thought I was being clever at the time but looking back I believe I was actually communicating on a level just slightly higher than prelingual grunting. She was kind to me, though, and flattering, and she had the good sense, before I could make an actual ass of myself, to hang up on me."[42]

IN 2006, HARPER LEE turned eighty; Alice is ninety-five. They both wear hearing aids that go *Wheeee!* in diners at times and then they argue about whose is making the noise. They often debate whose turn it is to get the check, too, a discussion that usually ends with, "I'll get it this time, and you next time." Nelle dotes on her older sister, whom she calls

"Atticus in a skirt" because of Alice's achievements in law, particularly with regard to integrating the Methodist church over the years.[43] "Miss Alice has been legal counsel to the First Methodist Church of Monroeville since the early fifties," said Reverend Butts. "One of her friends asked another friend once: 'What do you suppose Alice would do if she got to Heaven and found out there were no Methodist committees meeting?' The friend said knowingly: 'She would call one!' "[44]

While Nelle is in Monroeville, she spends most of her time at home reading. Inside the entryway of the Lees' one-story brick ranch house are photographs of family members. But everywhere else are books: in a bookcase that takes up half the entrance hallway; in Alice's bedroom, off the kitchen; and in Nelle's blue bedroom, at the end of the hallway. In her room, the walls are devoted to built-in white bookshelves, floor to ceiling. There is a third bedroom, a guest bedroom, and it has bookshelves, too. As in Nelle's apartment in New York, there's no evidence of expensive furnishings that would indicate she is the author of the bestselling novel of the twentieth century. On the contrary, the Lees' home is unremarkable in every way.

"Those things have no meaning for Nelle Harper," Alice Lee said. "All she needs is a good bed, a bathroom and a typewriter. . . . Books are the things she cares about."[45] Several times a week, the sisters go to the post office to gather the mail, which often includes hundreds of letters addressed to Harper Lee. Alice brings along a blue plastic bag to put them in. If Nelle is alone, she sits in the car and reads many of them. A few she will reply to.

In New York, where she spends less and less time, Nelle is a Mets fan and an aficionado of museums. She's also very knowledgeable about the city's history, and stares out the windows of the buses she takes everywhere—she prefers them to taxis—examining the buildings and street scenes she has known for more than half a century. Her favorite outfit for excursions, say, to a used bookstore, is a running suit, sneakers, and a big purse slung across her front.

She likes anonymity, but she is not without a normal dollop of ego. "When Harper Lee was in Pensacola looking for a new outfit—and she's not a fancy woman—the clerk was showing her some item that was very expensive," said Darryl Pebbles, whose relatives are friends of Nelle's. "Lee said she'd rather see something plainer, which made the salesperson lose interest in her. A huffy scene followed and Lee became upset that she was treated so badly. After they had left the store, Lee said to her friend, 'For the first time in my life I wanted to pull out my credit card and let that woman see the name "Nelle Harper Lee" on it.' "[46]

She has never, in sixty years, attended a reunion of the sisters of Chi Omega house at the University of Alabama. "I've written to her many times," said Chi O classmate Carolyn Crawford, "and she's never acknowledged receipt of my letter."[47] But a street on campus is named for her.

An anecdote floating around on the Internet in 2005 said that a waiter at a party in New York recognized Harper Lee sitting by herself at a table. Unable to resist the temptation to express his admiration, he struck up a friendly conversation with her and asked the inevitable: "Why didn't you write another book?"[48]

"I had every intention of writing many novels," she reportedly said, "but I never could have imagined the success *To Kill a Mockingbird* would enjoy. I became overwhelmed." Every waking hour seemed devoted to the promotion and publicity surrounding the book. Time passed and she retreated from the spotlight, she said. She claimed to be inherently shy and was never comfortable in the limelight. Fame had never meant anything to her, and she was not prepared for what *To Kill a Mockingbird* achieved. Before she knew it, nearly a decade had passed and she was nowhere near finishing a new book. Rather than allow herself to be eternally frustrated, she simply "forgave herself" and lifted the burden from her shoulders of living up to the book. And she refused to pressure herself into writing another novel unless the muse came to her naturally.

A little more than a year after *To Kill a Mockingbird* was published, Nelle wrote to friends in Mobile, "People who have made peace with themselves are the people I most admire in the world."[49] From all indications, she seems to have done that.

Notes

1: THE MAKING OF ME

1. "Severe Snowstorm Hits East, Stalls Traffic, Shuts Schools; Many Firms Close Early," *Wall Street Journal,* 4 March 1960, 2.

2. John Beechcroft, "To Kill a Mockingbird," *Literary Guild Book Club Magazine,* August 1960, 1–2.

3. "Traffic Ticket Report," *Saturday Review,* 6 August 1960.

4. Hubert A. Johnson, *To Kill a Mockingbird* uncorrected proof, Spring 1960, Special Collections, Charlottesville: University of Virginia.

5. "Mocking Bird Call," *Newsweek,* 9 January 1961, 83.

6. E. B. White, *Here Is New York* (New York: Harper and Brothers, 1949).

7. *New York City Guide and Almanac, 1957–1958* (New York: New York University Press, 1957–58).

8. Geoffrey Mohan, "Suburban Pioneers," part 1 of "Long Island: Our Story," *Newsday,* 28 September, 1997.

9. Robert Daley. "It's Like a Plate of Spaghetti Under New York Streets," *Chicago Tribune,* 7 February 1960, 20.

10. Truman Capote, *Breakfast at Tiffany's* (New York: Random House, 1950), 1.

11. "Rubbish in Manhattan Streets" (letter to the editor), *New York Times,* 11 May 1949, 28.

12. At the November 8, 1962, Mount Holyoke 125-year anniversary commemoration, Lee received an honorary doctorate. As part of the ceremony, her bookstore

experience was mentioned. Most sketches of her adult life begin with her working at an airline.

13. Maryon Pittman Allen (former U.S. senator from Alabama), letter to author,
30 November 2003.

14. Marianne M. Moates, *A Bridge of Childhood: Truman Capote's Southern Years*
(New York: Henry Holt, 1989), 103–4, 106.

15. George Thomas Jones, "Courthouse Lawn Was Once Kids' Playground," in
Happenings in Old Monroeville, vol. 2 (Monroeville, AL: Bolton Newspapers,
2003), 163.

16. Eugene Walter, as told to Katherine Clark, *Milking the Moon* (New York:
Three Rivers Press, 2001), 93.

17. Drew Jubera, "To Find a Mockingbird," *Dallas Times Herald,* n.d. (1984).

18. Michael Brown, "Fall River Hoedown," in *New Faces of 1952* (this rendition
from Chad Mitchell Trio recording "Mighty Day on Campus").

19. Harper Lee, "Christmas Means to Me," *McCall's,* December 1961, 63.

20. Ibid.

21. Ibid.

22. Ibid.

23. Ibid.

24. "Alumna Wins Pulitzer Prize for Distinguished Fiction," University of Alabama *Alumni News,* May–June 1961, n.p.

25. Harper Lee, letter to Huntingdon College, 26 January 1961.

26. "Annie L. Williams, Authors' Agent, Dies," *New York Times,* 18 May 1977, 94.

27. Howard Fast, *Being Red: A Memoir* (Boston: Houghton Mifflin, 1990), 161.

28. "Authors' Agent, Dies."

29. Leonard Lyons, "Gossip from Gotham," *Washington Post,* 14 February 1945, 14.

30. Douglas Roberts, interview with author, 21 November 2004.

31. Annie Laurie Williams papers, Rare Book and Manuscript Library, Columbia
University, New York, Pamela Barnes to Harper Lee, 31 March 1960, box 149,
folder L.

32. "Traffic Ticket Report."

33. Ibid.

2: "ELLEN" SPELLED BACKWARD

1. George Thomas Jones, "Young Harper Lee's Affinity for Fighting," letter to
EducETH "Teaching and Learning," educeth.ethz.ch/, 7 December 1999, accessed 17 January 2002.

2. Freda Roberson Noble, letter to author, 18 September 2002.

3. George Thomas Jones, "Queen of the Tomboys," in *Happenings in Old Monroeville,* vol. 1 (Monroeville, AL: Bolton Newspapers, 1999), 125.

4. Truman Capote, "The Thanksgiving Visitor," in *A Christmas Memory, One
Christmas, and The Thanksgiving Visitor* (New York: Modern Library, 1996).

5. Taylor Faircloth, interview with author, 17 March 2003.

6. Fred Roberson Noble, letter to author, 18 September 2002.

7. *Monroeville: The Search for Harper Lee's Maycomb* (Charleston, SC: Arcadia
Publishing, 1999), 69.

8. Ibid., 40.

9. Harper Lee, *To Kill a Mockingbird* (1960; reprint, New York: Warner Books, 1982), 253.

10. " 'Luckiest Person in the World,' Says Pulitzer Winner," *Birmingham News,* 2 May 1961, n.p.

11. *Harper Lee's Maycomb,* 26.

12. Patricia Burstein, "Tiny, Yes, But a Terror? Do Not Be Fooled by Truman Capote in Repose," *People Weekly,* 10 May 1976, 12–17.

13. Lee, *Mockingbird,* 144.

14. Charles Ray Skinner, interview with author, 22 December 2002.

15. Marie Rudisill, with James C. Simmons. *The Southern Haunting of Truman Capote* (Nashville, TN: Cumberland House, 2000), 192.

16. Clark, *Milking the Moon,* 40.

17. *National Archives and Records Service,* College Park, MD, Fifteenth Alabama Infantry files. I am also indebted to the Johnson County Genealogical and History Society in North Carolina; and genealogists Kevin L. Privette, Margaret Lee, Larry Kea, and Tiffany Harmon for sharing their research about the Virginia, North Carolina, and Alabama Lees.

18. *Ninth Annual Catalogue of the Alabama Girls' Industrial School, Montevallo, Alabama, 1904–1905* (Montgomery, AL: The Brown Printing Co.), 20.

19. Ibid., 38.

20. Harper Lee to Caldwell Delaney, 30 December 1988.

21. Kathy Painter McCoy, *Letters from the Civil War: Monroe County Remembers Her Rebel Sons* (Monroeville, AL: Monroe County Heritage Museums, 1992).

22. Centennial edition of the *Monroe Journal,* Monroeville, AL, 22 December 1966, 23C.

23. Alice Lee, letter to author, 8 November 2005.

24. Lee, *To Kill a Mockingbird,* 136.

25. Marie Faulk Rudisill, interview with author, 21 December 2005.

26. Charles Ray Skinner, interview with author, 22 December 2002.

27. Mary Tucker, interview with Monroe County Historical Museum, Monroeville, AL, 7 July 1998.

28. Truman Capote, "Christmas Vacation," in *Conjunctions: 31,* ed. Bradford Morrow and Peter Constantine (New York: Bard College, 1998), 139–77. Capote retitled "Mrs. Busybody," and handed it in as a school assignment.

29. Lawrence Grobel, *Conversations with Capote* (New York: New American Library, 1985), 54. Said Capote, "Mrs. Lee was quite an eccentric character. Mr. Lee was wonderful, but Mrs. Lee—who was a brilliant woman, she could do a *New York Times* crossword puzzle as fast as she could move a pencil, that kind of person—was an endless gossip."

30. Rudisill, interview with author, 15 December 2005.

31. Betty Martin, interview with author, 5 November 2005.

32. Rudisill, with Simmons, *Southern Haunting,* 191.

33. Rudisill, interview with author, 15 December 2005.

34. Lee, *Mockingbird,* 6.

35. Rudisill, interview with author, 21 December 2005.

36. George Thomas Jones, letter to author, 11 January 2003.
37. Gerald Clarke, *Capote: A Biography* (New York: Simon and Schuster, 1988), 14. I am indebted to Clarke's excellent biography of Capote for much of the information about Truman's parents and the Faulk home.
38. Ibid., 24.
39. Rudisill, with Simmons, *Southern Haunting*, 241–42.
40. Gloria Steinem, " 'Go Right Ahead and Ask Me Anything' (And So She Did): An Interview with Truman Capote," *McCall's*, November 1967, 76–77, 148–52, 154.
41. *Harper Lee's Maycomb*, 70.
42. Thomas Daniel Young, introduction to part III of *A History of Southern Literature*, ed. Louis D. Rubin, Jr., et al. (Baton Rouge: Louisiana State University Press, 1985), 262.
43. "Biographical Memoranda in Reference to A. C. Lee," 9 February 1927, Alabama Department of Archives and History, Montgomery, Alabama.
44. Lee, *Mockingbird*, 133.
45. Joseph Deitch, "Harper Lee: Novelist of the South," *Christian Science Monitor*, 3 October 1961, 6.
46. Roy Newquist, *Counterpoint* (Chicago: Rand McNally, 1964), 407.
47. Moates, *Bridge of Childhood*, 116.
48. Randy Schulkers, letter to author, 25 February 2005.
49. Rudisill, with Simmons, *Southern Haunting*, 193.
50. Jubera, "To Find a Mockingbird."
51. Wayne Greenhaw, "Capote Country," *Alabama on My Mind* (Montgomery, AL: Sycamore Press, 1987), 103.
52. Jones, "Meyer Katz Found His Dream in Monroeville," *Happenings*, vol. 1, 135.
53. Lee, *Mockingbird*, 101.
54. "Old Monroe County Courthouse," Monroe County Heritage Museums, Monroeville, AL, n.d., n.p.
55. Steinem, "Go Right Ahead."
56. Truman Capote papers, box 7, folders 11–14, New York Public Library. Lee introduces her notes on the research for *In Cold Blood*, "These Notes Are Dedicated To The Author of The Fire and the Flame . . . ."
57. Newquist, *Counterpoint*, 407.
58. George Plimpton, *Truman Capote: In Which Various Friends, Enemies, Acquaintances and Detractors Recall His Turbulent Career* (New York: Anchor, 1998), 10.
59. Truman Capote, *The Grass Harp* (New York: Random House, 1951).
60. *United States Federal Census*, 1930, National Archives and Records Administration, T626, 2,667 rolls, Washington, D.C.; also, George Thomas Jones, letter to author, 16 March 2004.
61. Roberson Noble, letter to author, 18 September 2002; also, Jones, letter to author, 8 October 2002.
62. Skinner, interview with author, 22 December 2002.
63. Lee, *To Kill a Mockingbird*, 12.

64. Plimpton, *Capote,* 14.
65. Joseph Blass, letter to author, 10 September 2002.
66. Rudisill, with Simmons, *Southern Haunting,* 190.
67. Jubera, "To Find a Mockingbird."
68. Joseph Blass, letter to author, 10 September 2002.
69. Ibid.
70. Ibid.
71. George Thomas Jones, letter to author, 16 August 2004.
72. Moates, *Bridge of Childhood,* 61–62.
73. A. C. Lee, "This Is My Father's World," 1952. Bounds Law Library, University of Alabama, Tuscaloosa, AL.
74. Rudisill, interview with author, 15 December 2005.
75. Truman Capote, *Other Voices, Other Rooms* (1948; reprint, New York: Vintage/Random House, 1994), 132.

3: WITHOUT "FINISHING TOUCHES"

1. Moates, *Bridge of Childhood,* 169.
2. Claude Nunnelly, interview with author, 7 December 2003.
3. George Thomas Jones, "Courthouse Lawn Was Once Kids' Playground," in *Happenings in Old Monroeville,* vol. 2 (Monroeville, AL: Bolton Newspapers, 2003), 140.
4. Freda Roberson Noble, letter to author, 25 April 2003.
5. Sue Philipp, interview with author, 9 March 2004.
6. Roberson Noble, letter to author, 25 April 2003.
7. Ibid.
8. Jubera, "To Find a Mockingbird."
9. Roberson Noble, letter to author, 25 April 2003.
10. Ibid.; also, *Harper Lee's Maycomb,* 41.
11. Harper Lee, "Springtime," *Monroe Journal,* 1 April 1937, n.p.
12. Jubera, "To Find a Mockingbird."
13. Dr. Wanda Bigham, letter to author, 9 April 2004.
14. "Election Results," *Monroe Journal,* 12 August 1926, 3.
15. Vernon Hendrix, "Firm Gives Books to Monroe County," *Montgomery Advertiser,* 23 December 1962, 1D.
16. *Journal of the House of Representatives of Alabama,* 1935, House bill 191, 418–19.
17. Ibid., 424–25 and 2753–54.
18. George Painter, "The Sensibilities of Our Forefathers: The History of Sodomy Laws in the United States," at the Web site SodomLaws.org. According to Painter, "Representative A. C. Lee (D.-Monroeville) . . . was absent on the vote on the first sterilization bill and voted in favor of the second bill. He also voted in favor of an amendment to ban voluntary sterilization for purposes of contraception and against an amendment to prohibit sterilization of those in whose favor a jury has rendered a verdict."
19. "Literary Laurels for a Novice," *Life,* 26 May 1961, 78A–78B.
20. Jane Kansas, "To Kill a Mockingbird and Harper Lee: Alice Finch Lee," mockingbird.chebucto.org.bio.html. Kansas offers the most comprehensive

site about *To Kill a Mockingbird* on the Internet because of her indefatigable research and fascination with the novel.

21. Alice Lee, speech presented at Maud McLure Kelly Award Luncheon (award given to Miss Lee, Mobile, AL, 18 July 2003).
22. Ibid.
23. Elizabeth Otts, "Lady Lawyers Prepare Homecoming Costumes," *Crimson White,* 26 November 1946, 14.
24. Rhoda Coleman Ellison, *History of Huntingdon College, 1854–1954* (Tuscaloosa: University of Alabama Press, 1954), 250.
25. Catherine Helms, letter to author, 14 June 2003.
26. Emily R. Grace, letter to author, 26 March 2003.
27. "Tests," *Huntress* (Huntingdon College), 11 October 1944, 1.
28. William M. Pearson, letter to author, 6 April 2003.
29. Jeanne Foote North, letter to author, 17 February 2003.
30. Ibid.
31. Catherine Helms, letter to author, 18 June 2003.
32. Catherine Helms, interview with author, 29 March 2003.
33. Mary Tomlinson, interview with author, 30 April 2003.
34. Mary Tomlinson, letter to author, 2 November 2005.
35. Martha Brown, interview with author, 5 July 2003; Tina Rood, letter to author, 16 February 2003.
36. Catherine Helms, letter to author, 20 June 2003.
37. Mary Nell Atherton, interview with author, 25 February 2003.
38. Ibid.
39. Emily H. Anthony, interview with author, 23 February 2003.
40. Harper Lee, "Nightmare," *Prelude* (Huntingdon College literary magazine), Spring 1945, 11.
41. Lee, *Mockingbird,* 118.
42. Harper Lee, "A Wink at Justice," *Prelude* (Huntingdon College literary magazine), Spring 1945, 14–15.
43. Ann Richards, interview with author, 14 March 2003.
44. *Harper Lee's Maycomb,* 18–19.
45. Florence Moore Stikes, letter to author, 26 April, 2003.

4: *RAMMER JAMMER*

1. Barbara Moore, letter to author, 13 December 2003.
2. Mildred H. Jacobs, letter to author, 6 December 2003.
3. Barbara Moore, letter to author, 13 December 2003.
4. "Chi Omega," *The Corolla* (University of Alabama at Tuscaloosa yearbook), 1946, 231.
5. Polly Terry, interview with author, 31 January 2003.
6. Mary Anne Berryman, interview with author, 5 February 2003.
7. Jane Benton Davis, interview with author, 8 March 2004.
8. Mary Anne Berryman, letter to author, 3 February 2003.
9. Ibid.
10. Polly Terry, interview with author, 31 January 2003.

11. Jane Benton Davis, interview with author, 8 March 2004.

12. Harper Lee, "Caustic Comment," *Crimson White,* 2 August 1946, 2.

13. Polly Terry, interview with author, 5 February 2003.

14. Barbara Moore, letter to author, 13 December 2003.

15. Harper Lee, "Caustic Comment," *Crimson White,* 16 August 1946, 2.

16. Ibid.

17. Mildred H. Jacobs, interview with author, 7 December 2003.

18. John T. Hamner, "This Mockingbird Is a Happy Singer," *Montgomery Adver-tiser,* 7 October 1960, n.p.

19. Harper Lee, "Caustic Comment," *Crimson White,* 28 June 1946, 2.

20. Laurie Maxwell, "Editorials, 'Week in Review' Rank High Among Readers of C-W, Survey Shows," *Crimson White,* 12 July 1946, 2.

21. Letter to the editor, "Caustic Comment," *Crimson White,* 2 August 1946, 2.

22. Harper Lee, "Alabama Authors Write of Slaves, Women, GIs," *Crimson White,* 1 October 1946, 2.

23. Ernest Maygarden, letter to author, 3 December 2003.

24. Vincent Lauria, interview with author, 10 December 2003.

25. Myrlie (Mrs. Medgar) Evers, with William Peters, *For Us, the Living* (Jackson: University Press of Mississippi, 1996), 27.

26. "We Bequeath Our Anti-Klanism," editorial, *Crimson White,* 16 August 1946, 2.

27. Hamner, "Happy Singer," n.p.

28. Harper Lee, "What Price Registration?" *Crimson White,* 13 June 1946, 2.

29. Betty McGiffert, interview with author, 3 February 2003.

30. " 'Little Nelle' Heads Ram, Maps Lee's Strategy," *Crimson White,* 8 October 1946, 1.

31. "Farrah's Eyes Are On You, Barristers," *Crimson White,* 16 August 1946, 8.

32. James B. Sellers, *History of the University of Alabama,* revised and edited by W. Stanley Hoole (Tuscaloosa: University of Alabama Press, 1975), 219.

33. Elizabeth Otts, "Lady Lawyers Prepare Homecoming Costumes," *Crimson White,* 26 November 1946, 14.

34. Elise Sanguinetti, interview with author, 5 November 2005.

35. Harper Lee, "Now Is the Time for All Good Men (A One-Act Play)," *Rammer Jammer,* October 1946, 7, 17–18.

36. "Literary-est Part of US Is South," *Crimson White,* 29 March 1947, 5.

37. Harper Lee, "Some Writers of Our Times," *Rammer Jammer,* November–December 1945, 14.

38. Harper Lee, "Revision," *Rammer Jammer,* November–December 1945, 18.

39. Lee, "Writers," 14.

40. Wayne Greenhaw, "Learning to Swim," in *The Remembered Gate: Memoirs by Alabama Writers,* ed. Jay Lamar and Jeanie Thompson (Tuscaloosa: University of Alabama Press, 2002), 101.

41. Ibid., 102.

42. Helen Norris, interview with author, 18 March 2004.

43. Thomas Hal Phillips, interview with author, 14 December 2002.

44. Harper Lee to Hudson Strode, 6 March 1961, Hudson Strode Papers, Hoole Library, University of Alabama at Tuscaloosa, box 1207, folder L.

45. Timothy Hoff, "Influences on Harper Lee: An Introduction to the Symposium," *Alabama Law Review* 45 (Winter 1994): 389.

46. Helen Norris, interview with author, 18 March 2004.

47. John T. Hamner, interview with author, 29 April 2005.

48. Winzola McLendon, "Nobody Mocks 'Mockingbird' Author: Sales Are Proof of Pudding," *Washington Post,* 17 November 1960, B12.

49. Carney Dobbs, letter to author, 5 December 2002.

50. Jimmy Faulkner, "How the Monroe Journal Was Purchased from Gregory Peck . . . Sort Of," Jimmy Faulkner's "Mumblings," 26 June 2003, www.siteone.com/columns/faulkner.

51. "A Final Word of Appreciation," *Monroe Journal,* 26 June 1947, 4.

52. Daniel J. Meadors, interview with author, 9 March 2004.

53. Mary Lee Stapp, interview with author, 11 March 2004.

54. Jane Williams, interview with author, 12 March 2004.

55. Robert Woolridge, interview with author, 9 March 2004.

56. Marion Goode Shirkey, interview with author, 23 January 2003.

57. Olive Landon, interview with author, 16 March 2004.

58. Jane Williams, interview with author, 12 March 2004.

59. Jubera, "To Find a Mockingbird."

60. Jane Williams, interview with author, 12 March 2004.

61. "Miss Nelle Lee Chosen to Attend Oxford," *Monroe Journal,* 29 April 1948, 1.

62. "Ten Liners Arrive or Depart Today," *New York Times,* 30 June 1947, 37.

63. Roy E. Hranicky, interview with author, 6 December 2004.

64. Robert W. Morgan, Jr., "Letter from France: Notes on Tourists, Students, Francs, and Politics," *Harvard Crimson,* 28 September 1948, n.p.

65. Roy E. Hranicky and Lois Belle White, *The Five H's* (privately printed, 1950), 15.

66. "Programme for the 1948 Delegacy for Extra-Mural Studies Summer School: 'European Civilization in the Twentieth Century,'" Oxford University Archives (CE 3/384), Bodleian Library, Oxford, England.

67. Marja Mills, "To Find a Mockingbird," *Chicago Tribune,* 28 December 2002, Midwest edition.

68. Ibid.

69. Olga Lee Ryan, letter to author, 22 April 2003.

70. Lee, *Mockingbird,* 7, 128–29.

5: *Atticus* Becomes *To Kill a Mockingbird*

1. Williams papers, box 210, author card files I–Q.

2. Don Lee Keith, "An Afternoon with Harper Lee," *Delta Review* (Spring 1966): 40–41, 75, 81–82.

3. Williams papers, box 210, author card files I–Q.

4. Ibid.

5. Williams papers, unsorted correspondence, 7 January 1961, unsigned, box 194.

6. Williams papers, box 210, author card files, I–Q.

7. "Nelle Harper Lee," in *Current Biography,* ed. Charles Moritz (New York: H. W. Wilson Co., 1961).

8. Williams papers, box 210, author card files I–Q.

9. Ramona Allison, " 'Mockingbird' Author Is Alabama's 'Woman of the Year,'" *Birmingham Post Herald,* 3 January 1962, n.p.

10. Williams papers, box 210, author card files I–Q.

11. Carter Wilson, interview with author, 19 November 2004.

12. Tay Hohoff, *Cats and Other People* (New York: Popular Library, 1973), 20.

13. Tay Hohoff, "We Get a New Author," *Literary Guild Book Club Magazine,* August 1960, 3–4.

14. Ibid.

15. *The Author and His Audience: 175th Anniversary J. B. Lippincott Company* (Philadelphia: J. B. Lippincott, 1967), 28.

16. Ibid.

17. Hohoff, "New Author," 3–4.

18. Williams papers, box 210, author card files I–Q.

19. Hohoff, "New Author," 3–4.

20. Newquist, *Counterpoint,* 412.

21. Hazel Rowley, "Mockingbird Country," *Australian's Review of Books,* 22 April 1999.

22. "Negro Held for Attacking a Woman," *Monroe Journal,* 9 November 1933, 1.

23. *United States Federal Census,* 1930, National Archives and Records Administration, Washington, D.C., T626, 2,667 rolls.

24. John N. Maxwell, interview with author, 9 July 2003.

25. *State of Alabama v. Walter Lett,* State Minutes of the Circuit Court, Monroe County Courthouse, Monroeville, Monroe County, Alabama (1934), 345.

26. Ibid.

27. "Lett Negro Saved from Electric Chair," *Monroe Journal,* 12 July 1934, 1.

28. C. E. Johnson, M.D. to Hon. B. M. Miller, governor, 20 July 1934, Death Cases (Executions, Reprieves and Communications) by Gov. B. M. Miller, Alabama State Archives, Montgomery, AL.

29. G. M. Taylor, M.D. to Hon. B. M. Miller, governor, 23 July 1934, Alabama State Archives, Montgomery, AL.

30. "Negro law," not taught in any law school or codified in any statute book, was a blur that whipped past black defendants. Part show, part legal twaddle, it rested, wrote southern historian Leon Litwack in *Trouble in Mind,* "largely on custom, racial assumptions, the unquestioned authority of whites, and a heavy dose of paternalism." The tone was set for a case involving a Negro when a judge appointed an attorney for the accused. Usually, counsel for the defense was a newly minted lawyer, a beginner, as A. C. Lee was in 1919.

31. George Thomas Jones, letter to author, 24 October 2003.

32. A. C. Lee, "This Is My Father's World," speech, Bounds Law Library, University of Alabama at Tuscaloosa.

33. Ray E. Whatley, "The Laborer," sermon delivered at First United Methodist Church, Monroeville, AL, 2 September 1951.

34. Ray E. Whatley, "A Brotherhood of Love," sermon delivered at First United Methodist Church, Monroeville, AL, 2 October 1952.

35. A. C. Lee, "This Is My Father's World."

36. Ray E. Whatley, "Some Reflections on Race Relations in the South," paper

presented to the Commission on Social Concerns of the First Methodist Church, Evanston, IL, 19 April 1965.

37. Ray E. Whatley, "My Brother's Keeper," sermon delivered at First United Methodist Church, Monroeville, AL, 8 February 1953.

38. Don Collins, interview with author, 1 April 2004.

39. Ray E. Whatley. "A Review of Personal Experiences in Racial Issues" (contributed to a project in Richmond, Virginia, about the history of integration), 11 January 1994.

40. J. M. Bonner, letter to the editor, *Tuscaloosa News,* 21 February 1956.

41. A. B. Blass, "Mockingbird Tales," *Legacy* (magazine of the Monroe County Heritage Museums), Fall/Winter 1999, 22.

42. Allison, " 'Mockingbird' Author."

43. Thomas Lane Butts, "An Introduction of Alice Finch Lee as Recipient of the 2003 Maud McClure Kelly Award by the Alabama Bar Association," Mobile, Alabama, 18 July 2003.

44. Harper Lee, *To Kill a Mockingbird,* 5–6.

45. Truman Capote, letter to Alvin and Marie Dewey, 12 August 1960. In *Too Brief a Treat: The Letters of Truman Capote,* ed. Gerald Clarke (New York: Random House, 2004), 290.

46. "Negro Accidentally Killed Last Friday," *Monroe Journal,* 16 February 1933, 1.

47. "Mad Dog Warning Issued for State," *Monroe Journal,* 28 June 1934, 2.

48. Truman Capote, letter to Alvin Dewey III, 4 July 1964, in Clarke, *Too Brief,* 401.

49. Lee, *To Kill a Mockingbird,* 6.

50. Phoebe Adams, review of *To Kill a Mockingbird* by Harper Lee, *Atlantic Monthly,* August 1960, 98–99.

51. W. J. Stuckey, *The Pulitzer Prize Novels: A Critical Backward Look* (Norman: University of Oklahoma Press, 1966), 194.

52. "Harper Lee Gets Scroll, Tells of Book," *Birmingham News,* 12 November 1961, n.p.

53. Hal Boyle, "Harper Lee Running Scared, Getting Fat on Heels of Success," *Birmingham News,* 15 March 1963.

54. *The Author and His Audience,* 29.

55. Sue Philipp, interview with author, 9 March 2004.

56. Marie Faulk Rudisill, interview with author, 21 December 2005.

57. *The Author and His Audience,* 28.

58. McLendon, "Nobody Mocks 'Mockingbird' Author."

59. *The Author and His Audience,* 28.

60. Wayne Greenhaw, interview with author, 20 March 2004.

61. Ibid.

62. Claude Nunnelly, interview with author, 7 December 2003.

63. Dr. Grady Nunn, letter to author, 1 December 2003.

64. Nicholas Delbanco, letter to author, 10 November 2004.

65. Kay Anderson, letter to author, 15 March 2004. As a student at Monroe County High School, Anderson heard Harper Lee tell the story of throwing the manuscript out the window, which Alice Lee denied. Several other former students

heard the same story over the years. The "for better or for worse" remark is from Newquist, *Counterpoint,* 405.

66. Dr. Grady Nunn, letter to author, 1 December 2003.

67. Williams papers, Williams to Harper Lee, 10 January 1959, uncatalogued correspondence, box 86.

68. Ibid.

69. Sarah Countryman, interview with author, 9 March 2004.

70. *Harper Lee's Maycomb,* 44.

71. "Wealthy Farmer, 3 of Family Slain," *New York Times,* 16 November 1959, 7.

72. Clarke, *Capote,* 319.

73. William Allen White, "A Story of the Highlands," quoted in Holly Hope, *Garden City: Dreams in a Kansas Town* (Norman: University of Oklahoma Press, 1988).

6: "See NL's Notes"

1. George Plimpton, "The Story Behind a Nonfiction Novel," *New York Times,* 16 January 1966, accessed at www.nytimes.com/books/97/12/28/home/capote-interview.html.

2. Capote papers, New York Public Library, Manuscripts and Archives Division, box 7, folders 11–14, n.d. These folders contain dated but not numbered typewritten notes by Harper Lee.

3. Ibid., 16 December 1959.

4. Alvin A. Dewey as told to Dolores Hope, "The Clutter Case: 25 Years Later KBI Agent Recounts Holcomb Tragedy," *Garden City Telegram,* 10 November 1984, compact disc.

5. Ibid.

6. Ibid.

7. Ibid.

8. Ibid.

9. Clarke, *Capote,* 322.

10. Crystal K. Wiebe, "Author Left Mark on State," *Lawrence Journal,* World.com, 3 April 2005.

11. Jon Craig, "The Clutter Family Murders, November 14–15, 1959," unpublished paper, Washburn University, 5.

12. Wiebe, "Author Left Mark."

13. Truman Capote papers, Library of Congress, Manuscript Division, box 4, ac. 14, 213, research material/interviews.

14. Harold Nye, interview with author, 30 December 2002.

15. "Scene of the Crime: Twenty-Five Years Later, Holcomb, Kansas Remembers 'In Cold Blood,'" *Chicago Sunday Tribune,* 11 November 1984, 33.

16. Ibid.

17. "In Cold Blood: An American Tragedy," *Newsweek,* 24 January 1966, 59–63.

18. Capote papers, New York Public Library, box 7, folders 11–14, 26 December 1959.

19. Bill Brown, letter to author, 10 February 2003.

20. Capote papers, New York Public Library, box 7, folders 11–14, n.d.
21. Clarke, *Capote,* 323.
22. Cliff Hope, interview with author, 5 April 2005.
23. Harold Nye, interview with author, 30 December 2002.
24. Capote papers, New York Public Library, box 7, folders 11–14, 20 December 1959.
25. Truman Capote, *In Cold Blood* (1965; reprint, New York: Vintage, 1994), 70.
26. Craig, "Clutter Family Murders," note 1. Clutter's remark comes from his files examined by the Finney County Sheriff's Department.
27. Capote papers, New York Public Library, box 7, folders 11–14, 20 December 1959.
28. Cliff Hope, interview with author, 5 April 2005.
29. Capote papers, Library of Congress, box 4, ac. 14, 213, research material/interviews; also, Capote papers, New York Public Library, box 7, folders 11–14, 20 December 1959.
30. Capote papers, New York Public Library, box 7, folders 11–14, 20 December 1959.
31. Ibid.
32. Melissa Lee, "Brother, Friends Object to Portrayal of Bonnie Clutter by Capote," *Lawrence Journal,* World.com, 4 April 2005.
33. Capote papers, Library of Congress, box 4, ac. 14, 213, research material/interviews.
34. Capote papers, New York Public Library, box 7, folders 11–14, 20 December 1959.
35. Capote, *In Cold Blood,* 17.
36. Capote papers, New York Public Library, box 7, folders 11–14, 20 December 1959.
37. Ibid.
38. Ibid.
39. Ted Hall, letter to author, 21 October 2002.
40. Capote papers, Library of Congress, box 4, ac. 14, 213, research material/interviews.
41. C. B. Palmer, "A Farmer Looks at Farming 1954," *New York Times Magazine,* 1 August 1954, 8, 23, 24.
42. Harold Nye, interview with author, 30 December 2002.
43. Capote papers, New York Public Library, box 7, folders 11–14, n.d.
44. Pat Johnson, letter to author, 23 October 2002.
45. Capote papers, New York Public Library, box 7, folders 11–14, n.d.
46. Ibid.
47. Ibid., 15 January 1960.
48. Ibid., 19 December 1959.
49. Ibid., 20 December 1959.
50. Ibid., 19 December 1959.
51. Ibid., 18 December 1959.
52. Ibid.

53. Nathaniel Pennypacker, "Massacre of the Clutter Family," *Front Page Detective,* April 1960, 76.
54. Capote, *In Cold Blood,* 13.
55. Plimpton, "Nonfiction Novel."
56. Cliff Hope, interview with author, 5 April 2005.
57. Hope, *Garden City,* 61.
58. Hope, "The Clutter Case."
59. Dolores Hope, letter to author, 8 June 2005.
60. Plimpton, "Nonfiction Novel."
61. Hope, *Garden City,* 23.
62. Alvin A. Dewey as told to Dolores Hope, "Finding the Killers 'Gave Me Peace of Mind,' " *Hutchinson News,* 11 November 1984, 7B.
63. Crystal K. Wiebe, " 'To Kill a Mockingbird' Author Helped Truman Capote Break the Ice in Kansas," *Lawrence Journal,* World.com, 3 April 2005.
64. Holly Hope, interview with author, 17 February 2005.
65. Dewey and Hope, "Finding the Killers," 16B.
66. Harold Nye, interview with author, 30 December 2002.
67. Capote papers, New York Public Library, box 7, folders 11–14, 26 December 1959.
68. Ibid.
69. Ibid.
70. Ibid., box 7, folder 8. Folder 8 contains some of Capote's notes.
71. Dewey and Hope, "Finding the Killers," 7B.
72. Capote papers, New York Public Library, box 7, folder 8.
73. Ibid., box 7, folders 11–14, n.d. (probably 31 December 1959).
74. Ibid., box 7, folder 8, n.d. (probably 31 December 1959).
75. Hope, "The Clutter Case."
76. Plimpton, *Capote,* 172.
77. Dan Holt, *Kansas Bureau of Investigation, 1939–1989* (Marceline, MO: Jostens, 1990), 70.
78. Capote papers, New York Public Library, box 7, folder 8, n.d.
79. Capote papers, New York Public Library, box 7, folders 11–14, n.d.
80. Ibid., 2 January 1960.
81. Ibid., box 7, folder 7, n.d.
82. Plimpton, "Nonfiction Novel."
83. Dolores Hope, letter to author, 21 February 2005.
84. Capote, *In Cold Blood,* 20.
85. George Steiner, "A Cold-Blooded Happening," *Guardian,* 2 December 1965.
86. Capote papers, New York Public Library, box 7, folders 11–14, 3 January 1960.
87. Capote papers, Library of Congress, Washington, D.C., box 4, ac. 213, interviews.
88. Harold Nye, interview with author, 30 December 2002.
89. Capote papers, New York Public Library, box 7, folders 11–14, 5 January 1960.
90. Ibid.
91. Ibid.

92. Ibid.

93. Truman Capote, letter to Alvin and Marie Dewey, 12 August 1960. In Clarke, *Too Brief,* 276.

94. Bill Brown, letter to author, 10 February 2003.

95. Capote papers, New York Public Library, box 7, folders 11–14, 6 January 1960.

96. Capote, *In Cold Blood,* 248.

97. Capote papers, New York Public Library, box 7, folder 8, 7 January 1960.

98. Ibid., box 7, folders 11–14, 7 January 1960.

99. Capote, *In Cold Blood,* 31.

100. Clarke, *Capote,* 326.

101. "In Cold Blood," *Newsweek,* 26 January 1966, 59–63.

102. Guy Louis Rocha, "Truman Capote's *In Cold Blood*: The Nevada Connection," *Las Vegas Review Journal,* 18 April 1999.

103. Capote, *In Cold Blood,* 244.

104. Capote papers, New York Public Library, box 7, folders 11–14, 7 January 1960.

105. Ibid., 9 January 1960.

106. Ibid., 11 January 1960.

107. Capote papers, Library of Congress, box 4, ac. 14, 421, 11 January 1960.

108. Capote papers, New York Public Library, box 7, folders 11–14, 11 January 1960.

109. Ibid., 11 January 1960.

110. Ibid.

111. Plimpton, "Nonfiction Novel."

112. Capote papers, New York Public Library, box 7, folders 11–14, 11 January 1960.

113. Ibid.

114. Ibid.

115. Harold Nye, interview with author, 30 December 2002.

116. Capote papers, Harold Nye to Truman Capote, 27 June 1962, New York Public Library, box 7, folder 8.

117. Ibid., box 7, folders 11–14, 15 January 1960.

118. Bill Brown, letter to author, 10 February 2003.

119. Harold Nye, interview with author, 30 December 2002.

120. Plimpton, *Capote,* 171.

121. Newquist, *Counterpoint,* 405.

122. Truman Capote, letter to Cecil Beaton, 21 January 1960, in Clarke, *Too Brief,* 276–77.

123. "Harper Lee Gets Scroll, Tells of Book," *Birmingham News,* 12 November 1961, n.p.

124. Don Kendall, "Clutter Sale Has Big Crowd," *Garden City Telegram*, 21 March 1960, 1.

125. Elon Torrence, interview with author, 6 May 2005. Torrence is a former Associated Press reporter who attended the trial.

126. Capote papers, New York Public Library, box 7, folders 11–14, 22 March 1960.

127. Ibid.

128. Ibid.

129. Ibid., 19 March 1960.

130. Mack Nations, "America's Worst Crime in Twenty Years," *Male,* December 1961, 30–31, 76–83.
131. Elon Torrence, interview with author, 6 May 2005.
132. Nations, "America's Worst Crime," 76–83.
133. Capote papers, New York Public Library, box 7, folders 11–14, n.d.
134. Mark Besten, "Too Hot for You? Take a Dip in Cold Blood," *Louisville Eccentric Observer,* 1 August 2001, 16.

7: *MOCKINGBIRD* TAKES OFF

1. Truman Capote, letter to David O. Selznick and Jennifer Jones, early June 1960, in Clarke, *Too Brief,* 284.
2. Michael Stillman, "19th Century Shop Offers Selections from New York Antiques Show," *Americana Exchange,* November 2004.
3. Williams papers, undated news release, early January 1960, box 86.
4. Newquist, *Counterpoint,* 405.
5. Frances Nettles, "Addenda," *Monroe Journal,* 16 June 1960, n.p.
6. Glendy Culligan, "Listen to That Mockingbird," *Washington Post,* 3 July 1960, E6.
7. Williams papers, Williams to Truman Capote, 3 August 1960, box 41.
8. Alden Todd, interview with author, 20 November 2004.
9. Frank H. Lyell, "Violence in Dixie," review of *Seed in the Wind* by Leon Odell, *New York Times,* 31 July 1960, BR23.
10. Capote, letter to Alvin and Marie Dewey, 10 October 1960, in Clarke, *Too Brief,* 299.
11. "Mocking Bird Call," *Newsweek,* 9 January 1961, 83.
12. Williams papers, W. D. Weinman to Harper Lee, 8 August 1965, box 86.
13. Hudson Strode papers, letter to Nelle Harper Lee, 24 January 1961, Hoole Library, University of Alabama at Tuscaloosa, box 1211, folder 158.
14. Wayne Greenhaw, interview with author, 20 March 2004.
15. Hohoff, *Cats and Other People,* 195.
16. Max York, "Throngs Greet Monroe Writer," *Montgomery Advertiser,* 13 September 1960, 3A.
17. Vernon Hendrix, "Author's Father Proud of 'Mockingbird' Fame," *Montgomery Advertiser,* 7 August 1960, 1B.
18. Capote, letter to Andrew Lyndon, 6 September 1960, in Clarke, *Too Brief,* 291.
19. Albin Krebs, "Truman Capote Is Dead at 59; Novelist of Style and Clarity," *New York Times,* 26 August, 1984, 1.
20. "Mocking Bird Call," 83.
21. Ibid.
22. Ibid.
23. June Maulding, "Harper Lee Remains Serene Over Success," *Mobile Register,* 17 September 1960, n.p.
24. Williams papers, unsigned letter to Harper Lee from secretary in Williams's office, 7 January 1961, box 86.
25. Deitch, "Novelist of the South," 6.

26. Hamner, "Happy Singer," n.p.
27. Letters to the editor ("Tell It to Old Grandma"), "Irked" by Tom Gardner, *Montgomery Advertiser,* n.d., n.p.
28. Hamner, "Happy Singer," n.p.
29. John T. Hamner, interview with author, 29 April 2005.
30. Charles Ray Skinner, interview with author, 22 December 2002.
31. Williams papers, unsigned letter to Harper Lee from secretary in Williams's office, 7 January 1961, box 86.
32. Williams papers, Maurice Crain to Harper Lee, 27 January 1961.
33. Williams papers, Williams to Harper Lee, "Saturday morning" (early January 1961), box 86.
34. Moates, *Bridge of Childhood,* 2.
35. Joel P. Smith, " 'Mockingbird' Author Looking for Characters?" *Eufaula Tribune,* 8 September 1960, 4.
36. Williams papers, letter to Harper Lee, and her reply, 5 January 1961, box 86.
36. "Prize Winner Remembered as Deflater of Phoniness," *Montgomery Advertiser,* 4 May 1961, n.p.
37. Nelle Harper Lee to Leo R. Roberts, January 1960, Archives and Information Center, Huntingdon College Library, Huntingdon Collection, Montgomery, AL.
38. Williams papers, Robert P. Richards to Williams, 8 November 1960, box 86.
39. Frances Kiernan, "No Apologies Necessary," *Atlantic Monthly,* April 2001.
40. Hendrix, "Author's Father Proud of 'Mockingbird' Fame."
41. Ibid.
42. Emma Foy, interview with author, 5 July 2003.
43. Williams papers, Williams to Nelle and Alice Lee, 28 January 1961, box 86.
44. Williams papers, Williams to Alan Pakula, 16 November 1960, box 86.
45. "Mockingbird Film May Begin in Fall," *Birmingham News,* 2 May 1961, n.p.
46. Williams papers, Williams to "Boaty" Boatwright, 25 June 1962, box 86.
47. Letter to the editor, "Spreading Poison," *Atlanta Journal,* 7 February 1961, n.p.
48. Williams papers, Williams to George Stevens, with note attached from Harper Lee, 8 August 1960, box 86.
49. Williams papers, Maurice Crain to Alice Lee, 22 March 1961, box 86.
50. Fred Gipson papers, Harry Ransom Humanities Research Center, University of Texas at Austin, Maurice Crain to Fred and Tommie Gipson, 7 April 1961, box 18, folder 4.
51. Murray Schumach, "Prize for Novel Elates Film Pair," *New York Times,* 19 May 1961, 26.
52. " 'Luckiest Person in the World,' Says Pulitzer Winner," *Birmingham News,* 2 May 1961, n.p.
53. "State Pulitzer Prize Winner Too Busy to Write," *Dothan Eagle,* 2 May 1961, n.p.
54. Strode papers, box 1211, folder 158.
55. "Luckiest Person," n.p.
56. "Mocking Bird Call," 83.
57. Capote to Alvin and Marie Dewey, May 22, 1961, in Clarke, *Too Brief,* 317.
58. Caldwell Delaney papers, University of South Alabama Archives, Mobile, AL, Nelle Lee to Helen Waterman, 20 November 1961.

59. Plimpton, *Capote,* 14.

60. "Senate Lauds Pulitzer Winner," *Montgomery Advertiser,* 20 May 1961, 7A.

61. James B. McMillan, review of *To Kill a Mockingbird* by Harper Lee, *Alabama Review,* July 1961, 233.

62. Delaney papers, Nelle Lee to Helen Waterman, 20 November 1961.

63. Williams papers, note to Harper Lee, 12 July 1961, box 86.

64. "Luckiest Person," n.p.

8: "OH, MR. PECK!"

1. Reed Polk, letter to author, 10 July 2003.

2. Scott McGee, Kerryn Sherrod, and Jeff Stafford, "To Kill a Mockingbird: The Essentials," Turner Classic Movies, www.turnerclassicmovies.com.

3. Deitch, "Novelist of the South," 6.

4. Charles S. Watson, *Horton Foote: A Literary Biography* (Austin: University of Texas Press, 2003), 114. Miss Lee didn't quite feel "indifference," as she claimed. In a letter to Helen Waterman, a friend in Mobile, dated November 20, 1961, Lee wrote: "Please forgive the long silence from Monroeville. I had to do some things that HAD to be done as soon as I returned—the most pressing task was doctoring the movie script" (Caldwell Delany papers, University of South Alabama).

5. Don Noble, *Bookmark: Interview with Horton Foote,* videocassette, Alabama Center for Public Television, Tuscaloosa, AL, 27 August 1998.

6. *To Kill a Mockingbird: Then and Now,* videocassette, Prince William County Public Schools, Manassas, VA, 25 April 1997.

7. M. Jerry Weiss, *Photoplay Guide: "To Kill a Mockingbird,"* NCTE Studies in the Mass Media (Champaign, IL: National Council of Teachers of English, 1963), 18.

8. *To Kill a Mockingbird* (commentary section), Universal City, CA: Universal Home Video, 1998, compact disc.

9. Williams papers, Williams to George Stevens, 23 May 1961, box 86.

10. Jones, "Stand Up, Monroeville, Gregory Peck Is Passin'," *Happenings,* vol. 2, 159–60.

11. Gary Fishgall, *Gregory Peck: A Biography* (New York: Scribner, 2002), 233.

12. Jones, "Stand Up," *Happenings,* vol. 2, 160.

13. Ibid., 160–61.

14. Dolores Hope, letter to author, 15 October 2002.

15. Thomas McDonald, "Bird in Hand," *New York Times,* 6 May 1962, 149.

16. Jane Kansas, "To Kill a Mockingbird and Harper Lee: Why the Site?" mockingbird.chebucto.org/why.html.

17. "Brock Peters, 'To Kill a Mockingbird' Actor, Dies at 78," *USA Today,* 23 August 2005.

18. *To Kill a Mockingbird* (commentary section), compact disc.

19. Barbara Vancheri, "Author Lauded 'Mockingbird' as a 'Moving' Film," *Pittsburgh Post-Gazette,* 20 February 2003.

20. Philip Alford, interview with author, 21 May 2004.

21. Murray Schumach, "Film Crew Saves $75,000 on Shacks," *New York Times,* 19 January 1962, 26.

22. Jane Kansas, "To Kill a Mockingbird and Harper Lee: The Film," mocking bird.chebucto.org/film.html.

23. Newquist, *Counterpoint,* 406.

24. Gipson papers, Tommie Gipson to Maurice Crain, 19 February 1962, box 18, folder 4.

25. Gipson papers, Maurice Crain to Tommie Gipson, 20 February 1962, box 18, folder 4.

26. Kansas, "To Kill a Mockingbird and Harper Lee: The Film."

27. Philip Alford, interview with author, 21 May 2004.

28. Ibid.

29. Vernon Hendrix, "Firm Gives Books to Monroe County," *Montgomery Advertiser,* 23 December 1962, n.p.

30. E. L. H., Jr., "The Obvious Is All Around Us," *Birmingham News,* 22 April 1962, n.p.

31. Capote, letter to Alvin and Marie Dewey, 5 May 1962, in Clarke, *Too Brief,* 348.

32. Joy Hafner-Bailey, interview with author, 21 December 2005.

33. Williams papers, Harold Hayes, *Esquire* editor, to Nelle Harper Lee (regarding "Dress Rehearsal," submitted by Lee), 27 October 1961, box 86.

34. Fishgall, *Gregory Peck,* 236.

35. Ibid.

36. Watson, *Horton Foote*, 143.

37. Fishgall, *Gregory Peck*, 236.

38. *To Kill a Mockingbird* (commentary section), compact disc.

39. Capote, letter to Alvin and Marie Dewey, 16 August 1962, in Clarke, *Too Brief,* 361.

40. Strode papers, Elise Sanguinetti to Hudson Strode, box 1211, folder 161.

41. Darryl Pebbles, interview with author, 9 February 2005.

42. "Harper Lee" Program from 1962 Founders Day, Mount Holyoke College Archives and Special Collections, South Hadley, MA, Honorary Degrees: Citations, folder 6.

43. "Chicago Press Call," *Overpress,* Chicago Press Club, March 1963.

44. Capote, letter to Donald Cullivan, 11 December 1962, in Clarke, *Too Brief,* 372.

45. Judith Martin, "To Lady Bird Johnson Alabama Is New Kin," *Washington Post,* 10 December 1962, B4.

46. Ibid.

47. Williams papers, "Author Praises Picture Made from Prize Novel," *New York Times,* n.d., n.p.

48. *To Kill a Mockingbird* (commentary section), compact disc.

49. Williams papers, Williams to Alice Lee, 16 February 1963, box 86.

50. *To Kill a Mockingbird* (commentary section), compact disc.

51. Dean Shackelford, "The Female Voice in *To Kill a Mockingbird*: Narrative Strategies in Film and the Novel," in *To Kill a Mockingbird: Modern Critical Interpretations,* ed. Harold Bloom (Philadelphia: Chelsea House, 1999), 121.

52. *Newsweek,* film review of *To Kill a Mockingbird,* 18 February 1963, 93.

53. Bosley Crowther, "Screen: 'To Kill a Mockingbird,'" *New York Times,* 15 February 1963, 10.

54. Colin Nicholson, "Hollywood and Race: *To Kill a Mockingbird*," in *Cinema and Fiction: New Modes of Adapting, 1950–1990,* ed. John Orr and Colin Nicholson (Edinburgh: Edinburgh University Press, 1992), 97.

55. Andrew Sarris, *Village Voice,* 7 March 1963.

56. Weiss, *Photoplay Guide: "To Kill a Mockingbird,"* 18.

57. Capote, letter to Alvin and Marie Dewey, 15 February 1963, in Clarke, *Too Brief,* 382.

58. Williams papers, Williams to Alice Lee, 16 February 1963, box 86.

59. Boyle, "Harper Lee Running Scared," n.p.

60. Williams papers, Williams to Alice Lee, 25 March 1963.

61. Dorothy and Taylor Faircloth, interview with author, 17 March 2003.

62. Joseph Blass, letter to author, 10 September 2002.

63. Dorothy and Taylor Faircloth, interview with author, 17 March 2003.

64. S. Jonathan Bass, *Blessed Are the Peacemakers: Martin Luther King, Jr.: Eight White Religious Leaders, and the "Letter from Birmingham Jail"* (Baton Rouge: Louisiana State University Press, 2001), 102–3.

65. Vernon Hendrix, "Harper Lee Cries for Joy at Peck's Winning of Oscar," *Montgomery Advertiser,* 10 April 1963.

66. Moates, *Bridge of Childhood,* 11.

9: The Second Novel

1. Williams papers, Williams to Alice Lee, 21 June 1963, box 86.

2. Ibid.

3. Strode papers, Therese Strode to Peggy (unidentified), 22 June 1963, box 1209, folder 48.

4. "Chicago Press Call."

5. Virginia Van der Veer Hamilton, *Alabama: A History* (reprint, New York: Norton, 1984).

6. Kay Wells, interview with author, 5 November 2005.

7. Allison, "Woman of the Year," n.p.

8. Donald Collins, interview with author, 1 April 2004.

9. Sam Hodges, "To Love a Mockingbird," *Mobile Register,* 8 September 2002.

10. Wes Lawrence, "Author's Problem: Friends," *Cleveland Plain Dealer,* 17 March 1964, n.p.

11. Williams papers, Williams to Alice Lee, 6 September 1963, box 86.

12. Williams papers, Alice Lee to Williams, 9 September 1963, box 86.

13. Williams papers, Williams to Alice Lee, 21 October 1963, box 86.

14. Ibid.

15. Newquist, *Counterpoint,* 208.

16. Amelia Young, "Her Writing Place Is Secret: 'Mockingbird' Author Working on Second Book," *Minneapolis Star,* 26 May 1963, n.p., Williams papers, box 86.

17. Lawrence, "Author's Problem."

18. James B. Simpson, *Simpson's Contemporary Quotations* (New York: Houghton Mifflin, 1988).

19. Boyle, "Harper Lee Running Scared," n.p.

20. Deitch, "Novelist of the South," 6.
21. Williams papers, Alice Lee to Williams, 14 November 1963, box 86.
22. Capote to Alvin and Marie Dewey, 14 February 1964, in Clarke, *Too Brief,* 393.
23. Young, "Her Writing Place Is Secret."
24. Ibid.
25. Capote to Bennett Cerf, 10 September 1962, in Clarke, *Too Brief,* 363.
26. Capote papers, New York Public Library, Harold Nye to Capote, 27 June 1962, box 7, folder 9.
27. Capote papers, Library of Congress, Washington, D.C., box 7, ac. 14, 213: research material/interviews. Robert J. Kaiser to Clifford R. Hope, Jr., 14 January 1963.
28. Capote to Alvin and Marie Dewey, 23 May 1964, in Clarke, *Too Brief,* 397.
29. Patrick Smith, "An Outspoken Critic," *Lawrence Journal,* World.com, 5 April 2005.
30. "Scene of the Crime: Twenty-Five Years Later, Holcomb, Kansas Remembers 'In Cold Blood.'" *Chicago Sunday Tribune,* 11 November 1984, 34.
31. Don Lee Keith, "An Afternoon with Harper Lee," *Delta Review* (Spring 1966), 41.
32. Harold Nye, interview with author, 30 December 2002.
33. Newquist, *Counterpoint,* 412.
34. Williams papers, Williams to Alice Lee, 3 August 1964, box 86.
35. Ibid.
36. Williams papers, Williams to Alice Lee, 1 September 1964, 86.
37. Gus Lee, letter to author, 2 December 2004.
38. Gus Lee, *Honor and Duty* (reprint, New York: Ivy Books, 1994), 149–50.
39. Ibid.
40. Joy Hafner-Bailey, interview with author, 15 December 2005.
41. Clarke, *Capote,* 354.
42. Holt, *Kansas Bureau of Investigation,* 71.
43. Capote to Cecil Beaton, 19 April 1965, in Clarke, *Too Brief,* 421.
44. Williams papers, Williams to Alice Lee, 7 May 1965, box 86.
45. *Harper Lee's Maycomb,* 19.
46. Keith, "An Afternoon with Harper Lee," 82.
47. Williams papers, Williams to Alice Lee, 7 June 1965, box 86.
48. Keith, "An Afternoon with Harper Lee."
49. Jubera, "To Find a Mockingbird."
50. Williams papers, Williams to Alice Lee, 5 August 1965, box 86.
51. Capote papers, New York Public Library, box 9, folder 1.
52. Harper Lee, "When Children Discover America," *McCalls,* August 1965, 76–79.
53. Nye, interview with author, 30 December 2002.
54. Wayne Lee, "Emotions Mixed Among Clutter Participants," *Hutchinson News,* 31 October 1965, n.p.
55. Williams papers, Williams to Alice Lee, 15 September 1965, box 86.
56. Williams papers, Williams to Alice Lee, 28 September1965, box 86.
57. Sarah Countryman, interview with author, 9 March 2004.
58. Williams papers, Williams to Alice Lee, 8 October 1965, box 86.
59. Ibid.

60. Wayne Greenhaw, letter to author, 1 November 2005.

61. R. Philip Hanes, interview with author, 6 December 2004.

62. Michael Shelden, "The Writer Vanishes," *Daily Telegraph,* 12 April 1997, n.p.

63. David Kipen, letter to author, 23 November 2005. Mr. Kipen is the National Endowment for the Arts Literature director.

64. "Mr. Bumble and the Mockingbird," editorial, *Richmond News-Leader,* 5 January 1966, 12.

65. "Author Harper Lee Comments on Book-Banning," *Richmond News-Leader,* 15 January 1966, 10.

66. R. Philip Hanes, interview with author, 6 December 2004.

67. Ibid.

68. Jimilu Mason, interview with author, 18 February 2005.

69. R. Philip Hanes, interview with author, 6 December 2004.

70. Ibid.

71. Darryl Pebbles, interview with author, 9 February 2005.

72. Sarah Dyess, letter to author, 10 December 2004.

73. William Smart, interview with author, 2 July 2004.

74. Karen Schwabenton, "Harper Lee Discusses the Writer's Attitude and Craft," *Sweet Briar News,* 28 October 1966, 3.

75. Charlotte Curtis, "Capote's Black and White Ball: 'The Most Exquisite of Spectator Sports,'" *New York Times,* 29 November 1966.

76. Williams papers, Maurice Crain to Ann Brun Ash, 3 January 1968, box 146, folder Ca.

77. Wayne Greenhaw, letter to author, 23 March 2005.

78. Paul Engle papers, Special Collections Department, University of Iowa Libraries, Harper Lee to Paul Engle, 20 August 1968, box 9.

79. Williams papers, Maurice Crain to Ted Lloyd, 24 February 1969, box 149, folder L.

80. Joy Hafner-Bailey, interview with author, 15 December 2005.

81. Williams papers, Williams to May Lou (unidentified), December 1970, box 149, folder L.

82. Williams papers, Williams to Harper Lee, 11 March 1971.

83. Capote to Alvin and Marie Dewey, 3 December 1961, in Clarke, *Too Brief,* 332–33.

84. Williams papers, Pamela Barnes to Mrs. Erskine Caldwell, 13 September 1971, box 146, folder C-Cu.

85. Dr. Grady H. Nunn, letter to author, January 4, 2005.

86. Peter Griffiths, letter to author, 26 April 2005. Mr. Griffiths was a researcher for the BBC in 1982, which visited Monroeville for a documentary about *To Kill a Mockingbird.*

10: QUIET TIME

1. Tom Radney, interview with author, 14 November 2005.

2. Jubera, "To Find a Mockingbird."

3. Tom Radney, interview with author, 14 November 2005.

4. Jubera, "To Find a Mockingbird."

5. Ralph Hammond, interview with author, 20 March 2005.

6. Burstein, "Tiny, Yes."

7. James Wolcott, "Tru Grit," *Vanity Fair,* October 2005, 166.

8. Dolores Hope, letter to author, 13 October 2002.

9. Tom Radney, interview with author, 14 November 2005.

10. Ibid.

11. Drew Jubera, "'Mockingbird' Still Sings Despite Silence of Author Harper Lee," *Atlanta Journal-Constitution,* 26 August 1990, M1 and M3.

12. Emma S. Foy, interview with author, 5 July 2003.

13. Jubera, "To Find a Mockingbird."

14. Ibid.

15. William Smart, interview with author, 2 July 2004.

16. Clarke, *Capote,* 22.

17. Harper Lee to Caldwell Delaney, 30 December 1988. Robert Hicks, author of *Widow of the South* (New York: Warner Books, 2005), found this letter between the pages of a used copy of Clarke's *Capote*.

18. "Story of Attempted Drowning Called False, Angers Harper Lee," *Tuscaloosa News,* 25 September 1997.

19. *Harper Lee's Maycomb,* 86.

20. Williams papers, Christopher Sergel to Williams, 5 January 1965, box 149, folder L.

21. "Harper Lee, Read but Not Heard," *Washington Post,* 17 August 1990.

22. The author participated as a juror during the play in Monroeville in May 2003.

23. Roy Hoffman, "Long Lives the Mockingbird," *New York Times,* 9 August 1998, BR31.

24. Dr. Wanda Bigham, former president of Huntingdon College, letter to author, 25 May 2004.

25. Harper Lee, foreword to the thirty-fifth-anniversary edition of *To Kill a Mockingbird* (New York: HarperCollins, 1993).

26. George Thomas Jones, letter to author, 30 August 2003.

27. Marja Mills, "A Life Apart: Harper Lee, the Complex Woman Behind 'A Delicious Mystery,'" *Chicago Tribune,* 13 September 2002, n.p.

28. Ibid.

29. J. Wes Yoder, "Debating the Details: Some Residents of Monroeville Prefer to Ponder the Fine Points of Famous Novel," *Expressions* (online magazine), Auburn University Journalism Department, 2001.

30. Judge Otha Lee Biggs, interview with author, 21 May 2004.

31. George Thomas Jones, letter to author, 30 August 2003.

32. Mills, "A Life Apart."

33. Jay C. Grelen, "Freaking Out the Talented Harper Lee," *Sun News* (Myrtle Beach, SC), 31 December 2002, C1.

34. Spike (columnist), "Scaring Harper Lee, No Time to Die, the Leaf Player Revisited," *Online Journalism Review,* 8 January 2003, Annenberg School for Communication, University of Southern California, Los Angeles, CA.

35. Kathy Kemp, "Mockingbird Won't Sing," *News & Observer,* 12 November 1997, E1.

36. Mark Childress, "Looking for Harper Lee," *Southern Living,* May 1997, 148–50.

37. Mary Tomlinson, letter to author, 2 November 2005.

38. Richard Chalfin, "The Day Harper Lee Came to See Me," *New York Observer,* 4 December 2000, 5.

39. Carla Jean Whitley, "Small-Town Q&A: Amanda McMillan," *Crimson White,* University of Alabama at Tuscaloosa, 9 October 2003, n.p.

40. Donald Collins, interview with author, 1 April 2004.

41. Jim Gilbert, "Cold, Cold Mockingbird," *Mobile Register,* 13 May 2001.

42. Jim Gilbert, "Cold, Cold Mockingbird: Postscript," www.weirdplots.com, March 2002, accessed 13 December 2005.

43. Reverend Thomas Lane Butts, remarks at "Maud McLure Kelly Award Luncheon" (award given to Miss Lee, Mobile, AL, 18 July 2003).

44. Ibid.

45. Mills, "A Life Apart."

46. Darryl Peebles, interview with author, 9 February 2005.

47. Carolyn Crawford, interview with author, 1 February 2003.

48. "One Version of the Harper Lee Story," Harperlee@yahoogroups.com (listserv), accessed 11 October 2005.

49. Caldwell Delaney papers, University of South Alabama Archives, Mobile, AL, Nelle Lee to Helen Waterman, 20 November 1961.

Bibliography

BOOKS

The Author and His Audience: 175th Anniversary J. B. Lippincott Company. Philadelphia: J. B. Lippincott, 1967.

Ayers, Edward L. *The Promise of the New South: Life After Reconstruction.* New York: Oxford University Press, 1992.

Bass, S. Jonathan. *Blessed Are the Peacemakers: Martin Luther King, Jr., Eight White Religious Leaders, and the "Letter from Birmingham Jail."* Baton Rouge: Louisiana State University Press, 2001.

Bloom, Harold, ed. *To Kill A Mockingbird: Modern Critical Interpretations.* Philadelphia: Chelsea House Books, 1999.

Capote, Truman. *Breakfast at Tiffany's.* New York: Random House, 1950.

———. *In Cold Blood.* 1965. Reprint, New York: Vintage, 1994.

———. *Other Voices, Other Rooms.* 1948. Reprint, New York: Vintage, 1994.

Cash, W. J. *The Mind of the South.* New York: Alfred A. Knopf, 1941.

Clarke, Gerald. *Capote: A Biography.* New York: Simon and Schuster, 1988.

———, ed. *Too Brief a Treat: The Letters of Truman Capote.* New York: Random House, 2004.

Collins, Donald E. *When the Church Bell Rang Racist: The Methodist Church and the Civil Rights Movement in Alabama.* Macon, GA: Mercer University Press, 1998.

Fishgall, Gary. *Gregory Peck: A Biography*. New York: Scribner, 2002.

Fleming, Walter L. *Civil War and Reconstruction in Alabama*. New York: Peter Smith, 1949.

Griffith, Lucille. *Alabama: A Documentary History to 1900*. Tuscaloosa: University of Alabama Press, 1968.

Grobel, Lawrence. *Conversations with Capote*. New York: New American Library, 1985.

Hamilton, Virginia Van der Veer. *Alabama: A History*. 1977. Reprint, New York: Norton, 1984.

Hohoff, Tay. *A Ministry to Man: The Life of John Lovejoy Elliot*. New York: Harper, 1959.

———. *Cats and Other People*. New York: Popular Library, 1973.

Hollowell, John. *Fact and Fiction: The New Journalism and the Nonfiction Novel*. Chapel Hill: University of North Carolina Press, 1977.

Holt, Dan. *Kansas Bureau of Investigation, 1939–1989*. Marceline, MO: Jostens, 1990.

Hope, Holly. *Garden City: Dreams in a Kansas Town*. Norman: University of Oklahoma Press, 1988.

Hranicky, Roy E. and Lois Belle White. *The Five H's*. Privately printed, 1950.

Inge, Thomas M. *Truman Capote Conversations*. Jackson: University of Mississippi Press, 1987.

Johnson, Claudia Durst. *To Kill a Mockingbird: Threatening Boundaries*. New York: Twayne, 1994.

Jones, George Thomas. *Happenings in Old Monroeville*. Volume 1. Monroeville, AL: Bolton Newspapers, 1999.

———. *Happenings in Old Monroeville*. Volume 2. Monroeville, AL: Bolton Newspapers, 2003.

Lee, Harper. *To Kill a Mockingbird*. 1962. Reprint, New York: Warner Books, 1982.

Litwack, Leon F. *Trouble in Mind: Black Southerners in the Age of Jim Crow*. New York: Alfred A. Knopf, 1998.

Malin, Irving. *Truman Capote's In Cold Blood: A Critical Handbook*. Belmont, CA: Wadsworth, 1968.

McCorvey, Thomas Chalmers. *Alabama Historical Poems*. Birmingham, AL: Birmingham Publishing Company, 1927.

Moates, Marianne M. *A Bridge of Childhood: Truman Capote's Southern Years*. New York: Holt, 1989.

Monroeville: Literary Capital of Alabama. Charleston, SC: Arcadia Publishing, 1998.

Monroeville: The Search for Harper Lee's Maycomb. Charleston, SC: Arcadia Publishing, 1999.

Moore, Albert Burton, ed. *History of Alabama and Her People*. 3 vols. Chicago: American Historical Society, 1927.

Morrow, Bradford and Peter Constantine, eds. *Conjunctions: 31. Radical Shadows: Previously Untranslated and Unpublished Works by 19th and 20th Century Masters*. New York: Bard College, 1998.

Nance, William L. *The Worlds of Truman Capote*. New York: Stein and Day, 1970.

Newquist, Roy. *Counterpoint*. Chicago: Rand McNally, 1964.

New York City Guide and Almanac, 1957–1958. New York: New York University Press, 1957–58.

O'Neill, Terry, ed. *Readings on* To Kill A Mockingbird. San Diego: Greenhaven Press, 2000.

Owen, Thomas McDory. *History of Alabama and Dictionary of Alabama Biography.* 4 vols. Chicago: S. J. Clarke, 1921.

Plimpton, George. *Truman Capote: In Which Various Friends, Enemies, Acquaintances and Detractors Recall His Turbulent Career.* New York: Anchor, 1997.

Rubin, Louis D., Jr., et al., eds. *A History of Southern Literature.* Baton Rouge: Louisiana State University Press, 1985.

Rudisill, Marie with James C. Simmons. *Truman Capote: The Story of His Bizarre and Exotic Childhood by an Aunt Who Helped Raise Him.* New York: William Morrow, 1983.

Sellers, James B. *History of the University of Alabama.* Revised and edited by W. Stanley Hoole. Tuscaloosa: University of Alabama Press, 1975.

Strode, Hudson. *Spring Harvest: A Collection of Stories from Alabama.* New York: Alfred A. Knopf, 1944.

Stuckey, W. J. *The Pulitzer Prize Novels: A Critical Backward Look.* Norman: University of Oklahoma Press, 1966.

Tindall, George Brown. *The Emergence of the New South 1913–1945. A History of the South.* Compiled and edited by Wendell Holmes Stephenson and E. Merton Coulter. Vol. X. Baton Rouge: Louisiana State University Press, 1967.

Van der Veer Hamilton, Virginia. *Alabama: A History.* Reprint, New York: Norton, 1984.

Walter, Eugene (as told to Katherine Clark). *Milking the Moon.* New York: Three Rivers Press, 2001.

Watson, Charles S. *Horton Foote: A Literary Biography.* Austin: University of Texas Press, 2003.

Watson, Fred S. *Piney Woods Echoes: A History of Dale and Coffee Counties, Alabama.* Enterprise, AL: Elba Clipper, 1949.

White, E. B. *Here Is New York.* New York: Harper & Brothers, 1949.

Williams, R. B., III. *The Day the Barn Almost Burned and Other Stories of Deep South Plantation Life in the 1940s.* Montgomery, AL: Court Street Press, 2000.

ARTICLES

Adams, J. Donald. Speaking of Books (column). *New York Times,* 2 June 1963, 270.

Adams, Phoebe. Review of *To Kill a Mockingbird* by Harper Lee, *Atlantic Monthly,* August 1960, 98–99.

Allison, Ramona. " 'Mockingbird' Author Is Alabama's 'Woman of the Year.' " *Birmingham Post Herald,* 3 January 1962.

"Alumna Wins Pulitzer Prize for Distinguished Fiction." University of Alabama *Alumni News,* May–June 1961.

Ames, Lynn. "Dispelling Misconceptions Between the North and the South." *New York Times,* 5 May 1996, WC2.

"Annie L. Williams, Authors' Agent, Dies." *New York Times,* 18 May 1977, O4.

"Annie Williams, Agent Who Sold 'Gone With the Wind.'" *Washington Post*, 20 May 1977, C8.

"Arts Council to Mull Grants, 1967 Budget." *Washington Post*, 11 February 1966, B3.

"Author Harper Lee Comments on Book-Banning." *Richmond News-Leader*, 15 January 1966, 10.

Beechcroft, John. "To Kill a Mockingbird." *Literary Guild Book Club Magazine*, August 1960, 1–2.

Besten, Mark. "Too Hot for You? Take a Dip in Cold Blood." *Louisville Eccentric Observer*, 1 August 2001, 16.

Blass, A. B. "Mockingbird Tales." *Legacy,* Fall/Winter 1999, 22.

Boyle, Hal. "Harper Lee Running Scared, Getting Fat on Heels of Success." *Birmingham News*, 15 March 1963.

Brady, Dave. "Harper Lee, Top Scientists Are Competition for 'Bear.'" *Washington Post*, 26 May 1963, C6.

Brian, Denis. "Truman Capote," in *Truman Capote Conversations*, ed. Thomas M. Inge. Jackson: University of Mississippi Press, 1987, 210–35.

"Brock Peters, 'To Kill a Mockingbird.' Actor, Dies at 78." *USA Today*, 23 August 2005.

Buder, Leonard. "Opportunities for Study in Europe." *New York Times*, 11 April 1948, E11.

Burstein, Patricia. "Tiny, Yes, But a Terror? Do Not Be Fooled by Truman Capote in Repose." *People Weekly*, 10 May 1976, 12–17.

Capote, Truman. "The Thanksgiving Visitor," in *A Christmas Memory, One Christmas, and The Thanksgiving Visitor*. New York: Modern Library, 1996.

Carroll, Maurice. "New York Plays Upbeat Host to Delegates." *New York Times*, 12 July 1976, 1.

Chalfin, Richard. "The Day Harper Lee Came to See Me." *New York Observer,* 4 December 2000, 5.

"Chicago Press Call." *Rogue*. Chicago Press Club. December 1963.

Childress, Mark. "Looking for Harper Lee." *Southern Living*, May 1997, 148–50.

"Christopher Sergel, Publisher of Plays and Playwright, 75." *New York Times*, 2 May 1993, B7.

Clemons, Walter. "The Last Word: The Pulitzer Non-Prize for Fiction." *New York Times*, 6 June 1971, BR55.

Cobb, Mark Hughes. "Native Stars Fall on Alabama Hall of Fame." *Tuscaloosa News*, 17 March 2001.

"Countries—One Brings Tractor Order." *New York Times*, 5 October 1948, 28.

Craig, Jon. "The Clutter Family Murders, November 14–15, 1959." Unpublished ms., Washburn University, 1979.

Crimmins, Margaret and Nancy L. Ross. "Kennedy Center's Opening—It'll Be a Starry Night." *Washington Post*, 5 September 1971, 135.

Crowther, Bosley. "Screen: 'To Kill a Mockingbird.'" *New York Times*, 15 February 1963.

Culligan, Glendy. "Listen to That Mockingbird." *Washington Post*, 3 July 1960, E6.

Curtis, Charlotte. "Capote's Black & White Ball: 'The Most Exquisite of Spectator Sports.'" *New York Times*, 29 November 1966, 53.

Daley, Robert. "It's Like a Plate of Spaghetti Under New York Streets." *Chicago Tribune*, 7 February 1960, 20.

Dare, Tim. "Lawyers, Ethics, and *To Kill a Mockingbird*." *Philosophy and Literature* 25 (April 2001), 127–41.

Deitch, Joseph. "Harper Lee: Novelist of South." *Christian Science Monitor*, 3 October 1961, 6.

Erisman, Fred. "The Romantic Regionalism of Harper Lee." *Alabama Review* 26 (1973), 122–36.

"Exchange Students Sail: But Only 105 Leave on *Marine Jumper* Under U.S. Plan." *New York Times*, 7 June 1947, 29.

Faulkner, Jimmy. "How the Monroe Journal Was Purchased from Gregory Peck . . . Sort Of." Jimmy Faulkner's "Mumblings." 26 June 2003. www.siteone.com/columns/faulkner.

Feeney, F. X. "A Tale of Three Parties: Recalling Truman Capote." *Truman Capote: In Which Various Friends, Enemies, Acquaintances and Detractors Recall His Turbulent Career* by George Plimpton. *LA Weekly*, 13–20 February 1998.

"1st Novel Wins Pulitzer Prize." *Washington Post,* 12 May 1961, A3.

Gilbert, Jim. "Cold, Cold Mockingbird." *Mobile Register*, 13 May 2001.

———. "Cold, Cold Mockingbird: Postscript." www.weirdplots.com. March 2002.

Going, William T. "Truman Capote: Harper Lee's Fictional Portrait of the Artist As an Alabama Child." *Alabama Review* 42.2 (April 1989), 136–49.

Greenhaw, Wayne. "Capote Country," in *Alabama on My Mind*. Montgomery, AL: Sycamore Press, 1987.

———. "Learning to Swim," in *The Remembered Gate: Memoirs By Alabama Writers*, ed. Jay Lamar, and Jeanie Thompson. Tuscaloosa: University of Alabama Press, 2002.

———. "Teacher and Friend," in *Alabama on My Mind*. Montgomery, AL: Sycamore Press, 1987.

Grelen, Jay C. "Freaking Out the Talented Harper Lee." *Sun News* (Myrtle Beach, SC), 31 December 2002, C1.

H., E. L., Jr. "The Obvious Is All Around Us." *Birmingham News*, 22 April 1962.

Hamner, John T. "This Mockingbird Is a Happy Singer." *Montgomery Advertiser*, 7 October 1960.

"Harper Lee Gets Scroll, Tells of Book." *Birmingham News*, 12 November 1961.

"Harper Lee Twits School Board in Virginia for Ban on Her Novel." *New York Times*, 16 January 1966, 82.

"Harper Lee, Read but Not Heard." *Washington Post*, 17 August 1990.

"Harper Lee's First Novel Sets the Whole Book World on Fire!" (advertisement). *New York Times*, 17 July 1960, 228.

Hechinger, Fred M. "Censorship Found on the Increase." *New York Times*, 16 September 1986, C7.

Hendrix, Vernon. "Author's Father Proud of 'Mockingbird' Fame." *Montgomery Advertiser*, 7 August 1960.

———. "Firm Gives Books to Monroe County." *Montgomery Advertiser*, 23 December 1962.

———. "Harper Lee Cries for Joy at Peck's Winning of Oscar." *Montgomery Advertiser*, 10 April 1963.

Hodges, Sam. "To Love a Mockingbird." *Mobile Register*, 8 September 2002.

Hoff, Timothy. "Influences on Harper Lee: An Introduction to the Symposium." *Alabama Law Review* 45 (Winter 1994), 389.

Hoffman, Roy. "Long Lives the Mockingbird." *New York Times Book Review*, 9 August 1998, 31.

Hohoff, Tay. "We Get a New Author." *Literary Guild Book Club Magazine*, August 1960, 3–4.

"Honors Are Given 13 Women by Mount Holyoke College," *New York Times*, 11 November 1962, 53.

"John Megna, 42, 'Mockingbird' Star." *New York Times*, 7 September 1995, B17.

Johnson, Claudia Durst. "The Secret Courts of Men's Hearts: Code and Law in Harper Lee's *To Kill a Mockingbird*." *Studies in American Fiction* 19 (Autumn 1991), 129–39.

Johnson, Hubert A. *To Kill a Mockingbird* uncorrected proof, Spring 1960, Special Collections, University of Virginia.

Jones, George Thomas. "Courthouse Lawn Was Once Kids' Playground," in *Happenings in Old Monroeville*. Volume 2. Monroeville, AL: Bolton Newspapers, 2003.

———. "Queen of the Tomboys." *Monroe Journal*, 6 May 1999.

———. "Stand Up, Monroeville, Gregory Peck Is Passin'," in *Happenings in Old Monroeville*. Volume 2. Monroeville, AL: Bolton Newspapers, 2003.

———. "Young Harper Lee's Affinity for Fighting." EducETH.ch (The English Page). 7 December 1999. www.educeth.ch/english/readinglist/leeh/remin. html#fight.

Jubera, Drew. "'Mockingbird' Still Sings Despite Silence of Author Harper Lee." *Atlanta Journal-Constitution*, 26 August 1990, M1, M3.

———. "To Find a Mockingbird." *Dallas Times Herald*, n.d. (1984).

Keith, Don Lee. "An Afternoon with Harper Lee." *Delta Review* (Spring 1966), 40–41, 75, 81–82.

Kemp, Kathy. "Mockingbird Won't Sing." *News & Observer*, 12 November 1997, E1.

Krebs, Albin. "Truman Capote Is Dead at 59; Novelist of Style and Clarity." *New York Times*, 28 August 1984.

Lapsley, James N. "Cultural Alienation: *In Cold Blood*." *Theology Today*, July 1966, 210–15.

Lawrence, Wes. "Author's Problem: Friends." *Cleveland Plain Dealer*, 17 March 1964.

Lazenby, Permilia S. "First United Methodist Church, Monroeville, Alabama: History" (church booklet). n.p., 1979.

Lee, Gus. *Honor and Duty*. Reprint, New York: Ivy Books, 1994.

Lee, Harper. "Springtime." *Monroe Journal*, 1 April 1937, 3.

———. "Nightmare." *Prelude*, Spring 1945, 11.

———. "A Wink at Justice." *Prelude*, Spring 1945, 14–15.

———. "Some Writers of Our Times." *Rammer Jammer*, November 1945, 14.

———. "What Price Registration?" *Crimson White*, 13 June 1946, 2.

———. "Caustic Comment" (column). *Crimson White*, 28 June 1946, 2 August 1946, 16 August 1946.

———. "Now Is the Time for All Good Men" (one-act play). *Rammer Jammer*, October 1946, 7, 17–18.

———. "Alabama Authors Write of Slaves, Women, GIs." *Crimson White*, 1 October 1946, 2.

———. *To Kill a Mockingbird*. 1960. Reprint, New York: Warner Books, 1982.

———. "Christmas Means to Me." *McCall's*, December 1961, 63.

———. Foreword to the 35th anniversary edition of *To Kill a Mockingbird*. New York: HarperCollins, 1995.

Lee, Melissa. "Brother, Friends Object to Portrayal of Bonnie Clutter by Capote." *Lawrence Journal-World*, 4 April 2005. www.ljworld.com.

Lee, Wayne. "Emotions Mixed Among Clutter Participants." *Hutchinson News*, 31 October 1965.

"Lett Negro Saved from Electric Chair." *Monroe Journal*, 12 July 1934, 1.

Letter to the editor. "Caustic Comment." *Crimson White*, 2 August 1946, 2.

Letter to the editor. "Spreading Poison." *Atlanta Journal*, 7 February 1961.

"Literary-est Part of US Is South." *Crimson White*, 29 March 1947, 5.

"'Little Nelle' Heads Ram, Maps Lee's Strategy." *Crimson White*, 8 October 1946, 1.

Lubet, Steven. "Reconstructing Atticus Finch." *Michigan Law Review* 97.6 (1999), 1339–62.

"'Luckiest Person in the World,' Says Pulitzer Winner." *Birmingham News*, 2 May 1961.

Lyell, Frank H. "One Taxi-Town." *New York Times*, 10 July 1960, BR5.

Lyons, Leonard. "Gossip from Gotham" (column). *Washington Post*, 14 February 1945, 14.

"Mad Dog Warning Issued for State." *Monroe Journal*, 28 June 1934, 2.

Maples, Ann. "Novels Look Bright Under the Tree." *Washington Post*, 27 November 1960, C16.

"Marine Tiger to Make Quick Turnaround and Substitute for Marine Jumper." *New York Times*, 9 Sepember 1948, 55.

Martin, Judith. "To Lady Bird Johnson Alabama Is New Kin." *Washington Post*, 10 December 1962, B4.

McCoy, Kathy. "*To Kill a Mockingbird*: The Great American Novel." *Legacy*, Monroe County Heritage Museums, 1994, 22–25.

McDonald, Thomas. "Bird in Hand." *New York Times*, 6 May 1962, 149.

McGee, Scott, Kerryn Sherrod, and Jeff Stafford. "To Kill a Mockingbird: The Essentials." Turner Classic Movies. www.turnerclassicmovies.com.

McLendon, Winzola. "Nobody Mocks 'Mockingbird' Author: Sales Are Proof of Pudding." *Washington Post*, 17 November 1960, B12.

McMillan, James B. Review of *To Kill a Mockingbird* by Harper Lee. *Alabama Review*, July 1961, 233.

Mills, Marja. "A Life Apart: Harper Lee, The Complex Woman Behind 'A Delicious Mystery.'" *Chicago Tribune*, 13 September 2002.

" 'A Ministry to Man: The Life of John Lovejoy Elliot,' a Biography by Tay Ho-hoff." *New York Times*, 7 January 1959, 30.

"Miss Nelle Lee Chosen to Attend Oxford." *Monroe Journal*, 29 April 1948, 1.

Mitgang, Herbert. "Books of the Times" (column). *New York Times*, 13 July 1960, 33.

"Mocking Bird Call." *Newsweek*, 9 January 1961.

"Mockingbird Film May Begin in Fall." *Birmingham News*, 2 May 1961.

Mohan, Gary. " 'Suburban Pioneers' in 'Long Island: Our Story.' " New York News-day.com. 2005.

Monroe Journal (Centennial Edition). 22 December 1966.

Morgan, Robert W., Jr. "Letter from France: Notes on Tourists, Students, Francs, and Politics." *Harvard Crimson*, 28 September 1948.

"Mr. Bumble and the Mockingbird." Editorial. *Richmond News-Leader*, 5 January 1966, 12.

Nations, Mack. "America's Worst Crime in Twenty Years." *Male,* December 1961.

"Negro Accidentally Killed Last Friday." *Monroe Journal*, 16 February 1933, 1.

"Negro Held for Attacking a Woman." *Monroe Journal*, 9 November 1933, 1.

"Nelle Harper Lee," in *Current Biography,* ed. Charles Moritz. New York: H. W. Wilson Co., 1961.

Nichols, Lewis. "In and Out of Books" (column). *New York Times*, 25 December 1960, BR8.

———. "In and Out of Books" (column). *New York Times*, 14 May 1961, BR8.

Nicholson, Colin. "Hollywood and Race: *To Kill a Mockingbird*," in *Cinema and Fiction: New Modes of Adapting, 1950–1990,* ed. John Orr and Colin Nicholson. Edinburgh: Edinburgh University Press, 1992.

Noble, Don. "Bookmark: Interview with Horton Foote." Videocassette. Alabama Center for Public Television. Tuscaloosa, Alabama. August 27, 1998.

"Novelist Lee to Join Arts Unit." *Washington Post*, 28 January 1996, C3.

O'Hagan, Andrew. "Good Fibs." *London Review of Books*, 2 April 1998. www.lrb.co.uk/v20/n07/ohag01_.html.

"One Version of the Harper Lee Story." Harperlee@yahoogroups.com (listserv), 11 October 2005.

Otts, Elizabeth. "Lady Lawyers Prepare Homecoming Costumes." *Crimson White*, 26 November 1946, 14.

Palmer, C. B. "A Farmer Looks at Farming 1954." *New York Times Sunday Magazine*, 1 August 1954.

Park, Mary Jane. "Truman's Aunt Tiny." *St. Petersburg Times,* 3 October 2000. www.sptimes.com/News/100300/Floridian/Truman_s_Aunt_Tiny.shtml.

Pennypacker, Nathaniel. "Massacre of the Clutter Family." *Front Page Detective*, April 1960.

Plimpton, George. "The Story Behind a Nonfiction Novel." *New York Times*, 16 January 1966. www.nytimes.com/books/97/12/28/home/capote-interview.

Prescott, Orville. "The Best of the Year: A Critic's Choice." *New York Times*, 4 December 1960, BR3.

———. "Books of the Times" (column). *New York Times*, 15 August 1960, 21.

"A Prize Novel Is Removed from School Reading List." *New York Times*, 4 December 1977, 26.

"Prize Winner Remembered as Deflater of Phoniness." *Montgomery Advertiser*, 4 May 1961.

Rhodes, Matthew W. "Truman Capote." *Legacy*, Monroe County Heritage Museums, 1994, 26–31.

Robertson, Nan. "Johnsons Hail the Creative Life with a Dinner at White House," *New York Times*, 14 December 1966, 55.

Rocha, Guy Louis. "Truman Capote's *In Cold Blood*: The Nevada Connection." Nevada State Library and Archives, Department of Cultural Affairs. dmla. clan.lib.nv.us/docs/nsla/archives/spec-feat.htm.

Romine, Dannye. "Truman's Aunt: A Bio in Cold Blood. *Chicago Tribune*, 5 June 1983, sec. 5, 1–2.

Rowley, Hazel. "Mockingbird Country." *Australian's Review of Books*, April 1999.

"Scene of the Crime: Twenty-Five Years Later, Holcomb, Kansas Remembers 'In Cold Blood.'" *Chicago Sunday Tribune*, 11 November 1984.

"School Reading Lists Shun Women and Black Authors." *New York Times*, 21 June 1989, B6.

Schultz, William Todd. "Why Did Truman Capote Write *Answered Prayers*?" Unpublished ms., Pacific University, 2004.

Schumach, Murray. "Film Crew Saves $75,000 on Shacks." *New York Times*, 19 January 1962, 26.

———. "Prize for Novel Elates Film Pair." *New York Times*, 19 May 1961.

Schwabenton, Karen. "Harper Lee Discusses the Writer's Attitude and Craft." *Sweet Briar News*, 28 October 1966, 3.

"Senate Lauds Pulitzer Winner." *Montgomery Advertiser*, 20 May 1961.

"Severe Snowstorm Hits East, Stalls Traffic, Shuts Schools; Many Firms Close Early." *Wall Street Journal*, 4 March 1960.

Shackelford, Dean. "The Female Voice in *To Kill a Mockingbird*: Narrative Strategies in Film and the Novel," in *To Kill a Mockingbird: Modern Critical Interpretations,* ed. Harold Bloom. Philadelphia: Chelsea House, 1999.

Smith, Joel P. "'Mockingbird Author Looking for Characters?'" *Eufaula Tribune*, 8 September 1960.

Smith, Patrick. "An Outspoken Critic." *Lawrence Journal-World*, 5 April 2005, www.ljworld.com.

Spike (columnist). "Scaring Harper Lee, No Time to Die, The Leaf Player Revisited." *Online Journalism Review*, 8 January 2003. Annenberg School for Communication, University of Southern California.

"State Pulitzer Prize Winner Too Busy to Write." *Dothan Eagle*, 2 May 1961.

Steinem, Gloria. "'Go Right Ahead and Ask Me Anything.' (And So She Did): An Interview with Truman Capote." *McCall's,* November 1967, 76–77, 148–52, 154.

Steiner, George. "A Cold-Blooded Happening." *Guardian*, 2 December 1965.

"Story of Attempted Drowning Called False, Angers Harper Lee." *Tuscaloosa News*, 25 September 1997.

"Strange Gods (Like TV) Buried in Church Rite." *Washington Post*, 13 July 1962, A3.

"Tay Hohoff, Author, Lippincott Officer." *New York Times*, 12 January 1974, 36.

"Ten Liners Arrive or Depart Today: Seven Vessels, Bringing 4,596 Passengers, Due from Europe and the Near East." *New York Times*, 30 June 1947, 37.

"They All Had a Ball at Capote's Party." *Washington Post*, 30 November 1966, D2.

"$300,000 Is Paid for 'Moon Is Down': Record Price Given by Fox for Screen Rights to the Drama by John Steinbeck." *New York Times*, 29 April 1942, 27.

"Traffic Ticket Report." *Saturday Review*, 6 August 1960.

Vancheri Barbara. "Author Lauded 'Mockingbird' As a 'Moving' Film." *Pittsburgh Post-Gazette*, 20 February 2003.

"We Bequeath Our Anti-Klanism," Editorial. *Crimson White*, 16 August 1946, 2.

"Wealthy Farmer, 3 of Family Slain." *New York Times*, 16 November 1959, 7.

Webb, Theresa Ellen. "The Aesthetics of Justice in Contemporary American Film." Unpublished diss., University of California–Los Angeles, 2002.

Weiler, A. H. "New Midtown Showcase—Other Film Matters." *New York Times*, 29 January 1961, X7.

Weiss, M. Jerry. *Photoplay Guide: "To Kill a Mockingbird."* NCTE Studies in the Mass Media. Champaign, IL: National Council of Teachers of English, March 1963.

White, Jean M. "The Council on the Arts: Beginning a Second Decade." *Washington Post*, 4 September 1974, B1.

Whitley, Carla Jean. "Small-Town Q&A: Amanda McMillan." *Crimson White*, 9 October 2003.

Wiebe, Crystal K. "Author Left Mark on State." *Lawrence Journal-World,* 3 April 2005. www.ljworld.com.

———. " 'To Kill a Mockingbird' Author Helped Truman Capote Break the Ice in Kansas." *Lawrence Journal-World,* 3 April 2005. www.ljworld.com.

Wolcott, James. "Tru Grit." *Vanity Fair*, October 2005.

Woodard, Calvin. "Listening to the Mockingbird." *Alabama Law Review* 45 (Winter 1994), 563–85.

Yoder, J. Wes. "Debating the Details: Some Residents of Monroeville Prefer to Ponder the Fine Points of Famous Novel." *Expressions* (online magazine), Auburn University Journalism Department, 2001.

York, Max. "Throngs Greet Monroe Writer." *Montgomery Advertiser*, 13 September 1960.

Young, Amelia. "Her Writing Place Is Secret: 'Mockingbird' Author Working on Second Book." *Minneapolis Star*, 26 May 1963.

Young, Thomas Daniel. Introduction to Part III in *A History of Southern Literature*, ed. Louis D. Rubin, Jr., et al. Baton Rouge: Louisiana State University Press, 1985.

Zoerink, Richard. "Truman Capote Talks About His Crowd." *Playgirl*, September 1975, 50–51, 54, 80–81, 128.

MEDIA

Dewey, Alvin A. as told to Dolores Hope. "The Clutter Case: 25 Years Later KBI Agent Recounts Holcomb Tragedy." Compact disc. *Garden City Telegram*, 10 November 1984.

Noble, Don. "Bookmark: Interview with Horton Foote." Videocassette. Alabama Center for Public Television, Tuscaloosa, AL, August 27, 1998.

"To Kill a Mockingbird" (commentary section). Compact disc. Universal City, CA: Universal Home Video, 1998.

" 'To Kill a Mockingbird': Then and Now." Videocassette. Prince William County Public Schools, Manassas, VA, April 25, 1997.

Acknowledgments

DURING THE WRITING OF THIS BOOK, MY WIFE, GUADALUPE, provided research assistance, editorial suggestions, and constant encouragement. In every sense of the word, she has been my helpmate. Outside of my family, whose members have expressed their support many times, my agent, Jeff Kleinman, accepted a book proposal on a topic that had no precedent and parlayed it into a most satisfying professional experience for this writer. And George Hodgman, the "show me" editor from Missouri at Henry Holt and Company, pressed for a better and better manuscript. I'm grateful for his patience and deft improvements to my writing. His editorial assistant, Supurna Banerjee, coordinated back-and-forth communications with ease and good humor; assistant director of publicity Annsley Rosner put her creativity at my disposal; and Chris O'Connell, production editor for the book, was enormously helpful and accommodating in keeping it on schedule.

A number of institutions made their archives available to me, and those angels in the reference department, as I once heard them called, located facts, photographs, and printed materials that were like hidden treasure to me. For this I thank the Alderman Library at the University of Virginia; Mount Holyoke College Archives and Special Collections; the New York Public Library, Manuscripts and Archives Division; the Hoole Library and Bounds Law Library at the University of Alabama; the Huntingdon College Archives and Information Center; the Columbia University Rare Book and Manuscript Library; the National Archives and Records Service, College Park, Maryland; the University of Montevallo Carmichael Library; the Rare Book, Manuscript, and Special Collections Library at Duke University; the University of South Alabama Archives; the Library of Congress Manuscript Reading Room; the Harry Ransom Humanities Research Center at the University of Texas at Austin; the Oxford University Archives, Bodleian Library; the Special Collections and Archives, Ralph Brown Draughon Library, Auburn University; the Alabama Department of History and Archives; the University of Iowa Special Collections; the University of North Carolina at Chapel Hill, Special Collections, Randall Library; the Wisconsin Historical Society; the Fales Library and Special Collections at New York University; the Evergreen Public Library, Lucy C. Warren Heritage Section, Evergreen, Alabama; the Finney County Public Library, Garden City, Kansas; and the Johnston County Genealogical and Historical Society, Smithfield, South Carolina.

My thanks also go to George Thomas Jones, town historian of Monroeville, Alabama. Mr. Jones, an old-fashioned southern gentleman, welcomed a stranger into sharing the lore of the town and the county he loves so well.

Any shortcomings or mistakes in this book are entirely my own, especially in light of the help I've received from a host of generous people, too many to be named here.

Index

Academy Awards, 221, 229–31
Adams, Phoebe, 128
Alabama, 12, 13, 16, 17–18, 22, 24,
    31–59, 90, 103, 117, 155, 205
    Freedom Ride, 197–98, 234
    Lee's roots and themes in, 21, 35,
        44–54, 116–18, 120–21, 126–28,
        185, 241, 244, 271–73
    Montgomery bus boycott, 197
    racism, 117–26, 196–98, 201, 233
    Scottsboro Boys trials, 117–18
    Till murder, 125
    To Kill a Mockingbird film
        premiere, 228–29
Alabama Council on Human Relations,
    124
Alabama Girls' Industrial School, 37,
    39
Alabama Journal, 186–87, 188
Alabama Literary Association, 199
Alford, Philip, 211–12, 214, 217,
    229
Algonquin Hotel, New York, 186
Allen, Fred, 16
Alley, J. P., 52
American Actors Theater, 205
American Friends Service Committee,
    105
Anderson, James, 211, 214
Anderson, Sherwood, 21
Anthony, Emily H., 79
Arlen, Harold, 22
Army Air Corps, 73–74, 100, 110
Ashida, Mrs. Hideo, 140–41, 149
Associated Press, 160, 178
Atherton, Mary Nell, 78, 79
Atlanta Journal-Constitution, 196
Atlantic, 128
Atticus Productions, 204, 232

Austen, Jane, 64, 105, 249
    Pride and Prejudice, 64
Avedon, Richard, 176

Badham, Mary, 212, 214, 217, 229
Baggett, Robert, 54
Baldwin Times, 101
Barnes, Pamela, 29
Barnett, J. B., 60, 102
Barnett, Ross, 220
BBC, 276
Beaton, Cecil, 175, 246
Beechcroft, John, 12–13
Behan, Brendan, 186
Bernstein, Elmer, 226
Berryman, Mary Anne, 84, 86
Bible, 67, 121, 123, 193
Biggs, Otha Lee, 275, 276
Bilbo, Theodore G., 91
Birmingham, 229
Birmingham News, 57
Birmingham School of Law, 68
Birmingham World, 57
Black and White Ball, 250, 251, 258–59
blacks, 41, 52
    civil rights, 125–26, 183, 196–98,
        219–20, 223, 229, 233–34
    Lee on racial injustice and, 79–81,
        90, 117–18, 120, 184, 196–97,
        206, 219, 222–23, 226, 229, 234,
        257
    Lett rape case, 118–20
    lynching, 118
    Scottsboro Boys trial, 117–18
    segregation, 90–91, 121, 126, 196
    slaves, 37, 90
    Till murder, 125
Blass, A. B., Jr., 62, 81–82, 125, 207
Blass, Joseph, 55–56, 228–29

Bodleian Library, 108
Boleware, Alfred R., 53–54
Boleware, Son, 53, 54, 189
Bonner, J. M., 125
Book-of-the-Month Club, 200
Bowen, Elizabeth, 108
Boyle, Hal, 228
Brentwood Productions, 204
Brewton Standard, 187
British Book Society, 200
British Overseas Air Corporation
    (BOAC), 20, 24, 26
Brodsky, Joseph, 117
Brown, Bill, 142, 167, 168, 174, 176
Brown, Joy, 23–24, 25–26, 114, 131,
    241, 242, 262
Brown, Martha, 78
Brown, Michael Martin, 23–24, 25–26,
    112, 113, 114, 116, 131, 241, 242,
    262
Bugg, Barnett & Lee, 38, 68, 70, 101,
    125, 236
Burns, Robert, 268–69
Butts, Thomas Lane, 126, 274, 277, 284

Calpurnia's Cookbook, 274–75
Capote, Joseph, 55
Capote, Truman, 14, 16–17, 96, 104–5,
    224, 237
    Alabama road trip with Lee, 259–60
    Answered Prayers, 266
    birth of, 43
    Black and White Ball, 250, 251,
        258–59
    childhood of, 16–17, 20, 31–35, 39,
        42–55, 57, 64, 113, 170, 196, 265
    "A Christmas Memory," 52
    Clutter killer interviews, 171–72
    Clutter murder research, 132–33,
        136–79, 237–40
    death of, 266
    decline into drugs and alcohol, 262,
        265–66, 270
    early writing, 40, 50–52
    at execution of Hickock and Perry,
        244–46

    fame sought by, 153, 186, 239–40,
        250, 266
    "The Fire and the Flame," 51
    The Grass Harp, 53
    homosexuality of, 44, 96
    In Cold Blood research and writing,
        136–79, 209–10, 237–40
    as inspiration for Lee's characters,
        34, 97, 127, 128, 180
    jealousy of Lee's success, 183,
        186, 200–201, 209–10, 218, 231,
        254
    Kansas expenses, 140–41
    Lee as assistant on *In Cold Blood,*
        136–79, 209–10, 237–40, 248,
        249, 253–54
    Lee as childhood friend of, 16–17,
        20–21, 31–35, 40, 44–55, 127,
        200, 270–71
    Lee as inspiration for characters of,
        59
    Lee in New York and, 19, 22–23,
        113
    Lee underappreciated for *In Cold
        Blood* work, 152–53, 239–40,
        253–54, 259
    "The Muses Are Heard," 133
    odd behavior of, 141, 154, 157
    "Old Mrs. Busybody," 40, 110
    Other Voices, Other Rooms, 16–17,
        59, 96, 109
    relationship with his mother, 35,
        42–44, 55
    "The Thanksgiving Visitor," 32
    To Kill a Mockingbird involvement,
        130–31, 254, 283
    train trip to Kansas with Lee,
        133–34, 154
Carroll, Margaret, 115
Carter, Jennings Faulk, 20–21, 46, 52,
    57, 61, 200
Carter, Mary Ida, 47, 48, 129
Cary, Joyce, 108
Cerf, Bennett, 133, 138, 238, 239
Chalfin, Richard, 280
Chappell, Gordon T., 81

Chasin, George, 218

Chaucer, Geoffrey, *The Canterbury Tales,* 64

Chicago, 134, 175, 221

Chicago Tribune, 182, 193, 274

Childress, Mark, 279–80

Christian Science Monitor, 186

Church, Roy, 160, 162, 165

civil rights, 125–26, 183, 196–98
   movement, 197, 219–10, 223, 229, 233–34

Civil War, 35, 36, 38

Clare, Myrtle T., 141

Clarke, Gerald, *Capote: A Biography,* 270–71

Clausell, Hattie Belle, 41

Clutter, Beverly, 147, 150, 151, 152, 176

Clutter, Bonnie, 139, 142, 146–47, 149, 151–52, 157, 161, 166

Clutter, Eveanna, 146, 147, 150, 151, 152, 176

Clutter, Herb, 139, 140, 142, 144–52, 153, 161, 166, 170, 176

Clutter, Kenyon, 139, 142, 147, 149, 150, 151, 161, 166

Clutter, Nancy, 139, 141–42, 147–48, 149, 150–52, 161–62, 164, 166, 170, 173

Clutter murders, 132–33, 136–79, 209–10, 237–40, 245, 250
   arraignment, 168–70
   arrests, 158–69
   Capote and Lee's investigation of, 136–79, 237–40
   confessions, 164, 166, 171
   crime scene, 145–50, 157
   execution of Hickock and Smith, 244–46
   final report, 245–46
   KBI investigation, 137–79
   killers interviewed by Capote and Lee, 171–72
   news media on, 141, 142, 160, 161, 165–74, 176–78
   trial, 165, 174, 175, 176–79
   weapons, 165–66

Collins, Donald, *When the Church Bells Rang Racist,* 124, 234

Columbia Journalism Review, 278

Columbia University, 71, 97

Communism, 117

Connor, Bull, 197, 229

Connor, Hank, 110

Connor, Herschel, 110, 269

Connor, Louise Lee, 13, 24, 34, 38, 41, 60, 66, 67, 110, 111, 190, 193, 233, 235, 269

Cooper, Gary, 191

Counterpoint (radio show), 240–41

Crain, Maurice, 12, 13, 26–30, 113–14, 132, 180–81, 186, 188, 189, 198, 199, 202, 213, 216, 232, 235, 242, 246–47
   "chaste affair" with Lee, 261
   illness and death of, 247, 259–62

Crimson White, 84, 88, 91, 92, 93, 94, 97, 99, 187

Cross, Ruth, 216

Crowther, Bosley, 227

Davis, Jane Benton, 85, 86

Day, Clarence, *Life with Father,* 27–28

Deal, Borden, 199

Dees, Maggie, 40

Dehn, Leone, 188–89

Deitch, Joseph, 186

Delaney, Caldwell, 270

Delbanco, Nicholas, 131

Delta Review, 247

Denton, Crahan, 210

Depression, 17, 33, 41, 44–46, 60, 126

Dewey, Alvin, 137–38, 155–60, 161–68, 170–75, 245–46, 250, 259
   friendship with Capote and Lee, 155–68, 174

Dewey, Marie, 155–60, 161, 164–65, 167, 237, 259

D'Harnoncourt, René, 260

Dobbs, Carney, 101

Drury, Allen, *Advise and Consent,* 188

Duntz, Clarence, 159, 160, 162, 165, 172–73
Duvall, Robert, 210–11

Eddins, E. O., 201
Edwards, Blake, 230
Eliot, T. S., 108
Engle, Paul, 249, 260
Esquire, 88, 216–17, 266
Evans, Estelle, 210
Ewalt, Clarence, 142
Ewalt, Nancy, 142

Faircloth, Taylor, 32, 228, 229
Fair Employment Practices Committee (FEPC), 122
Fallowfield, Julie, 272
Faulk, Jennie, 43, 51–53
Faulk, Lillie Mae, 34, 35, 42–44, 55
Faulk, Sook, 51, 52
Faulkner, Jimmy, 101–2
Faulkner, William, 76
Fenton, Robert M., 157
Fielding, Henry, 105
Finch, Alice, 37
Finch, Ellen, 36–37
Finch, James Cunningham, 36–37
Finney County Courthouse, 137, 169, 176–78
Fire Island, 241, 242, 250
Fix, Paul, 210
Fleming, Arthur, 177, 178
Foote, Horton, 205, 211, 218, 265
    To Kill a Mockingbird screenplay, 205–6, 231, 261
Foote, Jeanne, 75
France, 106, 107
Frankfurt, Stephen, 226
Freedom Ride, 197–98, 234
Freret, Jane, 91
Fugate, Caril, 140
Future Farmers of America, 105

Garden City Telegram, 142, 167, 174, 176
Gardner, Tom, 187

Georgia, 205
Germany, 106
Gettell, Richard Glenn, 220
Ghostley, Alice, 210
Gilbert, Jim, 283
Gilbert and Sullivan, 85
Gill, Brendan, 227
Gipson, Fred, 198–99, 261
    Old Yeller, 14, 198
Glock, William, 108
Golitzen, Alexander, 212
Graham, Kay, 258–59
Great Britain, 242
    Lee in, 105–8
Green, Logan, 177, 178
Greenhaw, Wayne, 97, 98, 130, 184, 253, 259, 263
    The Golfer, 130
Grelen, Jay C., 277–78
Griffiths, Peter, 263

Haldane, J. B. S., 108
Hale, Richard, 210
Hall, Radclyffe, *The Well of Loneliness*, 96
Hambone's Meditations, 52
Hammond, Mother, 74
Hammond, Ralph, 265
Hamner, John T., 89, 92, 99, 187, 188
Hanes, R. Philip, 253, 255–56
Hanover County School Board, *To Kill a Mockingbird* banned by, 254–55
Hare, Francis W., 69–70, 119
Harrison, Leigh, 104
Harvey, Paul, 271
Hayes, Harold, 217
Heflin, Howell T., 103
Helms, Catherine, 76, 77, 78, 82
Hersey, John
    A Bell for Adano, 28
    The Child Buyer, 188
    A Single Pebble, 14
Hickock, Richard, 158–75, 237–38
    confession, 164

execution of, 244–46
interviewed by Capote and Lee,
    171–72, 210
trial, 174, 175, 176–79
Hicks, Granville, 128
Hines, Anne, 61–62, 100
Hohoff, Tay, 14, 115–16, 184–85, 202,
    246, 262–63
    death of, 263
    as Lee's editor, 116, 129–32, 252,
        262–63
    A Ministry to Man, 115
Hood, James, 233
Hoole, W. S., 202
Hope, Clifford, 143, 144, 145, 148, 149,
    154–57, 238
    *Garden City: Dreams in a Kansas
        Town,* 156
Hopkins, Gerard Manley, 108
Hudson, Rock, 195, 204, 225
Huntingdon College, 62, 70, 73, 100,
    273
    Lee at, 70–72, 74–82, 191
Huntress, The, 77, 79
Hutchinson News, 142, 158, 174

In Cold Blood (Capote), 167, 170, 200,
    266, 267
    Capote and Lee as coworkers on,
        136–79, 209–10, 237–40, 248,
        249, 253–54
    dedicated to Lee, 253
    final phases of, 153, 237–40, 248,
        249, 250
    hunting scenario, 153
    Lee's contributions
        underappreciated by Capote,
            152–53, 239–40, 253–54, 259
    New Yorker serialization of, 250–51,
        253
    outline, 180
    power of, 163–64
    research and writing, 136–79,
        209–10, 237–40
Iowa Writers' Workshop, 249, 260
Italy, 106

Jacobs, Mildred, 83, 88
jazz, 21–22, 43
Jewell, Tony, 161
Johnson, Claudia Durst, 253
Johnson, Lyndon B., 224, 255
Jones, George Thomas, 32, 276
Jones, Jennifer, 180
Jones, Powell, 35
Jones, Mrs. Powell, 35
Jones, R. L., 101

Kansas, 133–35
    Clutter murders, 132–33, 136–79,
        209–10, 237–40, 245, 250
Kansas City Star, 142
Kansas State University, 134, 138, 142
Katz, Mrs. Clarence, 149
Katz, Miriam, 207, 209
Keith, Don, 247–48
Kell, Richard, 110
Kemp, Kathy, 278
Kennedy, Jacqueline, 181, 225
Kennedy, John F., 181, 220
Kennedy, Robert, 229
Kidwell, Susan, 142, 162, 163
Kimbrough, Edward, *Night Fire,* 90,
    97
King, Martin Luther, Jr., 124, 197, 223,
    233–34
Kirk, Claude, 103
Kiwanis Club, 69, 125
Knopf, Alfred A., 248
Knowles, John, *A Separate Peace,* 188
Ku Klux Klan, 48, 52, 57–58, 91, 125

Lamb, Charles, 105
Landon, Olive, 104
Lauria, Vincent, 90–91
Lee, A. C., 13, 16, 17, 18, 24, 35–38,
    55–59, 146, 192, 207, 225, 236
    Atticus character based on, 44–45,
        120–21, 185, 215, 229
    childhood of, 35–36
    death of, 185, 214–16
    deaths of his wife and son, 110
    gives Nelle a typewriter, 50–51

law career, 38, 50, 57, 60, 68, 80,
    120–26, 185
marriage of, 37–38, 41
morals of, 36, 44–45, 57–59, 60, 67,
    120–26, 215
newspaper career, 57–58, 64, 65, 66,
    75, 101–2
Peck and, 207–8
political career, 65–67, 75
on race relations, 57–58, 91, 120–26
relationship with daughter Nelle,
    16, 17, 19, 22, 33, 44–45, 50,
    58–59, 66, 100–101, 104, 109,
    185, 214–15
religious views of, 58–59, 67,
    121–24, 126, 215
Lee, A. Cowan, 110
Lee, Alice Finch, 13, 24, 33, 34, 41, 49,
    65–70, 75, 110, 192, 207, 271,
    276, 282, 285
as helpmate to her father, 65–70,
    111, 129
law career, 68–70, 101, 119, 236,
    284
as manager for Nelle, 192–93, 195,
    196, 232, 233, 235, 237, 242, 263,
    277
newspaper career, 65, 66
on race relations, 126
relationship with sister Nelle, 65, 70,
    111, 129, 192–93, 232–33,
    235–36, 283–84
Lee Cader Alexander, 36
Lee, Edwin, 13, 23, 34, 39, 41, 60, 66,
    67, 73, 127, 207, 236
death of, 13, 110–11, 122
marriage of, 99–100, 102
military career, 73, 100, 110
Lee, Edwin, Jr., 110
Lee, Frances Finch, 13, 16, 35, 36–38,
    207
childhood of, 37–38
death of, 109–10, 185
emotional and health problems, 16,
    39–42, 59, 66, 100, 102, 109, 270
marriage of, 36, 41

relationship with daughter Nelle,
    16, 39–42, 44, 59, 70, 109–11,
    270–71
Lee, John, 36
Lee, Mary, 110
Lee, Nelle Harper
adolescence, 60–65, 67, 70
agents of, 12, 26–30, 113–14, 132,
    180–81, 186, 189, 191–95, 199,
    202, 232, 242, 259–62
Alabama roots and themes of, 21,
    35, 44–54, 116–18, 120–21,
    126–28, 185, 231, 244, 271–73
ancestry, 35–39
athleticism, 77, 78
birth of, 39
BOAC job, 20, 24, 26
Browns' Christmas loan to, 25–26,
    114, 116, 262
as Capote's assistant on *In Cold
    Blood,* 136–79, 209–10, 237–40,
    245, 248, 249, 253–54
Capote as childhood friend of,
    16–17, 20–21, 31–35, 40, 44–55,
    127, 200, 270–71
Capote as inspiration for characters
    of, 34, 97, 127, 128, 180
Capote in New York and, 19, 22–23,
    113
"The Cat's Meow," 114
"Caustic Comment" column, 89–91
celebrity of, 186, 274–80, 285
"chaste affair" with Maurice Crain,
    261
childhood of, 16–18, 31–59, 270
Clutters' killers interviewed by,
    171–72
in college, 16, 17, 62, 70–72, 74–82,
    83–108, 191
Counterpoint interview, 240–41
death of Capote, 266
death of her brother, 110–11
death of her father, 214–16
death of her mother, 109–10
drinking of, 22, 99, 129, 185, 270
early writing, 50–52, 64, 79–81

education of, 16, 17, 31–33, 55, 60, 62–65, 70–72, 74–82, 83–108

film of *Mockingbird* and, 195, 205, 213–14, 221–22, 224, 225–31, 232

finances managed by sister Alice, 192–93, 195, 196, 232, 233, 235, 237, 242, 277

"The Fire and the Flame," 51

first rejection letter, 216–17

first typewriter, 50–51, 55

foul mouth of, 76, 78

hand injury and operations, 243, 249, 251

in high school, 60, 62–65, 70

Hohoff as editor of, 116, 129–32, 252, 262–63

honorary degrees, 220–21, 273

humor and, 89, 97, 112

at Huntingdon College, 70–72, 74–82, 191

as inspiration for Capote's characters, 59

in Kansas with Capote, 136–69, 236–40

"The Land of Sweet Forever," 112

law studies, 70, 75, 81, 92, 93, 99, 100–105, 108–9, 221–22

legacy of, 271–85

literary influences on, 64, 105, 108, 240

The Long Goodbye, 115

"Love—In Other Words," 201, 249

men and, 61, 93, 105, 261

move to New York, 16, 17, 109

National Council on the Arts, 255–57

in New York, 11–15, 18–30, 112–33, 180–82, 202, 236, 264–65, 284

"Nightmare," 80

nonconformism of, 33, 35, 39, 55, 61, 76–77, 84, 237

"Now Is the Time for All Good Men," 94–95

at Old Stone House, 132, 188, 189, 216, 232–33, 235, 237, 242

at Oxford, 105–8

pen name, 129

physical appearance of, 34, 61, 76, 77, 83, 84, 85–87, 103, 137, 188, 243, 278, 281, 284

post–*Mockingbird* writing, 201, 216–17, 218, 224, 236, 248–50, 267–70, 285

pretense disliked by, 45, 61, 78, 99, 190, 237

as Pulitzer Prize winner, 98, 199–201, 209–10

on race relations, 79–81, 90, 117–18, 120, 184, 196–97, 206, 219, 222–23, 226, 229, 234, 257

as *Rammer Jammer* editor and contributor, 91–99

as recluse later in life, 248–49, 264–66, 272–85

relationship with her father, 16, 17, 19, 22, 33, 44–45, 50, 58–59, 66, 100–101, 104, 109, 185, 214–15

relationship with her mother, 16, 39–42, 44, 59, 70, 109–11, 270–71

relationship with sister Alice, 65, 70, 111, 129, 192–93, 232–33, 235–36, 283–84

The Reverend, 267–70

"A Roomful of Kibble," 112

scholarships funded by, 282

second novel difficulties, 216–17, 218, 222, 224, 232, 236–37, 247–63, 271, 285

smoking of, 76, 78, 85, 93

"Snow-on-the-Mountain," 112, 113–14

"Some Writers of Our Times," 95–97

speeches and lectures, 236, 242, 243–44, 257–58

"spitfire" image of, 61–62

"Springtime," 64

success of *To Kill a Mockingbird,* 12–14, 28–29, 181–202, 218–19, 285

tax situation, 237, 241–42

"This Is Show Business," 112

tomboy image of, 41, 61–62, 77, 85, 331–34

train trip to Kansas with Capote, 133–34

at University of Alabama, 81, 83–99, 102–5, 187

"The Viewer and the Viewed," 112

"When Children Discover America," 249

"A Wink at Justice," 80–81

writing habits and methods, 20–21, 26, 128, 237, 240, 258

see also To Kill a Mockingbird (book)

Lee, Sara Anne McCall, 61–62, 75, 82, 100, 102, 110, 236

Lee, Theodocia, 36

lesbianism, 96

Lett, Walter, 118–20

Liebowitz, Samuel, 117

Life magazine, 67

Lippincott (A. B.) publishers, 14, 114–15, 206, 210, 225

early interest in To Kill a Mockingbird, 114–16

To Kill a Mockingbird contract and advance, 116, 129, 131–32

To Kill a Mockingbird publication, 180–83

Literary Guild, 12, 14, 29, 182, 200

Lowery, Naomi, 118–19

Lucy, Autherine, 125

Lyell, Frank, 182

Lyndon, Andrew, 133

Lyon, Kenneth, 143, 144, 145, 148, 149

MacDonald, Betty, The Egg and I, 114

MacIntosh, Mavis, 27

Mademoiselle, 91

Male magazine, 178

Malone, Vivian, 233

Manchester, William, A Rockefeller Family Portrait, 14

Mann, Thomas, 108

March on Washington, 233–34

Marine Jumper, 106

Masters, Edgar Lee, 21

Maxwell, John N., 119

Maxwell, W. M. "Willie Jo," 267–70

Maxwell Airfield, 72, 73, 74, 110

Mayes, Bill, 88, 91

Maygarden, Ernest, 90

McCall's magazine, 23, 249

McClain, James, 138, 142, 143

McCoy, Whit, 103–4

McCullers, Carson, The Member of the Wedding, 192

McGiffert, Betty, 93

McKinley, Alice, 32, 40–41, 235

McMillan, James B., 201

McNeil, Mrs. Leighton, 32–33

Meador, Daniel J., 103

Megna, John, 212, 214

Memphis, 117

Meredith, James, 219–20

Methodist Church, 121–26, 215, 219, 234, 274, 284

Miller, B. M., 119, 120

Miller, Glenn, 74, 89

Mississippi, 90, 91

racism, 219–20

Mitchell, Margaret, Gone With the Wind, 27, 202

Mitgang, Herbert, 182

Moates, Marianne M., A Bridge of Childhood: Truman Capote's Southern Years, 20

Mobile Register, 40, 52, 57, 271, 277, 283

Monroe County Bank, 66, 102, 120, 207

Monroe County Courthouse, 49–50, 119, 120

Monroe County Heritage Museums, 273, 274–75

Monroe County High School, 60, 62–65, 257

Monroe County Library, 225

Monroe Journal, 16, 34, 38, 49, 57, 58, 64, 65, 66, 67, 101–2, 104, 105, 118, 120, 127, 182, 228

Monroeville, Alabama, 13, 16, 17–18, 31–35, 37–59, 60–70, 109, 129,

182, 187, 188–90, 236, 246–47,
        265, 271, 284
    as inspiration for *To Kill a
        Mockingbird,* 44–48, 54, 116–18,
        120–21, 126–28, 185
    Lett rape case, 118–20
    modernization of, 195, 196, 212
    success of *To Kill a Mockingbird*
        and, 182, 185, 188–91, 199, 203–4,
        207–9, 219, 225, 228, 246, 271–80
Monroeville Elementary School, 31–33,
        44, 57
Montgomery Advertiser, 57, 119, 190,
        215
Montgomery bus boycott, 197
Moore, Barbara, 83, 87
Moore, Florence, 82
Mount Holyoke College, 220–21
Mulligan, Robert, 193–96, 198
    as *To Kill a Mockingbird* director,
        206–7, 210–15, 218, 226
Munro, Irene, 75
Murphy, Jay, 103
Murphy, Rosemary, 210

National Association for the
        Advancement of Colored People
        (NAACP), 197, 223
National Council on the Arts, 255–57,
        260
Nations, Mack, 178
New Orleans, 43, 155
Newquist, Roy, 240–41
Newsweek, 170, 186, 189, 200, 227
New York City, 11–17, 106
    Lee in, 11–15, 18–30, 112–33,
        180–82, 202, 236, 264–65, 284
    Lee moves to, 16, 17, 109
    1950s arts scene, 21–24
    To Kill a Mockingbird film
        premiere, 225–26
New York Daily News, 28
New Yorker, 133, 227
    Capote's Clutter murders article for,
        133, 138, 142, 175, 176, 250–51,
        253

New York Public Library, 19
New York Sun, 96
New York Times, 29, 132, 139, 150, 182,
        206, 227
    "The Story Behind a Nonfiction
        Novel" interview, 154
    To Kill a Mockingbird on bestseller
        list, 182, 193
New York World Telegram, 182
Norris, Helen, 98
Nunn, Grady H., 130, 131
Nunnelly, Claude, 61, 130
Nye, Harold, 141, 143, 150, 157, 159,
        160, 165, 173, 174, 238, 240,
        250–51

Old Stone House, West Hartland,
        Connecticut, 132, 188, 189, 216,
        232–33, 235, 237, 242, 259, 262
Otis, Elizabeth, 27
Overton, Frank, 210
Oxford University, 105–8

Pakula, Alan, 193–96, 198, 225
    as *To Kill a Mockingbird* producer,
        204–7, 210–15, 218
Panell, Anne Gary, 257
Paramount Pictures, 194
Parks, Rosa, 197
Parnell, Sylvia, 87
Passani, Veronique, 207, 209
Paton, Alan, 216
Patterson, John, 103, 197–98
Patton, George, 100
Paxton, Collin Wilcox, 210
Payne, "Jumping Jack," 103
Pebbles, Darryl, 257, 284
Peck, Gregory, 191, 203–4, 225, 269
    as Atticus Finch in *To Kill a
        Mockingbird,* 203–7, 213–14,
        217–18, 222, 226, 229, 231
    Lee and, 255–57
Persons, Archulus Julius, 42–44, 55, 61
Peters, Brock, 211, 214
Philipp, Sue, 63, 128–29
Phillips, Thomas Hal, 98, 99

Plimpton, George, 154, 155, 277
Polk, L. Reed, 110, 203–4
Prelude, 79
Pulitzer, Joseph, 199
Pulitzer Prize, 98, 199–201, 209–10
Pynchon, Thomas, 115

racism, 57–58, 90–91, 118–26, 183,
    196–98
    Klan, 48, 52, 57–58, 91, 125
    Lee on, 79–81, 90, 117–18, 120, 184,
        196–97, 206, 219, 222–23, 226,
        229, 234, 257
    Lett rape case, 118–20
    religion and, 121–26
    Scottsboro Boys trials, 117–18
    Till murder, 125
    University of Mississippi
        desegregation, 219–20
    See also segregation
radio, 16, 46, 161, 265
Radney, Tom, Sr., 267–70
railroad, 38, 134, 175
Rammer Jammer, 87, 88–99, 187, 247,
    265
    "Caustic Comment" column, 89–91
    Lee as editor of, 91–99
Random House, 133, 138, 238
rape, 117, 118–19
    Lett case, 118–20
    Scottsboro Boys trials, 117–18
    as theme in *To Kill a Mockingbird,*
        117–18, 120, 184
Reader's Digest, 14, 242
Reader's Digest Condensed Books, 12,
    14, 28, 182, 200
Reed, Emily Wheelock, 201
religion, 58, 67, 71, 121–24, 126
Richards, Robert P., 191
Richmond News-Leader, 254
Roberson, Freda, 32
Roberts, Leo R., 191
Robinson, Earl, 167
Rodgers and Hammerstein, 85
Rood, Tina, 78
Rorem, Ned, 170

Rosborough, Jane Hybart, 33
Rudisill, Marie Faulk, 35, 39, 42, 56,
    59, 129
Rupp, Bobby, 150, 151, 154, 163, 173
Ryland, Cecil, 132

Salter, Edward, 101
Sanford, Logan, 137, 160–61, 164, 165,
    167
Sanguinetti, Elise, 94, 99, 219
    The Last of the Whitfields, 219
Sarris, Andrew, 227
Sartre, Jean-Paul, 108
Saturday Review, 128
Sawyer, Elliott, 54
Schrader, M. C., 169, 170
Schulkers, Robert F., *Seckatary
    Hawkins,* 46–47, 51
Scottsboro Boys trials, 117–18, 120
Searcy, Hubert, 71
segregation, 90–91, 121, 126, 196, 234
    bus, 90–91, 197
    school, 197, 219–20, 233
Sergel, Christopher, 271
Shakespeare, William, 53, 97–98, 106,
    184
Shawn, William, 133, 142
Shirkey, Marion Goode, 104
Siegel, Stanley, 265–66
Simms, Louise, 22
Simms, Zoot, 22
Skinner, Charles Ray, 34, 54, 188, 208
slavery, 37, 90
Smith, Harrison, 177, 178, 239
Smith, Lillian, *Strange Fruit,* 90
Smith, Margaret Chase, 220
Smith, Perry, 158–75, 237–38
    confession, 166, 171
    execution of, 244–46
    interviewed by Capote and Lee,
        171, 173–74, 210
    trial, 174, 175, 176–79
Smith, Rayford, 62
South, 44–45, 90, 241
    Depression-era, 44–46
    Lee's roots and themes in, 21, 35,

44–54, 116–18, 120–21, 126–28,
185, 241, 244, 271–73
racism, 90–91, 117–26, 196–98, 229,
233–34
Reconstruction-era, 94, 95
Scottsboro Boys trials, 117–18
slavery, 90
Southern Christian Leadership
Conference, 229
Stabler, Anna, 52–53
Stallworth, Nicholas, 49
Stapp, Mary Lee, 103
Starkweather, Charles, 140
Steinbeck, John, 27, 255, 257
The Moon Is Down, 27
Stevens, Roger, 255–56
Stevenson, Adlai, 181
Stewart, Bill, 101–2
stock market crash (1929), 65
Stoecklein, Alfred, 144, 145
Stratemeyer, Edward, *The Rover Boys,*
46
Stribling, T.S., 95
Birthright, 95
Stringer, Polly, 151
Strode, Hudson, 97–99, 184, 199, 219
Shakespeare class, 97–99, 184
Stuckey, W.J., *The Pulitzer Prize
Novels: A Critical Backward
Look,* 128
Student Nonviolent Coordinating
Committee, 197
Supreme Court, U.S., 117, 225, 237–38
Brown v. Board of Education, 197
Sutherland, Edwin Van Valkenberg,
243
Sweet Briar College, 257–58, 270
Swift, Harriet, 56

Tate, Roland, 176–77
Taylor, A.J.P., 108
television, 141, 195
on Clutter murder case, 141
Tennessee Commercial Appeal, 182
Terry, Polly, 84, 86, 87
Texas, 27, 28

Till, Emmett, 125
Todd, Alden, 183
To Kill a Mockingbird (book), 12–14,
33, 34
adapted for film, 205–6
Atticus character, 44–45, 114, 117,
120–21, 127, 185, 203–6, 213,
215, 217–18, 226, 229
Aunt Alexandra character, 110, 206
banned by schools, 254–55
as bestseller, 182–83, 193, 199, 219
Boo Radley character, 54, 127, 146,
189, 211
British editions, 242, 281, 282
Calpurnia character, 54
Capote as inspiration for, 34, 97,
127, 128, 180
Capote's involvement with, 130–31,
254, 283
critics and reviews on, 12–13, 128,
182–83, 186–88
cultural significance of, 198
Dill character, 35, 127, 128, 180, 212
drafts, titles, and revisions, 114–16,
126–32, 183
film of. *See To Kill a Mockingbird*
(film)
galleys, 175–76
Jean Louise character and narrative
techniques, 127–28
Jem character, 127, 211
Klan imagery, 48
Lee's Alabama roots portrayed in,
21, 35, 44–48, 54, 116–18,
120–21, 126–28, 185, 244, 271–73
Lippincott contract and advance,
116, 129, 131–32
Lippincott's early interest in,
114–16
as Literary Guild selection, 12, 14,
29, 182
Monroeville annual theatrical
performances of, 271–73
Monroeville reactions to, 182, 185,
188–91, 199, 203–4, 207–9, 219,
225, 228, 246, 271–80

mother absent in, 42, 205
movie rights, 191–96
narrative point of view in, 127–28, 226, 227
Popular Literary paperback, 242
publication, 180–83
Pulitzer Prize for, 98, 199–201, 209–10
racial prejudice and justice themes, 79–81, 117–18, 120, 184, 196–97, 206, 219, 226, 229, 257
rape theme, 117–18, 120, 184
as Reader's Digest Condensed Book selection, 12, 14, 29, 182
sales, 14, 184, 191, 199, 202, 210, 219, 242
on school reading lists, 234–35, 254–55, 257
Scout character, 45, 47, 127–28, 212, 226
signed copies and first editions, 281–82
success of, 12–14, 28–29, 181–202, 218–19, 285
title chosen for, 129
Tom Robinson character, 117, 211, 218, 272
tourism, 274–75
translations, 200, 242
To Kill a Mockingbird (film), 30, 203–31, 235, 273
Academy Awards, 221, 229–31
casting, 191, 195, 198–99, 204, 210–12
critics on, 226–27
editing, 218
Gregory Peck as Atticus Finch in, 203–7, 213–14, 217–18, 222, 226, 229, 231
premieres, 225–29
production, 209–14, 217–18
publicity, 224, 227, 232
release, 221–22
rights to, 191–96
screenplay, 205–6

Tomlinson, Mary, 77, 280
tourism, 274–76
Tracy, Spencer, 198
Traywick, Leonard, 104
Trevor-Roper, H. R., 108
Tucker, Mel, 218
Tuscaloosa News, 125
Tutwiler, Julia, 37, 39
20th Century Fox, 27

United Press International, 160
Universal Studios, 204, 207, 213, 218
University of Alabama, 62, 184, 185, 187, 190, 201, 236, 265, 273
Chi Omegas, 84–86, 285
Lee at, 81, 83–99, 102–5, 187
racism, 125, 233
University of Mississippi, 219–20
Updike, John, *Rabbit, Run,* 188

Van Meter, Marcia, 202
Van Vleet, Gerald, 141, 145, 146, 148, 149
Village Voice, 227
Vogue, 201, 249
voting rights, 125

Wallace, George, 233
Walter, Eugene, 22, 35
    The Untidy Pilgrim, 22
Warner Brothers, 27
Warren Hotel, Garden City, Kansas, 136–37
Washington Post, 182, 200, 224
Watson-Burkett, Gladys, 63–65, 75, 108, 132, 251–53
Wells, Floyd, 158, 159
Wells, Kay, 234
West, Duane, 165, 167, 168, 170, 177, 238, 239
West Point, 243–44
Whatley, Ray E., 110–11, 121–25
    on racial issues, 121–25
White, E. B., 15
White, William Allen, 135

Wilder, Alec, 184
Williams, Annie Laurie, 27–30, 112–13,
    131–32, 180–81, 183, 186, 188,
    189, 191–95, 199, 202, 206, 216,
    225, 227–28, 232, 235, 247,
    251–52, 259–62, 271
Williams, Garth, *The Rabbits'*
    Wedding, 201
Williams, Jane, 103, 104, 105
Windham, Donald, 266

Windom, William, 210
Windsor, Kathleen, 216
    Forever Amber, 28
Women's College of Alabama, 65, 70
Woolf, Virginia, 108
World War I, 39
World War II, 28, 60, 68, 71, 100, 194
    end of, 83, 105

Yarbrough, James, 191

About the Author

CHARLES J. SHIELDS, a former teacher, has been a reporter for public radio, a journalist, and the author of nonfiction books for young people. He and his wife, Guadalupe, reside in Barboursville, Virginia.